Dissimilar Coffee Frontiers

African History

VOLUME 9

The titles published in this series are listed at *brill.com/afh*

Dissimilar Coffee Frontiers

Mobilizing Labor and Land in the Lake Kivu Region, Congo and Rwanda (1918–1960/62)

By

Sven Van Melkebeke

BRILL

LEIDEN | BOSTON

Cover illustration: Lake Kivu (August 2016) taken from Shangugu (Rwandan side of the Lake). Photo by the author.

Library of Congress Cataloging-in-Publication Data

Names: Melkebeke, Sven Van, author.
Title: Dissimilar coffee frontiers : mobilizing labor and land in the Lake Kivu Region, Congo and Rwanda (1918–1960/62) / by Sven Van Melkebeke.
Description: Leiden ; Boston : Brill, [2020] | Series: African history, 2211–1441 ; volume 9 | Includes bibliographical references and index.
Identifiers: LCCN 2020023493 (print) | LCCN 2020023494 (ebook) | ISBN 9789004428157 (paperback) | ISBN 9789004428492 (ebook)
Subjects: LCSH: Coffee industry--Kivu, Lake, Region (Congo and Rwanda)--History--20th century. | Coffee plantations--Kivu, Lake, Region (Congo and Rwanda)--History--20th century. | Coffee growers--Kivu, Lake, Region (Congo and Rwanda)--History--20th century. | Kivu, Lake, Region (Congo and Rwanda)--Economic conditions--20th century--Regional disparities.
Classification: LCC HD9199.A3533 K586 2020 (print) | LCC HD 9199.A3533 (ebook) | DDC 338.1/73730967517--dc23
LC record available at https://lccn.loc.gov/2020023493
LC ebook record available at https://lccn.loc.gov/2020023494

Typeface for the Latin, Greek, and Cyrillic scripts: “Brill”. See and download: brill.com/brill-typeface.

ISSN 2211-1441
ISBN 978-90-04-42815-7 (paperback)
ISBN 978-90-04-42849-2 (e-book)

To those who never stopped believing in me …

Contents

Illustrations and Tables

Images

Diagrams

Maps

Tables

Acknowledgments

Although researching and writing can at times be a solitary activity, this book would never have been possible without the help and support of a lot of people.

First and foremost I would like to thank Eric Vanhaute. After I had finished my Master thesis at Ghent University, he invited me to work on a research project (funded by Ghent University). This book is primarily the result of this research project. Eric supervised my initial PhD project and continued to support me during the book project. Although some decisions I made sometimes contrasted with his opinion, he always let me find my own way and was always ready to give me advice, feedback and the confidence to continue. In addition to the sustained efforts of Eric, I also want to underline those of William Clarence-Smith, Ulbe Bosma, Guy Vanthemsche, Felicitas Becker, Baz Lecocq and Gillian Mathys. Their feedback and insights were a big support in the development of my argument, my theoretical framework and a critical attitude. The same is true for the feedback of the anonymous reviewers. Their remarks and suggestions were very helpful in improving the initial manuscript.

Discussions and meetings with former colleagues also contributed to refining some issues. In the monthly meetings of the research group ECC (Economies – Comparisons – Connections) I was able to expand my own views by listening to other people talking about their research. I also presented some of my own texts during these meetings, and the feedback from group members was always helpful as it enabled me to fine-tune and/or alter my own perspectives.

The people I shared an office with also deserve special mention. Distracting informal conversations were perhaps as important as, or even more important than, the ECC meetings in my continuing the effort of writing the initial PhD project and this book project. A very special mention goes to Pieter De Reu. From the moment I started to work on my PhD, we shared common interests. As a result we talked a lot and very often about non-work-oriented matters. Now, Pieter has become a close friend – a PhD and ultimately a book can also lead to unexpected results. I would also like to thank Hans Blomme (Ghent Centre for Digital Humanities) for designing the majority of the maps used in this book.

Furthermore, I appreciate the help of Raf Storme, who works in the basement of the archives of the Belgian Federal Public Service Foreign Affairs where I did most of my archival research. His assistance in locating (even uninventoried) and sometimes even deciphering sources was indispensable.

Bishop Emmanual Ngendahayo also deserves gratitude. Thanks to him I was able to visit magnificent Rwanda and to see the extraordinary beauty of Lake Kivu. During my visit, I stayed in both Gisenyi and Shangugu. I visited coffee plantations, which was very special to me, because I finally saw what I had been working on for years.

Last but not least, my appreciation goes to my friends and family, and particularly to my girlfriend, Sarah. With her optimistic attitude she showed me that there is more in life than writing a book. Moreover, whenever I suffered or even had had enough of it, she always succeeded in cheering me up.

Finally, words of thanks to the people I have unintentionally forgotten to mention but who were also important in accomplishing this book. Now it only remains for me to say that all mistakes in this work are my own, and solely my own.

Abbreviations

AAB	African Archives Brussels
AI	Affaires Indigènes
AIMO	Affaires Indigènes et Main-d'œuvre
CFL	Compagnie des Chemins de Fer des Grands Lacs Africaines
CFS	Congo Free State
CIM	Société Générale pour favoriser le Développement du Commerce, de l'Industrie et des Mines
CNKi	Comité National du Kivu
CSK	Comité Spécial du Katanga
GG	Gouvernement Général
HAV	homme(s) adulte(s) valide(s) (able-bodied men)
HCB	Huileries du Congo Belge
INEAC	Institut National pour l'Etude Agronomique du Congo belge
MGL	Compagnie Minière des Grands Lacs
MO	main-d'œuvre
OCIRU	Office des Café Indigènes du Ruanda-Urundi
ONU	Organisation des Nations Unies
RACB	Rapport Annuel Congo Belge
RARU	Rapport Annuel Ruanda-Urundi
RMCA	Royal Museum for Central Africa
SAAK	Société Auxiliaire Agricole du Kivu
SAB1, SAB2	State Archives of Belgium 1 and 2
TEPSI	(Commission du) Travail Et du Progrès Social Indigène
Unaki	Union Agricole du Kivu
UNOG	United Nations Office at Geneva
WFAR	White Fathers Archives Rome

Introduction

According to the 2015 Food and Agriculture Organization of the United Nations statistical pocketbook on coffee, both global coffee production and consumption have increased substantially over the past fifty years. As shown in this publication, Brazil is the undisputable leader, with 2965 million tons produced in 2014. The first African producer is ranked seventh in the table, with 270 million tons cultivated in the same year. Zooming in on former Belgian Africa, the Democratic Republic of the Congo, Rwanda and Burundi are major producers. In 2014 they produced 31 million, 20 million and 36 million tons of coffee respectively.[1]

Despite the importance of Central Africa in the global coffee market, the historical background of coffee production in this region is still poorly understood. However, examining the development of coffee production in various regions would be very relevant, not only because of the central role coffee played in the global economy but also because it is one of the most "valuable internationally traded agricultural commodities in history."[2] Both development and production of this commodity involved many colonial powers, especially in colonial Africa, yet in the literature coffee is rarely treated as a colonial product.[3] Historically, one of the specificities of coffee is that it was grown exclusively in tropical countries, while consumption was chiefly limited to countries in the northern hemisphere. In that way, coffee production contributed to a new division of labor based on the mobilization of abundant supplies of land and labor, linking local producers to consumers in other continents, and thus integrating coffee cultivators in the modern world-system.[4] Considering the role coffee as a commodity played in the expansion of capitalism and the integration of rural populations in the world-system, this book aims to focus on

1 For these data see: S.N., *FAO statistical pocketbook coffee 2015* (Rome: FAO, 2015): 14; 42; 46; 65; 74 and 147.

2 Steven Topik and William Gervase Clarence-Smith, "Introduction: Coffee and global development," in *The global coffee economy in Africa, Asia, and Latin America 1500–1989*, ed. William Gervase Clarence-Smith and Steven Topik (Cambridge; New York: Cambridge University Press, 2003): 2.

3 Ibid.

4 Immanuel Wallerstein, *World-systems analysis. An introduction* (Durham; London: Duke University Press, 2007 [2004]): 23; Edward B. Barbier, *Scarcity and frontiers. How economies have developed through natural resource exploitation* (Cambridge; New York: Cambridge University Press, 2011): 418; Jeffrey G. Williamson, "Land, labor and globalization in the Third World, 1870–1940," *Journal of Economic History* 62, no. 1 (2002): 79; and Catherine M. Tucker, *Coffee culture: local experience, global connections* (New York; London: Routledge, 2011): Chapter 5.

 | DOI:10.1163/9789004428492_002

how the coffee production sector developed in the region around Lake Kivu. By using a comparative framework, the aim is to show the different ways in which labor and land were mobilized and commodified on both sides of the lake in order to produce for the export market, what factors had an impact on this labor and land mobilization/commodification (policy and coercion, for instance, but also the degree of African agency), and what role different colonial actors (the state but also African chiefs, African planters, European planters, agronomists, etcetera) played in these processes.[5]

The emphasis in this book is on private production for the market, which means that only minor attention is paid to ways that coffee was processed, and no attention is paid to export. Moreover, I also do not focus on missions; even though missions in colonial Africa were important in the initial phase of spreading the crop (see Chapter 1), they hardly cultivated for the market. Furthermore, although Belgian Africa was respected for its agricultural/ experimental research, the scientific aspect of coffee production is ignored mainly because those institutions' prime focus was not on market production as such, but rather on seeking ways to improve production factors by refining varieties, improving yields, introducing fertilizers, etcetera. Hence, scientific institutions only contributed indirectly to export production in the Lake Kivu region.

1 Relevance of This Research

1.1 *A Historiographical Sketch of Belgian Africa*

According to two historiographical articles, there has been little enthusiasm among historians for the Belgian colonial past.[6] This statement applies to the colony, but also to the Belgian mandate, although recently this situation seems to have changed.[7] Moreover, nearly all literature on Belgian Africa is written

5 It goes without saying that none of these categories of actors was static, or homogeneous. For instance, there were not only small planters cultivating only a few hectares, but there were also large companies occupying hundreds of hectares; agronomists were barely trained in the early years, but training improved toward the end of the colonial period. However, more research is needed to characterize these different actors, their experiences, their social background and so on.

6 Guy Vanthemsche, "The historiography of Belgian colonialism in the Congo," in *Europe and the World in European historiography*, ed. Csaba Lévai (Pisa: CLIOHRES, 2006); and Hein Vanhee and Geert Castryck, "Belgische historiogafie en verbeelding over het koloniale verleden," *Journal of Belgian History* 32, no. 3–4 (2002).

7 For example: at Ghent University alone, five PhDs have been successfully defended in recent years, focusing on socio-economic history: Sven Van Melkebeke, "'Changing grounds.' The development of coffee production in the Lake Kivu region (1918–1960/62). The colonial state,

within the framework of the nation-state.[8] This means that a comparative perspective (either cross-border or more in general) is lacking, or that historical regions are ignored. Consequently, this bibliographical sketch will be divided into sections summarizing relevant literature on the Belgian Congo and, secondly, relevant literature on Ruanda-Urundi. However, similarly to Mathys' recent work, this book aims to surpass colonially imposed borders, even though the development of different coffee production systems along the Congo–Rwanda border – primarily plantations in eastern Congo and primarily smallholder cultivation in Ruanda-Urundi – and the way archival material is stored and preserved do not make this an easy task. I will come back to these two aspects further on in this introduction. For now, suffice it to say that despite differences and variations in socio-cultural patterns (for example different languages), along the border people still lived in the same historically interlinked region, known as the "Lake Kivu space,"[9] with social, economic and political ties and overlap.[10] By comparing the east and west sides of Lake Kivu, this book will contribute not only to "going beyond" imposed borders but also to what Topik and Clarence-Smith have urged for: comparisons between different coffee economies, which (metaphorically) should yield rich harvests.[11]

labor, land and production for the world market" (Unpublished PhD dissertation, Ghent University, 2017); economic-fiscal history: Bas De Roo, "Colonial taxation in Africa. A fiscal history of the Congo through the lens of customs (1886–1914)" (Unpublished PhD dissertation, Ghent University, 2016); socio-political history: Gillian Mathys, "People on the move. Frontiers, borders, mobility and history in the Lake Kivu region 19th–20th century" (Unpublished PhD dissertation, Ghent University, 2014); socio-cultural history: Myriam Mertens, "Chemical compounds in the Congo: pharmaceuticals and the 'crossed history' of public health in Belgian Africa (ca. 1905–1939)" (Unpublished PhD dissertation, Ghent University, 2014); socio-economic history: Petra Vervust, "The limits of colonial symbolic power. Ethnicization and racialization in Rwanda 1890–1960" (Unpublished PhD dissertation, Ghent University, 2010).

8 There are exceptions – for instance, socio-economic works stressing the importance of the Lake Kivu region: David Newbury, "Lake Kivu regional trade in the nineteenth century," *Journal des Africanistes* 50, no. 2 (1980) and Bernard Lugan, "Les pôles commerciaux du lac Kivu à la fin du XIXe siècle," *Revue Française d'Histoire d'Outre-Mer* 64, no. 235 (1977). Or socio-political works: Mathys, "People on the move. Frontiers, borders, mobility and history in the Lake Kivu region 19th–20th century" and Gillian Mathys, "Bringing history back in: past, present, and conflict in Rwanda and eastern Democratic Republic of Congo," *Journal of African History* 58, no. 3 (2017).

9 Jean-Pierre Chrétien, *The Great Lakes of Africa. Two thousand years of history* (New York: Zone Books, 2006 [2003]): 195.

10 Mathys, "People on the move. Frontiers, borders, mobility and history in the Lake Kivu region 19th–20th century": 133.

11 Topik and Clarence-Smith, "Conclusion: new propositions and a research agenda": 408.

As for the literature on the Belgian Congo, Vanthemsche argues that in general the Belgian colonial world has received far less attention than the CFS (Congo Free State).[12] Despite this, there is some literature on Belgian Congolese cash crops other than coffee (primarily palm oil and cotton) and on other economic sectors, such as railways or minerals (copper in particular).[13] However, publications emphasizing the mobilization of both land and labor in the coffee production sector are rare. General literature on the Belgian Congo pays little direct attention to coffee production in the Kivu, or fails to mention it.[14] The more economically oriented literature focuses on European capital investment,[15] global economic performances[16] or agricultural development in a broad sense,[17] without paying specific attention to coffee. Nevertheless, there are specific studies on coffee production in regions other than the Kivu.[18]

---

12 Vanthemsche, "The historiography of Belgian colonialism in the Congo": 106.

13 For example: Osumaka Likaka, *Rural society and cotton in colonial Zaire* (Madison: University of Wisconsin Press, 1997); Jules Marchal, *L'histoire du Congo 1910–1945. Travail forcé pour le cuivre et pour l'or, pour le rail, pour l'huile de palme*, 3 vols. (Borgloon: P. Bellings, 1999–2001); Charles Perrings, *Black mineworkers in Central Africa: industrial strategies and the evolution of an African proletariat in the copperbelt, 1911–1941* (London: Heinemann, 1979). and S.E. Katzenellenbogen, *Railways and the copper mines of Katanga* (Oxford: Clarendon Press, 1973).

14 For instance: Jean Kestergat, *Quand le Zaïre s'appelait Congo. L'aventure coloniale belge* (Bruxelles: Paul Legrain, 1985); Robert Cornevin, *Historie du Zaïre. Des origines à nos jours* (Bruxelles; Paris: Hayez, 1989); Isidore Ndaywel è Nziem, *Histoire générale du Congo. De l'héritage ancien à la République Démocratique* (Paris: Duclot, 1998); Georges Nzongola-Ntalaja, *The Congo: from Leopold to Kabila: a people's history* (London; New York: Zed Books, 2002); David Renton, David Seddon, and Leo Zeilig, *The Congo: plunder and resistance* (London; New York: Zed Books, 2007); and David Van Reybrouck, *Congo. Een geschiedenis* (Amsterdam: De bezige bij, 2010).

15 For instance: Jacques Depelchin, *From the Congo Free State to Zaire (1885–1974). Towards a demystification of economic and political history* (London: CODESRIA, 1992) and Frans Buelens, *Congo 1885–1960. Een financieel-economische geschiedenis* (Berchem: EPO, 2007).

16 For example: André Huybrechts, *Bilan économique du Congo* (Paris: L'Harmattan, 2010), but also Gaston Vandewalle, *De conjuncturele evolutie in Kongo en Ruanda-Urundi van 1920 tot 1939 en van 1949 tot 1958* (Ghent: RUG. Hogere school voor handels-en economische wetenschappen, 1966), focusing on Ruanda-Urundi as well.

17 For instance: Jeannôt Mokili Danga Kassa, *Politiques agricoles et promotion rurale au Congo-Zaïre (1885–1997)* (Paris: L'Harmattan, 1998) and the work of a former agronomist who extends his focus to Ruanda-Urundi as well: Vladimir Drachoussof, ed., *Le developpement rural en Afrique Centrale 1908–1960/1962. Synthèse et réflexions*, 2 vols. (Bruxelles: Fondation Roi Baudoin, 1991).

18 For coffee: see Eric de Dampierre, "Coton noir, café blanc. Deux cultures du Haute-Oubangui à la veille de la loi-cadre," *Cahiers d'Etudes Africaines* 1, no. 2 (1960) and Mokili K. Mbuluyo, "La culture du café et le développement de l'Uele," *Cahiers d'Outre-Mer* 39, no. 154 (1986).

Apart from this, there is some additional literature that focuses on the mobilization of land and/or labor in general, or in other commodity sectors.[19]

However, literature remains scarce on the mobilization of land and labor in the coffee sector in the Kivu and the role played by colonial actors. Hence, this book seeks to bridge (a) geographical as well as (a) thematic gap(s). More broadly speaking, since the 1970s, publications on the Kivu region are not abundant. Since the publication of a historical overview in 1980[20] there seems to have been little new historical research, at least until very recently.[21] However, this does not mean that the coffee sector in the Kivu has not been examined yet. Scholars refer to labor, labor conditions and land, but they usually focus on the period before World War II, thereby missing major changes;[22] or they examine the entire plantation economy from a geographical perspective and not coffee as such;[23] or they stress rural protest and forms of resistance against European rule;[24] or they are more interested in the commodity chain

19 For example: Julia Seibert, *In die globale Wirtschaft gezwungen. Arbeit und kolonialer Kapitalismus im Kongo (1885–1960)* (Frankfurt; New York: Verlag, 2016); Samuel H. Nelson, *Colonialism in the Congo basin, 1880–1940* (Athens (Ohio): Center for International Studies, 1994); and Piet Clement, "The land tenure system in the Congo, 1885–1960: actors, motivations and consequences," in *Colonial exploitation and economic development. The Belgian Congo and the Netherlands Indies compared*, ed. Ewout Frankema and Frans Buelens (London; New York: Routledge, 2013). For the cotton sector see Likaka, *Rural society and cotton in colonial Zaire*. For the palm oil sector see Benoît Henriet, "The concession experience. Power, ecology and labour in the Leverville circle (Belgian Congo, 1911–1940)" (Unpublished PhD dissertation, Université Saint-Louis Bruxelles, 2016).

20 Chubaka Bishikwabo and David Newbury, "Recent historical research in the area of Lake Kivu: Rwanda and Zaïre," *History in Africa* 7 (1980).

21 Renewed interest in the Kivu region is coming from works such as Mathys, "People on the move. Frontiers, borders, mobility and history in the Lake Kivu region 19th–20th century" or Nicole Eggers, "Kitawala in the Congo: religion, politics and healing in 20th–21st century Central Africa" (Unpublished PhD dissertation, University of Wisconsin, 2013).

22 David Northrup, *Beyond the bend in the river: African labor in Eastern Zaire 1865–1940* (Athens (Ohio): Center for International Studies, 1988); Cirhagarhula Bashizi, "Processus de domination socio-économique et marché du travail au Bushi (1920–45)," *Enquêtes et Documents d'Histoire africaine* 3 (1978); or Chubaka Bishikwabo, "Un aspect du colonat au Congo belge: le sort des travailleurs du Kivu (1900–1940)," *Genève-Afrique* 16, no. 2 (1977–78).

23 Jean-François Drevet, "Les plantations Européenes dans le Kivu d'altitude" (Unpublished PhD dissertation, Université de Paris, 1977).

24 Bycyalimwe Mararo, "Land conflicts in Masisi, Eastern Zaire: the impact and aftermath of Belgian colonial policy (1920–1989)" (Unpublished PhD dissertation, Indiana University, 1990), and Cirhagarhula Bashizi, "Pouvoirs publics, plantations européennes et réactions paysannes au Sud-Kivu (1920–1960)," in *Ambiguités de l'innovation: sociétés rurales et technologies en Afrique Centrale et Occidentale au XXe siècle*, ed. Bogumil Jewsiewicki and Jean-Pierre Chrétien (Québec: SAFI Press, 1984).

approach.[25] But none of these contributions satisfactorily "crosses the border" by comparing with or connecting to coffee production on the Rwandan side of Lake Kivu.

Literature on Rwanda has focused even less on coffee, the way land and labor were integrated in the capitalist world-system, and what role colonial actors played in this process. For Burundi, on the other hand, such literature does exist.[26] Literature on Rwanda can be divided into a German part (until World War I) and a Belgian part (starting from 1916). Although the Germans initiated private coffee production on a very limited scale (*infra*), literature on the German period pays little or no attention to it, as it is oriented more toward socio-political events and the "discovery" of Lake Kivu by the German count Von Götzen.[27] Most literature on the Belgian period continues to follow a more socio-political input, although some publications (by Newbury, for instance) do pay sufficient attention to coffee, land and labor.[28] Other literature stresses particular periods, but also from a socio-political angle and hardly mentioning coffee production.[29]

Moreover, there is little literature on the Rwandan economy during the colonial period, except for Dorsey's dissertation.[30] This work discusses coffee, land and labor mobilization, but does not treat the entire colonial period.

25 Guillaume Léonard, "Un divorce belge. Expériences contrastées du planteur belge de café au Kivu (1945–1960)," in *L'Afrique belge aux XIXe et XXe siècles. Nouvelles recherches et perspectives en histoire coloniale*, ed. Patricia Van Schuylenbergh, Catherine Lanneau, and Pierre-Luc Plasman (Bruxelles; Berne; Berlin: P.I.E. Peter Lang, 2014).

26 For instance: Alexandre Hatungimana, *Le café au Burundi au XXe siècle: Paysans, argent, pouvoir* (Paris: Karthala, 2005) and Deogratias Nsavyimana, "La mobilisation de la force de travail au Burundi sous le mandate belge (1920–1940)" (Unpublished PhD dissertation, Université Catholique de Louvain, 1989).

27 See for instance: Helmut Strizek, *Geschenkte Kolonien: Ruanda und Burundi unter deutscher Herrschaft* (Berlin: Christoph Links Verlag, 2006); Bernard Lugan, *Cette Afrique qui était allemande* (Paris: Jean Picollec, 1990); and Gudrun Honke, ed., *Au plus profond de l'Afrique: le Rwanda et la colonisation allemande 1885–1919* (Wuppertal: Peter Hammer Verlag, 1990).

28 For instance: Innocent Nsengimana, *Le Rwanda et le pouvoir européen (1894–1952). Quelles mutations?* (Bern: Peter Lang, 2003); Catharine Newbury, *The cohesion of oppression. Clientship and ethnicity in Rwanda, 1860–1960* (New York: Columbia University Press, 1988); and many works of Lermarchand – to cite only one, René Lemarchand, *Rwanda and Burundi* (London: Pall Mall Press, 1970).

29 For example: Alison Liebhafsky Des Forges, *Defeat is the only bad news: Rwanda under Musinga, 1896–1931* (Madison: University of Wisconsin Press, 2011); Jean Rumiya, *Le Rwanda sous le régime du mandat Belge: 1916–1931* (Paris: L'Harmattan, 1992); or F. Nkundabagenzi, *Rwanda politque, 1958–1960* (Bruxelles: CRISP, 1961).

30 Learthen Dorsey, "Rwandan colonial economy, 1916–1941" (Unpublished PhD dissertation, Michigan State University, 1983).

Moreover, many arguments made by Dorsey are generalizing and do not specifically refer to the coffee sector around Lake Kivu. Furthermore, literature on coffee production in Rwanda often has a socio-political perspective (for instance by stressing the changing roles of chiefs, or even relating coffee production directly to the genocide of 1994).[31] Finally, except for the works of Mathys and Newbury, relevant existing literature on the colonial period lacks nuance in the sense that the focus is often not on the areas bordering Lake Kivu.[32]

1.2 *Theoretical Framework*

In addition to filling thematic and geographical gaps and in the historiography of former Belgian Africa, this book also aims to engage in two related theoretical debates: on commodity frontiers[33] and on empire.

Over the past five hundred years, the expansion of capitalism has resulted in the incorporation and transformation of vast rural zones in its attempt to acquire the "four cheaps" – labor, food, energy and raw materials[34] – or, in other words, in capitalism's ability to cheaply appropriate and reorganize these four hitherto uncommodified aspects. This integration is often seen as globalization, as a process of "becoming" more homogeneous. However, with regard to Africa, Frederick Cooper argues that integration here actually created more rather than less fragmentation.[35] In world-system analysis, the expansion of capitalism is very often focused on core regions. Peripheries are taken into account, but only from within the perspective of the core.[36] Such approaches have been subject to criticism. Mignolo, for example, argues that world-system analysis is blind to what he calls "colonial difference": differences in knowledge (production), culture, socio-economic systems. Imposing knowledge deemed

31 Laurien Uwizeyimana, "Rôle politique de la caféiculture au Rwanda," *Etudes Rurales*, no. 180 (2007) and Isaac A. Kamola, "The global coffee economy and the production of genocide in Rwanda," *Third World Quarterly* 28, no. 3 (2007).

32 Mathys, "People on the move. Frontiers, borders, mobility and history in the Lake Kivu region 19th–20th century" and Newbury, *The cohesion of oppression. Clientship and ethnicity in Rwanda, 1860–1960*.

33 Recently, a new network (Commodity Frontiers Initiative) has been created by Eric Vanhaute, Ulbe Bosma and Sven Beckert. This network has expertise on a wide range of commodities, covering all principle producing regions of the world from the early modern period to the present day (https://wigh.wcfia.harvard.edu/ commodity-frontiers-initiative).

34 Jason W. Moore, *Capitalism in the web of life. Ecology and the accumulation of capital* (London; New York: Verso, 2015).

35 Frederick Cooper, "What is the concept of globalization good for? An African historian's perspective," *African Affairs* 100, no. 399 (2001).

36 Hanne Cottyn, "A world-systems frontier perspective to land: exploring the uneven trajectory of land rights standardization in the Andes," *Journal of World-Systems Research* 23, no. 2 (2017).

more advanced and the presumed right to subject populations have obscured the story of the periphery.[37] Cooper is scathing about the mechanistic nature of world-systems theory and insistent that with every attempt to understand integration, tracing place-specific tensions and struggles is paramount.[38] This critique has inspired scholars, such as Thomas Hall, to refine existing theorization.[39] According to Hall, peripheries are as important to study as core regions if we want to understand the modern capitalist world-system. Although changes that happen in peripheries as a result of incorporation are often at least directed by core regions, some processes of change are best observed in peripheries. Where core (the expanding world-system) and external zones "meet," a frontier, and hence a periphery, develops. In frontiers, two societal systems come into contact with each other, interacting and transforming each other, albeit with asymmetrical power relations.[40] Colonialism is a perfect example of the expansion of the world-system and the incorporation of "new" populations. A frontier thus has to be understood as the process of incorporation, whereas the specific places where this incorporation happens are frontier zones. Even though frontiers do have a spatial component,[41] they are never stable or fixed and are constantly shifting in search of new and cheaper

37 Walter D. Mignolo, *Local histories/global designs: coloniality, subaltern knowledges, and border thinking* (Princeton: Princeton University Press, 2000).

38 Frederick Cooper, "Africa and the world economy," in *Confronting historical paradigms. Peasants, labor, and the capitalist World System in Africa and Latin America*, ed. Frederick Cooper, et al. (Madison: University of Wisconsin Press, 1993): 95–98.

39 See in particular: Thomas D. Hall, "Frontiers, ethnogenesis and world-systems: rethinking the theories," in *A world-systems reader. New perspectives on gender, urbanism, cultures, indigenous peoples, and ecology*, ed. Thomas D. Hall (Lanham (Maryland): Rowman & Littlefield Publishers, 2000): 237; Thomas D. Hall, "(Re)periphalization, (re)incorporation, frontiers, and non-state societies: continuities and discontinuities in globalization processes," in *Globalization and global history*, ed. Barry Gills and William Thompson (London; New York: Routledge, 2006): 104; and Thomas D. Hall, "Incorporation into and merger of world-systems," in *Routledge handbook of world-systems analysis: theory and research*, ed. Salvatore J. Babones and Christopher K. Chase-Dunn (London; New York: Routledge, 2012). 48.

40 For instance: Thomas D. Hall, "Puzzles in the comparative study of frontiers: problems, some solutions, and methodological implications," *Journal of World-Systems Research* 15, no. 1 (2009): 25; Thomas D. Hall, "Lessons from comparing the two Southwests: Southwest China and Northwest New Spain/Southwest United States," *Journal of World-Systems Research* 19, no. 1 (2013): 25; and Hanne Cottyn, "Renegotiating communal autonomy. Communal land rights and liberal land reform on the Bolivian altiplano. Carangas, 1860–1930" (Unpublished PhD dissertation, Ghent University, 2014): 20.

41 Saskia Sassen, "When the center no longer holds: Cities as frontier zones," *Cities* 34 (2012).

opportunities.[42] This kind of frontier expansion provides new sources of land and labor, for example for production purposes.[43] As Barbier argues, necessary conditions for successful frontier-based development are: firstly, institutional preconditions, for example the possibility to use coerced labor; secondly, the development of specialized activities; and thirdly, economic development, for instance by using (or rather expropriating) agricultural land and by limiting free competition.[44] Clearly these conditions are nourished by unequal power relations and state intervention.

In order to extend the theorization of processes of incorporation, interaction and transformation, Jason Moore introduced the concept of the commodity frontier. By focusing on the production (and distribution) of one specific commodity (in his case sugar) he examines the reorganization of geographical spaces at the margins of the world-system.[45] According to Moore, commodity frontiers extensively transformed existing land and labor patterns,[46] for instance by (partially) commodifying both. Moreover, this scholar argues, commodity frontiers were extremely effective in the rise of capitalism because on these frontiers "a relatively small volume of capital, backed by territorial power, could appropriate a very large basket of nature's gifts."[47] In this book, nature's gift coffee is the commodity, a good that has a value and a price and that is traded globally.

As mentioned, (commodity) frontier zones' main characteristic is interaction: two different societal systems meet and affect each other. Incorporation into the capitalist world-system is never one-directional: there is always feedback from populations that are being incorporated.[48] This feedback manifests

42 Hall, "(Re)periphalization, (re)incorporation, frontiers, and non-state societies: continuities and discontinuities in globalization processes": 99.

43 Barbier, *Scarcity and frontiers. How economies have developed through natural resource exploitation*: 7.

44 Ibid: 21.

45 Jason W. Moore, "Sugar and the expansion of the Early Modern world-economy: commodity frontiers,ecological transformation, and industrialization," *Review (Fernand Braudel Center)* 23, no. 3 (2000): 410.

46 Ibid: 412.

47 Jason W. Moore, "Madeira, sugar, and the conquest of nature in the 'first' sixteenth century, Part II. From regional crisis to commodity frontier, 1506–1530," *Review (Fernand Braudel Center)* 33, no. 1 (2010). 4.

48 For more on feedback see: Cottyn, "Renegotiating communal autonomy. Communal land rights and liberal land reform on the Bolivian altiplano. Carangas, 1860–1930": 44–49; Hall, "Lessons from comparing the two Southwests: Southwest China and Northwest New Spain/Southwest United States": 25; and Hall, "(Re)periphalization, (re)incorporation, frontiers, and non-state societies: continuities and discontinuities in globalization processes": 106.

itself in the form of both contestation (resistance, sabotage, fleeing) and alliance (treaties, marriage, economic collaboration). In this context, Kardulias introduced the concept of negotiated peripherality. By this, he means that thanks to their agency, people in the periphery are able to negotiate with representatives of expanding states. People at the margins of the world-system "can and do determine the nature and extent of interaction with core polities to at least some degree."[49] The consequence of this is that incorporation is always partial, and results in the creation of a new hybrid system combining elements of the incorporator and the incorporated. The impact of capitalist expansion for rural populations in peripheries is unpredictable.[50] The outcome of incorporation depends on differences in existing local conditions (for example economies or socio-political structures). In short, (commodity) frontier zones are perfect means through which to study interactions and negotiations about commodification (of labor and land, for instance) and socio-cultural assimilation.[51] Thus, focusing on those involved in the production of commodities makes it possible to understand how global history has been built up from the agency of local actors.[52]

Nevertheless, incorporation into the capitalist world-system is based on unequal power relations. During the imperialistic period, capitalism expanded and incorporated vast new zones in Africa. Tropical frontier expansion, which started in the 1870s, was based on abundant supplies of cheap labor and land.[53] Moreover, imperial powers were convinced of their superiority over "barbaric" indigenous people and initiated numerous ways of reorganizing incorporated areas after the European example, often by use of force. Burbank and Cooper define this as "arrogance of power" while Scott argues that reorganizing and simplifying existing structures was meant to make societies more comprehensible and more controllable.[54] During this phase of incorporation, European

49 Nick Kardulias, "Negotiation and incorporation on the margins of world-systems: examples from Cyprus and North America," *Journal of World-Systems Research* 13, no. 1 (2007): 76.

50 Cottyn, "Renegotiating communal autonomy. Communal land rights and liberal land reform on the Bolivian altiplano. Carangas, 1860–1930": 72.

51 Michael L. Galaty, "World-systems analysis and anthropology: a new détente?," *Reviews in Anthropology* 40, no. 1 (2011): 14.

52 Jonathan Curry-Machado, "Global histories, imperial commodities, local interactions: an introduction," in *Global histories, imperial commodties, local interactions*, ed. Jonathan Curry-Machado (Houndsmills; New York: Palgrave Macmillian, 2013): 6.

53 Barbier, *Scarcity and frontiers. How economies have developed through natural resource exploitation*: 415–416.

54 Jane Burbank and Frederick Cooper, *Empires in World History. Power and the politics of difference* (Princeton; Oxford: Princeton University Press, 2010): 288; and James Scott,

colonizers behaved like empires, as "large political units, expansionist or with a memory of power extended over space, polities that maintain[ed] distinction and hierarchy as they incorporate[d] new people."[55] Two things are important here. Firstly, empire not only entails economic incorporation but also attempts to impose political/social/cultural structures. Secondly, as opposed to many teleological interpretations of world history with expanding European nation-states and more homogenization, Burbank and Cooper stress the importance of difference as well as the role of local actors (indigenous people, but also settlers, for instance) in shaping empire.[56]

According to the same authors, states like Belgium and Portugal had a special interest in empire because they were small actors on the European scene, as opposed to Britain and France.[57] Consequently, in this book, I will put particular emphasis on the role of the state and the local coffee actors involved. More precisely, I will focus on the way the state operates on the ground rather than theorizing about colonial states as such.[58] This requires a focus on labor/land mobilization/commodification policies and on the active intervention of the state in labor/land mobilization/commodification, but also on feedback from different coffee (African and European) actors and how this influenced these processes.

Empire is created out of heterogeneity and preserves difference. This means that empires had changing sets of rules and employed various strategies in different places at the same time.[59] However, it would be wrong to conceive of empire, or in this book the Belgian colonizer, as one entity. There was not one colonial state. Not only do we have to take into account regional differences and diverging forms of feedback, but we also need to consider contradictions and conflicts between different actors on the ground.[60] Similarly to the creation of a frontier, empire is the result of negotiation, cooperation, adaptation

---

Seeing like a state. How certain schemes to improve the human condition have failed (New Haven; London: Yale University Press, 1998).

55 Burbank and Cooper, *Empires in World History. Power and the politics of difference*: 8.

56 Ibid: 13–14.

57 Ibid: 344.

58 Comaroff suggests that colonial states should be conceived as "processes of becoming": as a state (institutional order) and a statement (ideological project); see: John L. Comaroff, "Reflections on the colonial state, in South Africa and elsewhere: factions, fragments, facts and fictions," *Social Identities: Journal for the Study of Race, Nation and Culture* 4, no. 3 (1998): 346.

59 Frederick Cooper, *Africa in the world: capitalism, empire, nation-state* (Cambridge (Massachusetts): Harvard University Press, 2014): 40.

60 Frederick Cooper, *Colonialism in question. Theory, knowledge, history* (Berkeley; Los Angeles; London: University of California Press, 2005): 51.

to localities and the reconciliation of actors with different interests. A focus on the local – in this case study on labor/land mobilization/commodification in the colonial territories bordering Lake Kivu – is vital to better understanding the development of empire and commodity frontiers in world history.

This book aims to contribute to existing theory on frontier (zones) and empire by offering an empirical case study, since "empirical studies of frontiers can contribute to refined world-systems theorizing."[61] The integration of these interrelated theoretical concepts leads to the central question: how did coffee production around Lake Kivu develop? Combining commodity frontier zones and empire allows me to examine the ways labor and land were mobilized and commodified; how existing patterns were altered and/or adapted to coffee production for the export market; what sets of rules were used on both sides of Lake Kivu; which roles different actors on the ground (most importantly the colonizing state, but also colonists, African notables and people working in the coffee sector themselves) played; and, finally, what kind of feedback Africans offered and how all of this had an impact on the further evolution of the coffee sector. The main argument of this book is that coffee production in the commodity frontier zones around Lake Kivu developed and evolved differently between east and west, not only as a result of existing local differences (precolonial, demographic) that were enhanced during the colonial period (with a judicial component), but also as a result of compromises between, and feedback from, several actors involved. Despite harmonizing tendencies inherent in capitalism, these two factors – difference and compromise – resulted in two main diverging production systems (plantations and smallholders) – or in two divergent hybrid systems, and consequently in dissimilar ways of mobilizing labor and land, as well as different ways of empire-building (different sets of rules on both sides of the lake). However, empire is created out of heterogeneity, which also resulted in "internal difference," or, in the existence of both smallholders *and* plantations on both sides of the lake, requiring different sets of rules in the same place, at the same time.

2 Geographical and Temporal Scope

In addition to explaining the importance of the Kivu region as a coffee producer it is also essential to elaborate on the different varieties of coffee. In the last decade of the nineteenth century, *Liberica* coffee was introduced in the western Congo and grown on plantations, for instance in the vicinity of

61 Hall, "Puzzles in the comparative study of frontiers: problems, some solutions, and methodological implications": 37.

Léopoldville. But when Belgium took over the CFS in 1908, production of this variety was almost completely abandoned, and in the following decades, *Liberica* would not become a major variety.[62]

In the late nineteenth century, another variety, *Robusta*, was discovered in the Congo basin.[63] Immediately after its discovery, this variety was cultivated by colonial agents in the vicinity of their administrative posts. But, as opposed to what was the case in Angola for example, interest in *Robusta* cultivation was lacking until shortly before World War I.[64] However, after World War I, *Robusta* would become the major variety produced in the Belgian Congo (see Chapter 1).

The second major coffee variety in Belgian Africa after World War I was *Arabica*. The main differences between these two varieties are illustrated in the following quote:

> The *Arabica* is a coffee with beautiful [red] shades, large beans, excellent aroma, with a beneficial return because it competes with the luxurious coffees of Nicaragua, Venezuela, Guatemala and Mexico. However, yield per tree is smaller. On the other hand, the Congolese *Robusta* is a coffee with an incontestable lesser quality, lower price, brownish shade.[65]

Even though yields per hectare were higher for *Robusta*, *Arabica* has/had the advantages of a better-quality coffee and obtained higher prices on the international markets.[66] Furthermore, the latter only thrives in specific regions where factors such as temperature, humidity, altitude, soil, etcetera are appropriate. Conditions in the regions bordering Lake Kivu are perfect for its

62 Edgar Van der Straeten, *L'agriculture et les industries agricoles au Congo belge* (Bruxelles: Editons L. Cuypers, 1945): 150.

63 For more see especially: Edmond Leplae, *Les plantations de café au Congo belge: leur histoire (1881–1935), leur importance actuelle* (Bruxelles: Van Campenhout, 1936).

64 Angola's success in *Robusta* production in the nineteenth century is even considered the first African coffee boom; see: Jelmer Vos, "The first African coffee boom: Angolan Robusta, c.1820–c.1900" in *II CHAM International Conference* (Universidade Nova de Lisboa, 2015).

65 H. Kermans, "Les cafés du Congo belge," *Bulletin Agricole du Congo Belge* 21, no. 3 (1930): 954–955.

66 Estimations made at the end of the 1930s show that *Robusta* yields could be twice as large as *Arabica* yields. Moreover, more than *Robusta*, *Arabica* yields very much depend(ed) on climate conditions (rainfall), soil quality, altitude (recommended between 1650 and 2150 meters above sea-level), and especially maintenance; see: Edmond Leplae, *La culture et le rendement d'une plantation de café au Congo belge* (Bruxelles: Imprimerie industrielle et financière, 1928).

cultivation. From this point of view, a focus on the Lake Kivu region is also legitimized.

However, as opposed to *Robusta*, *Arabica* did not originate in Belgian Africa. In Chapter 1, I discuss the spread and the way *Arabica* arrived in the Kivu region. The global diffusion of *Arabica* was based on human decisions,[67] in particular those of missionary fathers. But for now, suffice it to say that in the Kivu region, *Arabica* was nearly the only variety cultivated. After the starting point of World War I, *Arabica* coffee developed into a major export crop and played a primordial role in the economic development of the Lake Kivu region.[68] Even though *Arabica* arrived in the Kivu region in the early twentieth century, sustained market production did not start until after World War I. It should be stressed, however, that Germany made a limited attempt to start coffee cultivation to the east of the lake, shortly before World War I. But to the west of the lake, there was no *colonisation agricole* before the war, except for some limited tests around administrative posts.[69] The endpoint of this book is the formal end of the colonial period (1960/2) which meant the end of empire or the change of territorial power from Belgium to three independent states.

Another reason why a study of this region is required is because the Lake Kivu region is a curious case, urging for comparison to be made. After World War I, plantations were the main mode of production on the Congolese side, while on the Rwandan side a smallholder coffee economy was the dominant mode of production. Although there were hybrid forms (for instance Africans engaging other Africans in Rwanda; see Chapter 4), here I define a plantation as an enterprise run by white settlers on concessionary (mostly large) estates using African wage labor, while smallholders are understood as independent (though mostly obliged) producers, cultivating the land around or in the vicinity of their homesteads using family labor. Chapter 2 will discuss the reasons for this distinction.

3 Coffee Cultivation in Belgian Africa

In order to get a full understanding of the way land, and in particular labor, was mobilized and commodified in the coffee sector around Lake Kivu, a focus on

67 Steven Topik and Allen Wells, *Global markets transformed, 1870–1945* (Cambridge (Massachusetts); London: Harvard University Press, 2012): 219.

68 In 1977, for example, 64% of the total Rwandan export still consisted of coffee; see: François Bart, "Le café dans l'agriculture rwandaise: l'exemple de Kidahiré (Runyinya)," *Cahiers d'Outre-Mer* 33, no. 132 (1980): 303.

69 Emile Vandewoude, *Documents relatifs à l'ancien district du Kivu, 1900–1922* (Léopoldville: Section Documentation Bureau Archives, 1959): 31.

how the crop was cultivated is essential.[70] The export of *Arabica* was preceded by an intensive process. After existing vegetation had been cleared, the land was arranged in order to facilitate planting or sowing. Poles were placed at regular intervals to indicate spots of planting or sowing. For *Arabica*, intervals varied between 1.8 and 3 meters. This step had a high labor demand, as it took an estimated 130 days of work per laborer per hectare.

After these preparatory steps, coffee was either sown directly on the land (large-scale plantations of 500 hectares and more) or in nurseries, followed by a transplantation of seedlings (a method used by small-scale plantations and smallholders). With both procedures, plants started to germinate after three to four weeks. From this moment on, a daily or twice-daily inspection was required in order to remove weeds. In the second method, workers had to dig holes before seedlings could be transplanted (after six to eight months). Usually, holes had a diameter of about 60 centimeters and a depth of 30 to 60 centimeters. A few days after the careful transplantation of seedlings, the holes were refilled. This "sewing-planting" phase required an estimated sixty-five days of work per laborer per hectare.

After this labor-intensive initial phase, coffee bushes blossomed. In general, it took two to three years before *Arabica* started to produce berries, with a maximum yield after five to six years (*Robusta* took three years).[71] During this period, attentive and careful maintenance of the bushes was indispensable for the success of the harvests. Labor input was lower than during the initial stage. Estimations show that only fifty to sixty days of work per worker per hectare per year were required. One important maintenance aspect consisted of regularly fertilizing the land, preferably with organic material (cattle manure and/or compost). From the mid-1930s onwards chemical fertilizers were used as well. Besides fertilizing, the almost continual controlling and removing of weeds was equally crucial. Especially in the first months after planting/sowing, removing weeds was intensive. However, once coffee bushes had reached a considerable size, so that the branches provided enough shadow to protect the trunk, weeding intensity declined. Maintenance of coffee bushes also included

70 This section is mainly based on: Edmond Leplae, "Prix de revient et rendements probables de plantations au Congo belge," *Bulletin Agricole du Congo Belge* 14, no. 4 (1923); Leplae, *La culture et le rendement d'une plantation de café au Congo belge*; J. Courcelles, "Etablissement d'une plantation de café arabica au Kivu," *Bulletin Agricole du Congo Belge* 28, no. 2 (1937); Van der Straeten, *L'agriculture et les industries agricoles au Congo belge*; and Hatungimana, *Le café au Burundi au XXe siècle: Paysans, argent, pouvoir*: 354–386.

71 *Arabica* bushes could produce until the age of twenty and, in exceptional cases, even thirty years old. After their productive life, these plants were replaced by new ones. Replacement of plants also happened during the cultivation process, for example, when plants were diseased.

recurrent fighting of diseases and insects (*antestia* for example). *Robusta* was more resistant and required less disease/insect control. Finally, the pruning and topping of bushes required attention as well, because well-pruned bushes produced on a more regular basis, and had qualitatively better berries. Moreover, non-topped bushes could reach a height of six to eight meters. For this reason, *Arabica* bushes were topped at one to three meters.

As opposed to *Robusta*, *Arabica* harvests were limited to once every year. Harvesting berries was also labor-intensive and lasted two to three, sometimes even four, months (June–August). Despite the absence of estimations, harvest periods resulted in high labor peaks (including women and children in the process). There were two methods of harvesting coffee: either by removing all berries from the branch with one stroke followed by separating mature berries from immature or rotten ones and from leaves and other waste; or by only picking mature berries. Laborers were provided with a basket to collect berries. Even though this method required more labor power, picking could be carried out more carefully, sorting out good and bad berries was not necessary and, moreover, bushes suffered less, which had a positive impact on the quality of future harvests.

The way plantations processed berries differed from the approach of smallholders. The latter processed manually (but in the 1950s mechanization entered as well, for example machines to remove shells), the former mostly mechanically (at least since the end of the 1920s). After harvesting, smallholders dried berries for about fifteen days in the open air and turned them around several times a day. When berries were dry enough, the shell was removed manually; sometimes (but not always) beans were fermented for two to three days; after that they were cleaned and prepared for sale. Coffee berries originating from plantations, on the other hand, were usually not dried on the spot but transported to processing factories shortly after the harvest. Shells were removed mechanically without drying, in so-called *dépulpeurs*. At the end of the 1930s, twenty-three such *dépulpeurs* existed in eastern Congolese Costermansville Province. After removal of the chorion, beans were fermented in large concrete vessels, followed by a mechanized drying process which lasted only a day. Finally, they were cleaned and prepared for the export market.

One final word about cultivation: as in many other coffee-producing regions in the world, in Belgian Africa coffee was rarely cultivated as a monocrop.[72] In most cases food crops (for instance bananas) were planted between the bushes, on smallholder plots as well as on plantation land. But next to food crops, from the mid-1930s onwards plantations (but some smallholders too) started

72 Topik and Clarence-Smith, "Conclusion: new propositions and a research agenda": 393.

to diversify even more by planting additional cash crops (for example tea and/or quinine). Polyculture was not only a measure to remedy increasing soil exhaustion but, in the aftermath of the global crisis, also a spread of risk. This is similar to how many coffee plantations in Kenya, for example, reacted after the crisis.[73]

4 Methodology and Sources

This book builds upon a wide array of largely untapped archival sources.[74] The majority of these records stem from administrations in both the Belgian Congo and Ruanda-Urundi and are kept by the Belgian Federal Public Service Foreign Affairs (African Archives) in Brussels (AAB).[75] The first general methodological issue with these sources is that they are sometimes difficult to access – I deal with particular methodological issues in the different chapters of this book. Parts of the sources are not inventoried yet, which means that future research might reveal new data on the development of the coffee sector around Lake Kivu. For instance, there is a large "temporary classification" section.[76] The only access to these sources is a vague list. Hopefully, documents in this section contain data on smallholder coffee cultivation in eastern Congo, which is mostly lacking in this research. Secondly, some sources have been inventoried and bundled in sometimes rudimentary inventories, which means that gaining insight into what value particular sources have and whether they are feasible for this research took quite some time. Moreover, since I am dealing with European and African coffee cultivators, it is necessary to know what these categories mean (*supra*). The problem is that sources do mention "European agriculture," which means plantations, but do not differentiate when referring to "African agriculture." For example, obligatory cultivation is often confused

73 Paul van Zwanenberg, "Kenya's primitive colonial capitalism: the economic weakness of Kenya's settlers up to 1940," *Canadian Journal of African Studies* 9, no. 2 (1975): 288.

74 I have translated original French citations into English in order to improve the consistency of the text. Possible translation errors are my own and only my own.

75 For an overview of these archives see: Bérengère Piret, "Reviving the remains of colonization – the Belgian colonial archives in Brussels," *History in Africa* 42 (2015). Furthermore, in 2015, it was decided to transfer all African Archives to the State Archives of Belgium. However, due to a lack of budget, the archives have not been moved yet and will not be transferred in the near future either.

76 De Roo, "Colonial taxation in Africa. A fiscal history of the Congo through the lens of customs (1886–1914)": 21.

with independent production.[77] Smallholders are often represented as people producing coffee freely, even though cultivation was imposed. Consequently, familiarity with the context of the source is crucial.

For an exhaustive source list, I refer the reader to the end of this book. The aim here is to stress which sources I used most and what their particular contribution was. For both the Belgian Congo and Ruanda-Urundi, I consulted territorial annual reports (*Rapports Annuels des Territoires*).[78] These reports contain a lot of information relevant to this book: numbers for instance, but also information about recruitment and sometimes labor conditions.

For the Belgian Congolese Kivu, I supplemented these annual reports with reports produced by the provincial council. These councils shed light on the discussions between different parties (state, planters, missions). Moreover, I consulted numerous dossiers from the inventories Agri (*Agriculture*) and AIMO (*Affaires Indigènes et Main-d'œuvre*) in order to reconstruct land and labor mobilization and commodification. The former were useful to detect the importance of the Comité National du Kivu (CNKi) in land issues, for example, whereas the AIMO files contain not only inspection reports but also correspondence from and with administrations, inspectors and planters, all revealing interesting data on labor conditions.

Important additional sources for the mandate were found in the RWA inventory. Coffee reports – containing technical data but also information on land organization and land use, for example – greatly contributed to this book. Reports sent to the United Nations as well as reports of Visiting Missions (since 1948 the UN visited mandates every three years) are important sources as well. Territorial and even chieftaincy council meetings (these sources are absent or not yet inventoried for the colony) shed light on how chiefs and African notables experienced coffee cultivation and how they thought the sector should evolve. Furthermore, the AIMO files classified in this inventory contributed greatly to my insight into plantation labor conditions in general.

On the one hand, I supplemented these documents with other files held in the African Archives, as well as with dossiers located in other archival depots.

77 For an overview of different categories of African agriculture during the colonial period see: Sven Van Melkebeke, "Dualisme ou dynamisme? Une analyse de l'économie rurale congolaise durant l'Entre-deux-guerres," *Journal of Belgian History* 43, no. 2–3 (2013). Although this publication refers to the Belgian Congo, it can be applied to Ruanda-Urundi as well.

78 The Belgian Congo was administratively divided into provinces, each province into districts and each district into several territories (*territoire*). A territory consisted of several chieftaincies (*chefferie*). Ruanda-Urundi, in turn, was divided into two residences (Ruanda and Urundi), each residence into territories and each territory into chieftaincies.

In order to get a better understanding of the incentives of companies and parastatal organizations, I consulted sources in the State Archives of Belgium (SAB1 and SAB2). At the United Nations Office in Geneva (UNOG), I studied legal texts in order to grasp the judicial difference between a colony (Congo) and a mandate (Ruanda-Urundi) and the impact of this difference on the initial development of the coffee sector. Finally, the online Derscheid collection holds additional material on governmental policy in Shangugu.[79] On the other hand, there are sources that might seem relevant to a project that aims to contribute to the historiography of Belgian Africa, but that I did not use: the missionary sources and dossiers preserved at the Royal Museum for Central Africa (RMCA) in Tervuren.

With regard to missions, I have already claimed that missions were important in the early stages of the spread of *Arabica* in Belgian Africa, but that they did not cultivate for the export market. There is ample evidence (production figures) for this in annual reports. Nevertheless, I visited the White Fathers Archives in Rome (WFAR) with the particular intention of finding more detailed information on labor and land mobilization and the role of empire in this process. I was able to consult some diaries, but the benefit–cost ratio of this particular kind of archival research was too limited. As fathers wrote about people visiting them or about their visiting villages, about temperatures and rainfall, or about their own coffee fields, the contribution to the argument of this book would be very limited.[80] Moreover, most data on labor and land issues mentioned in these diaries are also available in the sources I did use.

Archival documents preserved by the RMCA are principally focused on the CFS and on (a bulky collection of) private dossiers. The records of individuals (agronomists in particular) might have been valuable for the scope of this book. Therefore, I started reading private files. However, I soon realized that, besides personal notes, such files also contained a lot of technical data incomprehensible for a historian lacking botanical knowledge. Moreover, the bank accounts and reports on trips and visits to scientific stations I consulted suggested that such documents were of little value for the scope and the argument of this research.[81]

79 Materials in this collection were collected by Jean-Marie Derscheid, a zoologist and wildlife conservationist who undertook historical research on Rwanda and eastern Congo from 1924 to 1939. Among other things, he is notable for having criticized Belgian colonial agricultural policies.

80 WFAR, Diaires de Rugari, Kabare, Mibirizi et Nyamasheke; D.OR 103/56, D.OR 100/56, D.OR 120/85 and D.OR 120/86.

81 See for instance: RMCA, Collection Privé, Papiers Pierre Staner, no. 79 : 6.

Finally, I did not consult archives in either the Congo or Rwanda. National Archives in Kinshasa and Kigali are difficult to use. This is all the more true for local archives around Lake Kivu, where records are nonexistent, difficult to access, affected by violence in the region or in very bad shape. In many cases preserved archives lack inventories or are transferred. Sources were sometimes deliberately destroyed during war periods, or documents were used by soldiers to make fire (for cooking, for instance).[82] In other cases, archives are ill-preserved, as they are sometimes held in barns exposed to humidity, heat, insects, etcetera. This was not an insurmountable problem, as most records relevant to this research are held in Belgian archives. However, I did visit some coffee plantations in Rwanda. With the help of a guide and a chauffeur, I was able to visit coffee cultivators in both Gisenyi and Shangugu, both situated nearby Lake Kivu. This site visit was very informative, because it allowed me to experience what I had been working on for a couple of years. Rwandan people involved in current-day coffee production explained that coffee is still cultivated in a way that is roughly similar to the method used in the colonial period, although production is mainly organized in cooperatives. Cultivators buy seedlings from the cooperatives, they plant coffee around their homes and, after the harvest, they sell the beans to the cooperatives. The major difference with the colonial period is that, today, the post-harvest steps are done by the cooperative. Washing the harvested beans and preparing them for the market is no longer done by small producers themselves but by people working for the coffee cooperatives. Moreover, in Shangugu, many large-scale plantations were destroyed during the genocide of 1994. Even though coffee remains the main export product for Rwanda as a whole, tea production has made considerable progress since then.

5 Administrative Note

As already explained, the geographical focus in this book is on the Lake Kivu area, or more precisely the colonial territories bordering the lake. I do not take into account minor adaptations to territorial borders in the course of the colonial period, but some major changes require explanation.

On the Congolese side of Lake Kivu, three territories have been examined: Rutshuru in the north, Masisi in the middle and Kabare in the south.[83] However,

82 Mathys, "People on the move. Frontiers, borders, mobility and history in the Lake Kivu region 19th–20th century": 25.

83 Throughout the text I consistently use these names, although in the sources other names were used as well, especially before the 1930s. Kabare was referred to as Banya-Bongo or Unya-Bongo, Masisi as Bahunde-Wanianga and Rutshuru as Bahutu.

from 1945 onwards, Kabare was split up and transformed into two distinct territories: Kabare and Kalehe (see Map 1). I have not researched the latter territory in detail (except for the quantitative Chapter 1) because, firstly, there are only nine annual reports left for Kalehe and, secondly, despite nuances, many of the features relevant to the coffee sector there are similar to those in Kabare. From 1954 onwards, Masisi was also divided into two territories: Masisi and Walikale (see Map 2). I have not examined the latter territory because, from 1954 onwards, annual reports are lacking and, in addition, in Walikale mining was more important than coffee production.

On the Rwandan side of Lake Kivu, I also analyzed three territories: Gisenyi in the north, Kibuye in the middle and Shangugu in the south.[84] However, due to a lack of financial resources, on January 1, 1936, the Belgian administration decided to eliminate Kibuye and split up this territory. Kibuye was absorbed by neighboring territories (Gisenyi, Shangugu and Nyanza). But from February 1, 1953, onwards, the territory was reinstated (see Map 2). This means that during the period 1936–1953, there were only two Rwandan territories that bordered Lake Kivu.

A final "administrative" remark. After World War I, the former German colonies of Rwanda and Burundi became a mandate of Belgium: Ruanda-Urundi. Up until 1945, it was called a mandate, but from that point onwards, the official denotation (and perspective) changed to "trusteeship."[85] European trusteeholders were urged to put more emphasis on political development, which had to result in future self-government. More international control would be initiated (for instance, from 1948 onwards there was to be a visiting mission every three years). Moreover, the United Nations charter stated that people living in trusteeships should prevail and not the metropole. In practice, however, in Ruanda-Urundi, the shift in policy went very slowly, and was often only half-and-half. Partly because of this, I continue to use the term "mandate" for the entire colonial period, even though after 1945 Ruanda-Urundi should be properly called a "trusteeship." The consistent use of the term is also for clarity, in order not to overwhelm readers with a surplus of judicial/administrative terms and definitions.

---

84 In what follows I use those names. Except for Kibuye (Lubengera), names seem to have changed little or not at all, as opposed to the Belgian Congo. The spelling of territorial names could vary, however: Cyangugu or Kisenyi, for instance.

85 Filip Reyntjens, *Pouvoir et droit au Rwanda: droit public et évolution politique, 1916–1973* (Tervuren: Musée Royal de l'Afrique Centrale, 1985): 210.

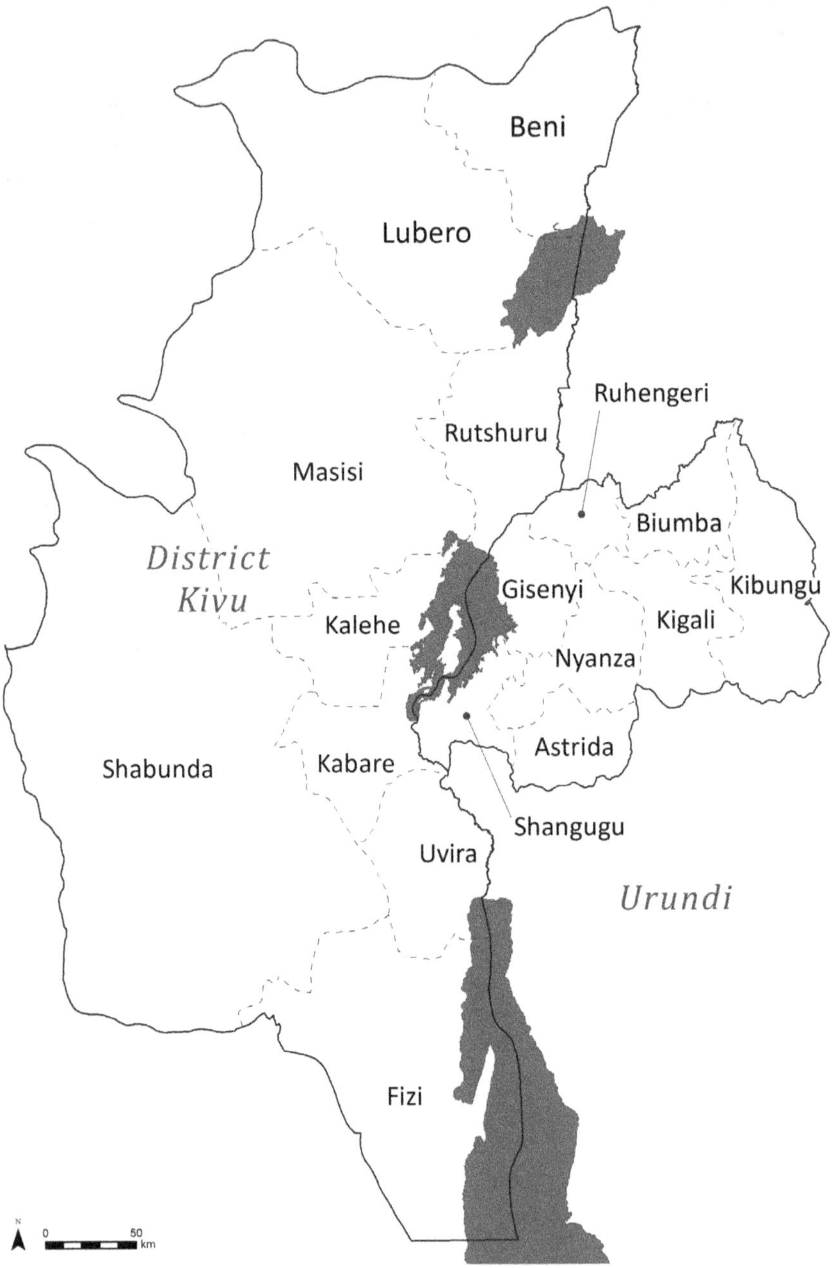

MAP 1 Colonial territories (*territoires*) around Lake Kivu in 1945
Note: Full line: district/residence; dotted line: territory.

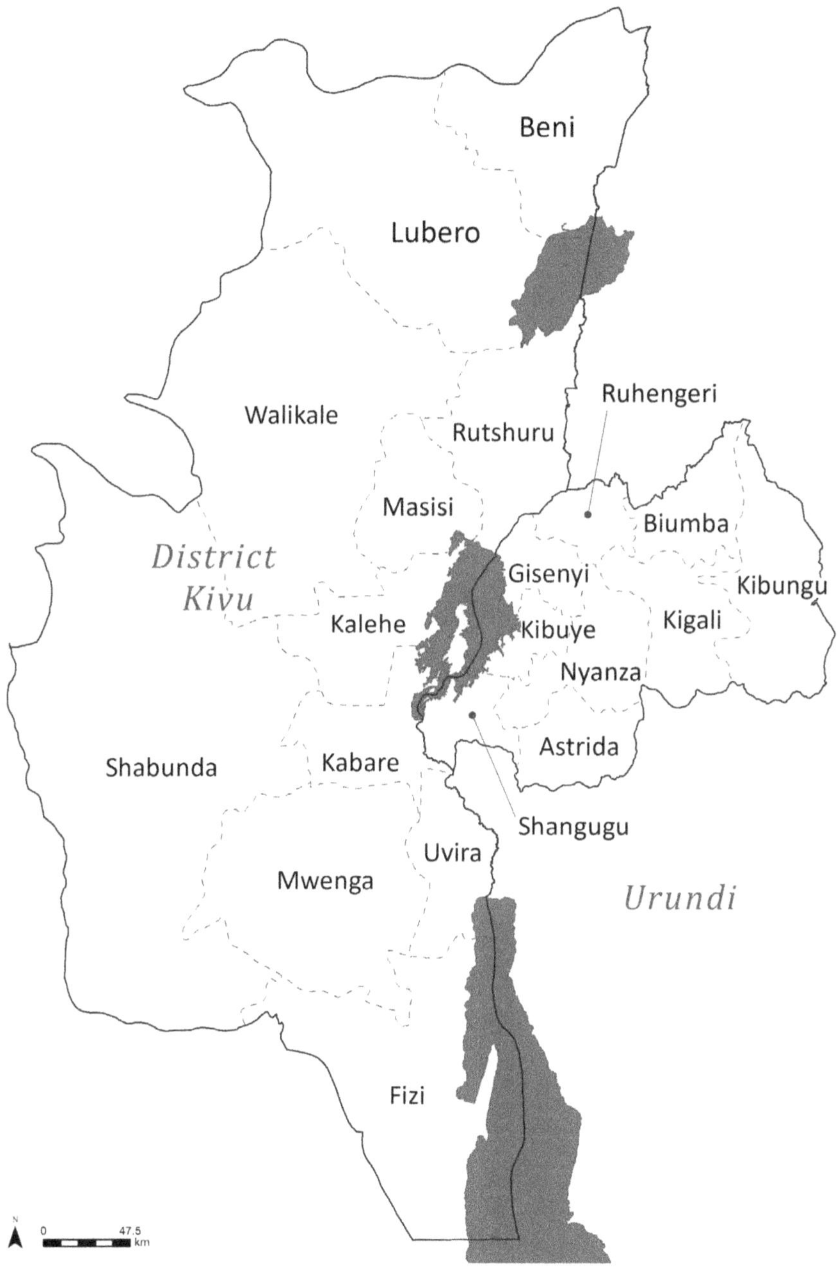

MAP 2 Colonial territories around Lake Kivu in 1955
Note: Full line: district/residence; dotted line: territory.

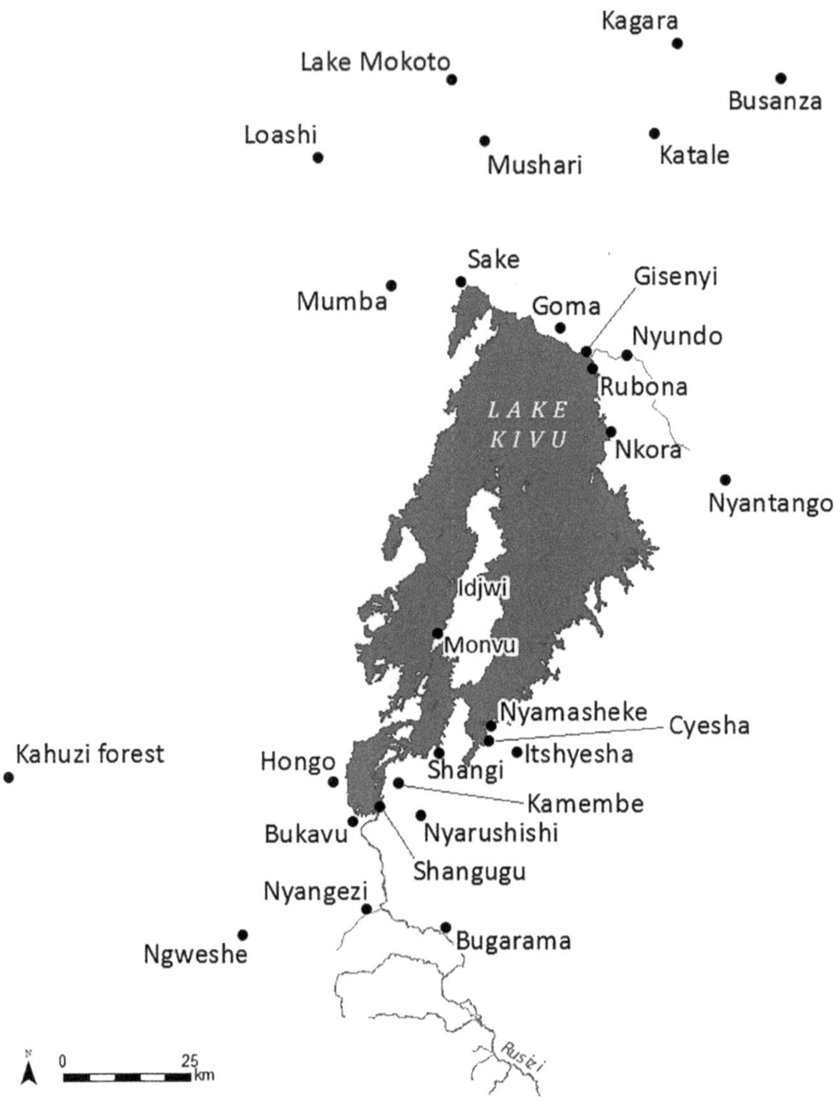

MAP 3 Indicative map with places mentioned in the text

6 Outline

The aim of this book is to compare two regions separated by a colonially imposed border, but still belonging to one historical complex. Although the classification of the sources is clearly marked by the colonial period (*supra*), comparisons allow the transcending of colonial demarcations and contribute to a better historical understanding of coffee production on a global scale. To be more concrete, by comparing the two sides of Lake Kivu, I use the colonially instigated border as a mirror. At the same time, I try to grasp the Lake Kivu region as one region, by tackling issues that apply across the Congolese–Rwandan border. As opposed to "incorporated comparisons" offering the occasion to compare over time and space,[86] "comparison" here means reciprocal comparison[87] between localities in the same period and the same zone. By asking the same set of questions of the Congolese and the Rwandan side, more light will be shed on the development of the coffee commodity frontier and the role of empire in the Lake Kivu region in the colonial period.

A short prelude offers an overview of precolonial communities in the Lake Kivu region, and precedes the six chapters of this book.

Each of these chapters is set up thematically, although I have also tried to maintain a chronological structure in each chapter as much as possible. Part 1, "Structural basis," consists of two chapters. In these chapters, I present a macroeconomic analysis of the coffee sector around Lake Kivu. Part 2, "On the ground," contains the four remaining chapters in which labor and land issues will be tackled at length and in detail.

Chapter 1 offers a quantitative approach to the coffee sector in the former Belgian colonial sphere.[88] The aim is not only to situate this sector in the global coffee economy but also, by presenting figures regarding production, the size of land used in the coffee sector and the amount of laborers involved over time, to answer criticism formulated in 2000 about the lack of use of quantitative data in African history.[89]

Chapter 2 explains the difference between plantations based in the west and smallholders based in the east of the Lake Kivu coffee sector. This chapter analyzes and evaluates different possible explanations in order to determine the most plausible reasons for the divergence in economic development.

86 See: Philip McMichael, "Incorporating comparison within a world-historical perspective: an alternative comparative method," *American Sociological Review* 55, no. 3 (1990).

87 Based on Gareth Austin, "Reciprocal comparison and African history: tackling conceptual Eurocentrism in the study of Africa's economic past," *African Studies Review* 50, no. 3 (2007).

88 Parts of the first and second chapter are also published in: Sven Van Melkebeke, "Divergence in rural development: the curious case of coffee production in the Lake Kivu region (first half twentieth century)," *African Economic History* 46, no. 2 (2018). I thank the editors of this journal for their permission to reprint.

89 David Newbury and Catharine Newbury, "Bringing the peasants back in: agrarian themes in the construction and corrosion of statist historiography in Rwanda," *The American Historical Review* 105, no. 3 (2000): 834.

Moreover, this chapter also elaborates on "reversed modes of production" – plantations in western Rwanda and smallholders in eastern Congo.

Chapter 3 focuses on land. By comparing land mobilization for the coffee sector in both the colony and the mandate, similarities and differences will be highlighted. Attention will be paid to disputes between different local actors and tensions over land. Precolonial conditions will be considered too, because these contributed to the way land tenure evolved during the colonial period.

Chapter 4 unravels the various ways in which coffee labor was mobilized: the ways people were recruited or the limitation of competition in the colony, the ways people in Rwanda were incorporated into cash-crop production for the export market, and also the ways Rwandan plantations attained sufficient laborers. Precolonial labor mobilization will also receive attention because, especially for Rwanda in the start-up epoch, Belgium relied strongly on African notables and existing patterns of labor in order to incorporate rural cultivators.

Chapter 5 scrutinizes labor commodification. It focuses on labor treatment and labor relations. Labor categories in both the colony and the mandate will be analyzed. This chapter also pays attention to the working conditions of both plantation workers and smallholders, as well as to their remunerations and their purchasing power. Similarly to the previous chapter, a particular emphasis will be put on the role of the state in relation to other actors on the ground.

The final chapter is particularly devoted to the feedback from Africans involved in the coffee sector, even though in previous chapters "the African side" is not ignored. Placing this chapter at the end might give the false impression that Africans' struggles are an afterthought. Africans' reactions to capitalism were not just defensive reactions but one of the parameters within which labor recruitment had to function.[90] Consequently, feedback should be understood as a loop influencing coffee labor and land mobilizations as much as these mobilizations influenced Africans' livelihoods. Contrary to the three previous chapters, this chapter presents the Lake Kivu region as one region because much of the feedback was trans-border and/or broadly similar along the border. The first part of this chapter zooms in on the "weapons of the weak." Forms of resistance, sabotage, migrations, etcetera will be discussed. The second part stresses the way people reacted to the entrance of capital, how coffee workers reorganized subsistence activities and made use of markets to increase incomes, and how they continued to trade despite the delineation of a border.

In the conclusion, I recapitulate the main insights offered in this book and connect its empirical underpinnings to the main argument.

---

90 Cooper, "Africa and the World Economy": 126 and 133.

PRELUDE

The Lake Kivu Region in the Nineteenth Century

Lake Kivu is part of the African Great Lakes region. Notwithstanding the cohesion within this "interlacustrine" region (in the form of social/political/religious resemblances), regional diversity is equally prominent.[1] The Lake Kivu region is situated between two distinct mountain ranges: the Congo-Nile divide to the east of the lake and the Mitumba Mountains to the west. This topographical feature was helpful in shaping a natural geographical zone of shoreline people.[2] Consisting of regions in what is now eastern Congo and western Rwanda, this zone was (and still is) regarded as culturally distinct from the Congolese forest zone and from people east of the Congo-Nile divide.[3]

Although there are arguments for labeling the Lake Kivu region as one historical zone, focusing on similarities would blur political, social and cultural diversity within the region. This prelude will therefore present an analytical overview of the communities and social-political structures around Lake Kivu in the decades prior to colonization. The goal is to give not an exhaustive overview but rather a brief analytical sketch in order to provide contextualization for what follows in the subsequent chapters.

The indicative Map 4 shows that the Lake Kivu region harbored several, often interlinked, political/cultural zones in the second half of the nineteenth century. But there were no fixed boundaries between these zones; realms of influence could shift (through conquest for instance); and, moreover, some communities succeeded in stay outside these zones. Furthermore, living in a certain zone did not imply a definitive geographical identity: living in Buhavu, for example, did not equate with "being a Havu." Fluidity and mobility, both geographical and social, were characteristic of the area around precolonial Lake Kivu. Not only were there several social-political and economic ties but people were also able to shift between cultural "identities."[4] As such, I intend to use these categories only for reasons of readability, because categorizing people in the years prior to the colonial period is somewhat anachronistic:

---

1 Chrétien, *The Great Lakes of Africa. Two thousand years of history*: 23–25.

2 David Newbury, *Kings and clans: Ijwi Island and the Lake Kivu Rift, 1780–1840* (Madison: University of Wisconsin Press, 1991): 23.

3 David Newbury, "'Bunyabungo': the western Rwandan frontier, c.1750–1850," in *The African frontier: the reproduction of traditional African societies*, ed. Igor Kopytoff (Bloomington: Indiana University Press, 1987): 165–166.

4 Ibid, especially Chapters 9–11.

 | DOI:10.1163/9789004428492_003

MAP 4 Some "cultural" zones in the Lake Kivu region, circa second half nineteenth century
SOURCE: BASED ON NEWBURY, *KINGS AND CLANS: IJWI ISLAND AND THE LAKE KIVU RIFT, 1780–1840*: 22

present-day ethnic categories are not a mere continuation from precolonial times.[5] A recent article claims that colonizers misconceived complexities

5 Mathys, "People on the move. Frontiers, borders, mobility and history in the Lake Kivu region 19th–20th century": 51.

associated with fluidity and mobility. In the colonial period, cultural zones became integrated into *chefferies* and *territoires*, and as such the colonial state assumed that a "cultural group" occupied a certain territory with clear boundaries and with a rigid centralized political organization.[6] But, as the remainder of this prelude suggests, that was hardly the case.

1 Lake Kivu's Communities

In spite of variations and nuances, communities in the Lake Kivu region were broadly organized in either kinship-based or non-kinship-based structures on the eve of colonization. On the one hand, lineages (corporate groups with a shared descent) or clans (groups with a common identity) governed small areas independently of each other. On the other hand, small polities (kingdoms) bringing together different lineages/clans reigned over larger areas. These polities were ruled by a king (*mwami*), and the organizing principle was not kinship but rather ritual claims to the productivity of the land and the wellbeing of the population.[7] However, what the late Vansina observes for precolonial Rwanda also applies to the regions west of the lake: social-political structures were not rigid and were often fluid, and moreover, these two main types of organization often interacted with each other.[8]

Bushi, to the southwest of Lake Kivu, is the first example of the coexistence of several forms of organization. Despite relative cultural homogeneity, Bushi was not a unified political entity in the nineteenth century. Covering an area of about 4600 square kilometers, Bushi consisted of seven kingdoms, of which only Kabare and Ngweshe were more or less centralized.[9] As well as these kingdoms, Bushi also harbored several independent polities with ties to either Kabare or Nwgeshe.[10] The more centralized nature of social-political organization, especially in Kabare and Nwgeshe, is demonstrated by two features: the

6 Mathys, "Bringing history back in: past, present, and conflict in Rwanda and the Eastern Democratic Republic of Congo": 475–479.

7 David Newbury, "Precolonial Burundi and Rwanda: local loyalties, regional royalties," *International Journal of African Historical Studies* 34, no. 2 (2001): 290. Newbury refers to communities to the east of Lake Kivu, but the situation to the west was comparable.

8 Jan Vansina, *L'évolution du royaume rwanda des origines à 1900* (Bruxelles: Académie Royale des Sciences d'Outre-Mer, 2000): 92.

9 Chubaka Bishikwabo, "Le Bushi au XIXe siècle: un peuple, sept royaumes," *Revue Française d'Histoire d'Outre-Mer* 67, no. 246–247 (1980): 89–90; and Richard Sigwalt, "The early history of Bushi. An essay in the historical use of genesis traditions" (Unpublished PhD dissertation, University of Wisconsin, 1975): 11.

10 Pierre Colle, *Essai de monographie des Bashi* (Bukavu: Centre d'Etude de Langues Africaines, 1971): 257.

existence of perpetual kingship and of a certain stratification. When a king died, he was succeeded by his son. But in absence of a legal successor or in cases where the son was a minor, it was instead the queen-mother who governed with a regency council, until her son was old enough or powerful enough to replace her.[11] Moreover, some regions of Bushi were characterized by distinct socio-economic classes: for example, rich men who had at least three sons, a few cows and an entourage belonged to the class of the *Bagula*.[12]

More to the north, in Buhavu and Butembo, a similar mix of different types of organization existed. In the first zone, independent groups and small kingdoms coexisted and interacted. In many ways the Havu shared more characteristics (cattle contracts, for example) associated with present-day Burundi than with Bushi or modern Rwanda.[13] Butembo, on the other hand, shared features with Bushi and Havu.[14] In the course of the nineteenth century, clan structures evolved into several small kingdoms in which ritual claims gained importance but where centralization was very weak, as people within these realms were too itinerant to allow for an institutionalization of power.[15]

In the Tembo kingdoms, kings were referred to not as *mwami* but as *mubake*, which was also the case in Buhundu.[16] This latter zone to the northwest of Lake Kivu was not a unified political entity but rather a place of relative cultural unity in roughly the second half of the nineteenth century. As well as independent polities, Buhundu consisted of several clans which had been evolving into small kingdoms, although it is unclear when this evolution happened. Nevertheless, even in the early twentieth century there were several small kingdoms (Bunyungu, for instance) with mutual ties and, similarly to in Bushi, the Hundu also seem to have applied a form of perpetual kingship.[17] However, in this region matrilineal succession seems to have been prominent, because here the king was often succeeded by his sororal nephew – which more resembles polities of the east of Lake Kivu.

---

11 Elinor Sosne, "Of biases and queens: the Shi past through an androgynous looking glass," *History in Africa* 6 (1979): 233.

12 Colle, *Essai de monographie des Bashi*: 256.

13 Newbury, *Kings and clans: Ijwi Island and the Lake Kivu Rift, 1780–1840*: 149.

14 Chubaka Bishikwabo, "La politique indigène au Congo-belge et son application au Kivu: de la légitimé à l'illégitimé (1900–1945)," *Zamani* 1 (1984): 62.

15 Newbury, *Kings and clans: Ijwi Island and the Lake Kivu Rift, 1780–1840*: 50–51; and Mathys, "People on the move. Frontiers, borders, mobility and history in the Lake Kivu region 19th–20th century": 319 (footnote 75).

16 A different notion for "king," with broadly the same function as a *mwami*, points to a different origin, as *mubake* seems to have been imported from Buganda (Leo Viaene, "L'organisation politique des Bahunde," *Kongo-Overzee* 18, no. 1 (1952): 8).

17 Ibid: 9.

On the other side of the lake, in what is now western Rwanda, similar patterns can be distinguished. In Bugoyi, social and political life was regulated through lineage/clan lines in the decades prior to colonization. These groups coexisted and had ties with small kingdoms such as Bushiru, where ritual justification of kingship and matrilineal succession featured.[18] People in Bugoyi also had different kinds of ties with people in Buhundu, from commercial to social ties (land clientship, for instance). Also, many inhabitants of Bugoyi seem to have roots in regions to the west of the lake.[19]

In Kinyaga, the organizing principle for political and social life in the middle of the nineteenth century was a patchwork of lineages and clans that were autonomous but had mutual ties. Lineages protected their members (and their cattle), lineage heads possessed moral authority and political hierarchy was lacking.[20] Similarly to in Bugoyi, people in Kinyaga often had several ties with people living in Bushi, and mobility between these two cultural zones was high. This even resulted in the emergence of a small independent kingdom called Bukunzi. According to Mathys, this kingdom claimed its origins in areas to the west of Lake Kivu and many people coming from Bushi inhabited this kingdom – including elites linked to Ngweshe who had fled internal struggles.[21]

2 Peculiarities of the Region

Communities in the Lake Kivu region evolved and diversified internally in the centuries before the second half of the nineteenth century, despite the rather static sketch presented above. Moreover, before the eighteenth century this region was part of the forest cultural zone of the Kivu Rift Valley and resembled Congolese hinterland communities. It was characterized by a relatively egalitarian society, little social hierarchy, a lot of mobility, and an economy primarily based on gathering, hunting, and fishing. However, over the course of the eighteenth and nineteenth centuries the limits of this zone moved from the east of Lake Kivu to west of it (Mitumba Mountains). From then on, the

18 Newbury, "Precolonial Burundi and Rwanda: local loyalties, regional royalties": 291.

19 Mathys, "People on the move. Frontiers, borders, mobility and history in the Lake Kivu region 19th–20th century": 56.

20 Newbury, *The cohesion of oppression. Clientship and ethnicity in Rwanda, 1860–1960*: 95–96; and Newbury, "Ethnicity in Rwanda: the case of Kinyaga," *Africa: Journal of the International African Institute* 48, no. 1 (1978): 18–19.

21 Mathys, "People on the move. Frontiers, borders, mobility and history in the Lake Kivu region 19th–20th century": 51.

Lake Kivu region developed into a transitional zone between the Congolese forest zone and central Rwanda.[22]

In addition to these evolutions, two changes coming from the east had a major impact on the social-political and economic structures of the region in the course of the nineteenth century. Because these two changes also influenced the development of coffee production in the colonial period, it is important to discuss them concisely in this "precolonial prelude."

From about 1870, Arab troops commanded by Tippu Tip occupied parts of present-day eastern Congo – establishing control most effectively in Uele and Maniema[23] – during the so-called Zanzibari colonization.[24] While advancing through the region, the Zanzibari not only caused material damage by burning down habitations. They also captured people – usually men but also women who then were incorporated into the raiders' harems – and enslaved them. These slaves were then forced to work as porters, servants, soldiers or plantation workers. Although the Zanzibari did not succeed in establishing control over the regions bordering the lake, changes in existing patterns of labor mobilization also affected labor systems of communities near to Lake Kivu.

The second major change came from the established Nyiginya Kingdom in central Rwanda. Here, some kind of social stratification with elites (possessing luxury goods and more cattle, for instance) already existed in the seventeenth century. In the course of the eighteenth century, stratification developed further and elites succeeded in establishing a centralized, hierarchical kingdom by developing a court, by organizing permanent armies, and by acquiring all land and cattle.[25] Up until the middle of the eighteenth century, people living in the Kivu region had no contact with this Central Court. But from then on, army groups were installed – albeit irregularly and not everywhere at once – in areas that were not yet integrated into the kingdom. Army leaders, appointed by the Central Court, performed military and administrative duties and sent tribute collected from lineages to the Central Court.[26] Backed by a growing military apparatus the Central Court tried to establish control in regions in what is now eastern Rwanda. One implication of this was that many people

22 Newbury, *Kings and clans: Ijwi Island and the Lake Kivu Rift, 1780–1840*: 16–17.

23 Melvin E. Page, "The Manyema hordes of Tippu Tip: a case study in social stratification and the slave trade in Eastern Africa," *International Journal of African Historical Studies* 7, no. 1 (1974).

24 See in particular: Northrup, *Beyond the bend in the river: African labor in Eastern Zaire 1865–1940*: 23–36.

25 Jan Vansina, *Antecedents to modern Rwanda. The Nyiginya kingdom* (Madison: University of Wisconsin Press, 2004): 32 and 67.

26 Newbury, "'Bunyabungo': the western Rwandan frontier, c.1750–1850": 169.

fled westwards in an attempt to escape incorporation into the Nyiginya Kingdom with its growing social-political centralization. Yet these "refugees" shared political and cultural attributes related to central Rwanda and subsequently developed ties with the Central Court. In this way, these people were *de facto* vanguards in expanding centralized structures to the east of Lake Kivu.[27]

However, prior to the reign of Rwabugiri (from 1867 until his death in 1895), regions on the fringe of the Nyiginya Kingdom were relatively autonomous. These regions indeed felt the influence of the Central Court but were not yet part of the precolonial Rwandan state.[28] With Rwabugiri, the expansion of the kingdom intensified. This was a period of increased violence: not only in order to force people in newly incorporated regions to pay tribute to the Central Court, but also the assassination of notables who contested infiltration by the royal armies.[29] Besides sending armies to areas not yet incorporated into his kingdom, Rwabugiri also installed residences in those regions (including Bugoyi and Kinyaga) in order to accelerate subjection. Evidence suggests that Rwabugiri even managed to place residences in regions to the west of Lake Kivu, such as Buhundu. From there, Rwabugiri allegedly attempted to control the commercial ivory trade and was possibly also interested in slaves.[30] Moreover, the king also tried to establish control over Bushi and Idjwi island. Rwabugiri launched three expeditions to Bushi in an attempt to control this zone, but he did not fully succeed. Idjwi was placed under effective control of the Central Court until Rwabugiri's death. With the king's death, the Nyiginya Kingdom immediately lost control over both Idjwi and Bushi.[31]

The expansion of the Rwandan state under Rwabugiri should not be over- or underestimated. On the one hand, this process was gradual, often contested, regionally uneven and ongoing when the colonial period started.[32] On the eve of colonization, some regions that are part of present-day Rwanda were already fully incorporated, while in others state structures were still fragile. On the other hand, this process intensified the expansion of hierarchical, centralized structures, including new forms of clientship, and new systems of labor mobilization and land tenure, that both proved to be crucial for the development of the coffee sector in (western) Rwanda. This will be discussed at length in the following chapters.

27 Ibid: 170–171.
28 Vansina, *L'évolution du royaume rwanda des origines à 1900*: 78.
29 Ibid: 70–71; and Vansina, *Antecedents to modern Rwanda. The Nyiginya kingdom*: 164–165.
30 Vansina, *Antecedents to modern Rwanda. The Nyiginya kingdom*: 170.
31 Ibid: 173 and 176–177.
32 Ibid: 194–195.

PART 1

Structural Basis

CHAPTER 1

Coffee Production: From the Global to the Local

1 The Roots

The aim of this part is not to write another "coffee history," as there already is a vast literature on this theme.[1] Rather, the goal is to present a short summary of the global spread of the *Arabica* and the way in which this variety eventually entered the Lake Kivu region. This first chapter offers a quantitative approach to the development of the coffee commodity frontier in the former Belgian colonial sphere. By presenting figures regarding production, the size of land used and the number of laborers involved, I will situate the coffee sector around Lake Kivu within the global coffee economy.

1.1 *"Out of Africa"*

Coffee was cultivated for regional markets in Abyssinia from the fifteenth century onwards. The crop quickly spread to Yemen, and for the next three centuries coffee was grown and marketed almost exclusively in those two Red Sea regions.[2] Only in the late seventeenth century did Europeans succeed in breaking the Arabian monopoly. The Dutch introduced the crop in Indonesia (Java), and by the 1720s, French and Dutch scientists had examined it in their botanical gardens in Paris and Amsterdam before introducing it in their overseas colonies (Suriname, Martinique, Réunion, etcetera).[3] Next, the *Arabica* spread from Réunion to Madagascar and subsequently to mainland Eastern Africa at the end of the nineteenth century.[4] Coffee was also introduced in other parts of the world from the eighteenth century onwards. Up until the last quarter of

---

1 See for instance: Lucette Chabouis, *Le livre du café* (Paris: Bordas, 1988); Frédéric Mauro, *Histoire du café* (Paris: Editions Desjonquères, 1991); Gordon Wringley, *Coffee* (Harlow: Longman, 1988); or Antony Wild, *Coffee: a dark history* (New York; London: W.W. Norton & Company, 2004).

2 Steven Topik, "The integration of the world coffee market," in *The global coffee economy in Africa, Asia, and Latin America 1500–1989*, ed. William Gervase Clarence-Smith and Steven Topik (Cambridge; New York: Cambridge University Press, 2003): 25. And Topik and Wells, *Global markets transformed, 1870–1945*: 219.

3 Topik, "The integration of the world coffee market." 27–28. See also Carey Watt, "'A world of history in your cup': teaching coffee as global commodity c.1400–2000," *World History Bulletin* 28, no. 2 (2012): 17.

4 For an analysis of the coffee production in Réunion and Madagascar, see: Gwyn Campbell, "The origins and development of coffee production in Réunion and Madagascar, 1711–1972,"

 | DOI:10.1163/9789004428492_004

the nineteenth century, coffee was a luxury item, produced by a few and consumed by the happy few. From that moment, however, and parallel with the rise of imperialism, a global coffee market emerged. This resulted in coffee's "conversion" from a luxury product to a "pure" commodity.[5] In response to the ascendency of coffee as a mass commodity, new zones of coffee cultivation emerged in Latin America, Asia, Oceania and Africa (including the Kivu).[6]

1.2 *African "Comeback" and the "Birth" of the Kivu Coffee*

After its global diffusion, *Arabica* "re-entered" Africa and made its way to the Kivu region. In the late nineteenth and early twentieth centuries, "a small body of priests and lay brothers could play an important role in the initial stages of the diffusion of what is now one of East Africa's major exports."[7] Indeed, apart from a handful of colonial administrators, Christian missionaries played the decisive role in the distribution of coffee seedlings on the East African mainland. In the 1870s, after Father Charles Gommeninger (Saint-Esprits order) traveled to the island of Réunion, he introduced *Arabica* seeds on the Tanzanian shoreline.[8] About two decades later, *Arabica* traveled to the Kilimanjaro region, thanks to Father Auguste (Charles' brother).[9] In the final decade of the nineteenth century, the crop spread rapidly. Thanks to missionary fathers, land was brought into cultivation not only in Tanzania, Kenya and Uganda, but also around Lake Kivu. As early as 1891, the first *Arabica* plantations emerged around the posts of the White Fathers in Bujumbura (east Lake Tanganyika),

---

in *The global coffee economy in Africa, Asia, and Latin America 1500–1989*, ed. William Gervase Clarence-Smith and Steven Topik (Cambridge; New York: Cambridge University Press, 2003).

5 Watt, "'A world of history in your cup': teaching coffee as global commodity c.1400–2000": 18.

6 See, among many others: for Central America, William H. Hempstead, *The history of coffee in Guateamla* (Bogota: Villegas Asociados, 2001); for Latin America, Marcos Palacios, *Coffee in Colombia, 1850–1970. An economic, social, and political history* (Cambridge: Cambridge University Press, 1980).; for Asia, Jan Breman, *Mobilizing labour for the global coffee market. Profits from an unfree work regime in colonial Java* (Amsterdam: Amsterdam University Press, 2015); for Oceania, Paige West, *From modern production to imagined primitive: the social world of coffee from Papua New Guinea* (Durham (North Carolina): Duke University Press, 2012); for Africa, Brad Weiss, *Sacred trees, bitter harvests. Globalizing coffee in Northwest Tanzania* (Portsmouth: Heinemann, 2003).

7 J.A. Kieran, "The origins of commercial Arabica coffee production in East Africa," *African Historical Studies* 2, no. 1 (1969). 67.

8 Ibid: 54.

9 Ibid: 59–61.

and in 1893 the first beans entered the southeastern Congo (west Lake Tanganyika), before spreading further to the north.[10]

Although *Arabica* was unknown in both Ruanda-Urundi and the Kivu in the precolonial period, in the 1930s botanists discovered unknown coffee varieties in both regions. An expedition of the SAAK[11] (Société Auxiliaire Agricole du Kivu) in the Kahuzi forest – situated west of Bukavu in the Mitumba Range – had revealed the existence of a variety with some resemblances to the *Arabica*. The president of the SAAK immediately asked for the creation of a *zone de protection* around the location where this *Coffea Kivuensis* was found in order to examine this seemingly indigenous variety.[12] Near the center of Rwanda, botanists discovered another unknown variety (*Coffea Becquetii*). But whether this type was introduced in precolonial times or grew spontaneously was a question scientists were unable to answer in the mid-1930s.[13] It is also unclear whether Africans cultivated these varieties in precolonial times. Nevertheless, neither variety was ever cultivated for the market and consequently they are of no further significance for this book.

Coffee cultivation was not limited to missionaries before World War I. As in colonial Tanzania, German administrators distributed seedlings to small farmers in Rwanda and Burundi, enabling these farmers to pay their taxes.[14] Chiefs and sub-chiefs, on the other hand, succeeded in developing large estates with laborers cultivating the coffee as a form of *corvée* labor.[15] The choice of smallholder production was based on the British cotton production system in Uganda, and as such, "the Germans excluded both the possibility of European colonization in these populated regions and the prospect of a workforce exodus to the coast: they opted instead for making a profit from African labor onsite."[16] However, as Alexandre Hatungimana points out, despite the attempts of the Germans in the early twentieth century, coffee cultivation was still scarce in Rwanda and Burundi before the 1930s, and was limited to the vicinity of the military-administrative posts.[17]

10 R.P. Watteyne, "Le café du Kivu," *Bulletin Agricole du Congo Belge* 21, no. 3 (1930): 939.
11 The SAAK (founded 1929) was a large company active in coffee production across the entire Kivu district. It also engaged in processing harvests and scientific research.
12 AAB, Agri, Compagnies, CNKi (650), Lettre du président de la SAAK à la CNKi, 24/5/1932.
13 Georges Molitor, "L'introduction et le développement de la culture du caféier Arabica chez les indigènes du Ruanda-Urundi," *Le Matériel Colonial* 27, no. 6 (1937): 159.
14 Ralph A. Austen, *Northwest Tanzania under German and British rule. Colonial policy and tribal politics, 1889–1939* (New Haven; London: Yale University Press, 1968): 55.
15 Chrétien, *The Great Lakes of Africa. Two thousand years of history*: 258.
16 Ibid: 259.
17 Hatungimana, *Le café au Burundi au XXe siècle: Paysans, argent, pouvoir*: 79 and 106.

To the west of Lake Kivu in eastern Congo, private coffee cultivation started only after World War I, with expansive growth from the mid-1920s onwards. The main reason for this "late" valorization (compared with other cash crops in the rest of the Belgian Congo) is the military occupation of the region and the protection of the border with German East Africa.[18] Hence, there was a lack of economic interests before the war. The military campaign against the Germans changed this situation significantly. Belgian Congolese troops, supported by British soldiers, managed to defeat German troops in the border region east of the lake in 1916.[19] This campaign "had revealed to many the potential for European colonization in the hitherto neglected district of Kivu, whose volcanic soils, salubrious climate, abundant African labor, and physical beauty favored European agriculture, especially coffee plantations and cattle raising (both pioneered well before the war at the White Fathers' missions)."[20]

It is hardly surprising that, immediately after World War I, the two first colonists establishing coffee plantations west of Lake Kivu (Dierckx and Baselen) were former members of the Belgian military. Other European planters (mostly Belgian) followed the example of these "founding fathers" to the extent that some authors label the mid-1920s the beginning of the "rush of colonists."[21] Indeed, from that moment on the plantation economy in the Kivu expanded substantially. While in 1924 there were only eleven *colons agricoles* in this region, at the end of the 1930s the number of settlers had reached approximately 160.[22]

The German attempts to stimulate coffee production in Rwanda and Burundi did not continue straightforwardly after the war. First of all, there was the difficult political-administrative situation of the former German colonies. Up until 1924, a series of discussions and diplomatic consultations between Belgium, Great Britain and the United States were detrimental for both regions' economies. The different geopolitical actors finally reached an agreement on the status of Rwanda and Burundi in 1925. From then on, these

18 See for further details and other border-related issues in this area: Mathys, "People on the move. Frontiers, borders, mobility and history in the Lake Kivu region 19th–20th century."

19 Ingeborg Vijgen, *Tussen mandaat en kolonie. Rwanda, Burundi en het Belgische bestuur in opdracht van de Volkenbond (1916–1932)* (Leuven: Acco, 2005): 49.

20 Northrup, *Beyond the bend in the river: African labor in Eastern Zaire 1865–1940*: 148. As Northrup indicates, this potential was not unknown to Europeans before World War I, as the presence and the experiments with coffee of fathers suggest.

21 Ibid, and Michael B. Ost, "Agricultural laborers in Kivu, 1919–1939" (Unpublished Master thesis, University of Wisconsin, 1979): 11–12.

22 Bogumil Jewsiewicki, "Le colonat agricole européen au Congo-belge, 1910–1960: questions politiques économiques," *Journal of African History* 20, no. 4 (1979). 562–564. The 160 *colons* in the Kivu district represented one third of the total number of agrarian colonists in the Belgian Congo (479).

two formerly unattached regions were tied together into the Belgian mandate of Ruanda-Urundi.[23]

Secondly, similarly to in colonial Tanzania, Belgians tried to diversify cash-crop cultivation before fully concentrating on coffee.[24] Mandate administrators attempted to popularize coffee in the early 1920s, but were opposed mainly by sorcerers and notables (*infra*).[25] Due to the failure of the obligatory cultivation of palm oil, red pepper, castor oil and tobacco, the Belgian administration resolved upon turning coffee into the driving force of the economic *mise en valeur* from the 1930s onwards – despite initial resistance.[26] In order to achieve that goal, colonial officials launched seven consecutive coffee campaigns between 1931 and 1938. Using local (sub-)chiefs and various missions as role models, the Belgian government aimed at familiarizing Africans with a cash-crop economy.[27] Additionally, chiefs not only acted as "teachers" using customary labor systems. In close collaboration with European agronomists, African "coffee monitors" (see Chapter 4) and policemen, chiefs supervised and strictly controlled coffee producers in the remainder of the colonial period.[28] As in the area to the west of Lake Kivu, the coffee sector grew rapidly. In 1937, 50 to 70% of all taxpayers in the whole of Ruanda-Urundi were cultivating coffee on small pieces of land.[29]

2 Producing for the Global Market

The previous pages suggest that east and west of Lake Kivu two different coffee production systems developed. In eastern Congo a plantation economy – run by white settlers on concessionary (usually large) estates using African wage

23 For a more detailed analysis of this "mandate issue," see especially: Vijgen, *Tussen mandaat en kolonie. Rwanda, Burundi en het Belgische bestuur in opdracht van de Volkenbond (1916–1932)*.

24 The British also tried to diversify export commodity production by forcing Africans to cultivate cotton and chili peppers in the early 1920s. However, as in Ruanda-Urundi, these efforts were unsuccessful (Austen, *Northwest Tanzania under German and British rule. Colonial policy and tribal politics, 1889–1939*: 137).

25 S.N., "Le développement de la culture du café dans les milieux indigènes du Ruanda-Urundi," *Servir* 10, no. 3 (1949): 106–107.

26 Hatungimana, *Le café au Burundi au XXe siècle: Paysans, argent, pouvoir*: 72–73 and 79.

27 Ibid: 159.

28 Ibid: 162–170. For a general overview of the compulsory cultivation system in the Belgian Congo, see: Jan Vansina, *Being colonized: the Kuba experience in rural Congo, 1880–1960* (Madison: University of Wisconsin Press, 2010). For an excellent case study, see: Likaka, *Rural society and cotton in colonial Zaire*.

29 Chrétien, *The Great Lakes of Africa. Two thousand years of history*: 277.

labor – developed into the dominant mode of production. In Ruanda-Urundi on the other hand, African smallholders – tilling the land around or in the vicinity of their homesteads using mostly family labor – eclipsed European production.[30] The various possible and probable reasons for this difference will be the focus of the next chapter. This second part of the first chapter examines the meaning of Lake Kivu as a coffee producer on a global scale after World War I. How important was the Kivu region in the global commodity battle? How much land was required to compete on a global level? How many laborers were involved in the coffee sector?

2.1 *Global Coffee Production after World War I*

With more than 400 years of "experience" and growth, the coffee sector and its global production had already reached a significant level at the start of the twentieth century – as can be seen in Table 1 (indicating averages per year).

TABLE 1 World coffee production (1921–1960)

	Tons (own calculation)
1921–1925	1414423
1926–1930	1952626
1931–1935	2304461
1936–1940	2293949
1941–1945	1791768
1946–1950	2202182
1951–1955	2557913
1956–1960	3623337

Source: Based on Mario Samper and Radin Fernando, "Historical statistics of coffee production and trade from 1700 to 1960," in *The global coffee economy in Africa, Asia, and Latin America 1500–1989*, ed. William Gervase Clarence-Smith and Steven Topik (Cambridge; New York: Cambridge University Press, 2003): 417

30 In this case smallholders could be seen as independent free producers cultivating for their own account. However, as the remainder of this book demonstrates, freedom was lacking (due to rigid rules and control) and therefore smallholders should be understood as obligatory cultivators. See, for a more detailed categorization: Van Melkebeke, "Dualisme ou dynamisme? Une analyse de l'économie rurale congolaise durant l'Entre-deux-guerres": 158–165. Although this article concerns the Belgian Congo, it is equally applicable to the mandate.

In less than half a century, the global coffee production level more than doubled to reach an average of 3.6 million tons per year in the second half of the 1950s. However, caution is required, firstly, because these figures do not distinguish between *Robusta* and *Arabica* (the two major coffee varieties). Secondly, these figures represent averages and therefore obscure booms and slumps. Thirdly, this table aims at representing the total amount of coffee produced all around the globe, but it is not unthinkable that some errors may have occurred, especially before World War II when standardization was not yet commonplace as it is nowadays. Hence, the above figures are indicative rather than given facts, but they nonetheless can and do indicate general trends.

Total coffee production increased globally until the mid-1930s. From that moment on, the average level decreased until the end of World War II. After the war and in a time span of only fifteen years, global production doubled. Its regression during World War II can hardly be a surprise, but the high level of production during the Great Depression is remarkable, not least because the average coffee price fell sharply and did not recover until the post-World War II period.[31] Coffee producers may have answered or anticipated this by increasing their production levels. What is certain is that during the crisis global demand for coffee declined, causing overproduction. In an effort to stabilize prices on the international markets, Brazil – dominating the global coffee sector since the middle of the eighteenth century, and still today – decided to burn almost ten million pounds of stocked coffee.[32] Although the attempt of the Brazilian government was unsuccessful and prices continued to be unstable, it had far-reaching consequences, even for the coffee sector in the Kivu region (see Chapter 3).

A closer look at the output of the world's largest (mostly *Arabica*) coffee producer in the first half of the twentieth century enables me to compare and put the Kivu region into a broader perspective later in this chapter. As opposed to the Kivu area, the Brazilian success story was written in the postcolonial epoch.

In addition to its very favorable factor endowments (climate, vast areas of virgin land, etcetera), Brazil used large-scale plantations using slave labor (*fazenda*) to develop a successful and world-leading coffee sector in the course of the eighteenth and nineteenth centuries.[33] After the abolition of slavery in

31 Ibid: 457–458.

32 Topik and Wells, *Global markets transformed, 1870–1945*: 240.

33 Denise Douzant-Rosenfeld and Pernette Grandjean, "Planteurs et plantations. Le système de l'exploitation caféière en Amérique latine," *Etudes Rurales*, no. 180 (2007); and Hildete Pereira de Melo, "Coffee and development of the Rio de Janeiro economy, 1888–1920," in *The global coffee economy in Africa, Asia, and Latin America 1500–1989*, ed. William Gervase

TABLE 2 Brazilian coffee production (1921–1960)

	Tons (own calculation)
1921–1925	888443
1926–1930	1290905
1931–1935	1402327
1936–1940	1298405
1941–1945	748883
1946–1950	916493
1951–1955	978439
1956–1960	1593804

Source: Based on Samper and Fernando, "Historical statistics of coffee production and trade from 1700 to 1960": 422

1888, the coffee sector continued to grow and Brazil retained its leadership in the world market. Table 2 – and again those figures should be approached with caution – demonstrates that Brazil was responsible for half or more of the total global coffee production until World War II. During and after the war, Brazil's share in the world market dropped, but in the second half of the 1950s almost half of the coffee produced globally was once again "made in Brazil."

2.2 *Belgian Africa's Capacity*

In this section I analyze coffee production in the Belgian Congo and Ruanda-Urundi in order to sketch the importance of the coffee sector in Belgian Africa on a global scale. I will distinguish not only between European (plantation) and indigenous (smallholder) production but also between *Arabica* and *Robusta*, for the colony and the mandate as well.

2.2.1 Methodological Remarks

The figures used in this and the next section are drawn partly from archival material and partly from published sources. It is important to stress again that they must be read with caution, for several reasons. First of all, the consulted sources are not always explicit about what the figures represent. For instance, in some reports production figures are falsely equated with export figures. Before exportation, coffee was either stored for a few months in order to dry it or

Clarence-Smith and Steven Topik (Cambridge; New York: Cambridge University Press, 2003).

deliberately retained from the export market awaiting more stimulating prices (whether or not established by the government; see Chapter 5) – which often happened with Rwandan smallholders. In those cases I had to either search for more accurate figures or leave an unfortunate gap (meaning no data) in the tables.

A second reason concerns the accuracy of the figures. Stockpiling coffee in storehouses is not the only issue that can cause inaccuracies in annual production statistics; hiding at least part of the harvest might have the same result. Furthermore, especially before World War II, figures are often estimations. This comment applies not only to production figures but also, for example, to censuses or tax revenues. This does not mean that such figures are completely unworkable, but they have to be used as indicators rather than as established facts.

Finally, one of the consequences of focusing on a border region is the undeniable – often illicit, from a colonial perspective – existence of cross-border operations. Although the populations of east and west of Lake Kivu belonged to broadly different cultural zones (speaking different languages for example), they were still interlinked, and the zones overlapped in many ways.[34] I am referring not only to cross-border economic or social relations (like family ties, marriage ties, etcetera) but also to contraband. Once the plantation sector in the Kivu was well established, people (whether laborers or not) sometimes stole coffee and smuggled the cash crop into Rwanda (and vice versa; see Chapter 6 for a more detailed analysis). Consequently, production figures may be inaccurate as coffee produced west of Lake Kivu may have entered Ruanda-Urundi statistics. Although smuggled quantities were likely small, it should be kept in mind.

2.2.2 European versus African[35]

Table 3 gives an overview of the annual coffee production level (*Arabica* and *Robusta*) in the Belgian colony and the mandate after World War I. Before putting these figures into a global context, some comments are required.

Firstly, the coffee sector in the Belgian Congo originated in the early stages of the Congo Free State (CFS). Production levels remained low until 1927. From this point onwards, however, there was a remarkable increase in production

34 Mathys, "People on the move. Frontiers, borders, mobility and history in the Lake Kivu region 19th-20th century" 133.

35 Sources for Table 3, Diagrams 1 and 2, and the discussion in this section: AAB, Agri, Café, Statistiques (516), Dossier "Statistiques Café," [1955]; S.N., *Rapport annuel sur l'activité de la Colonie du Congo Belge pendant l'année…, 1920–58* (Bruxelles); and S.N., *Rapport sur l'administration Belge du Ruanda-Urundi pendant l'année…, 1920–61* (Bruxelles).

TABLE 3 European and African coffee production (tons), Belgian Congo and Ruanda-Urundi (1920–1961)

	Belgian Congo		Ruanda-Urundi	
	European	African	European	African
1920	100			
1921	54			
1922	71			
1923	87			
1924	160			
1925	324	42		
1926	459	86		
1927	623	130		30
1928	3211	145		50
1929	3984	158		60
1930	6079	121		50
1931	6401	103		70
1932	6797	49		88
1933	9954	71		152
1934	13345	168		223
1935	14312	165		450
1936	18075	220		1200
1937	19619	554	108.2	2000.08
1938	21087	579	135	3208
1939	21096	785	163	4950.7
1940	23076	926	601	6150
1941	22626	967	242	7559
1942	23131	761	695	10778
1943	21471	690	694	8057
1944	20003	650	263	10341
1945	20222	719	1343	4861
1946	20170	766	685	9867
1947	21874	543	1256	8570
1948	18002	763	311	8093
1949	19002	1108	178	7354
1950	19490	1306	449	11466
1951	19931	1619	416	12822
1952	19418	1901	355	9620

	Belgian Congo		Ruanda-Urundi	
	European	African	European	African
1953	20742	1958	413	10661
1954	25616	2706	379	9978
1955	26008	596[a]	249	21459
1956	38102	567[a]	292	18036
1957	42299	756[a]	987	29138
1958	52382	1408[a]	412	25113
1959			500	36125
1960			420	20255
1961			653	23161

a Only Kivu Province, so the total indigenous production in the Belgian Congo must have been higher.

capacity. Hence, 1928 can be seen as the definitive start of the Congolese coffee sector. I will return to this point in the following section when distinguishing between *Robusta* and *Arabica*. The second observation concerns indigenous production in the Belgian Congo. Although figures are lacking until 1925, it is clear that indigenous production was not prohibited. Congolese smallholders surely were limited in their activities[36] but they managed to increase their production (except from the early 1930s). There is clear evidence in the sources that such restrictions were based on racist images of Africans as bad agriculturists (see the section "Smallholding in eastern Congo" later in this chapter for more details).

In Ruanda-Urundi, as opposed to the colony, European coffee production was insignificant and its production capacity never came close to the level of African production. Moreover, I was unable to find any European production figures until 1937, despite the availability and accessibility of relevant sources. Does this mean that European production figures up to this point are lacking? Or does it simply mean that there was just not enough to report? The latter

36 See for instance: Bashizi, "Pouvoirs publics, plantations européennes et réactions paysannes au Sud-Kivu (1920–1960)": 141, who points out that smallholders in Kivu were not allowed to plant more than one hundred coffee bushes per person.

seems more likely, because African production figures are available from 1927. Thus European production must have been negligible until at least the mid-1930s. Furthermore, the production level in Ruanda-Urundi remained rather stable until 1931, and was even lower than in the Belgian colony. From 1932, however, smallholders in the mandate took the lead and soon became major (*Arabica*) coffee producers. Finally, in 1954–1955, production in the mandate more than doubled, while in 1959–1960 it almost halved. Annual production figures may fluctuate due to "bad" and "good" harvest years, but can such differences be explained merely by looking at this factor? Unfortunately, I was not able to find any plausible explanation for these two extraordinary leaps in the sources.

The first issue catching the eye is the divergent paths of development (see Diagrams 1 and 2) between the Belgian colony and the mandate – respectively European- and African-oriented. One could say that the coffee sector in the Congo is the mirror image of that in Ruanda-Urundi. During and in the aftermath of the Great Depression, coffee production in Belgian Africa continued to grow despite falling prices. In the mandate, the colonial economy – including the coffee sector – had only just started to emerge, so the effects on wage labor employment must have been minimal. But in the colony, the crisis caused a sharp rise in dismissals and a drop in employment figures.[37] However, the coffee sector in the Kivu (see next section) – and the Congolese agricultural sector in general[38] – was an exception to this trend. Furthermore, the coffee sector in both territories grew steadily until World War II. Both colony and mandate had difficulties after the war, which lasted for about a decade. From the mid-1950s onwards, the coffee sector recovered in both the Congo and Ruanda-Urundi, exceeded pre-WWII levels very rapidly and eventually boomed. This was partly due to the ten-year plan. This development plan was intended to improve infrastructure and to raise productivity, both aimed at improving the living standard of the African population in Belgian Africa. The plan was launched in the colony (1949) and in a modified form in the mandate (1951). However, one of

37 See: Buelens, *Congo 1885–1960. Een financieel-economische geschiedenis*: 236; and Bogumil Jewsiewicki, "The great depression and the making of the colonial economic system in the Belgian Congo," *African Economic History*, no. 4 (1977): 158. The latter explains that, for example, in the Katanga Province the number of Congolese industry workers decreased from 73000 in 1930, to 27000 in 1933.

38 This was partly because compulsory cultivation (initiated in 1917) was expanded by the colonial government during the crisis, but also because dismissed laborers were obliged to return to their home village and cultivate a certain cash crop (see Jewsiewicki, "The great depression and the making of the colonial economic system in the Belgian Congo": 160).

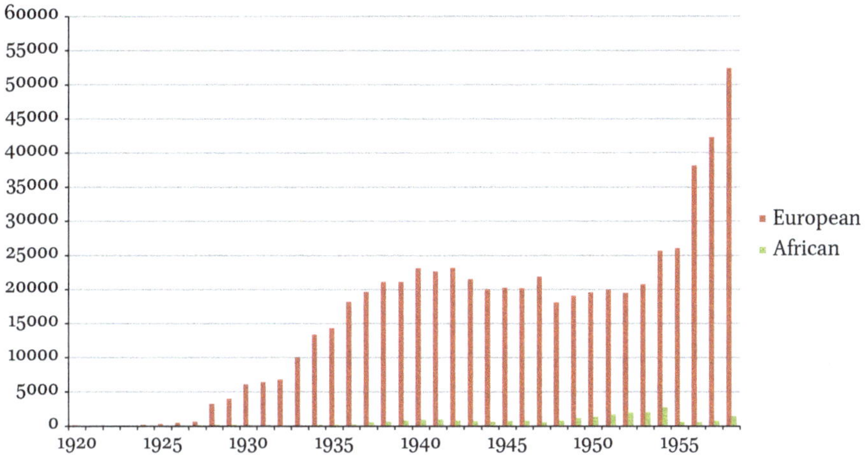

DIAGRAM 1 Coffee production in the Belgian Congo (1920–1958)

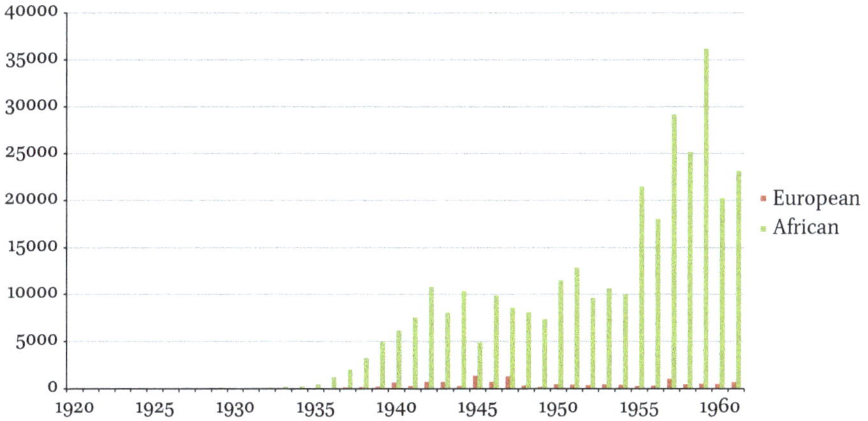

DIAGRAM 2 Coffee production in Ruanda-Urundi (1920–1961)

the intentions of these development plans – improving productivity – did not have the desired results for indigenous agriculture in the Congo, unlike in Ruanda-Urundi, but it did work for the European agricultural sector in the colony.[39] Hence, raising productivity, in combination with improved infrastructure and better cultivation methods, increased production levels in both the colony and the mandate.

39 Guy Vanthemsche, *Genèse et portée du "Plan décennal" du Congo belge (1949–1959)* (Bruxelles: Académie Royale des Sciences d'Outre-Mer, 1994): 48.

Belgian Africa's coffee production was negligible on a global scale, at least until 1928. In 1938, the colony and the mandate produced some 25000 tons together (to recall: this is European and African, *Robusta* and *Arabica*), which corresponds to approximately 1% of world production. Belgian Africa managed to produce about 32500 tons, at that time about 1.4% of the global figure, after World War II (1947). At the end of the colonial period (1958), some 78000 tons were being produced, or 2.1% of the "global cup of coffee." Despite fluctuations in production figures, both globally and locally, the share of Belgian Africa in world coffee production statistics increased in the course of the first half of the twentieth century. Although Belgian Africa was not a major producer compared to "giants" such as Brazil, which produced about half of world production, it certainly became a more important producer on a global level. Moreover, for the entire Kivu region, *Arabica* coffee was (and still is) a major export crop. Hence, examining the development of this sector on a local level is more than justified.

2.2.3 *Arabica* versus *Robusta*[40]

The distinction between *Arabica* and *Robusta* is made to demonstrate that the colony and the mandate are each other's mirror image in terms of not only the implemented production system (see *supra*) but also the major coffee varieties cultivated (see also Diagram 3 and 4). Belgian Africa's coffee sector does not owe its strength in the world market to only one variety: both major coffee varieties thrived. However, in the region I am investigating here, *Arabica* had an absolute dominant role; this will be clarified in the next section of this chapter.

As already mentioned briefly, in the Belgian Congo (*Robusta*) coffee cultivation started in the 1880s. In the lower Congo, colonial agents experimented with coffee bushes in the vicinity of their administrative posts.[41] But the rubber boom, starting in the 1890s, reoriented the focus, and the interest in coffee diminished rapidly.[42] Planters only regained interest in the coffee sector in 1911. In the metropole as well as the colony, propaganda was spread to convince potential planters of the "delights" of planting coffee. Another incentive was

40 Sources for Table 4, Diagrams 3 and 4, and the discussion in this section: AAB, Agri, Café, Statistiques (516), Dossier "Statistiques Café," [1955]; S.N., *Rapport annuel sur l'activité de la Colonie du Congo Belge pendant l'année…, 1920–58*; and S.N., *Rapport sur l'administration Belge du Ruanda-Urundi pendant l'année…, 1920–61*.

41 Edmond Leplae, "Native agricultural policy and European agriculture in the Belgian Congo," *Journal of Royal African Society* 38, no. 152 (1939): 365.

42 Leplae, *Les plantations de café au Congo belge: leur histoire (1881–1935), leur importance actuelle*: 6–16.

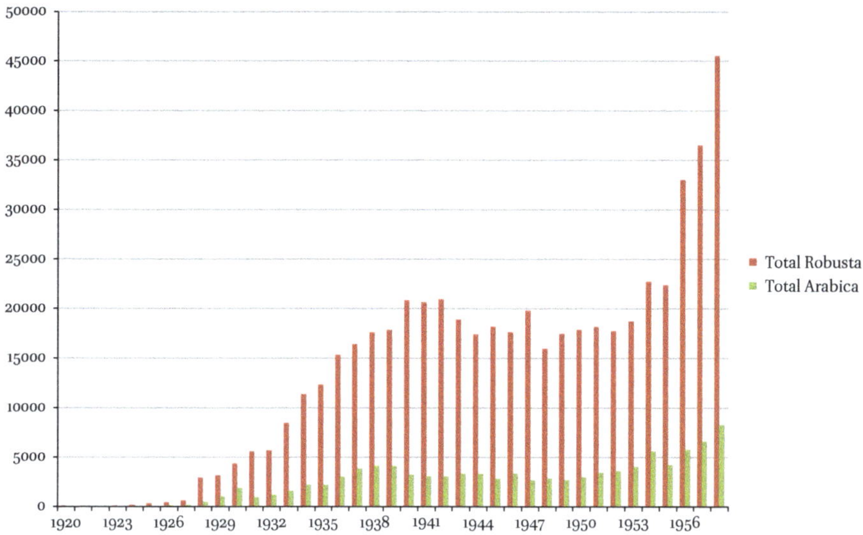

DIAGRAM 3 *Arabica* and *Robusta* production, Belgian Congo (1920–1958)

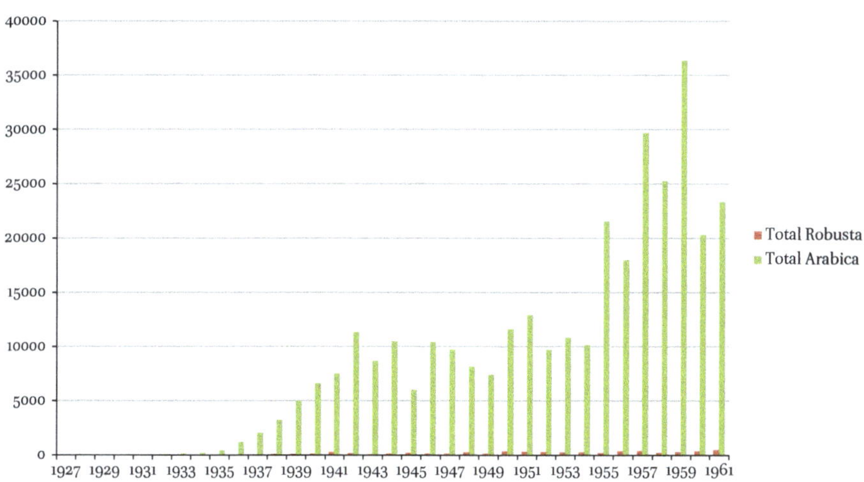

DIAGRAM 4 *Arabica* and *Robusta* production, Ruanda-Urundi (1927–1961)

the development of experimental stations – such as Lula in Stanleyville – aimed at helping planters grow and process their coffee properly. Thanks to these measures, the (*Robusta*) coffee sector began to flourish after World War I, followed by the emergence of *Arabica* – mostly in the elevated eastern parts of

TABLE 4 *Arabica* and *Robusta* production (tons), Belgian Congo and Ruanda-Urundi (1920–1961)

	Belgian Congo				Ruanda-Urundi			
	Robusta		*Arabica*		*Robusta*		*Arabica*	
	European	African	European	African	European	African	European	African
1920	100							
1921	54							
1922	71							
1923	81		6.1					
1924	143		17					
1925	274	42	50					
1926	359	65	101	20				
1927	509	88	114	42				30
1928	2791	115	420	30				50
1929	2964	158	1020					60
1930	4200	121	1879					50
1931	5464	103	937					70
1932	5595	49	1202					88
1933	8378	71	1576					152
1934	11171	168	2174					223
1935	12148	165	2164					450
1936	15080	220	2995					1200
1937	15833	554	3786		60	0.6	48.2	2000
1938	17004	579	4083		107	8	28	3200
1939	17025	785	4071		118	0,7	45	4950
1940	19877	926	3199		157		444	6150
1941	19623	967	3003		215	74	27	7485
1942	20118	761	3013		171		524	10778
1943	18183	690	3288		100		594	8057
1944	16717	650	3286		145	14	118	10327
1945	17429	719	2793		145	61	1198	4800
1946	16849	766	3321		86	67	599	9800
1947	19215	543	2659		78	70	1178	8500

	Belgian Congo				Ruanda-Urundi			
	Robusta		*Arabica*		*Robusta*		*Arabica*	
	Euro-pean	**Afri-can**	**Euro-pean**	**Afri-can**	**Euro-pean**	**Afri-can**	**Euro-pean**	**Afri-can**
1948	15160	763	2842		210	63	101	8030
1949	16616	808	2386	300	93	54	85	7300
1950	16825	1015	2665	291	327	23	122	11443
1951	16795	1340	3136	279	287	47	129	12775
1952	16082	1661	3336	240	239	50	116	9570
1953	17023	1683	3719	275	212	50	201	10611
1954	20469	2289	5147	417	202	50	177	9928
1955	22398		4206		150	60	99	21399
1956	32979		5690		153	224	139	17812
1957	36489		6566		156	265	831	28873
1958	45508		8282		191	60	221	25053
1959					226	80	274	36045
1960					254	135	166	20120
1961					336	168	317	22993

the Congo – from the mid-1920s onwards.[43] That both varieties were cultivated in the colony from this point on explains the 1928 "take-off" of the Congolese coffee sector. Clearly, the *Robusta* as well as the *Arabica* sector was European-oriented (plantations). An upward trend marks both varieties during the colonial period, although the *Robusta* sector seems to have grown at a quicker pace. Smallholders managed to produce both varieties for the export market. Their share increased, especially from the 1950s onwards, although not as much as expected under the ten-year plan.

In Ruanda-Urundi, *Robusta* cultivation was of minor importance in the colonial period. This variety was only significant in some lower areas (for instance the Rusizi plain partly situated in the Shangugu territory). However, in the

43 Ibid: 94.

early 1920s – the experimental stage – the mandate administration did actually try to urge the diffusion of the lower-value *Robusta*. The 1922 report of the Shangugu territory, for example, mentions the establishment of a *Robusta* nursery, the variety of which "the administration of Ruanda recommends [...] diffusion in preference to any other varieties."[44] But the attempt was unsuccessful[45] (except in regions of lower altitude) and the government targeted *Arabica* from this point onwards. However, as already mentioned, up until the 1930s cultivation of the latter was not successful or widespread. Only fathers growing coffee for their own subsistence, chiefs using *corvée* labor to work their coffee plots and the remainder of the modest German attempts are worth mentioning. Moreover, the European sector in the mandate was secondary to African production. Private entrepreneurs and missionaries managed to grow *Arabica* as well as *Robusta*, but what really stands out is the overwhelming dominance of smallholder *Arabica* production.

In the 1920s, elites and their "subjects" alike resisted the introduction of coffee. The former believed that coffee production would be a threat to their power. The latter were afraid that growing coffee would interfere with food production, which would result in increasing food insecurity.[46] Despite this objection, the mandate administration started to impose coffee cultivation in two consecutive stages.[47] Why and how coffee was imposed on smallholders will be discussed at length in the following chapters. For now, suffice it to say that the campaign of 1931–1932 was reserved for chiefs and sub-chiefs, urged to plant at least 1000 and 250 *Arabica* plants respectively. From 1932–1933, the diffusion of seedlings was extended to other layers of the population as well. Before the start of the campaigns, in 1931, Rwanda counted 457546 bushes. After the fourth campaign, in 1934–1935, already 4038450 bushes had been planted in the northern part of the mandate. The seventh, and also final, campaign of 1937–1938 resulted in the establishment of a further 1400500 new bushes.[48] Although the campaigns started in the early 1930s, production figures only rose from 1936 onwards due to coffee plants requiring four to six years to mature. Once coffee

44 AAB, RARU, Shangugu Territoire, Rapport Général, 1922, no. 100(2).

45 Ibid, 1925, no. 100(4).

46 Dorsey, "Rwandan colonial economy, 1916–1941": 169.

47 Hatungimana, *Le café au Burundi au XXe siècle: Paysans, argent, pouvoir*: 127.

48 These figures are drawn from AAB, Agri, Café, Statistiques (516), Dossier "Statistiques Café," [1955]. I once again stress that caution is required. They can be used to demonstrate only trends rather than given facts. Moreover, Dorsey also provides figures with regard to the campaigns, but his results differ from the ones I have used here (see: Dorsey, "Rwandan colonial economy, 1916–1941": 194).

cultivation had been firmly established, figures show an overall upward tendency in the mandate until the end of the colonial period.

2.3 *The Kivu Region*

Having established Belgian Africa's importance as a coffee producer on a global scale and stressed its significance in both *Robusta* and *Arabica* cultivation, in the following section I zoom in on the local scale. The Kivu region is the region *par excellence* for producing the latter major variety. Therefore, in the remainder of this book *Robusta* is left out for the greater part; *Arabica* is the center of interest.

2.3.1 Production

Diagram 5 clearly demonstrates the importance of the colonial Kivu district in producing *Arabica* for the world market. The red "Congo-line" depends on the blue "Kivu-line," because, in the colony, 75 to 80% on average of the total production of this variety was cultivated west of Lake Kivu. It is unnecessary to make a similar statement (or diagram) for Ruanda-Urundi, as the previous paragraph showed the predominance of *Arabica* in the entire mandate.

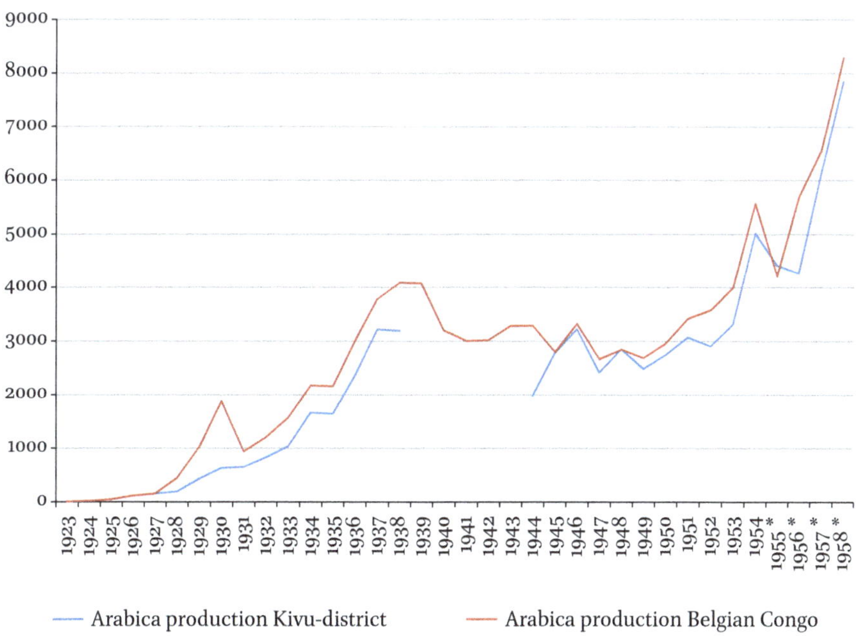

DIAGRAM 5 *Arabica* production, Kivu district and Belgian Congo (1923–1958)
SOURCES: SEE TABLES 4 AND 5

TABLE 5 European and African *Arabica* production (tons), Kivu district (1923–1958)

	European	African		European	African
1923	6.1		1941		
1924	17		1942		
1925	50		1943		
1926	100	20	1944	1985	
1927	114	42	1945	2506	282
1928	194		1946	2758	462
1929	434.9		1947	2214.7	200
1930	623.7		1948	2640	207
1931	643.3		1949	2185.3	295
1932	793	20	1950	2378	368
1933	1005.2	26	1951	2877	190.8
1934	1641	16	1952	2904	
1935	1641		1953	3065	242
1936	2346		1954	4469	543
1937	3163	48	1955[a]	3849	562
1938	3149	41	1956[a]	3917	344
1939			1957[a]	5619	533
1940			1958[a]	6901	937

Source: AAB, Agri, Café, Statistiques (516), Dossier "Statistiques Café," [1955] and S.N., *Rapport annuel sur l'activité de la Colonie du Congo Belge pendant l'année…, 1920–58*

a Note: Figures for Kivu Province, includes the Maniema district.

In addition to earlier remarks, some specific issues need to be addressed here. For the colony (as opposed to the mandate), I was unable to find figures per territory. Hence, the references to the Kivu district. Consequently, based on these figures, it is impossible to determine which colonial territory had the largest capacity. The literature suggests nevertheless that the Kabare territory dominates, while the production ability of the Masisi territory gained strength especially after World War II.[49] Figures are also lacking for the period 1939–1943, but when the "Kivu-line" follows the "Congo-line" as it does in other years, it may be expected that coffee production in this district dropped from the late

49 Bashizi, "Processus de domination socio-économique et marché du travail au Bushi (1920–45)": 6.

1930s onwards, while remaining stable until the early 1950s. From this point on a new boom emerged. This indicates that coffee production in the Kivu district followed the growing international demand for African commodities and raising prices on the markets, both starting in the late 1940s.[50]

A more detailed look at the coffee sector in the Kivu district shows that there was already some European export-oriented production in the early 1920s. Early-established *colons* succeeded in cultivating for the market. However, it was not until 1927 – and the "rush of colonists" – that the European plantation economy started to develop fully. Production increased at least until the late 1930s, while it took the plantation sector about seven years to recover from World War II. The pre-war level was attained in the 1950s, and the European sector continued to grow until the end of the colonial period.

African production, on the other hand, was not prohibited (but was surely restricted) in the entire colonial period. How indigenous production began and evolved during the colonial period will be discussed in Chapter 2. For now, suffice it to say that indigenous production capacity remained low, at least until the end of World War II, but that after the war several attempts were made to stimulate African cultivation.

For the eastern shore of Lake Kivu, records are more nuanced and detailed than Congolese sources, offering the possibility of focusing on territorial production figures. The issue with the Rwandan figures is that they do not distinguish between African and European production. Most of the figures in the consulted reports represent the total annual production in the territory. This is not a major concern because, as already demonstrated in previous sections, European coffee production in the mandate was unimportant compared to indigenous production. However, some of the (agricultural) reports do pay attention to European production figures, however small. Therefore, it is possible to have some indications of the relative importance of this coffee-cultivating segment in the mandate. As it turns out, only in the Shangugu territory were Europeans able to install a coffee sector of any significance (see Chapter 2).

That most figures are lacking for Kibuye is no surprise, since the territory was absorbed by neighboring territories for some time (see Introduction). The trends in Table 6 are nonetheless clear, despite some gaps. Both Gisenyi and Shangugu produced coffee before the start of the campaigns.[51] As already

50 J. Forbes Munro, *Africa and the international economy, 1800–1960: an introduction to the modern economic history of Africa south of the Sahara* (London; Totowa: Dent, 1976): 177–178.

51 Due to the importance of tobacco cultivation, Gisenyi's "coffee adventure" started later compared with Shangugu. Already produced and traded in precolonial times, tobacco continued to be an important trade good during the colonial period in the northern Lake

TABLE 6 Coffee production (tons) in Gisenyi, Kibuye and Shangugu (1925–1959)

	Gisenyi	Kibuye	Shangugu		Gisenyi	Kibuye	Shangugu
1925			3.6	1943	550		447
1926				1944			
1927			3	1945			
1928			1.2	1946	481		
1929	1.3			1947	395		450
1930			10	1948	330		427
1931	1.98		12	1949	540		491.8
1932	5.2		12.6	1950	711		716.5
1933			25	1951	700		1050
1934	12.3		39.7	1952			1085
1935	32.2			1953		259	1052
1936	32.3		118.8	1954		436	946
1937	194		262.5	1955		546.8	1179.5
1938	300		266.4	1956			
1939			200	1957			2000
1940			377	1958		920	1350
1941	683		516.3	1959			2600
1942			346.6				

Sources: For Gisenyi: AAB, RARU, Gisenyi Territoire, Rapport Général, 1929; 1931; 1934–38; 1943; 1946–51, no. 87(16); 87(17); 87(20); 87(21); 87(22); 87(23); 87(24); 88(3); 88(6); 88(7); 88(8); 88(9); 88(10); 88(11); Rapport Agriculture, 1932; 1941, no. 90(9); 90(16). For Kibuye, ibid, Kibuye Territoire, Rapport Général, 1958, no. 82(5); Rapport Agriculture, 1953–55, no. 82(23); 82(24); 82(25). For Shangugu, ibid, Shangugu Territoire, Rapport Général, 1925; 1927–28; 1930–34; 1936–43; 1948; 1952; 1957–58, no. 100(4); 100(6); 100(7); 100(9); 100(10); 100(11); 100(12); 100(13); 101(2); 101(3); 101(4); 101(5); 101(6); 101(7); 101(8); 101(9); 102(1); 102(5); 102(8bis); 102(9); Rapport Agriculture, 1947; 1949–51; 1953–55, no. 105(17); 105(19); 105(20); 105(21); 105(23); 105(24); 105(25); AIMO Report, 1959, no. 103(12)

stressed, those “early birds” were, next to a handful of fathers, mostly chiefs using *corvée* labor. After and during the campaigns, coffee production increased in both territories, until the outbreak of World War II. The war restrained

Kivu area. From as far as Masisi, people travelled to trade tobacco for *butega* (bracelets serving as currency). Once coffee cultivation was firmly installed, tobacco lost ground but did not disappear; see: AAB, RARU, Gisenyi Territoire, Rapport Général, 1926, no. 87(14), and, for the precolonial period: Bernard Lugan and Raphaël Mutombo, “Le tabac du Bugoyi dans le Rwanda ancien: une culture commerciale dans une société d'autosubsistance,” *Africa-Tervuren* 29, no. 1–2 (1983).

growth, but from the 1950s onwards coffee production revived in western Rwanda. Data for the 1950s are lacking for Gisenyi but, if the figures in Table 6 are reliable, in Shangugu coffee production doubled despite ups and downs.

Gisenyi and Shangugu produced more or less similar quantities from the late 1930s onwards. Comparing their share to the total production figure for the entire mandate reveals that the two territories managed to deliver about 300 tons each in 1938. This means that each territory delivered about 9% of the total mandate production. Both territories' share dropped after World War II. In 1950, Gisenyi and Shangugu produced about 700 tons each, equaling about 5.8% of the total amount. Some years later, in 1958, Shangugu alone managed to produce 5.4% of the total mandate quantity (1350 tons). That same year the "reborn" Kibuye territory (1953) accounted for 920 tons, or 3.6% of the total. In other words, similarly to the Kivu district, the Rwandan territories bordering Lake Kivu were major *Arabica* coffee producers in the colonial period.

2.3.2 Land Mobilization: Quantitative Approach

Clearly the Kivu region held a prominent place in cultivating *Arabica* coffee. But now the question arises of how much land was used in order to produce those quantities. I intend to put the Kivu region in a broader perspective as I did with the production figures. This means that surfaces (land used for coffee cultivation) for the entire colony and mandate will appear as well.

Before getting to the heart of the matter, some additional remarks are required again. First of all, the surfaces discussed below do not always concern *Arabica* alone. The sources I consulted sometimes fail to distinguish between the two major varieties. Therefore, it would be impossible to make general statements were it not for the minor role *Robusta* played in this region. For pragmatic and practical reasons I chose not to distinguish between land already in cultivation and land newly brought into cultivation. Only documents relating to the entire Belgian Congo make that distinction. Hence, in order not to complicate things even further, "coffee land" means *all* land, already producing or not, planted with coffee.

Similarly to production figures in the previous section, figures referring to surfaces planted with coffee do not concern the territory level for the Belgian Congo. This means that Table 7 refers to the Kivu district. However, I have managed to find documents from 1939 listing concessions per territory in the district. That enabled me to at least give an indication of what surface was occupied in what territory.

Arabica surfaces planted in the Kivu district give some indications for the surfaces planted in the entire colony. As argued above, the Kivu guaranteed the lion's share of overall Congolese production, which is clearly demonstrated by looking at the European surfaces. However, focusing on the African surfaces complicates things.[52] The figures I found for the 1920s represent not only the Kivu district but the entire Oriental Province, and are likely rough estimations. Moreover, they include *Robusta* surfaces (albeit a small proportion) as well. This methodological issue also concerns the first half of the 1950s. Figures for the 1930s are available for the Kivu but not for the colony. Furthermore, a close inspection of Table 7 shows that, for the years 1943–1944, 1949 and 1953–1954, the size of African surface planted with coffee is the same for the Belgian Congo and for the Kivu district. Is this merely a coincidence, due to the fact that for 1953–1954, *Robusta* surfaces are included? Was there only *Arabica* smallholding in the Kivu district for the other years? Or did an agent abusively take the

TABLE 7 *Arabica* coffee surfaces (hectare), Belgian Congo and Kivu district (1927–1958)

	Belgian Congo		Kivu	
	European	African	European	African
1927			1350	
1928			841 (1)	265 (1) (2)
1929			1905 (1)	337 (1) (2)
1930			5443 (1)	486 (1) (2)
1931			6000	310 (1) (2)
1932	12188		8373	64
1933	12977		9158.7	58.5
1934	15819		11365.7	85
1935	17985		12715	200
1936	18354		13475	627
1937	18770		14663	743.27
1938	19519		14918	765
1939	16639	1243		
1940	17017	1243		
1941	13808	836		
1942	13331	730		
1943	11280	843		843
1944	11222	783	9575	783

52 African coffee cultivation in the Kivu district was especially important in the northern territories of Beni and Lubero (see Chapter 2). These regions were less suitable for European colonization, as opposed to the territories focused on in this book.

	Belgian Congo		Kivu	
	European	African	European	African
1945	11209		9541	
1946	10945		9256	
1947	9815		9453	769
1948	10659	1477	8715	747
1949	10125	883	8593.5	883
1950	10718	1308	9210	932 (2)
1951	11740	1331	10155	1209 (2)
1952	12571	1476	10826.5	1460 (2)
1953	14252	1823	12353	1823 (2)
1954	14807	2188	12757	2188 (2)
1955	17082		14238	2861.2 (2)
1956	13110		14810 (2)[a]	1719 (2)[a]
1957	14512		10598[a]	2187[a]
1958	16525		11802[a]	2773[a]

Sources: AAB, Agri, Café, Statistiques (516), Dossier "Statistiques Café," [1955] and S.N., *Rapport annuel sur l'activité de la Colonie du Congo Belge pendant l'année…, 1920–58*

[a] Notes: Figures for Kivu Province, includes the Maniema district; (1) Oriental Province includes the districts Kivu, Maniema, Stanleyville, Aruwimi, Kibali-Ituri, Uele-Itimbiri and Uele-Nepoko; (2) *Arabica* + *Robusta* surface.

Kivu for the entire colony? Hence, it is very risky to draw any conclusions from the figures for African surfaces, except for the fact that African coffee cultivation was not prohibited.

In Diagram 6, the steep ascending blue line in the period 1927–1938 reflects the "rush of colonists" and the concessions they obtained/alienated. Land layout in the Kivu district changed rapidly – although with local variations – and the area planted with coffee multiplied by a factor of ten in only one decade. From 1939 until the end of World War II figures are lacking, but the postwar trend suggests that less land was planted with coffee. This decrease was a consequence of the Brazilian effort to stabilize prices. The colonial administration anticipated this by limiting cultivated surfaces and trying to increase productivity in both the colony and the mandate (see Chapter 3). The Kivu district succeeded in reaching the same level of land cultivated for coffee production in the 1950s, in order to follow the increased international demand for coffee (*supra*).

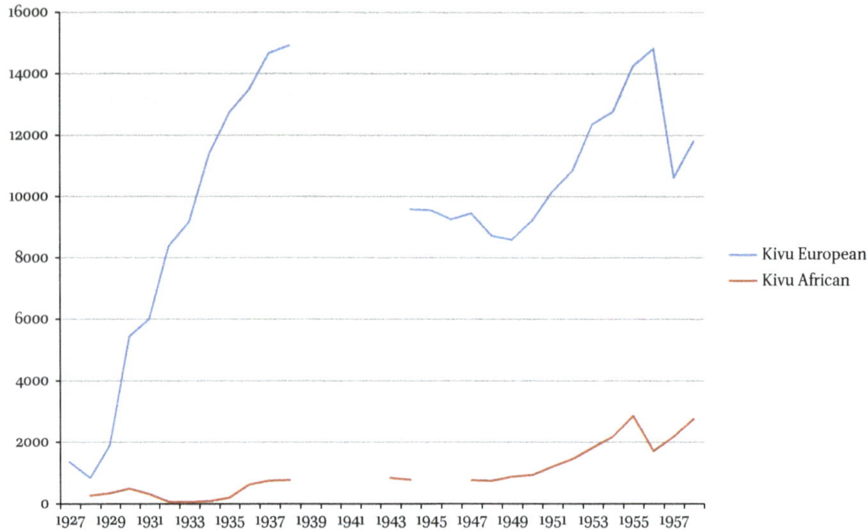

DIAGRAM 6 Surface (hectare) planted with coffee in the Kivu district, European and African (1927–1958)
SOURCES: SEE TABLE 7

The colonial Kivu district more or less corresponds to the present-day North- and South-Kivu Provinces, measuring respectively 59483 square kilometers and 65070 square kilometers, or 12455300 hectares together – almost four times the size of Belgium.[53] However, large parts of this area are inaccessible to coffee cultivation due to the presence of forests, other cash crops (tea, for instance), residences, unsuitable or infertile land, the National Albert Park, indigenous land for food crops, etcetera. Consulted sources fail to give figures, or even estimations, on the size of these "no-go zones." What I have found, on the other hand, are figures concerning the number of *colons*. Starting with eleven in 1924, their presence in the Kivu district grew to about 160 by the end of the 1930s.[54] The district accommodated 314 agrarian colonists in 1953, while their number reached 736 in 1958,[55] the majority of whom were running a

53 Figures from: S.N., "https://monusco.unmissions.org/sites/default/files/north_kivu.factsheet.eng_.pdf." (12/05/2016), and: S.N., "https://monusco.unmissions.org/sites/default/files/south_kivu_factsheet._eng.pdf." (12/05/2016).

54 Jewsiewicki, "Le colonat agricole européen au Congo-belge, 1910–1960: questions politiques économiques": 562–564.

55 AAB, RACB, Kivu Province, Conseil de Province, 1954 and 1959, no. 40(2) and 43(2).

coffee plantation.[56] The point is that relatively few coffee planters succeeded in developing a – for this region – important plantation sector. Except for plantation companies and some large-scale private planters, the average size of concessions was limited.

A 1939 document offers the opportunity to catch a glimpse of the situation on a territorial level. In the most prominent coffee-producing Kabare territory, eighty-two European planters were producing coffee on 7602 hectares.[57] This means that, on average, a coffee field in Kabare had a size of 92 hectares. In that same year Kabare measured 1052000 hectares, which means that 0.7% of the territory was covered with coffee plants.[58] This gives a good impression of the actual size of the plantation sector at a given time, but in turn blurs the concentration of coffee estates in the two major *chefferies* of the territory, Kabare and Ngweshe.[59]

With regard to the cultivated African surfaces in the Kivu district, there is far less to say. Keeping the nature of the consulted sources in mind, this is hardly a surprise. Moreover, some figures are debatable. The only thing that can be said with certainty is that smallholder coffee cultivation increased in the course of the 1950s thanks to the efforts of the colonial administration to encourage African coffee production. I will return to this issue in Chapter 2.

Quantifying land mobilization in Ruanda-Urundi is even more problematic. Figures are available for the entire mandate, albeit rather incomplete for African *Arabica* surfaces before the end of World War II. Information on the territorial level, on the other hand, is very sketchy. The consulted sources are mostly silent about African cultivated coffee surfaces: only scattered data are retraceable. This is no surprise as such, because coffee was cultivated mostly around people's homesteads, intercropped with other (food) crops. Consequently, measuring surfaces was/is difficult and likely relied on estimations (for the territorial as well as the mandate level). The territorial reports contain more data with reference to European surfaces, in spite of the minor role they played in producing coffee in the mandate.

56 As one of the consequences of the global crisis, a majority of coffee planters abandoned monoculture and diversified cash-crop production with, for example, quinine (important during World War II) and tea. Tea, in particular, became more significant after World War II (Paul Beghin, *Geleide verandering in een Afrikaanse samenleving. De Bushi in de koloniale periode* (Brussel: Koninklijke Academie voor Overzeese Wetenschappen, 1974): 37).

57 AAB, Agri, Café, Correspondance (517), Dossier "Situation des plantations de café," 30/10/1939.

58 Ibid, RACB, Kabare Territoire, Rapport AIMO, 1940, no. 99.

59 Bashizi, "Processus de domination socio-économique et marché du travail au Bushi (1920–45)": 6.

Table 8 indicates that, for the entire mandate, European coffee surfaces were small. With a peak of only 775 hectares of *Arabica* land – or only the size of a regular village – in 1956, this segment requires little emphasis. The 1939 decree did somewhat stabilize European land use. African surfaces were scarce during the coffee campaigns of the 1930s, based on the few figures that are available. However, figures reveal an increase in land planted with coffee bushes after World War II. In only one decade (1950–1961) the total surface more than doubled.

With 26338 square kilometers and 27834 square kilometers – or 5417200 hectares – respectively present-day Rwanda and Burundi are twice the size of Belgium.[60] Taking this larger picture into account, the total acreage planted with coffee in, for instance, 1934 amounted to only 0.05% of the mandate. In

TABLE 8 *Arabica* coffee surfaces (hectare), Ruanda-Urundi (1927–1961)

	European	African		European	African
1927	300 (1)		1945	1027 (2)	
1928			1946	919 (2)	
1929	760 (1) (2)		1947	1102 (2)	18000
1930		160 (1)	1948	464	18250
1931	923 (2)	450	1949	464	19000
1932	878 (2)		1950	514	20700
1933	1317 (2)		1951	531	25794
1934	1330 (2)	1700	1952	597	31025
1935	1415 (2)		1953	537	30405
1936	1258 (2)		1954	697	29539
1937	1240 (2)		1955	658	31490
1938	1197 (2)		1956	775	34687
1939	1155 (2)		1957	765	38625
1940			1958	627	40688
1941			1959	627	43109
1942			1960	627	43817
1943			1961	627	43969
1944	1031 (2)				

Sources: AAB, Agri, Café, Statistiques (516), Dossier "Statistiques Café," [1955] and S.N., *Rapport sur l'administration Belge du Ruanda-Urundi pendant l'année…, 1920–61*
Notes: (1) Only Rwanda; (2) *Arabica* + *Robusta* surface.

60 Figures from: S.N., "http://data.un.org/CountryProfile.aspx?crName=Burundi." (16/05/2016) and S.N., "http://data.un.org/CountryProfile.aspx?crName=Rwanda." (16/05/2016).

1960 the surface accounted for 0.8% of the total countries' size. Considering the same remarks made with respect to the Belgian Congo – land unsuitable for cultivation due to forests, waterways, sheer mountains, cattle land – the importance of smallholder coffee-producing clearly increased in a time period of only one generation.

An overview of cultivated African surfaces on a territorial level is nearly impossible, as Table 9 suggests. However, if the territories bordering Lake Kivu followed the evolution of the entire mandate, then cultivated coffee surfaces are likely to have been increasing, at least since World War II.

European estates are easier to comment on. Similarly to the entire mandate, there is a relative stabilization of the size of surfaces after 1939. However, what really strikes the eye here is the importance of Shangugu.[61] About half of the total European land planted with coffee was situated in this territory in 1933–1934.

TABLE 9 *Arabica* coffee surfaces (hectares) in Gisenyi, Kibuye and Shangugu (1925–1955)

	Gisenyi		Kibuye		Shangugu	
	European	African	European	African	European	African
1925						4.04
1926						
1927						
1928				17		16
1929				17	39	16
1930				20	360	15
1931		15		15	367	27
1932		26	3,5	50	291	33
1933					615	122.1
1934					614.5	
1935						
1936	9,7	1626			334	
1937					94	
1938					132.75	
1939						
1940	13.3				268.9	
1941	11.1	800			265	

61 I am not the first one to stress the relative importance of this territory in European coffee cultivation, see for example: Newbury, *The cohesion of oppression. Clientship and ethnicity in Rwanda, 1860–1960*: especially Chapter 8.

TABLE 9 *Arabica* coffee surfaces (hectares) in Gisenyi, Kibuye and Shangugu (1925–1955) (*cont.*)

	Gisenyi		**Kibuye**		**Shangugu**	
	European	**African**	**European**	**African**	**European**	**African**
1942	7.3				354.5	
1943	7.73				298.9	
1944	8.33				291.9	
1945	8.19				314.2	
1946					216.5	
1947	14.88				423	
1948	14.88				282	
1949	10.03				283.5	
1950	21.45				302	
1951	21.85				310.5	
1952	18.62				327.5	
1953	11.8		2.61		363	
1954	8		2.17		434	
1955	12.62				452	

Sources: For Gisenyi, AAB, RARU, Gisenyi Territoire, Rapport Agriculture, 1931–32; 1936; 1940–45; 1947–55, no. 90(8); 90(9); 90(11); 90(15); 90(16); 90(17); 90(18); 90(19); 90(20); 90(21); 90(22); 90(23); 90(24); 90(25); 90(26); 90(27); 90(28); 90(29). For Kibuye, ibid, Lubengera Territoire, Rapport Agriculture, 1928–32, no. 80(15A+B); 80(16); 80(17); 80(18); 80(19); ibid., Kibuye Territoire, Rapport Agriculture, 1953–54, no. 82(23); 82(24). For Shangugu, ibid, Shangugu Territoire, Rapport Général, 1925; 1933–34; 1936, no.100(4); 100(12); 100(13); 101(2); Rapport Agriculture, 1928–32; 1937–38; 1940–55, no. 105(1); 105(2); 105(20); 105(3); 105(23); 105(4); 105(5); 105(7); 105(8); 105(10); 105(11); 105(12); 105(13); 105(14); 105(15); 105(16); 105(17); 105(18); 105(19); 105(20); 105(21); 105(22); 105(23); 105(24); 105(25)

Its share even increased later on. In the mid-1950s, Shangugu accounted for two thirds of the total European *Arabica* coffee acreage in the mandate. Consequently, a focus on this territory is justified. The first issue that demands explanation is the high figures for 1933–1934 compared with other years. This is the result not of an overestimation by the responsible agent or the inclusion of *Robusta* surfaces, but rather of the presence of Protanag – a plantation company trying to develop large-scale coffee cultivation, in addition to a processing branch and the cultivation of other cash crops (for more, see Chapter 2).[62]

62 Ibid, Shangugu Territoire, Rapport Général, 1933–34, no. 100(12) and 100(13).

Secondly, in 1937, apparently there was a dramatic setback in the area planted with coffee despite the fusion between Shangugu and part of the Kibuye territory. Unfortunately, the sources I consulted do not allow me to give a reasonable explanation, except for a possible overestimation in the previous year.

These methodological issues aside, European coffee land clearly was much smaller than in the settler district of the Kivu (in absolute and relative figures). According to Mararo, Shangugu's size was about 1600 square kilometers or 160000 hectares in 1929.[63] This means that European coffee land represented only 0.02% of the territory – and at that time the proportion of African land was even smaller. Due to the merger of Shangugu and part of Kibuye, the territory accounted for 2610 square kilometers or 261000 hectares in 1949.[64] With 0.11% of the total size, European coffee cultivation was limited at the end of the 1940s, even in this prominent "European territory." Moreover, only three coffee colonists resided in Shangugu in 1939, while in 1958, 27 *colons agricoles* – of which only a few were actively engaged in cultivating *Arabica* – populated the territory.[65]

2.3.3 Labor Mobilization: Quantitative Approach

Having demonstrated the production capacity of the Lake Kivu region and shown how much land was required to achieve that capacity, in the final section of this first chapter I aim to indicate the size of the coffee labor force. This task requires even more attention and caution than with the above figures. Data are scarce, and for the greater part sources do not specify what kind of laborers are represented. This is why in this section, I focus on figures referring to the dominant mode of production: plantations in the colony and smallholders in the mandate.

The fragmentary Table 10 presents the number of agricultural wage laborers in the Kivu district as well as the territories bordering the lake. The first issue is that these data concern land laborers *sensu largo*, which means that not only coffee plantation workers are included but also tea or quinine workers. It is extremely hard to find exact figures representing only coffee plantation workers in the sources. However, as the coffee sector was the most prominent agricultural sector in the Kivu region, presumably the larger part of those laborers were involved in coffee cultivation. The second issue is that it is unclear whether the above figures represent agricultural laborers as such – tilling the land, harvesting, etcetera – or whether they also include people active in the

63 Mararo, "Land conflicts in Masisi, Eastern Zaire: the impact and aftermath of Belgian colonial policy (1920–1989)": 138.

64 AAB, RARU, Shangugu Territoire, Rapport Général, 1949, no.102(2).

65 Ibid, 1939 and 1958, no. 101(5) and 102(9).

processing of the coffee beans and thus *de facto* factory workers. Finally, do these figures only deal with regular workers or do they include temporary

TABLE 10 Agricultural laborers in Kivu district, Kabare, Kalehe, Masisi and Rutshuru (1919–1954)

	Kivu	Kabare	Kalehe	Masisi	Rutshuru
1919	68				
1920					
1921					
1922	650				
1923					
1924					
1925	2539				
1926					
1927					
1928	22001				
1929					
1930					
1931					
1932					
1933	23831[a]				
1934	23202[a]				
1935	21009[a]				
1936	24932[a]				
1937	25852				3976
1938	25712				3560
1939	32191				
1940	32469				
1941	33799				
1942					
1943	28601				
1944	32615				
1945					
1946	42349				
1947					
1948					

	Kivu	Kabare	Kalehe	Masisi	Rutshuru
1949					
1950	54468[a]	16524	6177	9562	8936
1951		16448	5324	10808	10798
1952		18471	5522	10907	9817
1953		15066	5337	12085	11299
1954				12508	12389

Sources: Kivu district: Northrup, *Beyond the bend in the river: African labor in Eastern Zaire 1865–1940*: 148; Ost, "Agricultural laborers in Kivu, 1919–1939": 102; and AAB, RACB, Kivu Province, Conseil de Province, 1944–45; 1947; 1951, no. 194(5); 195(1); 39(2); 39(4). Territories: ibid, Kabare Territoire, Rapports AIMO, no. 99; ibid, Kalehe Territoire, Rapports AIMO, no. 103; ibid, Masisi Territoire, Rapports AIMO, no. 143; and ibid, Rutshuru Territoire, Rapports AIMO, no. 163

a Figures for Kivu Province, thus includes the Maniema district.

workers as well? Most likely only regular male laborers are included. I will return to the various labor categories in Chapter 5.

Although data are shaky and for the territorial level only available from the 1950s onwards, some remarks are possible. For instance, about 75% of the agricultural labor force of the Kivu Province was situated in the territories bordering Lake Kivu in 1950, which underscores the agricultural importance of this area. Comparing the number of workers with the (estimated) population size gives an impression of the impact of the agricultural (coffee) sector on the Africans involved, bearing in mind that only a limited percentage of the able-bodied men (HAV) could be described as in wage labor. An estimated 1 million people were living in the Kivu district in 1928, which means that about 2% were working in the agricultural sector. In 1938, 980175 people lived in the district. Hence, about 2.6% were employed in the agricultural sector. The entire Kivu Province was home to 1627703 people, of whom 3.3% gained an income as an agricultural wage worker in 1950.[66]

A focus on the territorial level reveals that the impact of agricultural wage labor is even more pronounced. The population figure of Kabare is estimated

66 For the figures for the Kivu district/Province see the respective annual reports: S.N., *Rapport annuel sur l'activité de la Colonie du Congo Belge pendant l'année…, 1920–58*: 1928; 1938; and 1950.

at 250505 in 1950,[67] which means that in this territory about 6.6% of the population was active in the agricultural sector. In the 1945 established territory of Kalehe, counting 75486 people in 1953, approximately 7% of the population was active in the agricultural sector.[68] In Masisi, about 6% of the total population number of 198454 was involved in land labor in 1953.[69] Rutshuru offers the possibility of approaching agricultural labor in a more "evolutionary" way.[70] In 1936, the territory was estimated to be home to 57550 inhabitants while, in 1937, there were supposedly 4000 people active in salaried agriculture, or about 7%. According to the 1950 annual report, 99685 people inhabited Rutshuru, while 8936 people were engaged in the agricultural sector, or about 9% of the population. In absolute terms, the size of the workforce increased but so did the population size, which suggests a relative stable size of the agricultural workforce during the colonial period, at least in Rutshuru.

The difference between the above figures and the following Rwandan figures is that the latter are specifically on coffee cultivators[71] and not the sum of all agricultural workers – which means that people working for Europeans are not included. The relative stability of the agricultural labor force on the Congolese side of Lake Kivu is also applicable to the Rwandan side, at least with regard to coffee producers. Only Shangugu suffered from a (relative and absolute) decrease in smallholder cultivators, compared with the total size of the population. Unfortunately, the figures in Table 11 are as fragmentary as those for the Congolese labor force, except for Shangugu.

Even though these figures represent coffee cultivators as such, sources do not specify the kind of producers. They do not explain whether smallholders were cultivating coffee as their only professional occupation or whether they produced only temporarily, possibly in combination with other sources of income. Moreover, it is more than obvious that these numbers are estimations. Taking Shangugu as an example, there were allegedly as many farmers in 1940 as in 1943 and only one less in the period 1944–1947. The splitting off of Kibuye in 1953 reduced the smallholder force in Gisenyi but not in Shangugu.

In both Gisenyi and Shangugu, the number of people involved in coffee production rose rapidly once the campaigns started in the early 1930s. Afterwards,

67 AAB, RACB, Kabare Territoire, Rapport AIMO, 1950, no. 99.

68 Ibid, Kalehe Territoire, Rapport AIMO, 1953, no. 103.

69 Ibid, Masisi Territoire, Rapport AIMO, 1953, no. 143.

70 Figures from: ibid, Rutshuru Territoire, Rapport AIMO, 1936 and 1950, no. 163.

71 Table 11 indicates HAV producing coffee: 1000 smallholders means 1000 HAV. However, the subsequent chapters will make clear that family members (not included in those figures) often assisted in the production process and, hence, 1000 smallholders refers to 1000 households.

TABLE 11 Coffee smallholders in Gisenyi, Kibuye and Shangugu (1932–1955)

	Gisenyi	Kibuye	Shangugu		Gisenyi	Kibuye	Shangugu
1932	293			1944			26637
1933			5910	1945			26637
1934				1946			26637
1935				1947			26637
1936				1948			
1937	28880			1949			
1938	29119		26315	1950			
1939				1951	25500		19903
1940			26638	1952	25959		21337
1941			26638	1953	17884	16453	
1942			26638	1954	19516	16330	20305
1943			26638	1955	19436	17125	19814

Sources: For Gisenyi, AAB, RARU, Gisenyi Territoire, Rapport Général, 1932; 1937–38, no. 87(18); 87(23); 87(24); Rapport Agriculture, 1951–55, no. 90(25); 90(26); 90(27); 90(28); 90(29). For Kibuye, ibid, Kibuye Territoire, Rapport Agriculture, 1953–55, no. 82(23); 82(24); 82(25). For Shangugu, ibid, Shangugu Territoire, Rapport Général, 1933; 1938, no. 100(12); 101(4); Rapport Agriculture, 1940–47; 1951–52; 1954–55, no. 105(10); 105(11); 105(12); 105(13); 105(14); 105(15); 105(16); 105(17); 105(21); 105(22); 105(24); 105(25)

the size of the force appears to have stagnated and even decreased in the early 1950s in spite of rising production capacity. It is impossible to say (due to a lack of data) whether people used more land to achieve this (see *supra*). However, evidence suggests that producers were allowed to plant more than the initial fifty-four bushes (Chapter 3), which indicates that either more land was indeed used or that plants were placed closer to each other. Labor productivity might have increased as well (see Chapter 5), but the most likely explanation is a combination of several factors.

The annual report for 1939 estimates the population size of Gisenyi[72] at 293000, which means that about 10% of the population was engaged in coffee production, full-time or as an additional occupation. In 1950, the population of this territory had dropped to 259922. With 25500 recorded cultivators this again equals 10%. More to the south, in Shangugu,[73] an even larger part of the

72 Figures from: AAB, Gisenyi Territoire, Rapport Général, 1939; 1950, no. 87(25); 88(10).

73 Figures from: ibid, Shangugu Territoire, Rapport Général, 1936; 1940; 1957, no. 101(2); 101(6); 102(8bis).

population was involved in compulsory coffee cultivation. There were 157711 people living in this territory in 1936. With some 26000 smallholders, 16% of the population was producing for the world market. Four years later, with the outbreak of World War II, the population number dropped to 149825. With still some 26000 coffee producers, 17% of the population was engaged in coffee cultivation. However, in 1957, Shangugu housed no more than 20000 producers, or 12% of the total population size. Although this is still a large proportion of the population, is not clear why there was a relative decrease in this territory. Perhaps people had found other ways to earn a cash income (see following chapters). The proximity and great appeal of Bukavu might offer a plausible explanation.

3 Conclusion

Even though *Arabica* was already cultivated in the fifteenth century, it did not develop into a mass commodity until the last quarter of the nineteenth century. After a long global journey, *Arabica* re-entered the African continent. Simultaneously with the "promotion," in terms of quantities produced, of this coffee variety (from luxury to mass product), a new coffee commodity frontier zone emerged around Lake Kivu. Missionary fathers played a decisive role in the introduction and initial stages of coffee cultivation in the region, especially before World War I. Once *Arabica* had entered, the Lake Kivu region developed into an important agricultural region in Belgian Africa.

On a global scale, Belgian Africa's share in coffee production doubled throughout the colonial period, from 1% at the end of the 1930s to about 2.1% in the late 1950s (while global production multiplied by 1.5). Referring to coffee production calls for a distinction between *Robusta* and *Arabica*. For the whole of Belgian Africa, the former was quantitatively the most important variety, although the latter was primordial in the Lake Kivu region (and Ruanda-Urundi by extension). Moreover, regarding *Arabica* production, it was this region that pointed the way. This chapter also demonstrates that the colony and the mandate were each other's mirror image. European plantations dominated in eastern Congo, while in neighboring Ruanda-Urundi the smallholder sector prevailed. The next chapter will focus on this divergence and the possible/plausible reasons for it.

In both the Congolese and the Rwandese territories bordering the lake, coffee production increased until the late 1930s, stalled until the 1950s and then regained strength. In the colony, growth in production in the 1950s was partly the result of African smallholders increasing their share in the production figures.

A focus on land mobilization revealed that in the Kivu there was a sharp rise in (European) land used for coffee production until the late 1930s. Similarly to the production figures, land mobilization slackened in the 1940 (partly caused by the limitation of coffee surfaces, see Chapter 3), while in the 1950s more land was brought into cultivation once again. African land nearly tripled in the last decade of the colonial period. Crossing the border to the Rwandese regions bordering Lake Kivu, it is striking that Shangugu, in particular, was relatively important for European coffee production, albeit of minor importance compared with African production or the European sector in the Congolese Kivu. Furthermore, it is harder to quantify smallholder coffee land because most Africans cultivated coffee in the vicinity of their habitations. Nevertheless, based on available data, it seems that there was a sharp rise in the amount of land used for coffee farming after World War II.

As for the quantitative approach to coffee labor, data are very shaky and scarce but there are some indications. Even though it is not possible to determine how many laborers the coffee plantation sector in colonial Kivu consisted of, it seems that, in relative terms, the agricultural labor force remained quite stable during the colonial period and that the majority of agricultural laborers resided in the regions bordering the lake. In the Rwandan territories bordering the lake, the size of the coffee-cultivating labor force also remained stable in the period under study. But figures indicate that relatively more people were involved in the coffee sector on the Rwandan side of Lake Kivu than on the colonial side.

CHAPTER 2

Explaining the Divergence

In the previous chapter I outlined the quantitative differences between the Belgian Congo and Ruanda-Urundi. Not only did I compare the entire colony with the mandate, I also compared the regions bordering Lake Kivu with each other. In this way, I was able to show that the difference in production systems was experienced by "neighbors" as well. People who lived in the same historically interlinked region, known as the "Lake Kivu space,"[1] who had (social, economic, political) ties in the precolonial as well as the colonial epoch, were active in a different mode of production. In this second chapter my aim is to explain qualitatively why there were divergences between east and west of Lake Kivu. Although some plausible explanations refer to the colony and/or the mandate as a whole because some issues are simply not region-specific, I refer to the Kivu region – the geographical core of this book – as much as possible.

I am well aware that this chapter is open to debate because it is very hard – if not impossible – to identify *the* central explanatory factor for the divergence. As is often the case, the explanation is complex and multifaceted. Nevertheless, there are factors that are more determining and/or plausible than others.

The first section of this chapter will analyze the historiographical debate with regard to this "divergence issue." There is already a vast literature dealing with diversity in economic development, which I intend to summarize briefly before focusing on the case study of this book. In the second section, I will weigh the various possible explanation factors against each other. The final part aims to reverse the roles: this means that the focus will shift from the dominating systems to other modes of production (smallholder cultivation in eastern Congo and plantations in western Rwanda).

1 Historiography: Divergence in Rural Production Systems

Around the world, people – from smallholders to plantation workers and all categories in between – have cultivated cash crops (sugar, cocoa, coffee, etcetera) in various ways. However, a rural economy is never monolithic, as there is

1 Chrétien, *The Great Lakes of Africa. Two thousand years of history*: 195.

 | DOI:10.1163/9789004428492_005

always a coexistence between plantations and smallholders.[2] This implies that classifying such an economy as a whole blurs the local complexity involved. On the other hand, categorization offers scholars an opportunity to determine the dominant mode of production, allowing them to more sharply accentuate contrasts and similarities between production systems.

Scholarly literature on rural development tends to stress "financial" factors in order to explain diversity. While focusing on the production of a wide range of crops (cocoa, rubber, coffee), William Clarence-Smith mainly stresses the "cost-effectiveness" factor in his explanations. According to Clarence-Smith, smallholders were able to produce more cheaply than plantations. They were much more cost-effective as they could function on (free) family labor, for instance, and consequently had the ability to outcompete expensive plantations.[3] Similar explanations can be found with regard to sugar. Ralph Shlomowitz argues that it was mainly a plantation activity. On the one hand, harvesting sugar cane was easier to control when it was done collectively. On the other hand, the required processing material was only cost-effective when it was used for large-scale production. Both these factors gave the sugar cane plantation sector a comparative advantage.[4] In nineteenth-century India, smallholders outcompeted plantations. Unlike plantations, smallholders not only intercropped coffee with food crops but also used labor more efficiently (less labor input, hence lower costs).[5] One scholar, studying the coffee economy in Nicaragua, believes that the degree of risk determined the dominant mode of production. When plantations fail, this means a loss of investment. In my opinion this is a weak argument, because the failure of a company involves unemployment and a loss of income as well. When smallholder production fails, people will have to return to subsistence farming (only) and/or turn to

2 Frederic L. Pryor, "The plantation economy as an economic system," *Journal of Comparative Economics* 6 (1982): 291.

3 William Gervase Clarence-Smith, "Plantation versus smallholder production of cocoa: the legacy of the German period in Cameroon," in *Itinéraires d'accumulation au Cameroun*, ed. Peter Geschiere and Piet Konings (Paris: Karthala, 1993), and "Rubber cultivation in Indonesia and the Congo from the 1910s to the 1950s: divergent paths," in *Colonial exploitation and economic development. The Belgian Congo and the Netherlands Indies compared*, ed. Ewout Frankema and Frans Buelens (London; New York: Routledge, 2013).

4 Ralph Shlomowitz, "Plantations and smallholdings: comparative perspectives from the world cotton and sugar cane economies, 1865–1939," *Agricultural History* 58, no. 1 (1984): 11–12.

5 Bhaswati Bhattacharya, "Smallholdings versus European plantations: the beginnings of coffee in nineteenth-century Mysore (India)," in *Embedding agricultural commodities using historical evidence, 1840s–1940s*, ed. Willem van Schendel (Oxon; New York: Routledge, 2017): 66.

wage labor, according to Charlip.[6] In these examples, governments (whether colonial or not) seem to be able to opt for and/or institutionally support or discourage a particular production type.

These examples are part of a major debate in historiography that contributes to a better understanding of the reasons for diversity in global economic development (as part of the Great Divergence debate).[7] The New Institutional Economy approach stresses the importance of (European) institutions for economic development. Spearheaded by two influential articles published by Daron Acemoglu, Simon Johnson and James Robinson, New Institutional Economists emphasize the idea of long-term economic underdevelopment as a structural consequence of colonialism.[8] According to Acemoglu, Johnson and Robinson, and followed by scholars such as Nathan Nunn,[9] pauperization of many regions in the global South was caused by the (lack of) installment of European-oriented institutions. They argue that regions appropriate for long-term European settlement (for example North America) created institutions – property rights in particular – to escape from the previously less favorable situation. On the other hand, in regions where settlement proved to be more difficult (due to the climate, for example), Europeans either installed extractive institutions or maintained the existing, unproductive, local institutions. Both of these approaches allegedly hamper long-term economic growth (for example Latin America and Africa).

Many historians of colonialism in Africa have criticized such explanatory models for overgeneralizing specific historical trajectories, oversimplifying causation processes and minimizing the agency of indigenous actors.[10] These scholars stress that the diversity of local conditions (environmental, political,

6 Julie Charlip, "Small farmers and coffee in Nicaragua," in *The global coffee economy in Africa, Asia, and Latin America 1500–1989*, ed. William Gervase Clarence-Smith and Steven Topik (Cambridge; New York: Cambridge University Press, 2003) 253.

7 See: Peer Vries, *Escaping poverty. The origins of modern economic growth* (Goettingen: V & R Unipress, 2013).

8 Daron Acemoglu, Simon Johnson, and James A. Robinson, "The colonial origins of comparative development: an empirical investigation," *American Economic Review* 91, no. 5 (2001), and "Reversal of fortune: geography and institutions in the making of the modern world income distribution," *Quarterly Journal of Economics* 117, no. 4 (2002).

9 This scholar argues that the Atlantic slave trade and its consequences were one of the main causes for the underdevelopment of contemporary Sub-Saharan Africa, see: Nathan Nunn, "Historical legacies: a model linking Africa's past to its current underdevelopment," *Journal of Development Economics* 83, no. 1 (2007), and "The long-term effects of African's slave trades," *Quarterly Journal of Economics* 123, no. 1 (2008).

10 See among others: Gareth Austin, "The 'Reversal of Fortune' thesis and the compression of history: perspectives from African and comparative economic history," *Journal of International Development* 20, no. 8 (2008); Cooper, *Africa in the world: capitalism, empire, nation-state*.

economic, social)[11] and the divers reactions of people (indigenous populations, settlers)[12] to colonialism and capitalism have resulted in historically and regionally divers and uneven paths of incorporation into the modern world economy. In addition, one all-encompassing colonial state (assumed by New Institutional Economists) was lacking.[13] It is more fruitful to acknowledge the existence of multiple local political constellations as a consequence of local differences and the feedback of local populations.[14] Consequently, colonial governments were forced to adapt (economic) policy to divers local specificities.[15]

This chapter endorses the critique on the overgeneralizing New Institutional Economy approach. Local conditions are key in understanding the different paths of coffee production. The development of the coffee sector had to be accommodated to different local settings. Historiography on the Kivu region has not yet treated the diversity issue in depth. Explanations offered in existing scholarship are usually limited to one factor. In this chapter, I argue that monocausal explanations are insufficient to understanding this complex divergence. By adding new empirical evidence to the existing literature, I advance a multifaceted alternative model: the production of coffee around Lake Kivu differed primarily because of an interplay of differences in land availability and in indigenous precolonial institutions (landholding system) that were enhanced during the colonial period due to judicial differences.

2 The Lake Kivu Region: Why Diversity?

2.1 *Environmental Factors?*

The climate differs greatly between the colony and the mandate. Most parts of the Congo have a warm continental equatorial climate. Vegetation roughly

11 Gareth Austin, "Resources, techniques, and strategies south of the Sahara: revising the factor endowments perspective on African economic development, 1500–2000," *Economic History Review* 61, no. 3 (2008); Anthony G. Hopkins, "The new economic history of Africa," *Journal of African History* 50, no. 2 (2009); and Patrick Karl O'Brien, "Colonies in a globalizing economy, 1815–1948," in *Globalization and global history*, ed. Barry Gills and William Thompson (London; New York: Routledge, 2006).

12 Several examples, especially from West Africa, demonstrate that initiatives taken by Africans as a reaction to market conditions resulted in economic growth during the "cash-crop revolution" (1890–1930) (Austin, "Resources, techniques, and strategies south of the Sahara: revising the factor endowments perspective on African economic development, 1500–2000": 612).

13 See for example: Jeffrey Herbst, *State and power in Africa: comparative lessons in authority and control* (Princeton: Princeton University Press, 2000).

14 Cooper, *Colonialism in question. Theory, knowledge, history*: 51.

15 Burbank and Cooper, *Empires in world history. Power and the politics of difference.*

classifies as savanna and tropical rain forest. High-altitude areas like the Kivu region and most parts of Rwanda and Burundi have a humid climate with irregular rainfall (between 1200 and 1800 millimeters per year); the vegetation is mostly grassland.[16] This difference can offer an explanation for the cultivation of different crops or different varieties of the same crop. *Robusta* was the dominant coffee variety in the colony while *Arabica* was dominant in the mandate and the colonial Kivu district. Furthermore, it would make sense that smallholder production would dominate in a tropical climate (large parts of the Belgian Congo) that is less appropriate for European settlement.

The Kivu region itself is located in the Western Great Rift (Albertine Rift), covered with mountains resulting from prehistoric tectonic movements. Consequently, the whole area has a moderate healthy climate and very fertile volcanic soil, perfectly suitable for *Arabica*, for example.[17] In other words, the territories bordering Lake Kivu have the same climate and fertile soil, have the same vegetation and are "blessed" with the same irregular rainfall. Yet there are different production systems. This observation runs counter to what Sokoloff and Engerman suggest in relation to the New World. They argue that initial conditions (the natural environment) determined whether plantation or smallholder production emerged. After establishment, both production systems developed divergent social-political organizations and varying degrees of inequality.[18] In this case study, environmental conditions around Lake Kivu are similar and thus inadequate to explain the development of different production systems in one region.

2.2 *Successful Examples?*

According to Shlomowitz, governments usually follow the example of others in order to initiate a certain crop accompanied by a certain economic organization, in a certain region.[19] This means that administrations (might) look to neighbors or predecessors who are developing or have developed (successful)

16 J.L. D'Hoore, *Soil map of Africa scale 1 to 5 000 000. Explanatory monograph* (Lagos: Commission for Technical Co-operation in Africa, 1964): 32. Although the Congo is vast, with different climate types and vegetation, the average temperature is estimated at between 25 and 31 degrees Celsius. For Rwanda and Burundi, the average is between 20 and 27 degrees Celsius.

17 Northrup, *Beyond the bend in the river: African labor in Eastern Zaire 1865–1940*: 32, 148; and Dorsey, "Rwandan colonial economy, 1916–1941": 14–17.

18 Kenneth L. Sokoloff and Stanley L. Engerman, "History lessons: institutions, factor endowments, and paths of development in the New World," *Journal of Economic Perspectives* 14, no. 3 (2000).

19 Shlomowitz, "Plantations and smallholdings: comparative perspectives from the world cotton and sugar cane economies, 1865–1939": 2.

production schemes in similar conditions (environmental, economic, political, etcetera).

In this case study, other East and Central African smallholder cash-crop production might serve as an example. According to Des Forges, Belgium was: "Dissatisfied with the results of earlier direct administration in the Congo, and impressed by the economy and efficiency of the British administration in Uganda."[20] However, the (mainly *Robusta*) coffee sector in Uganda emerged simultaneously with the development of this sector in Ruanda-Urundi in the 1930s.[21] Consequently, the mandate administration might have followed the example of another cash crop: cotton. Initiated by missionaries, from the early twentieth century onwards, cotton as a cash crop attracted the attention of the British colonial administration. From the outset, the British set up a chain of command reaching from the administrators to the chiefs.[22] The latter were then supposed to give directions and orders to their subjects.[23] Cotton cultivators in Uganda were controlled strictly, not only by administrators but also by agricultural officers and local chiefs. Planting directives were developed centrally and then diffused via a hierarchical chain of command.[24] Moreover, the British distributed cotton seeds freely and built experimental centers that served to educate local planters.[25] Finally, the British colonial administration systematically tried to convert tribute labor into cash taxes in order to free the potential labor force.[26]

A similar chain of command functioned in colonial Tanzania (Bukoba), initiated in the German period. Chiefs successfully distributed (*Robusta*) coffee seeds to their subjects; chiefs were also urged to give instructions and to control African cultivators.[27] However, when Tanzania became a British mandated territory, the newly installed administration extended and formalized the

---

20 Des Forges, *Defeat is the only bad news: Rwanda under Musinga, 1896–1931*: 158–159.

21 Michiel de Haas, "Measuring rural welfare in colonial Africa: did Uganda's smallholders thrive?" *Economic History Review* 70, no. 2 (2017): 609–610.

22 The chain of command the British installed was based on a pre-existing, sophisticated, centralized social-political system, especially in Buganda; see for example: Henri Médard, *Le royaume du Buganda au XIXe siècle. Mutations politiques et religieuses d'un ancien Etat d'Afrique de l'Est* (Paris; Nairobi: Karthala; IFRA, 2007).

23 Peter F.B. Nayenga, "Commercial cotton growing in Busoga district, Uganda, 1905–1923," *African Economic History*, no. 10 (1981): 178.

24 Ibid: 183.

25 Ibid: 178.

26 Michiel de Haas, "Measuring rural welfare in colonial Uganda: Why farmers would not work for wages," in *African Economic History Working Papers Series no. 18/2014* (2014): 22.

27 Austen, *Northwest Tanzania under German and British rule. Colonial policy and tribal politics, 1889–1939*: 94–96.

German system. Inspired by successful cash-crop production in Uganda, district officer/senior commissioner D.L. Baines (1916–1923) implemented a political-economic system borrowed directly from the northwestern neighbor in order to increase coffee cultivation in Bukoba.[28]

The success of the Ugandan cotton planters – exports rose from 1142 tons in 1906–1910 to 44632 tons in 1931–1935[29] – also had caught the attention of the Belgian government in Ruanda-Urundi. The smallholder system that the Belgians expanded, intensified and modified in the mandate resembles the described system in Uganda. The mandate government also depended on so-called "indirect rule" using a chain of command with chiefs as ultimate distributors of orders. Cultivators were controlled severely, and the bureaucracy also tried to convert traditional labor tribute systems into cash taxes in different stages (*infra*). Whereas compulsory cotton cultivation in the Belgian Congo was inspired by the Ugandan cultivation model,[30] neither published nor unpublished sources provide conclusive evidence that, as the British did in Tanzania, the mandate administration copied and adapted the Ugandan model for Rwandan coffee production.

2.3 *German Legacy?*

As mentioned in the previous chapter, Germany did imitate the Ugandan cotton cultivation system in Rwanda and Burundi, before World War I. Although the German attempts were limited, it cannot be denied that an embryonic infrastructure was already present when Belgium took over these former German colonies.[31] One scholar suggests that, subsequently, the Belgian mandate administration merely adopted this existing embryonic infrastructure.[32] However, focusing on the continuation of the German model alone fails to acknowledge additional explanations. This chapter demonstrates that, on the contrary, other factors were at least as important.

The German legacy might also be interpreted in another sense. After the defeat in World War I, Germany had to pay compensation and lost all its

28 Ibid: 133 and 137.

29 de Haas, "Measuring rural welfare in colonial Africa: did Uganda's smallholders thrive?": 610, figure 1.

30 Edmond Leplae, *Histoire et développement des cultures obligatoires de coton et de riz au Congo belge de 1917 à 1933* (Bruxelles: Goemaere, 1933): 23.

31 Initially, Germany was more interested in developing cotton production and intended to create a "second Uganda" (Jean-Pierre Chrétien, "Le 'désenclavement' de la région des Grands Lacs dans les projets économiques allemands au début du XXe siècle," in *Histoire sociale de l'Afrique de l'Est (XIXe–XXe siècle)*, ed. Département d'histoire de l'Université du Burundi (Paris: Karthala, 1991): 354).

32 Hatungimana, *Le café au Burundi au XXe siècle: Paysans, argent, pouvoir*: 109.

colonies in Africa. This may have upset colonial minds, which resulted in anti-propaganda campaigns. The German press systematically published articles emphasizing the inability of the Belgian authorities to rule over Ruanda-Urundi.[33] This propaganda even reached the League of Nations, and some members were suspicious of the Belgians' real intentions in the mandate. The Germans accused the Belgians of only being interested in the Rwandan population in order to support and develop the economy in the Belgian Congo. The Belgian representative in the League of Nations, Halewyck, responded to this accusation by stressing that the Belgians:

> did not want to make personal profits but that they organize their administration in such a way that the moral and material development of the indigenous populations will be assured. [...] Mistrust appears in the Commission concerning the intentions of Belgium with regard to Ruanda-Urundi; it is believed that the latter is exploited only for the benefit of the Congo. [...] Undoubtedly, it is inadmissible that the Congo would be denied the assistance of the mandate territories. But it is important to act cautiously and to avoid, by means of texts and decisions, the creation of a privileged status for our colony.[34]

The mandate government might have reacted to the German accusations by continuing to tie cultivators in Ruanda-Urundi to the land. Even though there are sufficient sources available to reconstruct the smear campaign Germany conducted against Belgium,[35] sufficient evidence is lacking that this campaign indeed urged the latter to install/continue a smallholder system.

2.4 *Cost-Effectiveness?*

Economically, the European colonists west of Lake Kivu (as in the rest of the Belgian Congo) were unimportant, unquestionably when compared with big

33 Vijgen, *Tussen mandaat en kolonie. Rwanda, Burundi en het Belgische bestuur in opdracht van de Volkenbond (1916–1932)*: 141, and David Newbury, "The 'Rwakayihura' famine of 1928–1929. A nexus of colonial rule in Rwanda," in *Histoire sociale de l'Afrique de l'Est (XIXe–XXe siècle)*, ed. Département d'histoire de l'Université du Burundi (Paris: Karthala, 1991): 283 (footnote 22).

34 AAB, RARU, Rapport sur l'administration belge au Ruanda-Urundi à la Commission permanente des Mandats, Lettre du ministre de la colonie au commissaire royale à Usumbura (annexe), 19/1/1926, no. 17(4).

35 See: ibid, Affaires Economiques, no. 3300/1936: this file contains several documents concerning the German campaign against the Belgian mandate administration, including letters, newspaper articles, etcetera.

mining companies with large amounts of cash.[36] However, the Great Depression of the early 1930s confronted the colonial administration in the Belgian Congo with problems. International coffee market prices plummeted (by 50%) and many *colons* faced financial difficulties. The majority of plantations were only able to survive thanks to financial contributions (loans, subsidies and even free concessions) from the government.[37]

One scholar suggests that financial difficulties in the colony explain why Belgium installed a smallholder production scheme in Ruanda-Urundi:

> Mr. de Heusch [the Belgian representative in the League of Nations] told the Permanent Commission that the costs were much higher for European producers than for Africans, and that this was a major factor in the administration's decision to discourage European operations [in the mandate].[38]

However, smallholder production was already the dominant (if not only) mode of production in Ruanda-Urundi before the Great Depression (see below). Therefore, the mandate administration could only have intensified smallholder production in Ruanda-Urundi. Secondly, why did the Colonial Council in Brussels refuse or fail to redirect coffee production to the west of Lake Kivu as well? If finance was such a major factor, as the quote suggests, then why not completely turn the coffee economy over to African hands? Consequently, a "financial" explanation alone is insufficient to explain the different paths of development.

2.5 *Famine of 1928–1929?*

As opposed to eastern Congo Kivu, Rwanda suffered from three famines in only thirty years: 1916–1918,[39] 1928–1929 and 1943–1944.[40] The so-called

36 The authority of the colonists should be understood in a political sense. The colonial administration wanted to maintain the (otherwise minimal) "white" presence in the colony via those *colons* which allowed the latter to impose their wishes to a certain extent (see Jewsiewicki, "Le colonat agricole européen au Congo-belge, 1910–1960: questions politiques économiques": 564).

37 Ibid: 563.

38 Dorsey, "Rwandan colonial economy, 1916–1941": 191.

39 See for instance: Bernard Lugan, "Causes et effets de la famine 'Rumanura' au Rwanda, 1916–1918," *Canadian Journal of African Studies* 10, no. 2 (1976). Eastern Congo Kivu, especially north of the lake, equally suffered from severe dearth in 1916–1918 (Northrup, *Beyond the bend in the river: African labor in Eastern Zaire 1865–1940*: 109).

40 See for example: Dantès Singiza, "Les réactions des autorités belges et locales face à la famine Ruzagayura (Rwanda, 1943–1944). Heuristique, méthodologie et premiers résultats," in

"Rwakayihura" famine of the late 1920s is decisive in this context. While this famine raged particularly in eastern Rwanda, its consequences were felt throughout the entire mandated area. The Belgian regime forced people to cultivate more food crops, including newly introduced ones like manioc.[41] Collective barns were installed in order to preserve seeds for the next planting season, and marshes were drained so that more land could be brought into cultivation.[42] But the famine of the late 1920s also served as a trigger to push through the obligatory cultivation of (mainly) coffee.[43] The ensemble of all of these measures was meant to provide the people of Ruanda-Urundi with more food crops as well as with cash income – both allegedly in order to prevent future famines.[44]

2.6 *Racially Defined Diversity?*

In Belgian colonial circles the idea circulated widely that a certain segment of the population of Rwanda (Tutsi) was superior to other ethnicities (Hutu and Twa) due to their alleged descent from more "developed" populations in Northern Africa (Egyptians in particular).[45] Not only did this Hamitic hypothesis favor Tutsi in nearly all societal branches, but it seems that the Belgians also applied this myth to justify the different modes of production between Rwanda and the Congo:

> Concerning coffee [cultivation], the situation in Ruanda is completely different from the Kivu. In the Kivu the population density is lower and the people are very backward: it is logical and necessary that the cultivation has to be done by colonists or companies, and that the natives merely

L'Afrique belge aux XIXe et XXe siècles. Nouvelles recherches et perspectives en histoire coloniale, ed. Patricia Van Schuylenbergh, Catherine Lanneau and Pierre-Luc Plasman (Bruxelles; Berne; Berlin: P.I.E. Peter Lang, 2014).

41 Jean-Luc Vellut, "La misère rurale dans l'expérience coloniale du Zaïre, du Rwanda, et du Burundi. Crises de subsistance et insuffisances alimentaires dans les possessions coloniales de la Belgique (ca.1920–1960)," in *The annual meeting of the African Studies Association* (Boston, December 7–10, 1983): 12.

42 Joseph Gahama, *Le Burundi sous administration belge: la période du mandat 1919–1939* (Paris: Karthala, 1983): 175–183.

43 Newbury, "The 'Rwakayihura' famine of 1928–1929. A nexus of colonial rule in Rwanda": 285.

44 Ibid.

45 For more on this myth see: Vervust, "The limits of colonial symbolic power. Ethnicization and racialization in Rwanda 1890–1960", especially Chapter 2. For a contemporary account: Albert Pagès, *Au Ruanda sur les bords du Lac Kivu (Congo Belge): un royaume hamite au centre de l'Afrique* (Bruxelles: Hayez, 1933).

> come into play as strictly guided laborers. In the Occupied Territories the population density is very high [...], the people are active and controlled by an intelligent race, the Xattusi. Here, the population nearly reaches the same level [of development] as the population in Abyssinia fifteen years ago. The plantations of certain chiefs [...] produce a coffee of good quality, often better than those of certain colonists or companies in the region.[46]

2.7 *Population Density – Land Availability?*

Rwanda and Burundi were (are) among the more densely populated areas in (Central) Africa. In the 1920s, Rwanda had a population density of about thirty-eight people per square kilometer, while in 1960 the average density had increased to 100 people per square kilometer.[47] This factor endowment is an exception in African economic history. In Sub-Saharan Africa, land was usually abundant and labor scarce; this resulted in the development of extensive agriculture, except for regions in the Great Lakes area and in West Africa.[48] Another characteristic is the uneven distribution of the population throughout Rwanda. For instance, the Central Plateau and the areas bordering Lake Kivu were (are) more densely populated than the areas in the east. In the interwar period, for example, some of these areas reached figures of up to 170 people per square kilometer.[49] The Congolese Kivu on the other hand was (is) less densely populated than Rwanda, with only the Kabare territory in the south approaching Rwandan averages.[50]

The higher population density in Rwanda offers a possible explanation for the installation of a smallholder coffee economy, as some scholars suggest: "it is necessary to keep in mind that the demography and the land system [see below] make a large-scale colonization unrealistic."[51] In the early 1930s, the governor of Ruanda-Urundi confirmed the lack of land in a letter addressed to the Secretary of the Colony:

---

46 AAB, Agri, Compagnies, *Société Auxiliaire Agricole du Kivu* (649), Note concernant l'application des zones de protection, [1932].

47 Reyntjens, *Pouvoir et droit au Rwanda: droit public et évolution politique, 1916–1973*: 21.

48 See: Austin, "Resources, techniques, and strategies south of the Sahara: revising the factor endowments perspective on African economic development, 1500–2000", and Herbst, *State and power in Africa: comparative lessons in authority and control*: 11.

49 Sven Van Melkebeke, "*More continuity than change.* Arbeid en arbeidsrelaties in de koffieplantagesector van Kivu tijdens het interbellum" (Unpublished Master thesis, Ghent University, 2012): 29.

50 Ibid.

51 Hatungimana, *Le café au Burundi au XXe siècle: Paysans, argent, pouvoir*: 124, and Dorsey, "Rwandan colonial economy, 1916–1941": 357.

> direct cultivation of coffee, by European colonists, is impossible in Ruanda-Urundi, even for small exploitations of 100 hectares and that because of a lack of fertile land [*bonnes terres*] in elevated regions where 9/10ths of the population is located.[52]

In 1926, the governor of the Oriental Province in the Belgian Congo made the opposite remark with regard to the installation of smallholders in his province, as he argued that "indigenous coffee cultivation is not recommendable in regions appropriate for European colonization [which means where land is available]." And, he added: "In fact, a very scattered coffee cultivation is difficult to surveil."[53]

The land issue in particular concerned the mandate administration throughout the colonial period. After World War II, the United Nations praised the mandate government for discouraging the installation of a higher number of European colonists, despite a rising demand for concessions.[54] This "land availability" explanation may seem plausible, but it raises some questions as well. If the lack of available, open land was the prime factor in the Belgian mandate government installing smallholder production in Ruanda-Urundi, then why did the authorities allow plantations to develop similar economic activities in parts of the mandate? Because some land was available for European colonization, even though only a handful of settlers were engaged in coffee cultivation (see Chapter 1). On the other hand, why was there a concentration and dominance of plantations in Kabare (the Congolese territory with a population density comparable to that of Rwanda)? The explanation is twofold: first, as opposed to Ruanda-Urundi, the Belgian Congo was not a mandate but a colony. This legal distinction had implications (see below) which help to explain why in the colony plantations could emerge in land-scarce regions. Secondly, path dependency also matters in the sense that once a plantation economy is initiated, the need to transform it is not self-evident. Moreover, in the Kivu district the political voice of the colonists (represented by the lobby group the Union Agricole du Kivu or Unaki[55]) was strong, and this explains the

52 AAB, Agri, Café, Café au Ruanda-Urundi (119/80), Lettre de Jungers (gouverneur de Ruanda-Urundi) au ministre de la colonie, 6/10/1932.

53 Ibid, Correspondance (340), Lettre de Moeller (gouverneur Province Orientale) au ministre de la colonie, 24/10/1926.

54 Ibid, RARU, Rapport sur l'administration belge au Ruanda-Urundi à la Commission permanente des Mandats, 1948, no. 20(4) and no. 20(4bis).

55 The Unaki consisted of plantation owners and exerted influence as a member of the Conseil de Province. However, consulting Unaki documents has revealed that large planters

continuation of the plantation economy, even though the local government did not always back colonists' aspirations.[56]

2.8 *Customary Land Tenure?*

As hinted at above, the existing land tenure system in Ruanda-Urundi was not appropriate for the installation of a plantation economy. This means that understanding the diverging paths of development in the Lake Kivu region is impossible without examining precolonial land relations. Before analyzing this crucial factor, it is important to stress that there was no such thing as *one* land tenure system, either in the Congolese Kivu or in Rwanda. The aim of this section is to highlight common features, as this must suffice to make the argument that precolonial conditions are significant for the divergent colonial modes of coffee production.

In the precolonial Congolese Kivu, centralization was not as marked as in some parts of Rwanda (especially the Nyiginya Kingdom in the center). Land was controlled by a community (lineage/clan) and distributed along community structures in exchange for cattle (tribute, gradually replaced by money in the colonial period). A common feature across the Kivu at the end of the nineteenth century was patron–client ties in which the granting of usufruct rights depended on loyalty and the payment of tributes to a chief – called *kalinzi* or *ikoro* depending on the region.[57] In the colonial period, a dual land tenure system emerged (see next chapter for more details on the processes underlying this dual model). On the one hand, the colonial administration claimed ownership of all vacant land and introduced a system of land registration and private ownership in order to regulate colonists' access to those lands. On the other hand, the legitimacy of the existing land tenure system was recognized, but only where land was already under the control of the customary

had a stronger voice than small planters. Consequently, the demands of the former were more and/or faster implemented by the government.

56 See: Ewout Frankema, Erik Green, and Ellen Hillbom, "Success and failure of European settler farming in colonial Africa," in *African Economic History Working Papers Series no. 16/2014* (2014). This paper claims that in settler regions in West, East and South Africa, settlers' ability to successfully develop agricultural activities depended on governmental support in accessing land and labor. However, settlers did not always receive support and, similarly to the Kivu case, their voice was only strong temporarily.

57 There were more land contract categories, but those mentioned were common throughout the (colonial) Kivu district; see: Kavuha Kalemaza, "Le développement de l'agriculture au Kivu colonial (1903–1940)" (Unpublished Master thesis, Université nationale du Zaïre (campus Lubumbashi), 1973): 76–79, and J. Hecq et al., *Agriculture et structures économiques d'une société traditionnelle au Kivu (Congo)* (Bruxelles: Publications de l'Institut National pour l'Etude Agronomique du Congo, 1963): 59–62.

authorities.[58] Thus, in theory, a distinction was applied between indigenous land – where access was still regulated via customary rules – and vacant land. In practice, however, this distinction was often blurred and native land alienated.[59]

Land relations in precolonial central Rwanda (Nyiginya Kingdom) differed from precolonial land tenure in the regions bordering Lake Kivu. Before the arrival of Europeans, the Nyiginya Kingdom had a rigid hierarchical structure with various types of patron–client ties and a private land tenure system with land granted by chiefs in exchange for tribute or *corvées*.[60] By 1900, in densely populated areas nearly all individual land (as opposed to other forms of land such as cattle land) was occupied, and people sometimes had to delay cultivation until a plot of land was available.[61] Next to this form of individual land tenure, there was also a collective system called *ubukonde*. A lineage established property rights over an arable estate by clearing it for the first time. Subsequently, lineage superiors distributed land in exchange for tribute, usually food. In regions further away from the center, land was not as important in the precolonial period as in central Rwanda. As Catharine Newbury brilliantly stresses when referring to Shangugu, there was enough arable land and many could settle and cultivate crops without establishing patron–client ties.[62] Lineage was still the organizing social-political entity.[63] Although centralization and hierarchy increasingly spread to these areas with the expeditions of Rwabugiri, this process was not completed until European colonization.[64]

Without denying variations and differences,[65] it seems that precolonial land relations in the Rwandan territories bordering Lake Kivu resembled those of the Congolese Kivu, rather than those of the Nyiginya Kingdom. Access to land

58 Koen Vlassenroot, "Land and conflict: the case of Masisi," in *Conflict and social transformation in Eastern DR Congo*, ed. Koen Vlassenroot, et al. (Ghent: Academia Press, 2004): 84.

59 James Robert Fairhead, "Fields of struggle: towards a social history of farming knowledge and practice in a Bwisha community, Kivu, Zaire" (Unpublished PhD dissertation, School of Oriental and African Studies, 1990): 88.

60 Jan Vansina, "Les régimes fonciers Ruanda et Kuba – une comparaison," in *African agrarian systems*, ed. Daniel Biebuyck (London: Oxford University Press, 1963): 352–354, and especially Vansina, *Antecedents to modern Rwanda. The Nyiginya kingdom*.

61 Vansina, "Les régimes fonciers Ruanda et Kuba – une comparaison": 352.

62 Newbury, *The cohesion of oppression. Clientship and ethnicity in Rwanda, 1860–1960*: 81.

63 Ibid: 95. The lineage continued to hold control over land due to rights established by clearing it for the first time (*ubukonde*).

64 Vansina, *Antecedents to modern Rwanda. The Nyiginya kingdom*: 194–195.

65 I. Reisdorff, *Enquêtes foncières au Ruanda* (s.l.: s.n., 1952). This survey presents a good overview of the evolution and differences in land systems in Rwanda from precolonial times until the late 1940s.

was regulated via lineage ties or even without any ties at all, as non-community members could get access to land as well. Although the centralizing tendency was spreading to the Rwandan regions close to Lake Kivu when colonization started, it was not yet completed. It was an ongoing process, and homogeneity was still lacking.[66] Rigid hierarchical institutions of the Nyiginya Kingdom were expanded by the colonizers, and the relative autonomy enjoyed by areas further away from the center was replaced by submission.[67]

The implementation of coffee, as a perennial crop, in combination with a persistent pressure on land availability during the colonial period made the expansion and continuation of a smallholder economy likely, but not a certainty. Land could still be expropriated, as happened in the colony, but this was far more difficult for the mandate administration due to legal limitations, as will be demonstrated in the following section.

2.9 *Mandate versus Colony?*

One of the consequences of the Treaty of Versailles was a change in the judicial-administrative status of Ruanda-Urundi. Hitherto belonging to Deutsch-Ostafrika, this area became a Belgian mandate (and later trusteeship) after World War I. According to Vijgen, this different legal status only mattered politically: Belgium assured the administration and applied indirect rule (B-mandate), while economically Ruanda-Urundi was a C-mandate, considered by Belgium as its own territory and, similarly to the colony, exploited directly.[68] If this is correct, the "mandate versus colony" argument cannot explain the difference between a plantation economy and a smallholder economy. Similarly, in the international literature some scholars doubt the impact of a mandate structure. Togo – another former German colony partly transformed into a mandate after the war – is an excellent example. Several authors stress the minor impact of the League of Nations on the policy in this mandated region. The permanent Mandate Commission only met a few times a year and, consequently, forced labor continued on a massive scale.[69] In more recent literature, several other authors seriously doubt the alleged minor

66 Vansina, *Antecedents to modern Rwanda. The Nyiginya kingdom*: 164–165.

67 Newbury, *The cohesion of oppression. Clientship and ethnicity in Rwanda, 1860–1960*: 24.

68 Vijgen, *Tussen mandaat en kolonie. Rwanda, Burundi en het Belgische bestuur in opdracht van de Volkenbond (1916–1932)*: 231.

69 See for instance: Gbédémah Seti Gableame, "L'échec de la politique française d'integration au Togo sous tutelle (1946–1960)," in *Les Togolais face à la colonisation*, ed. Nicoué Lodjou Gayibor (Lomé: Presses de l'Université de Bénin, 1994), and Leo De Haan, *La région des savanes au Togo. L'état, les paysans et l'intégration régionale (1885–1985)* (Paris: Karthala, 1993).

impact of the League of Nations. Without denying the continuation of forced labor in one form or another, they emphasize the greater participation by the local populations in policy-making, which restrained the French mandate government's freedom.[70]

With regard to Ruanda-Urundi, David Newbury suggests that supervision by the League of Nations (and later the United Nations) urged the mandate administration to proceed cautiously.[71] Does this mean that Rwandans had more freedom compared with their Congolese neighbors? In other words: was it more difficult for Belgians to expropriate land and (directly or indirectly) force Rwandans into (plantation) labor? And is it possible that, contrary to what Vijgen argues, the legal difference between the Belgian Congo and Ruanda-Urundi did influence the economic scope of the respective governments? Empirical evidence suggests that it did. In a provisional legislative text from 1921 the League of Nations stressed the significance of indigenous institutions (article 6):

> While establishing the rules concerning land tenure and the transfer of land property, the mandatary agrees to take indigenous rules and customs into account, to respect the laws and to preserve indigenous interests.[72]

Although one can rightly claim that similar laws existed in the Belgian Congo (on vacant versus indigenous land, for instance), a supervising mandate entity such as the League of Nations was absent in the colony. The impact of this legal difference is stipulated in a 1924 letter sent to Sir Frederick Lugard (Mandate Commission member at that time). The Mandate Commission had asked Belgium to annex a bulletin with laws applicable to Ruanda-Urundi to the annual mandate report. However, Henri Jaspar (the then Belgian Secretary of Foreign Affairs) had sent a bulletin with laws applicable to the colony. It contained decrees of no use in the mandate and of little value for the members of the Mandate Commission.[73]

---

70 See for example: Benjamin N. Lawrence, *Locality, mobility and "nation." Periurban colonialism in Togo's Eweland (1900–1960)* (Rochester; New York: University of Rochester Press, 2007), and Ulricke Schuerkens, *Du Togo allemand aux Togo et Ghana indépendants. Changements social sous régime colonial* (Paris: L'Harmattan, 2001).

71 Newbury, "The 'Rwakayihura' famine of 1928–1929. A nexus of colonial rule in Rwanda": 278.

72 UNOG, Fonds du Secrétaire – Section des Mandats (1), Projet révisé de mandat belge, 23/2/1921, no. 9/1025.

73 Ibid, Lettre du Rappard (président section mandats) à Sir Frederick Lugard, 11/2/1924, no. 9/1025.

When legislation on the government of the mandate was finalized in 1926, the mandate charter contained ordinances that had been rewritten and reformulated from earlier versions and perhaps somewhat softened, but the basic principles remained. Previous research confirms this argument by stressing that the mandatary had the right to impose legislation as if the mandate were its own territory, but that local conditions should be kept in mind.[74] As argued above, this is what Belgium did (had to do).

In the annual mandate reports written by Belgian administrators, the effect of the mandate issue is rarely stressed or even mentioned explicitly. This suggests that the legal difference between a colony and a mandate must have been self-evident for government agents. Starting in 1948, members of the Mandate Commission visited Ruanda-Urundi every three years. That way the legal difference with the colony was no longer only theoretical but, from the late 1940s on, empirical as well. Furthermore, some Belgian entrepreneurs were also aware of this delicate judicial issue and its consequences:

> It is nevertheless an act which will not escape the League of Nations' attention that, while practicing indirect [coffee] cultivation in Ruanda-Urundi [...], we shape a small landowner and not only a wage owner working for a colonist or a company, we assure the native's social evolution, and we create resources while maintaining his freedom.[75]

2.10 *Land, Locality and Legality as Prevailing Explanations*

Empirical evidence suggests that the availability of land in both the Belgian Congo and Ruanda-Urundi was one of the prime factors motivating the colonial administration to diversify the mode of production. Pressure on land in the mandate partly explains the development of a smallholder coffee production scheme. Moreover, bureaucracies were aware of this delicate issue throughout the entire colonial period in both the colony and the mandate. Furthermore, at least in central Rwanda, a hierarchal system of precolonial land relations perfectly appropriate for indirect rule in the mandate had already matured. This centralized land system was gradually implanted in other parts of Rwanda. The judicial difference also impacted the decision-making process, helping to explain the deviating paths that emerged around Lake Kivu. I have shown that the mandate structure had to be kept in mind at all

74 Filip Reyntjens, "Statut international et droit constitutionnel du Ruanda-Urundi," in *L'ordre juridique coloniale Belge en Afrique Centrale. Eléments d'histoire*, ed. Emile Lamy and Louis De Clerck (Bruxelles: Académie Royale des Sciences d'Outre-Mer, 2004): 69.

75 AAB, Agri, Café, Café au Ruanda-Urundi (119/80), Note du manager de *Platarundi* au gouverneur du Ruanda-Urundi, 14/9/1931.

times by the Belgian administration in order to keep Geneva (and later New York) satisfied. Consequently, it was far more difficult to alter existing precolonial social-economic relationships in Ruanda-Urundi. Hierarchical, individualized landholding, in combination with limited land availability and legal restrictions, serves as the prevailing explanatory factor. However, embedding agricultural commodities is not merely an act, it is an ongoing process.[76] This means that the aforementioned factors not only determined the development of two different production systems, but they also determined the further evolution of the coffee sector on both sides of the lake, with their diverging methods of land and labor mobilization and commodification – as will be demonstrated in the following chapters.

Other factors can be left out completely (environmental factors, for example), require caution or are of additional relevance in explaining the divergent modes of production. Not only did the myth of powerful Tutsi elites who were superior to other societal groups serve to legitimate reservation of nearly every attractive position, but the Hamitic hypotheses also played a role in diversifying the populations in Rwanda – able to cultivate coffee on their own, yet rigorously controlled – and eastern Congo Kivu – incapable of growing this cash crop. The famine of the late 1920s also contributed to the decision of the mandate bureaucracy to implement and/or intensify a smallholder production scheme in Ruanda-Urundi. "Financial" considerations may have contributed (indirectly) to the mandate government's decision to intensify the coffee smallholder structure (which was still in its infancy) in Ruanda-Urundi, as the crisis left the administration in the Congo with financial disillusionment. The German legacy in Ruanda-Urundi worked out well for the mandate administration because the Germans had already introduced the African population to the cultivation of coffee. Moreover, the anti-propaganda campaigns Germany launched against Belgium may have urged the mandate government to continue and intensify smallholder production. However, empirical evidence to support this hypothesis is lacking. Caution is also required with regard to the successful development of the cotton smallholder sector in neighboring Uganda. The administration in Ruanda-Urundi constructed a mode of production similar to that of Uganda, with a hierarchical chain of command based on the existing centrality and power of the chiefs in the Rwandan state. However, empirical evidence that links coffee production in the Belgian mandate to Ugandan cotton cultivation is lacking.

76 Willem van Schendel, "Embedding agricultural commodities: an introduction," in *Embedding agricultural commodities using historical evidence, 1840s–1940s*, ed. Willem van Schendel (Oxon; New York: Routledge, 2017): 5.

3 Diversity in Reverse

The previous chapter of this book presented a quantitative outline of the diverging trends in the development of the coffee sector. The first part of this chapter explained why on the western side of Lake Kivu a plantation economy and on the eastern side smallholder cultivation were the dominant modes of production. But as the figures in Chapter 1 demonstrate, on both sides of the lake the opposite mode of coffee production was not absent. This section elaborates on that aspect.

3.1 *Smallholding in Eastern Congo*

3.1.1 Until the 1930s

The colonial administration encouraged African coffee production before the "rush of colonists" in the mid-1920s. According to Kalemaza, colonial agents distributed coffee seeds to local chiefs as early as the beginning of the twentieth century. However, due to a lack of interest among the elites, this attempt to stimulate coffee cultivation was not successful at this stage.[77] It was not until the introduction of compulsory coffee cultivation – strongly advocated by Edmond Leplae (*infra*) – among local chiefs in 1922 that indigenous production commenced. As in Ruanda-Urundi, local chiefs used *corvée* laborers to till their lands, resulting in the first harvest in 1926.[78] In the following year the "invasion" of colonists started. This meant increasing opposition to indigenous cultivation, animated discussions and ultimately the abolition – except in some well-chosen zones – of forced coffee cultivation in 1931.[79]

Edmond Leplae was a prominent antagonist of free indigenous cultivation.[80] Already at the end of World War I he expressed this point of view, clearly emphasizing the backwardness of Africans as the reason why Europeans should develop Africa:

> Some are dreaming of reserving Central Africa for the Africans: it is a noble and generous idea, but unrealizable. Nowadays material progress is proceeding too fast so that backward races, like the black ones, have no

77 Kalemaza, "Le développement de l'agriculture au Kivu colonial (19031940)": 94.

78 Ibid: 104.

79 Ibid: 106–107.

80 Leplae (1868–1941) was an agricultural engineer and a professor at the university of Louvain. He was engaged in the colony from 1910 onwards. As president of the agricultural department at the Ministry of the Colony, he was responsible for the introduction of the *cultures obligatoires* in 1917. Leplae retired in 1933, and was decorated by the Belgian state for his merits (M. Van den Abeele, "Edmond Leplae," in *Biographie coloniale belge* (Bruxelles: Académie Royale des Sciences Coloniales, 1955)).

> chance to resist the irresistible progressive (slow or fast) invasion of civilized people, incomparably more active and more intelligent.[81]

What Leplae meant by this quote is that economic development in Belgian Africa should be controlled and/or managed by Europeans. Africans should become wage laborers in one way or another, working in European enterprises or in close cooperation with European firms. However, with the outbreak of the global crisis a serious debate unfolded in Belgian colonial circles between supporters and adversaries of plantation wage labor.[82] Opponents argued that plantations were too expensive and that land was expropriated from indigenous communities. They advocated the installment of independent smallholder cultivation. Supporters (Leplae, backed by colonists) refuted those arguments, for example by arguing that plantation labor was training for the employees, enabling them to better cultivate their own fields, or by saying that plantation owners provided their laborers with a piece of land in order to cultivate food crops.[83] The "cooperation" aspect is nevertheless more relevant in this part. "Collaboration" between Europeans and Africans was conceived as a European colonist or enterprise delivering seeds or plants (palm, coffee, cotton, etcetera) to Africans. The latter cultivated (or was forced to cultivate), maintained and harvested the crop. Subsequently, Europeans purchased the crop (usually at a low price) and eventually marketed the commodity.[84] It was in this way that the compulsory cultivation scheme introduced in the colony in 1917 functioned.[85] This "collaboration" also resembles the organization of cultivation in the Ruanda-Urundi (see Chapter 5).

Although Leplae's ideas do not allude to a region in particular, they are applicable to the colonial Kivu district. African production was still in its infancy and – similarly to in Ruanda-Urundi – mainly the privilege of chiefs in the 1920s. From 1927 onwards, *colons agricoles* were rushing in and had commenced installing a plantation economy, thereby pushing the fragile African coffee sector of the Kivu district into the background. The administration in

81 Edmond Leplae, "La colonisation agricole belge au Congo," *Bulletin Agricole du Congo Belge* 9, no. 1–4 (1918): 4.

82 A similar discussion also emerged in Uganda in the early twentieth century: Phares M. Mutibwa, "White settlers in Uganda: the era of hopes and disillusionment, 1905–1923," *Transafrican Journal of History* 5, no. 2 (1976): 114–115.

83 Edmond Leplae, "Faut-il, en Afrique centrale, repousser le salariat et les plantations européennes?" *Bulletin Agricole du Congo Belge* 22, no. 4 (1931).

84 Leplae, "La collaboration agricole entre Indigènes et Européens," *Bulletin Agricole du Congo Belge* 22, no. 4 (1931): 567.

85 See Likaka, *Rural society and cotton in colonial Zaire*, for a detailed analyses of the compulsory cultivation of cotton.

the Oriental Province backed colonists (and their debatable arguments; see *infra*), arguing that certain crops (like coffee) could not be cultivated by both colonists and smallholders. The local government wanted to create a "second Kenya" in the Kivu district with the installation of "gentleman farmers" on concessions with a limited surface.[86] Furthermore, the already-mentioned political strength of the colonists and their lobby association (Unaki) ensured the continuation of a plantation economy and the limitation of independent African coffee production from the 1930s onwards. Even "collaboration" was not yet under discussion in the Congolese territories near to the lake.

3.1.2 1930s–1950s

Numerous restrictions imposed on coffee smallholders in areas appropriate for European colonization define this period. As in colonial Kenya: "The designated role of African smallholders was mostly to service the domestic market and provide a rural subsidy to African laborers on settler estates, but not to compete with the settler sector."[87] Small African producers in eastern Congo were not prohibited from cultivating coffee. However, unlike plantations, they were not allowed to plant more than 100 trees per person; they were excluded from any financial support; they were denied access to loans in the aftermath of the global economic crisis; and they received half or only one third of the coffee price paid to plantations.[88]

The colonial administration backed the aspirations of the *colons*, at least for the production of coffee.[89] In the Kivu district, a "collaboration system" developed in which cotton and rice were cultivated by Africans and processed by Europeans from the early 1930s onwards.[90] Coffee, on the other hand, was

86 AAB, RACB, Province Orientale, Comité Régional, 1927, no. 49(1bis).

87 David Hyde, "'Paying for the emergency by displacing the settlers': global coffee and rural restructuring in late colonial Kenya," *Journal of Global History* 4, no. 1 (2009): 83.

88 Bashizi, "Pouvoirs publics, plantations européennes et réactions paysannes au Sud-Kivu (1920–1960)": 141–142; Jewsiewicki, "The great depression and the making of the colonial economic system in the Belgian Congo": 169; and Northrup, *Beyond the bend in the river: African labor in Eastern Zaire 1865–1940*: 147. According to Northrup, both administrative force and the government's belief that Africans were accustomed to a lower standard of living legitimized such a measure. It is, however, not unlikely that racist motives – Africans as bad agriculturists – also played a role.

89 A recent study on Southern Rhodesia argues that the development of the coffee sector was designed precisely to support white settlers' economic opportunities and to increase their incomes (Takesure Taringana, *Agrarian capitalism and the development of the coffee industry in colonial Zimbabwe 1900–1980* (Newcastle upon Tyne: Cambridge Scholars Publishing, 2018)).

90 AAB, RACB, Kivu Province, Conseil de Province, 1934, no. 37(5).

another story. Cooperation, let alone independent African cultivation, was the colonist's worst nightmare. The arguments Kivu colonists used to convince the local government of their right are omnipresent in the discussions of the provincial council. Moreover, the same arguments were also used by settlers in other colonies. In Kenya, for example, colonists argued that African coffee production would increase the risk of spreading diseases; that the quality of African coffee would be inferior to the high-quality coffee produced by Europeans; that Africans were unable to maintain their fields properly; or that there might be a risk that Africans would steal coffee beans from plantations and mix them with inferior beans they produced themselves, damaging the entire coffee sector.[91] Nevertheless, in the Kivu and Kenya alike, colonists' greatest anxiety was running the risk of losing potential laborers for their estates. In April 1934, a member of the Unaki explained this grievance in plain terms to the Council of the Costermansville Province:

> With reference to coffee, the Unaki is absolutely opposed to allowing natives to cultivate next to us. If we tolerate native coffee plantations next to ours, it is evident that very soon the native will realize that he is able to make as much money on his own as with us [as a wage laborer], and that would ruin us rapidly. It would be a big economic mistake to tolerate that. We already have difficulties in recruiting laborers; if we permit the native to settle next to us and to do the same thing as us, it is certain that the labor issue will intensify even more.[92]

Restrictions do not equal absence. Chiefs continued to cultivate, and a limited number of colonial agents were unable to control everything. Moreover, as the above quote suggests, in areas unsuitable for European colonization or with no (or few) Europeans settled, indigenous production was less vulnerable to the opposition of colonists and therefore to limitations. The two most important territories for smallholder production in this period were Beni and Lubero in north Kivu. Although those areas are outside the scope of this book, it is important to briefly digress, because they underline the argument that free smallholder coffee production was allowed only in areas not appropriate for European colonization. In 1935, the government started this program, and

91 Nicholas E. Makana, "Metropolitan concern, colonial state policy and the embargo on cultivation of coffee by Africans in colonial Kenya: the example of Bungoma district, 1930–1960," *History in Africa* 36 (2009): 316–317. Moreover, colonists in the Kivu used the same arguments to oppose Rwandan smallholder cultivation.

92 AAB, RACB, Kivu Province, Conseil de Province, 1934, no. 37(5).

about 207 hectares were brought into cultivation.[93] Indigenous production proved to be successful, since in 1940 the two territories produced 122 tons (*Arabica* and *Robusta*), while in 1949, the amount had increased by more than 50% to 295 tons (both varieties).[94] Beni and Lubero accounted for almost the entire smallholder coffee production in the Kivu district at the end of the 1940s (see figures in Chapter 1) and demonstrated that native coffee production in a settler region could develop into a successful story.

It should be stressed that smallholder production was installed not only in the extreme north of the district. In Rutshuru the local administration also intended to promote smallholder *Arabica* production in areas with no coffee plantations or other European establishments. The annual report of 1933 stipulates that in the densely populated Bwisha chiefdom (see Map 5), bordering Lake Kivu and Rwanda, land was lacking for European colonization. Consequently, the territorial administrator launched the idea of obliging the natives to cultivate coffee (fifty bushes per year per HAV) for a time span of three years.[95] This effort is similar to experiments in some Kenyan regions lacking European plantations or other forms of cash income in the 1930s. In southwestern Kenya, for example, an experiment successfully started also in 1933. From then on, the Gusii, living far away from European plantations, were allowed to plant 100 coffee bushes per person.[96]

In Rutshuru, however, "propaganda" in favor of native production was already abolished in 1936 for several reasons: the territory suffered from a malaria outbreak and the administration had to prioritize this issue, and coffee bushes were not maintained properly, or were even destroyed.[97] After 1936, the obligation to cultivate coffee in Bwisha had disappeared, and references in the sources are absent from this point onwards. However, it would be a mistake to assume that smallholder cultivation had vanished. People allegedly did not like compulsory coffee cultivation, but with the disappearance of the obligation, the dislike might have disappeared as well.

93 Ibid, Rutshuru Territoire, Rapport AIMO, 1936, no.37(7).

94 Ibid, 1941 and 1950, no. 38(4) and 39(3).

95 Ibid, Rutshuru Territoire, Rapport AIMO, 1933, no.163.

96 Carolyn Barnes, "An experiment with coffee production by Kenyans, 1933–48," *African Economic History*, no. 8 (1979): 199. I also refer to M.A. Ogutu, "Dualism and the development of coffee in Meru, Kenya, in 1930s," *Transafrican Journal of History* 8, no. 2 (1979), who analyzes the creation of experimental coffee smallholding districts, such as Meru, in regions with no European plantations nearby.

97 AAB, RACB, Rutshuru Territoire, Rapport AIMO, 1936, no. 163.

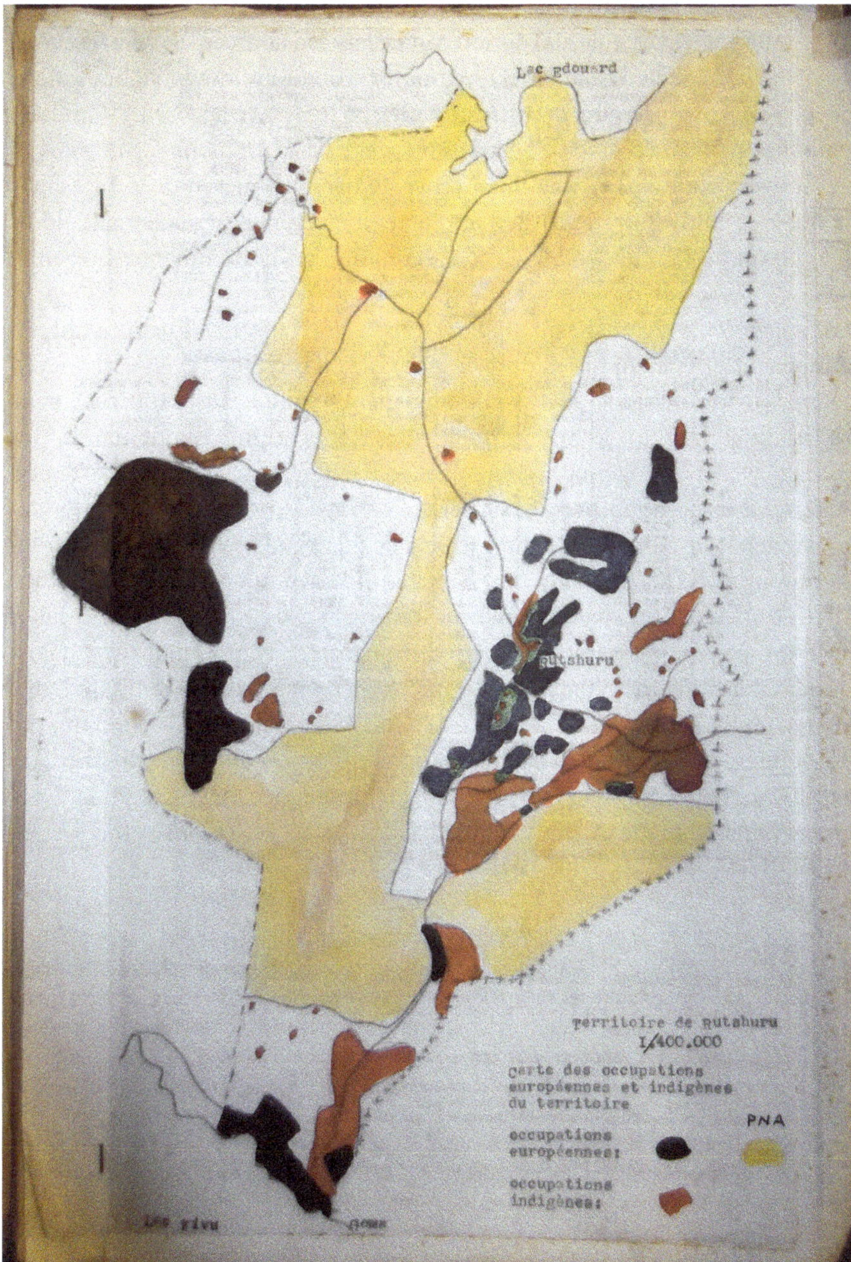

MAP 5 Land occupation in Rutshuru (1941). This map shows that in some regions, African land occupation was dense while in turn distances between European concessions and African villages sometimes were immense, which influenced labor patterns (see following chapters)

SOURCE: AAB, RACB, RUTSHURU TERRITOIRE, RAPPORT AIMO, 1941, NO. 163

3.1.3 1950s: Liberalization

The last decade of the colonial period can be labeled as an era in which several attempts were made by the Belgian administration to remove the limitations imposed on Africans trying to cultivate coffee on their own account.[98] Similarly to in other African colonies,[99] restrictions were eased, and one of the aims of the ten-year plan (1949) was to improve indigenous agriculture. In Kenya, smallholder cultivation flourished and after the colonial period smallholders even became "the backbone of an economy once dominated by white settlers."[100]

As suggested previously, smallholder coffee cultivation in Rutshuru did not disappear after 1936. In the mid-1950s, natives still produced even without obligation (or "promotion," as it is euphemistically called in the sources), even though they had to follow certain rules (concerning maintenance, for instance).[101] African agency also manifested itself in Masisi. In the Sake region (eastern Masisi) – an important settler area – the territorial administrator decided that native coffee cultivation should be managed by an agronomist from 1951 onwards.[102] This indicates that Africans did have some margin to produce coffee even before the 1950s. Moreover, starting in the early 1950s, a handful of (coffee or tea) colonists initiated something completely new and without governmental interference: tenancy.[103] A colonist, owner of a piece of land, distributed a plot (maximum one hectare) to an African farmer. As a tenant, the latter then received full responsibility and was supposed to cultivate the land as if it were his own (clearance, planting, maintenance, harvest). Finally, the harvest was sold to the owner, who paid a fixed price. For colonists this system

98 This does not mean that opposition to African cultivation had disappeared. In a 1956 article, the author adulates plantations because, according to him, they preserve better customary life (Joseph Goffin, "Les facteurs de développement et d'intégration des économies indigène et européenne au Congo belge et au Ruanda-Urundi," in *Vers la promotion de l'économie indigène. Compte rendu du colloque colonial sur l'économie indigène (9–13 janvier 1956)*, ed. Henri Janne (Bruxelles: Institut de Sociologie Solvay, 1956): 327).

99 See for Kenya: Hyde, "'Paying for the emergency by displacing the settlers': global coffee and rural restructuring in late colonial Kenya"; for French Cameroon: Martin Kuété, "Café, caféiculteurs et vie politique dans les hautes terres de l'Ouest-Cameroun," *Cahiers d'Outre-Mer* 61, no. 243 (2008): 295.

100 Frederick Cooper, *Africa since 1940: the past of the present* (Cambridge: Cambridge University Press, 2002): 93.

101 AAB, RACB, Rutshuru Territoire, Rapport AIMO, 1944, no. 163.

102 Ibid, Masisi Territoire, Rapport AIMO, 1950, no. 143.

103 See: Bycyalimwe Mararo, "Occupation économique du Kivu (1945–1959)" (Unpublished Master thesis, Université nationale du Zaïre (campus Lubumbashi), 1974): 149–151.

was cheaper than wage labor, and Congolese cultivators at least had a glimpse of working more freely.

A system that somewhat resembles tenancy is that of the *paysannats indigènes*,[104] already designed in the 1930s but unsuccessful until the end of World War II.[105] The *paysannats* aimed at intensifying native (food and export) production as follows:

> families were relocated in an effort to place their fields in a systematic layout and to place the center of the community nearer to existing roads in order to support the use of machinery and to facilitate the introduction of fertilizers, pesticides, superior crop rotation, and superior varieties, and to make supervision and guidance easier.[106]

Africans were thus moved, and had to (individually or collectively) cultivate a plot of land assigned by the administration. As Jewsiewicki points out, the premise of improving native agriculture was a way to reinforce control over the peasantry.[107] In other words, direct limitations were replaced by indirect ones. Jewsiewicki's view contradicts my argument of a liberalizing tendency in the regions bordering Lake Kivu during the 1950s. In those regions, *paysannats* did exist but they did not, however, include coffee production.[108] Food, cotton, palm products and tea were cultivated by means of these schemes. Migrants from Ruanda-Urundi even asked for financial support in Mushari (Rutshuru), as they intended to initiate a fishing *paysannat* in 1953. Due to a lack of money credit was refused and the plans rejected the year after.[109]

---

104 See Brecht Gunst, "Het Institut National pour l'Étude Agronomique du Congo belge. De integratie van de Congolese peasant in het kapitalistische wereld-systeem" (Unpublished Master thesis, Ghent University, 2012): 102–119, for an overview of the history, implementation and functioning of the *paysannats* in the Belgian Congo. For an extensive description of all *paysannats* in the colony and the mandate in the mid-1950s, see: Pierre Staner, "Les paysannats indigènes du Congo belge et du Ruanda-Urundi," *Bulletin Agricole du Congo Belge et du Ruanda-Urundi* 46, no. 3 (1955).

105 Huybrechts, *Bilan économique du Congo*: 53.

106 Marvin P. Miracle, *Traditional agricultural methods in the Congo Basin* (Stanford: Food Research Institute, 1964): E10.

107 Bogumil Jewsiewicki, "African peasants in the totalitarian society of the Belgian Congo, 1917–1960," in *Peasants in Africa, historical and contemporary perspectives*, ed. Martin A. Klein (Beverly Hills; London: Sage Publications, 1980): 58.

108 However, in Beni and Lubero coffee was indeed produced in *paysannats*, usually in rotation with food crops.

109 AAB, RACB, Rutshuru Territoire, Rapport AIMO, 1953 and 1954, no. 163.

The major difference between the *paysannats* (unsuccessful in this book's region of interest) and what is called "economic conversion" is that the latter attempt of the administration was based on free entrance. Starting in 1954, the local administration installed coffee smallholdings in Kabare, Masisi and Rutshuru, without, however, deliberately trying to damage European concessions.[110] The main reason for this turnaround in colonial thinking, and proof of declining restrictions, was a growing lack of fertile land:

> a program of "perennial crops" [based on volunteers] that constitutes another form of paysannat. The perennial crops are meant to increase the income of the planters. A consequence of this is a decrease in food crops until subsistence level. That way, we reduce overcultivation in saturated regions and permit the re-establishment of normal fallow periods.[111]

However, land availability was certainly not a "new" problem. The following chapter demonstrates that discussions concerning land occupation and "free" land were commonplace during the colonial period. The question is thus whether the drop in coffee prices (halved in only eight years) in the second half of the 1950s[112] was not the real, or at least an additional, incentive for the colonial administration to diversify the mode of production in the Congolese territories bordering Lake Kivu.

Whatever the underlying reasons of the local government in the Kivu might have been, "economic conversion" was successful. As the figures in the previous chapter show, indigenous coffee production as well as land occupied for coffee cultivation increased in the second half of the 1950s. While in 1955 the limitation of 100 bushes per person was still intact, in 1958 each native had the right to plant up to 500 bushes.[113] It is hardly a surprise that colonists were not amused by this evolution, which resulted in tensions with the government. The arguments used to block coffee smallholdings were no longer backed by the state. The dogma of only allowing smallholder coffee production in regions with little or no Europeans was also dismissed. Local administrators dreamed of an *occupation mixte* with European and African concessions next to each other, helping each other according to their respective capacities.[114] This, in

110 Ibid, Kivu Province, Conseil de Province, 1956, no. 41(2).

111 Ibid, Agri, Paysannats Indigènes, Kivu (82/8), Rapport concernant paysannats, 30/06/1958.

112 Hyde, "'Paying for the emergency by displacing the settlers': global coffee and rural restructuring in late colonial Kenya": 97.

113 AAB, RACB, Kivu Province, Conseil de Province, 1955 and 1958, no. 41(1) and 42(3).

114 Ibid, 1958, no. 42(3). People were displaced from saturated areas to regions with land still available, even within the Kivu district (see also Chapter 3).

turn, did not release the tension. On the contrary, as the following quote suggests:

> Concerning our relationship with certain representatives of the Territorial Administration, there is reason to complain about the fact that the latter is trying too often to expropriate us: exploitations of public domains, occupation of our colonization blocs [by natives] [...].[115]

3.2 *Plantations in Western Rwanda*

This section is not divided chronologically but rather geographically, as opposed to the previous section. The reason is that for the colony, there is a clear tendency in governmental politics concerning coffee smallholding throughout the colonial period. For the mandate, on the other hand, other aspects were intervening as well, as argued in the first part of this chapter. This means that, although on a limited scale, private European coffee planters – missions and scientific research stations are excluded – were present during the entire period of my research. Moreover, their presence depended on local conditions such as land availability and hence the presumed absence of pre-existing land relations.

3.2.1 *La petite colonisation*

With the exception of parts of Shangugu, most European coffee plantations in western Rwanda should be labeled as small, with a coffee surface not exceeding a few hectares – in the sources called *petite colonisation*. In Gisenyi, the first European *colon agricole* started his activities in 1933. A Greek had obtained a concession of 5.85 hectares in order to produce food for the emerging hotel sector in the region.[116] For the following years the consulted sources do not make any reference to private European producers, likely because there was simply nothing remarkable worth mentioning. Europeans established coffee plantations, only at the beginning of World War II. The agricultural report of 1940 mentions the presence of two planters (Belgian and Greek), each possessing a plantation of 1.5 hectares.[117] In the mid-1950s the same Belgian colonist was still producing coffee, but the size of his coffee plot was reduced to only

115 SAB2, Finoutremer, Documents CNKi (793), Procès-verbal comité de direction, 28/3/1958.

116 AAB, RARU, Gisenyi Territoire, Rapport Général, 1933, no. 87(19). For an overview of Greeks in Belgian Africa, see Georges Antippas, *Pionniers méconnus du Congo belge* (Bruxelles: Interprint, 2007).

117 AAB, RARU, Gisenyi Territoire, Rapport Agriculture, 1940, no. 90(15).

0.12 hectares. In a time span of fifteen years, the only thing that had changed in Gisenyi's European coffee sector was the replacement of the Greek planter by, apparently, a German planter possessing, at that time, a coffee acreage of 9 hectares.[118] This indicates that European coffee production was extremely rare in this territory. Moreover, a surface smaller than 2 hectares could be called a smallholding, but Europeans did not cultivate land around their homesteads and they did use African wage labor. Therefore, as small as these European concessions may have been, they should be seen as plantations.

The same arguments are true for Kibuye. The agricultural report of 1928 plainly states the following:

> We may, however, not lose sight of the fact that the introduction of new crops (we are talking about plantations […] like coffee) in the territory cannot be done on a large-scale […] we have to realize <u>that only small agrarian European exploitations</u> [small firms or colonists] are possible in the territory.[119]

It was extremely difficult for Europeans to obtain a concession in this territory due to the lack of available land as a consequence of the high population density and large volume of livestock (cattle and hence cattle land). However, only two years after the publication of the above-mentioned report, the CIM (Société Générale pour favoriser le Développement du Commerce, de l'Industrie et des Mines) did manage to receive a concession of 105 hectares, aspiring to create a coffee plantation.[120] But only one year after obtaining the concession, the firm decided to stop its coffee plantation tryout, because "local rural conditions and economic circumstances are unfavorable."[121] This quote refers not only to the crisis of the 1930s but also to a lack of land. When re-established in 1953, the Kibuye territory counted only one *colon agricole* cultivating coffee. On his concession of 10 hectares, the Swiss Matter only had 1 hectare planted

118 Ibid, 1955, no. 90(29). To be complete, after World War II, another Belgian colonist also established a coffee firm purchasing, (partly) processing and selling crops produced by native planters as well as *colons* active in the Congolese Kivu (see ibid, Rapport Général, 1948, no. 88(8)). As opposed to planters in eastern Congo, who usually processed their coffee in coffee-processing factories, but similarly to in Kibuye and Shangugu, European planters active in Gisenyi usually processed and sold their own coffee – which indicates the small-scale level they were working on in the mandate.

119 Ibid, Lubengera Territoire, Rapport Agriculture, 1928, no. 80(15A+B). Underlined in the original document.

120 Ibid, Rapport Général, 1930, no. 80(9). The CIM was a firm based in Goma and particularly engaged in Congolese non-agrarian activities such as trade.

121 Ibid, Rapport Agriculture, 1931, no. 80(18).

with *Arabica*.[122] The marginal presence of European coffee planters as well as the *petite colonisation* argument also apply to this territory.

3.2.2 Shangugu: The Exception Proves the Rule

As argued in the previous chapter, Shangugu was a relatively important European coffee production bastion. With half of the mandate's total European coffee acreage situated in this territory in the mid-1930s, and about two thirds in the 1950s, no further explanation is required. The question is thus: Why did European agrarian colonization prove to be more successful in this territory than in the two other territories bordering Lake Kivu?

Shangugu was the first region in Rwanda occupied by Europeans. In the mid-1890s, a few Belgian officers arrived on the eastern shores of Lake Kivu, while effective German colonialism started in 1898 with the establishment of the first military post in Shangi (see Image 1).[123]

Despite this early occupation, agrarian colonization was still limited during the 1920s. In 1928, 30 hectares was conceded to private (European and Asian) entrepreneurs. The company Protanag, established in 1927, held 175 hectares in concession, although the firm had asked for 7000 hectares of land dispersed

IMAGE 1 First German military post in Shangi
SOURCE: PERSONAL COLLECTION, 2016

122 Ibid, Kibuye Territoire, Rapport Agriculture, 1953, no. 82(23).

123 Newbury, *The cohesion of oppression. Clientship and ethnicity in Rwanda, 1860–1960:* 53 and 57.

over the territory.[124] Even though cattle raising was of greater interest to colonists in the early 1920s, 1928 was the year coffee cultivation started to spread across the territory. The territorial agent was convinced of the importance of European coffee production for the region, as he stated that local farmers started to realize the economic possibilities of the crop cultivated by both Protanag and colonists in the Kivu.[125] Implicitly, the administrator argued that non-Africans should function as an example to locals, thereby trying to legitimize their presence in the mandate.

This debatable argument about "functioning as an example" would never have convinced the League of Nations to allow Europeans to compete on a relatively significant scale with African coffee producers. The reason a company such as Protanag could develop its activities is that colonial representatives believed that in the 1920s, in parts of Shangugu, land was vacant (not used for African agriculture or grazing) – and thus available to Europeans – even though native rights to these lands were recognized:

> In the narrow sense of the word there is no vacant land free of any right and the exploitation by the natives is not expected. In the meantime, there is unoccupied land nearby the Great Forest [Nyungwe Forest], in the Impara, Bukunzi and Busoso provinces. At this moment this is the only land that can be put at the disposal of European enterprises.[126]

A 1929 letter from Protanag's manager to the deputy of the Resident in Bujumbura emphasizes the argument that land availability and hence local conditions were important:

> Mister Henry, head of the land rights department [*titres fonciers*] has informed me that the Government has decided not to grant any land to Protanag in the Nyarushishi region [...] insisting on the density of the population and the importance of the local livestock.[127]

Accordingly, Protanag succeeded in developing a coffee-producing branch in Shangugu, but the firm was never able to obtain the 7000 hectares it initially asked for. The total acreage of the firm amounted to 3414 hectares, of which

124 AAB, RARU, Shangugu Territoire, Rapport Général, 1928, no.100(7).

125 Ibid.

126 Derscheid Collection, University of Florida Digital Collection, Kamembe Territoire, Rapport avec réponses sur questions posé par M. le gouverneur du Ruanda-Urundi, 1929.

127 AAB, RWA, Colonisation, RWA(510), Lettre du président de Protanag au député du résident, 10/8/1929.

603.5 were planted with coffee in 1934.[128] As a consequence of financial issues, in combination with inadequate maintenance of their plantations, Protanag, as a coffee producer, ceased to exist in 1936–1937 and the state took over part of its concessions[129] in a failed attempt to reanimate the degenerated fields.[130]

In the meantime, colonists also tried to establish coffee plantations in Shangugu, although the peak of their presence should be situated after World War II. In 1941, only two *colons agricoles* (Italian brothers) were cultivating coffee next to other crops on a plot of land of 85 and 90 hectares.[131] Traveling around Shangugu in 1949, vice governor of Ruanda-Urundi Maurice Simon observed that land was seemingly still vacant and this was not the proper way to develop the mandate; according to him:

> During my last stay in the Shangugu territory, I have noticed [...] that between the big road Shangugu-Nyamasheke and the fringe of the forest [Nyungwe Forest] there are large surfaces of land practically free of any occupation. [...] At first sight these lands seem fertile and able to be used for cultivation. [...] in such a densely populated country [*sic*] like Ruanda-Urundi it is important not to neglect any arable land. [...] Two possibilities are to be anticipated: (1) intensive occupation by an organized *paysannat indigène*; (2) colonization by small-scale European agrarian colonists.[132]

The organization of a coffee/cotton *paysannat indigène* (situated in Bugarama) in an attempt to increase control over native production was not completed until 1957.[133] However, here the focus is on the European coffee segment after World War II. What catches the eye is the different meaning of "small-scale" colonization in Shangugu, compared with the other two Rwandan territories in this research. In this context "small" is not defined as a few hectares

128 Ibid, RARU, Shangugu Territoire, Rapport Général, 1934, no. 100(13).

129 Some of the concessionary land was also purchased by individual colonists who intended to establish a coffee plantation on their own (see ibid, Rapports Economiques et Agricoles (loose files), 1931–59, no. 104(3)).

130 Ibid, RWA, Colonisation, RWA(510), Rapport sur "Protanag," édité par agronome Dohogne, 21/4/1934, and ibid, RARU, Shangugu Territoire, Rapport Général, 1936, no. 101(2). In the sources, the name Protanag still appears for a few years after the state's takeover. It is possible that Protanag was still active as a processor of coffee or as a producer of walnuts, for instance, but the sources are unclear about this issue.

131 Ibid, 1941, no. 101(7).

132 Ibid, RWA, Colonisation, RWA(510), Lettre du vice-gouverneur Simon au administrateur territorial de Shangugu, 6/1/1949.

133 Ibid, RARU, Shangugu Territoire, Rapport Général, 1958, no. 102(9).

but rather as smaller than 100 hectares. The above example of the two Italian brothers already demonstrates this point. Information about European coffee producers in the 1950s only confirms this argument. Inspection reports drafted in 1953 offer an insight into the size of concessions in Shangugu. The Belgian colonist René Van De Voorde was granted a 70-hectare piece of land of which half was planted with coffee bushes. Another Belgian colonist, Jean Nemry, was the proprietor not only of a processing factory but also of the then largest European coffee plantation in Shangugu, measuring 90 hectares. At the end of the 1950s, the two Italian brothers were still active – albeit now joining forces on one instead of two concessions – planting coffee on a 80-hectare plot.[134]

The above paragraphs show that the European coffee sector was more significant in Shangugu than in Gisenyi or Kibuye. However, with only 0.11% of the total coffee-producing land surface in the late 1940s, the significance of the first territory should not be overestimated. Moreover, the fact that the size of European estates in the Rwandan territories bordering Lake Kivu differed substantially proves that colonial policy-making depended on local conditions – even more so in a mandate context. Even though United Nations experts did raise some questions about the size of the concessions, the mandate government claimed that in densely populated areas concessions could not exceed 75 hectares, whereas in less populated regions (such as Shangugu) the limit was officially set at 200 hectares.[135] The alleged availability of land – more pronounced in Shangugu than further to the north – and the supposed lack of native occupation explains why the supervising League of Nations (and later the United Nations) allegedly allowed Belgium to develop a European coffee-producing segment parallel to a successful African branch.

4 Conclusion

The purpose of this chapter was to examine and explain the differences in production systems in the Lake Kivu region. Although several possible factors may have contributed to diverging production systems, three in particular seem to be more plausible than others and therefore need to be considered as vital in understanding this critical issue. In (central) Rwanda, precolonial land relations were already rigid and hierarchically structured, perfectly appropriate to

134 This information stems from: ibid, RWA, AIMO(339), Shangugu rapports d'inspection, 1953–59.

135 Ibid, RARU, Rapport sur l'administration belge au Ruanda-Urundi à la Commission permanente des Mandats, 1947, no. 19(2).

indirect rule and the diffusion of orders via a chain of command. In combination with a higher population density and a resulting lack of available land in order to establish a large plantation economy, this meant that smallholder cultivation was the logical option. In addition, an administrative-judicial difference (between colony and mandate) confirmed existing variations. Even though some scholars doubt the actual impact of this judicial facet, for Belgian Africa it is clear that the possibilities for and objectives of Europeans were different.

This chapter highlighted plausible features that explain the divergent dominant modes of production in the Lake Kivu area. However, since the existence of a dominant production system does not exclude other modes, the chapter also elaborated upon what I called "diversity in reverse": smallholder coffee cultivation in eastern Congo Kivu and plantations in western Rwanda.

Regarding smallholder coffee cultivation in the colonial Kivu, three distinct periods stand out. The colonial government obliged Africans to cultivate coffee until the end of the 1920s. However, from then on, and simultaneously with the "rush of colonists," more and more limitations were imposed on Africans. In some areas, on the other hand, smallholder cultivation thrived, mainly due to a lack of European presence. In the 1950s limitations were gradually loosened, resulting in a growing smallholder sector.

The distinct feature of plantations in western Rwanda was their relative limited size, a consequence of a limited amount of available land. Shangugu was an exception, however. Especially in the eastern part of the territory, land allegedly proved to be vacant, which resulted in the development of more and larger plantations than in the other territories bordering Lake Kivu. The way(s) land was actually mobilized and used for the coffee sector in both the colony and the mandate will be discussed at length in the following chapter.

PART 2

On the Ground

CHAPTER 3

Mobilizing Land for the Coffee Sector

Outlining the main reasons for the development of different coffee production systems around Lake Kivu in the previous chapter demonstrated that land and pre-existing land systems played an important role during the colonial period. In eastern Congo, access to land for agricultural purposes differed from access in western Rwanda. As argued, in the mandate administrators had to keep in mind that a supervising entity was always lurking around the corner. Consequently, local conditions – such as the availability of land and existing precolonial relations – were much better preserved in the mandate than in the colony. Nevertheless, on both sides of Lake Kivu land occupation was altered and placed into a European idea of what a land tenure system should look like. This required direct state intervention in the way land was allocated and used.[1]

The aim of this chapter is to analyze the way(s) land was used to produce coffee during the colonial period. In doing so, I will not only briefly look at precolonial land tenure systems on both sides of the lake in order to show evolutions that accompanied the introduction and development of the coffee commodity frontier in this area. I will also stress major differences (but similarities as well) between the Congolese and the Rwandan Kivu in the colonial epoch, very well aware that in precolonial times a wide array of land systems and relations surrounded Lake Kivu.

The focus of this chapter is nevertheless on the colonial period. For pragmatical reasons (source material), I have chosen to make a geographical distinction. This distinction allows me to both discuss the same topics for the mandate and the colony, and draw comparisons between the two. Therefore, for both regions I will look at customary land tenure (partly a repetition of what has been said in Chapter 2); the introduction and implantation of coffee and its consequence for land use; land policy; and discussions, tensions and conflicts concerning land, for instance between settlers and the administration, or between unfairly treated natives and Europeans.

1 Henry Bernstein, *Class dynamics of Agrarian change* (Sterling: Kumarian Press, 2010): 43.

 | DOI:10.1163/9789004428492_006

1 The Congolese Kivu: Customary Land Systems and the Early Colonial Period

According to Colson, there were two principal land rights in most parts of precolonial Africa: (1) community rights, which meant that in order to support themselves and their dependents, individuals had the right to directly access and cultivate a piece of land controlled by a community to which they belonged; (2) particular rights, meaning that individuals had the right to "things" they had created (pots, craft products but also the produce of their land).[2] The community was the organizing principle; land distributed in usufruct and individual property were very rare, except in densely populated areas. The Asante in West Africa, for example, already had a land system based on individual property before the start of British colonization.[3] As argued in the previous chapter, the Rwandan Nyiginya Kingdom also knew an individual tenure system.

Zooming in on the region bordering Lake Kivu, a distinction has to be made between Bwisha (north), Buhundu (northwest) and Bushi (southwest). In Bwisha and Buhundu, vacant land was abundant and was the property of lineages and clans, its allocation was not permanent, and both regions were characterized by a high degree of mobility at the end of the nineteenth century.[4] In Bushi, the situation was different. Around the turn of the century, Bushi was not a unified kingdom but rather a collection of culturally related kingdoms, of which Kabare and Ngweshe were the most important ones.[5] This region was relatively densely populated and centralized, meaning that vacant land was scarcer and occupation more permanent. Despite the great variety and nuances in systems and relations, there seems to have been a resemblance in the way customary land was used and spread among community members.[6]

2 Elizabeth Colson, "The impact of the colonial period on the definition of land rights," in *Colonialism in Africa, 1870–1960. Volume 3: profiles of change: African society and colonial rule*, ed. Victor Turner (Cambridge; London; New York; Melbourne: Cambridge University Press, 1971): 194.

3 Gareth Austin, *Labour, land, and capital in Ghana: from slavery to free labour in Asante, 1807–1956* (Rochester: University of Rochester Press, 2005): 270.

4 See for Buhundu: Mararo, "Land conflicts in Masisi, Eastern Zaire: the impact and aftermath of Belgian colonial policy (1920–1989)": 41, and for Bwisha: Fairhead, "Fields of struggle: towards a social history of farming knowledge and practice in a Bwisha community, Kivu, Zaire"; 60–61.

5 Sigwalt, "The early history of Bushi. An essay in the historical use of genesis traditions": 11.

6 Even strangers could acquire a piece of land as soon as they became clients of the community chiefs. This shows, firstly, that land was a common good and, secondly, that concepts such as "community" and "lineage" were fluid, with the possibility of social mobility and

A community could establish control over land by expropriating it when it was abundantly available or by clearing it for the first time, as in Buhundu, for instance.[7] The same goes for Bushi, where similar notions existed of clans establishing land rights through "first clearance."[8] After control was secured, land was redistributed along community structures.[9] From lineage to over subchiefs to the lowest echelons, granting usufruct rights went hand in hand with paying tribute (cattle, food or goods) to higher-ranked chiefs. The latter had their own fields, usually cultivated by lower-ranked community members by means of *corvée* labor.

The above sentences are nothing more than a major simplification of the reality on the ground. Land tenure systems were complex, heterogeneous and disparate. However, in an attempt to make land rights more surveyable – or legible, as Mathys calls it[10]– a certain codification manifested itself during the nineteenth century. The system of *kalinzi* – paying a *droit de reconnaissance* (tribute) to a chief in exchange for the usufruct of a plot controlled by that chief[11]– first appeared in the core of Bushi, but was expanded during the colonial period over the then Kabare territory.[12]

For the majority of African communities, the colonial period meant increasing pressure on customary land tenure systems – the replacement of payment of tribute by money or commodification of land itself are perfect examples – and/or the expropriation of seemingly vacant land by colonial governments. Moreover, the complexity and diversity of land systems was not always fully understood by Europeans.[13] This, in combination with the demands of European

without fixed boundaries; see Frank Van Acker, "Where did all the land go? Enclosure & social struggle in Kivu (D.R. Congo)," *Review of African Political Economy* 32, no. 103 (2005): 81.

7 Leo Viaene, "L'organisation politique des Bahunde (II)," *Kongo-Overzee* 18, no. 2–3 (1952): 120.

8 Colle, *Essai de monographie des Bashi*: 235–236.

9 It should be stressed that in Bushi, access to land seems to have been more vertically integrated – which resonates with more centralized political structures (Sosne, "Of biases and queens: the Shi past through an androgynous looking glass": 226).

10 Mathys, "People on the move. Frontiers, borders, mobility and history in the Lake Kivu region 19th–20th century": 315.

11 Hecq et al., *Agriculture et structures économiques d'une société traditionnelle au Kivu (Congo)*: 31.

12 Chubaka Bishikwabo, "Mythes d'origine et croyances religieuses, bases d'une communauté de royauté interlacustre dans l'est du Zaïre," in *La civilisation ancienne des peuples des Grands Lacs. Colloque de Bujumbura (4–10 septembre 1979)*, ed. Unesco and Centre de la Civilisation Burundaise (Paris: Karthala, 1981): 76.

13 Johan Pottier, "'Customary land tenure' in Sub-Saharan Africa today: meaning and contexts," in *From the ground up: land rights, conflict and peace in Sub-Saharan Africa*, ed. Chris Huggins and Jenny Clover (Pretoria: ISS, 2005): 58–63.

colonists to receive land (to build plantations, for instance), urged the colonial government to make things more understandable and manageable.[14]

The Belgian colony was no exception to this trend. Already in the very first days of the creation of the CFS, discussions arose concerning land ownership. Land laws enacted from 1885 onwards did recognize existing customary land systems. However, the complexities, the absence of clearly defined borders and the dynamics of such systems were missed by European observers. Consequently, colonial land laws aimed at codifying and homogenizing existing land systems, and "theoretically enshrined a status quo where there was none."[15] Apart from the formal recognition, albeit often ignored, of indigenous rights, all land not inhabited or cultivated by natives was declared vacant and expropriated by the colonial state (*terres domaniales*).[16] The very restrictive definition of native land was extended only in 1906, when land inhabited, cultivated and exploited by Congolese was included as well. This meant that from this point on, vacant land such as forests was also considered native land by the colonial administration.[17] Clearly, the state controlled not only the process of primitive accumulation itself but, from the 1890s onwards, also the resources of those lands (minerals or agricultural products) and the fate of the people working these *terres domaniales*.[18] Already in this early colonial period, Belgian critical minds, such as lawyers and academics, were concerned about the validity of these state domains. They claimed that "before our arrival, indigenous communities possessed an immanent and privative right on land, judicially comparable to our property right." What they meant is that all land – even remote swamps or volcanoes – in one way or another related to a community or a village and thus that the installation of *terres domaniales* was in fact illegal.[19]

14 This is Scott's argument for how colonial states have tried to make subjected societies and communities more comprehensible by simplifying existing patterns and systems; see: Scott, *Seeing like a state. How certain schemes to improve the human condition have failed.*

15 Clement, "The land tenure system in the Congo, 1885–1960: actors, motivations and consequences": 89.

16 After opposition from companies and co-signatories of the Berlin Act, Leopold II modified the initial land laws by converting some vacant lands expropriated by the state into free trade zones.

17 Louis De Clerck, "Le régime foncier, le régime minier et le droit des biens," in *L'ordre juridique coloniale Belge en Afrique Centrale. Eléments d'histoire*, ed. Emile Lamy and Louis De Clerck (Bruxelles: Académie Royale des Sciences d'Outre-Mer, 2004): 256.

18 Bogumil Jewsiewicki, "Raison d'etat ou raison du capital: l'accumulation primitive au Congo belge," *African Economic History*, no. 12 (1983): 170.

19 Paul Coppens, "De la propriété collective vers la propriété individuelle," in *Vers la promotion de l'économie indigène. Compte rendu du colloque colonial sur l'économie indigène (9–13 janvier 1956)*, ed. Henri Janne (Bruxelles: Institut de Sociologie Solvay, 1956): 414.

Despite this criticism, the CFS unaffectedly granted concessions to missions and European companies. Even after 1908 and the takeover of the colony by the Belgian state, the granting of concessions continued and was even enhanced, despite the formulation of the Colonial Charter and the promise of an end to the abuses committed by the CFS.[20] The most famous example of a mismatch between theory and practice is the British concern Unilever, and especially its Belgian Congolese subdivision the Huileries du Congo Belge (HCB). In 1911, the HCB received concessions for no less than 750000 hectares of "vacant" land, divided into five circles situated across the northwest and west of the Belgian Congo in Bumba, Barumbu, Lusanga, Ingende and Basongo.[21]

The image presented here of how early colonial practices affected land tenure in the colony differs in some ways from what happened in the territories bordering Lake Kivu. As David Northrup argues, initially these areas were a gray zone, not belonging to the *terres domaniales* but definitely not a free trade zone either.[22] Until World War I, the colonial district lacked an effective administrative occupation. On the one hand, a handful of administrators accompanied by armed forces tried to pacify the insubordinate regions by means of military campaigns against local communities.[23] On the other hand, militaries protected the eastern periphery of the colony and tried to find an agreement with the Germans concerning the Congolese–Rwandan border (1910).

Despite the undesignated character of the area, some Belgian civilian colonists entered at the end of the nineteenth century. Most notable in this context are the counts d'Ursel, who engaged in trade activities in order to compensate for decreasing land rents in Belgium.[24] Because of the unclear judicial status of land, they acquired their plot by negotiation with local chiefs. Moreover, nearly all of the land European settlers aimed to occupy had to be negotiated over

20 Nelson, *Colonialism in the Congo basin, 1880–1940*: 114.

21 For more information, see: David Kenneth Fieldhouse, *Unilever Overseas: the anatomy of a multinational 1895–1965* (London: Croom Helm, 1978). Also Seibert, *In die globale Wirtschaft gezwungen. Arbeit und kolonialer Kapitalismus im Kongo (1885–1960)*: Chapter 7.

22 Northrup, *Beyond the bend in the river: African labor in Eastern Zaire 1865–1940*: 41.

23 Mathys, "People on the move. Frontiers, borders, mobility and history in the Lake Kivu region 19th–20th century": 126.

24 Buelens, *Congo 1885–1960. Een financieel-economische geschiedenis*: 515. I should also mention the failed attempt of the CFS to establish an Italian *colonat agricole* in the Kivu. Leopold II intended to create a buffer against the Germans by stimulating the emergence of a European planter branch in the early twentieth century. An experiment with forty Italian families failed because of the lack of governmental support to the families, while Italian deputes were often treated hostilely (S.N., *Comité National du Kivu 1928–1953. Vingt-cinquième anniversaire* (Bruxelles: Editons L. Cuypers, 1953): 46–48).

directly with native leaders up until 1927–1928.[25] The next section will make clear that after World War I, *terres domaniales* existed but that it was not until 1927–1928 that vast areas of supposedly vacant land were seized for the benefit of the developing a European-oriented agricultural sector.

1.1 *Changing Access to Land*

1.1.1 CNKi: Creating a Parastatal Entity

The colonial bureaucracy attempted to organize access to land for Europeans by granting concessions of 50–100 hectares in the early 1920s. These efforts, however, were still unsuccessful.[26] Random land acquisition continued and abuses were common, as a 1928 letter of Father Roelens – the vicar apostolic of Haut-Congo – explicitly states when talking about Kabare:

> In various places, land currently cultivated or destined for dry season crops, plantain plantations in full bloom, are conceded and even land currently occupied by indigenous houses. One [colonist] has made native chiefs declared all those lands vacant [...]. In order to obtain the chief's agreement one has made every effort. One has seduced them by the lure of personal gifts. One has exploited their childish attitude of wanting to possess certain European goods: automobiles, bikes, and even a bed or a pendulum clock.[27]

Unsurprisingly, when the "rush" of colonists reached its zenith (in 1927), land was expropriated massively and no one – the colonial administration included – was able to see the wood for the trees any more. In 1902, the colonial administration had founded the CFL (Compagnie des Chemins de Fer des Grands Lacs Africaines). Initially the CFL was granted the monopoly over 8 million hectares in order to exploit rubber and ivory gathering, but after World War I, the rising demand for land urged the colonial administration to revise the agreement, which it did in 1921. The CFL abandoned its previous rights and was compensated with 400000 hectares in the districts of Kivu and Ituri.[28] However, the CFL was particularly entrusted with the infrastructural *mise en œuvre*. Because this assignment was already hard enough, the CFL was not in a

---

25 Mararo, "Land conflicts in Masisi, Eastern Zaire: the impact and aftermath of Belgian colonial policy (1920–1989)": 100.

26 Fairhead, "Fields of struggle: towards a social history of farming knowledge and practice in a Bwisha community, Kivu, Zaire": 86.

27 AAB, Agri, Compagnies; sociétés; plantations, Colonisation au Kivu (657), Lettre de Père Roelens au ministre de la colonie, 27/6/1928.

28 E. Mendiaux, "Le Comité National du Kivu," *Zaïre*, no. 10 (1956): 803.

position to control or steer the "rush" and the explosive demand for land from 1927 onwards.[29] Consequently, the colonial administration – also unsuccessful in the early 1920s – decided to create a new parastatal entity to which the CFL transferred all land rights: the Comité National du Kivu or CNKi, a new entity in charge of a variety of activities but serving a double objective:

> […] one of the Committee's first acts was to halt the granting of new concessions while it sorted out the mess created by the land rush especially near the lake.[30]
>
> […] favoring the colonization of the region: knowing the right colonization, Belgian colonization.[31]

With its formation, the CNKi assumed responsibility for managing 12 million hectares (the size of the current North- and South-Kivu Provinces combined) of vacant land in the Kivu district – and initially also some land in Maniema. The CNKi was founded on the initiative of Secretary of the Colony Jaspar. The Secretary was entitled to appoint members and had the power of veto. Financially, the CNKi was set up with Belgian private capital (initially 100 million Francs).[32]

The CNKi had the right to exploit the areas it monopolized. From 1928 onwards, European colonists hoping to purchase or lease a plot of land in the fertile Kivu region had to appeal to this entity, with the exception of those interested in land outside the working area of the CNKi (see Map 6). For Africans, land controlled by the CNKi was inaccessible, except to some prominent figures. However, bad management and financial troubles resulted in several reforms in the early 1930s. The territory controlled by the CNKi was reduced in 1933 to "merely" 800000 hectares, and in 1943 to 300000 hectares. Moreover, at the same time, refinancing and a transfer of tasks to sub-branches were carried out by the administration.

1.1.2 Dual Land Tenure

The colonial administration started the process of land commodification in the early twentieth century, but the foundation of the CNKi proved to be the summit of this process. The dual land tenure system (briefly mentioned in the

---

29 Mararo, "Land conflicts in Masisi, Eastern Zaire: the impact and aftermath of Belgian colonial policy (1920–1989)": 74–75.

30 Northrup, *Beyond the bend in the river: African labor in Eastern Zaire 1865–1940*: 151.

31 Jean Stengers, *Le Congo, mythes et réalités. 100 ans d'histoire* (Gembloux: Duculot, 1989): 185.

32 S.N., *Comité National du Kivu 1928–1953. Vingt-cinquième anniversaire*: 158.

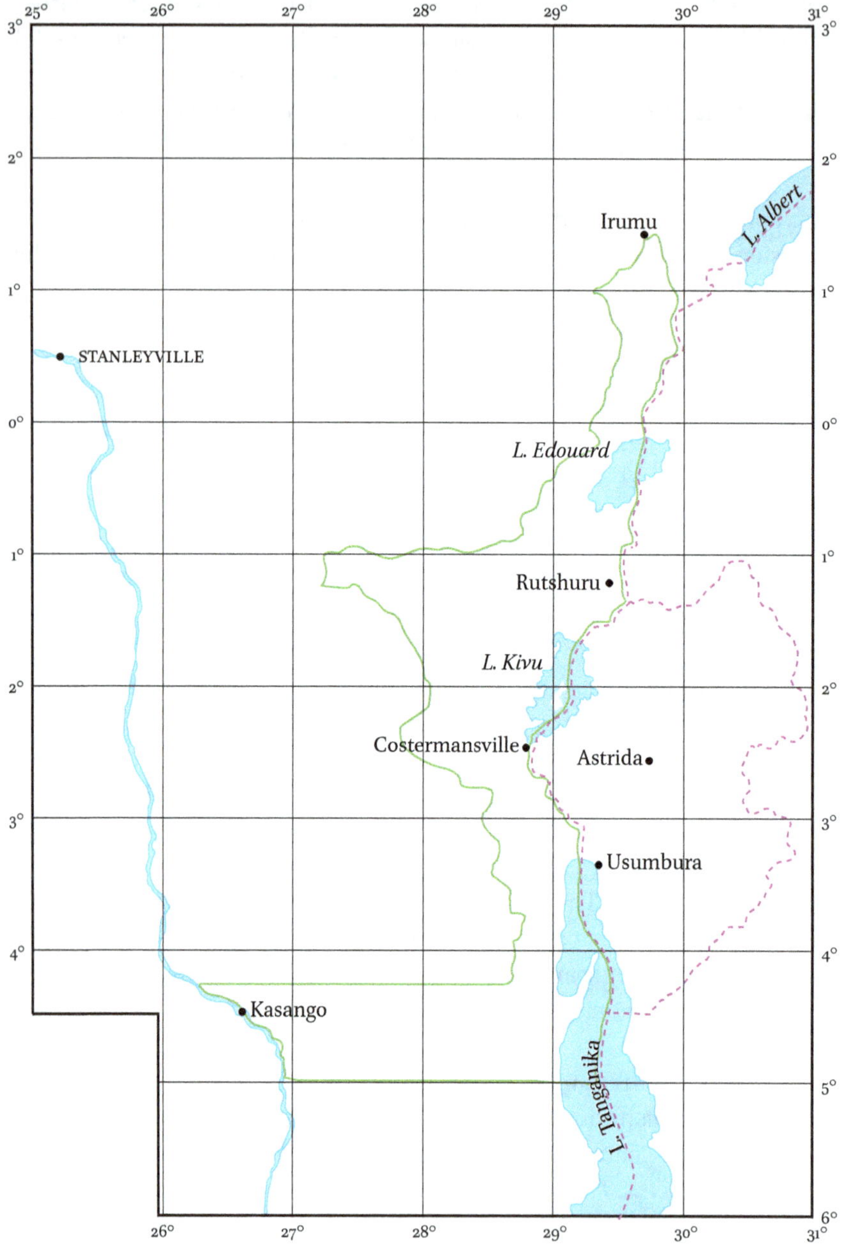

MAP 6 Initial working area of the Comité National du Kivu (July 1928)
SOURCE: REDRAWN FROM AAB, AGRI, COMPAGNIES, CNKI (650)

previous chapter) had reached maturity in the Kivu district. On the one hand, a system of land registration and private ownership emerged, while on the other, customary land tenure was recognized. Van Acker claims that this process "introduced a normative duality in the social meaning of land," which means that customary land defined social relations while in the capitalist economy land was an alienable marketable good.[33]

The colonial "vacant land" myth severely limited the expansion of customary land even though access to customary land remained more or less intact during the colonial period. In Kabare, for example, the system of *kalinzi* continued, but even here a certain monetization entered native customs. During and after the colonial period, tribute was paid no longer exclusively in goods (cattle) but also in money.[34] Moreover, the colonially imposed distinction between vacant (state) and native (occupied) land continued to exist up until 1973; in that year, Mobutu decided to introduce a new law considering all land as property of the Zairian state, thereby introducing registration and administrative procedures to acquire land, and equally compromising customarily evolved land tenure systems.[35]

Until the early 1950s, an increase in private African land ownership was slowed down anxiously by the colonial administration. Having Congolese "owning" their own plot instead of "using" it might have harmed (coffee) plantations, not only because of the possible loss of part of the labor reserve but also in creating competition. However, as a consequence of growing internal pressure and external events – such as bitter land conflicts in Kenya for instance – the colonial government changed policy, and from 1953 onwards Congolese legally had the right to possess land.[36] Even though there is a huge difference between what is legally possible and/or allowed and its practical realization, liberalizing Congolese farmers, in combination with an increasing demand for commodities such as coffee since the late 1940s, did have results in the Kivu district. As demonstrated in Chapters 1 and 2, from 1953–1954 onwards

---

33 Van Acker, "Where did all the land go? Enclosure & social struggle in Kivu (D.R. Congo)": 83.

34 Bulakali Nzigire, "Problème des terres dans l'occupation économique du Kivu (1918–1930)" (Unpublished Master thesis, Université nationale du Zaïre (campus Lubumbashi), 1972): 81.

35 Van Acker, "Where did all the land go? Enclosure & social struggle in Kivu (D.R. Congo)": 84.

36 Clement, "The land tenure system in the Congo, 1885–1960: actors, motivations and consequences": 99, and Mararo, "Land conflicts in Masisi, Eastern Zaire: the impact and aftermath of Belgian colonial policy (1920–1989)": 118–119.

the amount of African coffee cultivation increased. This enabled Africans to cultivate coffee, as previously, on land around their homesteads, but with the significant difference that this land was now their property.

The creation of the CNKi enabled European colonists to demand a plot of land from this institution, although the judicial ratification of granted land still remained the task of the colonial administration.[37] Concessions of up to 500 hectares could be established directly between a colonist and the CNKi; concessions of more than 500 hectares required a decree approved and signed by the Belgian king. With an average size of 92 hectares per coffee estate in Kabare at the end of the 1930s, large concessions were uncommon in the Kivu coffee sector. Only large companies (whether or not they were engaged in coffee production) could claim such huge areas. For instance, in the first half of the 1930s the SAAK possessed more than 20000 hectares of land, of which 1500 was planted with coffee, dispersed over the entire district.[38]

Every land agreement the CNKi issued stipulated a provisional occupation of one to nine years, and when after this term the conditions that were stipulated in the contract concerning land exploitation were met, a definitive sell or lease (of fifteen to thirty years) followed.[39]

Alongside purchasing or renting land from the CNKi, Europeans – the CNKi included – could also still negotiate directly with African chiefs in order to get access to native land. Even though there were regular discussions between the CNKi and colonists (*infra*), abuses continued to happen in these kinds of negotiations in particular. According to Fairhead, spoliation of native land was relatively easy between the creation of the CNKi (1928) and 1934.[40] Europeans corrupted not only Africans but also local agents; chiefs were bribed; vacancy inquiries were neglected, which resulted in the seizure of cultivated native land;[41] and in other cases, vacancy inquiries were considered a simple formality:

> certain applicants were confident in the results of the vacancy inquiries and already started to exploit the aspired lands.[42]

---

37 Mendiaux, "Le Comité National du Kivu": 805.

38 Ibid: 809, and S.N., *Comité National du Kivu 1928–1953. Vingt-cinquième anniversaire*: 194.

39 Mararo, "Land conflicts in Masisi, Eastern Zaire: the impact and aftermath of Belgian colonial policy (1920–1989)": 97. When the conditions of the contract were not met, the land returned to the CNKi without any form of compensation.

40 Fairhead, "Fields of struggle: towards a social history of farming knowledge and practice in a Bwisha community, Kivu, Zaire": 88.

41 Kalemaza, "Le développement de l'agriculture au Kivu colonial (1903–1940)": 82.

42 AAB, Agri, Compagnies, CNKi (650), Procès-verbal 26th réunion de la comité de direction du CNKi, 16/10/1928.

In order to counter illegal seizure of customary land, both in the Kivu and elsewhere, the colonial government formalized vacancy inquiries in 1934, making it more difficult to capture land, or at least giving the impression of doing so. Every demand was followed by a fixed procedure: an examination took place of which customary rights were established, in order to calculate fair compensation; the inquiry had to pass through divers administrative echelons and eventually resulted in a land transfer act after approval.[43] With some modifications, this procedure continued until the end of the colonial period. However, this does not mean that indigenous communities were all of a sudden treated as equal when negotiating the transfer of land. According to Clement, the only thing Congolese really had some leverage on was the fixation of the compensation to be paid, whereas local communities often equated the opening of an inquiry with an order to give up the land.[44]

The CNKi did not fancy the possibility of colonists being able to acquire land directly via native chiefs. As an internal document from 1937 suggests, the loss of profits from the sale or lease of land made the CNKi nervous, as did the loss of control over colonists involved in:

> colonists directly negotiating with natives. The CNKi disputes these new [*sic*] tendencies. The CNKi asks the Colony to oppose this for judicial and practical reasons. On the one hand, it is asserted, natives are not allowed to renounce a property right because they themselves are not authorized [without a vacancy inquiry]. On the other hand, natives, having sold the land they used to occupy, inevitably are going to occupy other lands belonging to the CNKi. At the end, it is thus the CNKi paying for the transaction, without any compensation.[45]

1.1.3 Squatters

While the emergence of a dual tenure system divided land into belonging either to the colonial state (or the CNKi) or to indigenous communities, both with the opportunity to sell it, the rise of a plantation economy also gave birth to a specific kind of access to land: squatting. Even though squatting is not about coffee land *sensu stricto*, it is a way in which settlers tried to tie labor to their coffee estate. In this context, squatting is defined as the practice of (a)

43 Clement, "The land tenure system in the Congo, 1885–1960: actors, motivations and consequences": 96–97.

44 Ibid: 98. However, Drevet demonstrates that prices paid to Africans were often extremely low; see: Drevet, "Les plantations Européenes dans le Kivu d'altitude": 107–108.

45 SAB2, Finoutremer, Documents CNKi (792), Rapport 4th direction générale – 1st direction, 23/11/1937.

local community or communities occupying a piece of land that in Western legal terms does not belong to them – in other words, a situation where local communities are living on a portion of concessionary land belonging to a European planter, while in exchange members of this community work for the planter. The plots thus occupied by locals could have belonged to them, but they disclaimed their rights by means of a transfer, or were forced to do so. However, in areas with a shortage of labor, for instance, Africans could also live on concessionary land without having any former connection to this land. Either way, in this context, squatting is an arrangement between a colonist and a community, with locals having the opportunity to continue or restart their previous activities (for instance subsistence agriculture). For a colonist, such a solution is benevolent because the costs of mobilizing labor are significantly lower. Obviously, squatting is not unique to the Belgian Congo. In Zanzibar at the end of the nineteenth century, for example, freed slaves were allowed to continue to live on the estate of their former owners, with retention of their huts and plots of land, while in exchange the squatters had to work for three to four days a week.[46]

A territory especially suitable for squatting was Rutshuru in the colonial period. As Map 5 in the previous chapter indicates, in most of this territory the distance between European plantations and native habitations, and thus potential labor, was vast. Hence, squatting was a common practice in this area:

> It would be completely different if the colonization area were close to inhabited areas. But that is generally not the case and native villages are often 3 to 5 hours [walking distance] removed from European concessions.[47]

Already in the early 1930s, administrative reports mention Africans residing on coffee concessions.[48] In 1936, the administrator of Rutshuru estimated that of a total of 57550 indigenous people, 5034 or about 10% were living on European plantations: 1684 men, 1508 women and 1842 children.[49] A year later, that

46 Frederick Cooper, *From slaves to squatters. Plantation labor and agriculture in Zanzibar and coastal Kenya, 1890–1925* (Portsmouth: Heinemann, 1997): 85. Some scholars claim that the roots of the Mau rebellion lay in the creation of a landless class in Kenya in the colonial period; see for example: Tabitha Kanogo, *Squatters and the roots of Mau Mau 1905–63* (Nairobi: East African Educational Publishers, 1993 [1987]).

47 AAB, RACB, Rutshuru Territoire, Rapport AIMO, 1937, no. 163.

48 Ibid, 1933.

49 Ibid, 1936.

number had increased to 8202.[50] In this area, people usually descended from villages high up in the mountains to work on European estates situated in lower areas; "these workers do not live in their natal or indigenous village any more, they gather on the concessions."[51] However, at the end of the 1930s local labor supply was no longer sufficient to "nourish" the European plantation sector. Therefore, labor had to be attracted from elsewhere – mostly from Lubero and Rwanda. These people also had access to land – either in labor camps or they built their own accommodations near to the concession – but they cannot be labeled as squatters, since they left as soon as their contract was over.

In sum, in Rutshuru squatters were usually people coming from other areas, deciding to settle – whether freely or not remains an open question – because plantations were too far away from their home villages. People also might have fled the increasing burden of *corvées* because of the scarcity of labor in Rutshuru. On the other hand, in the southern Kivu, in Kabare, squatting manifested itself differently. This territory was more densely populated than Rutshuru, meaning that less land was available. Already in the early colonial period, this was a cause of tensions between Europeans and Africans. Fertile land perfectly suitable for coffee cultivation was in many cases already occupied by local communities, which caused tensions between Africans and European in the "battle" over land (*infra*). A growing population, especially after World War II, and hence an even greater scarcity of available land, also caused problems within local societies. Without giving figures, the annual report of 1950 mentions people residing on European coffee estates. Because of a lack of customary land, these people migrated and looked for a new plot to cultivate and/or an income opportunity outside their village of origin, which was uncommon in this territory (see following chapters). They cultivated their own food crops and lived in "traditional Bashi huts and consequently they have the same way of living as the villagers."[52]

1.2 *Disputes over Land*

Despite a significant reduction in the amount of land it had to manage (*supra*), the CNKi still had the right to accumulate all profits it made by selling or leasing plots.[53] This led not only to speculation but also to quarrels with the *colons agricoles* or their lobby group, the Unaki.

50 Ibid, 1937.

51 Ibid.

52 Ibid, Kabare Territoire, Rapport AIMO, 1950, no. 99.

53 Mararo, "Land conflicts in Masisi, Eastern Zaire: the impact and aftermath of Belgian colonial policy (1920–1989)": 77.

In 1937, a discussion ensued in the provincial council over the fact that colonists in the Kivu district had to pay more for land managed by the CNKi than did colonists in Katanga for land controlled by a similar parastatal entity, the Comité Spécial du Katanga (CSK). The Unaki strongly advocated that CNKi tariffs should be the same as tariffs demanded for *terres domaniales*, or at least that the CNKi should compensate for the exaggerated prices. The Unaki also urged the colonial administration to control the CNKi more closely.[54] Unfortunately, the arguments of the colonists did not impress the CNKi or the local government. On the contrary, in the early 1950s the prices planters had to pay were still too high, even to the extent that some planters were hampered in their wish to develop or expand their concession:

> The Comity [CNKi] has chased off a young colonist hoping to obtain an extension in order to plant coffee, and declared to him that he must pay 17000 Francs per hectare. Is this favoring colonization?[55]

This suggests that land was relatively expensive in the Kivu district, which might explain the modest average plantation size demonstrated in Chapter 1. Colonists wanting to acquire land sometimes had to deal with the monopoly position of the CNKi. In the Belgian newspaper *La Libre Belgique*, debates between Kivu colonists and governmental entities were even represented as straight-out war.[56] What these debates show is conflicting interests: the CNKi, funded with private capital, tried to make as much profit as possible, while colonists hoped to acquire land as cheaply as possible. As Young argues, settlers were convinced that governmental institutions had to guarantee the conditions for their success.[57] On the other hand, the CNKi did also serve colonists' interests – not only by means of scientific research but also, for example in the second half of the 1950s, in the search for "new" land – situated outside the controlled area – appropriate for coffee cultivation.[58]

Disputes over land understandably also appeared between Africans and Europeans. According to Mararo, there were no land conflicts in Masisi in the

54 AAB, RACB, Kivu Province, Conseil de Province, 1937, no. 38(1).

55 Ibid, 1951, no. 39(4).

56 Léonard, "Un divorce belge. Expériences contrastées du planteur belge de café au Kivu (1945–1960)": 221–222. Colonists themselves did not have a good reputation in the Metropole either. In the press, they were often represented as "inhumans" treating their employees unfairly (ibid: 219).

57 Crawford Young, *The African colonial state in comparative perspective* (New Haven; London: Yale University Press, 1994): 119.

58 S.N., *Comité National du Kivu 1928–1953. Vingt-cinquième anniversaire*: 176.

colonial period because there still was enough vacant land.[59] In the early 1950s, however, local Bahunde notables openly complained about the appropriating activities of the CNKi. The latter not only prohibited natives from occupying land within a 3-kilometer radius of Lake Mokoto but also provisorily in the entire Mumba colonization bloc – both situated in the eastern part of the territory. Furthermore, according to the notables there was too much area allocated for future colonization.[60] The same dissatisfaction also troubled people living in Muvuny (a chieftaincy south of Gishari; see Map 7 in the next section). This area was occupied by 6483 families in 1953, but in order to cultivate sustainably, a further 7500 hectares was needed. This resulted in a rapid exhaustion of land. A total of 207 families had left the area in one year's time, but the CNKi continued to demand land in this region.[61]

In more densely populated Kabare, local notables not only contested European seizure activities but were also more reluctant to sell customary land to the Europeans. Already at the end of the 1930s, the territorial administrator estimated that local communities had at least 31000 hectares less than they needed in order to cultivate sufficient food and pasture their cattle.[62] A decade later the problem had only deteriorated. Nearly all land was occupied by local communities, while most of the land suitable for coffee production was already planted. At the same time, there was a rise in new requests for land. Some local chiefs, backed by the local colonial government, increasingly discouraged new demands, while others overtly refused to grant land to colonists any longer. The territorial administration was well aware of the land issue, and of the fact that chiefs needed to regain confidence in the government because otherwise it would become even more complicated for Europeans to negotiate land transfers.[63]

Land conflicts in the colonial era were always a sign of incompatible interests, not only between *colons* and the state (represented by a parastatal organization or not) but also between local communities and colonists, as the examples of Masisi and Kabare indicate. Nevertheless, the question can be raised whether chiefs protected their society's interests or rather their own. Seizure of land meant fewer possibilities to maintain customary social ties, less tribute,

59 Mararo, "Land conflicts in Masisi, Eastern Zaire: the impact and aftermath of Belgian colonial policy (1920–1989)": 235.

60 AAB, RACB, Masisi Territoire, Rapport AIMO, 1952, no. 143.

61 Ibid, 1953. Presumably, in this context, family refers to nuclear family.

62 AAB, RACB, Kabare Territoire, Rapport AIMO, 1939, no. 99.

63 Ibid, 1948 and 1949.

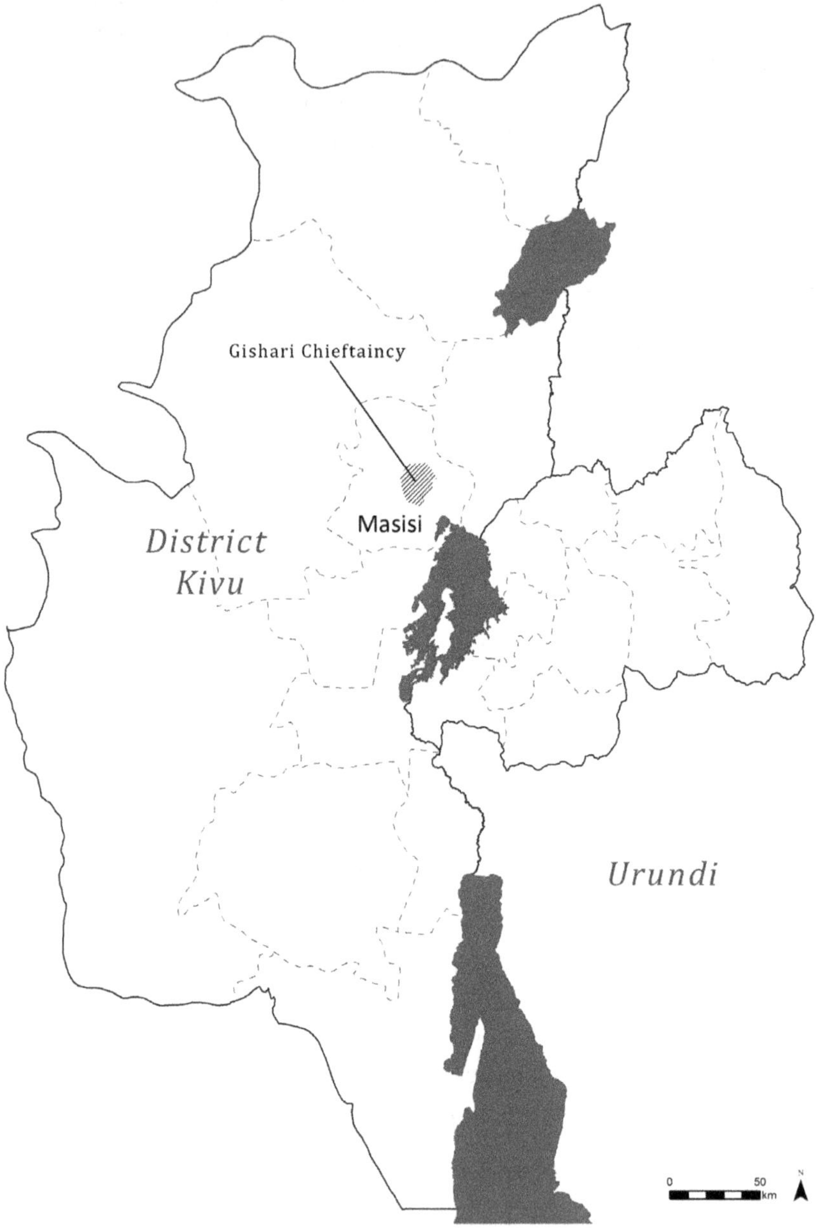

MAP 7 Gishari chieftaincy (1954)
SOURCE: BASED ON MARARO, "LAND CONFLICTS IN MASISI, EASTERN ZAIRE: THE IMPACT AND AFTERMATH OF BELGIAN COLONIAL POLICY (1920–1989)": 159–160

less control over people at work in the coffee plantation economy and, ultimately, less power.[64]

1.3 *The Role of the Local Administration*

According to Arrighi, settlers are unable to initiate a capitalist agricultural sector merely based on market mechanisms. In the initial phase of establishing a capitalist agriculture, they are financially not strong enough to purchase or lease land. Hence, the expropriation of land requires state intervention.[65] In Kenya and Rhodesia, the British colonial government created native reserves in order to facilitate land seizure by European colonists.[66] From the mid-1930s onwards, access to land within the reserves was regulated via customary rules, while in "European areas" market forces were at play.[67] The main reason why, especially in settler regions like the Kivu district, land was expropriated massively was to limit resources outside the capitalist agricultural sector and accordingly force people into wage labor.[68]

The division of land in the Belgian Congo into native land and *terres domaniales* resembles the British method but without the creation of native reserves – except for Katanga, where an experiment with native reserves started in the early 1920s but after heated discussion between colonial officials and protests by local notables was cancelled a few years later.[69] Moreover, it is doubtful whether land sales in the colony were merely regulated by market mechanisms. Colonists could negotiate with chiefs in order to acquire land in a context in which coercion and misleading was supposedly more common in determining a price than market forces. Even after introducing vacancy inquiries, land transfers were seldom an interaction between two legal equals. The same can be said about land allocated by the state. Especially in the case of the CNKi, land transfers were not (always) market-dependent.

---

64 Bashizi, "Pouvoirs publics, plantations européennes et réactions paysannes au Sud-Kivu (1920–1960)": 139.

65 Giovanni Arrighi, "Labor supplies in historical perspective: a study of the proletarianization of the African peasantry in Rhodesia," *Journal of Development Studies* 6, no. 3 (1970): 209.

66 Paul Mosley, *The settler economies. Studies in the economic history of Kenya and Southern Rhodesia 1900–1963* (Cambridge; New York: Cambridge University Press, 1983): 16.

67 Ibid: 25, and Ralph A. Austen, *African economic history: internal development and external dependency* (Oxford: James Currey, 2003 [1987]): 177–178.

68 Cooper, *From slaves to squatters. Plantation labor and agriculture in Zanzibar and coastal Kenya, 1890–1925*: 89.

69 Clement, "The land tenure system in the Congo, 1885–1960: actors, motivations and consequences": 92–95.

Partly outsourcing responsibilities to the CNKi did not mean that the local government in the Kivu no longer had control over land issues. As I have stated, various reorganizations had diminished the CNKi's surface to 300000 hectares. Part of this "lost land" went to related departments – such as the SAAK, for example – but the greater part was repurchased by the provincial administration.[70] That way the state not only re-strengthened its grip on land matter: it also freed land from the speculative endeavors of the CNKi and attempted to make it cheaper in order to favor colonization. Two things in particular show the impact of the state on (coffee) land-related issues, both starting in the 1930s. The first is the creation of a chieftaincy for Rwandan immigrants in Masisi. This was not about mobilizing coffee land *sensu stricto*, but about an attempt to attract (coffee) labor. The second is the limitation of coffee surfaces in both the colony and the mandate.

1.3.1 Gishari Chieftaincy

Both Masisi and Rutshuru were less densely populated than Kabare, which created problems for Europeans in mobilizing (coffee) labor. In Rutshuru, this problem was dealt with in two particular ways.[71] First, the local administration allowed Africans to cultivate coffee in areas with no plantations. The second solution was squatting, with people living on estate land. In Masisi, however, the local government attempted to solve the lack of labor in another way. It should be stressed that the solution benefited not only coffee plantations, but other European economic activities (pyrethrum plantations, for example) in the territory as well. According to the territorial administrator, in 1937:

> the major political event will be the introduction of a more or less enlarged contingent of Wania-Ruanda pastoralists, on vacant lands in the [Bahunde] chieftaincy. In case of success, the problem European colonization faced will no longer have its current edgy character and the Bahunde will be partly relieved of exploiting the region.[72]

The government thus created the chieftaincy of Gishari, measuring 37000 hectares, hoping to attract Rwandans laborers (see Map 7). The cooperation of territorial administrations and local chiefs in Rwanda, both hoping to relieve

70 AAB, RACB, Kivu Province, Conseil de Province, 1937, no. 38(1).

71 I also point to unsuccessful attempts of the territorial administration to transplant Rwandan labor, first mentioned in the reports in 1933 (Mathys, "People on the move. Frontiers, borders, mobility and history in the Lake Kivu region 19th–20th century": 178–179).

72 AAB, RACB, Masisi Territoire, Rapport AIMO, 1936, no. 142.

overpopulated regions, was also required. Moreover, in order to achieve this goal, the Kivu administration institutionalized certain benefits for the migrants: they were granted vacant land and pasture, provided with food in the first month after their arrival, and promised exemption from *corvée* labor for two years.[73] However, granting land was the first problem the administration had to deal with, because Gishari was situated within "CNKi territory." Legally, the local government was allowed to neutralize land controlled by the CNKi when it served a public purpose.[74] The installation of Rwandan migrants in Masisi was represented precisely in this way. The CNKi was not happy with this development and reacted by demanding compensation for the lost land.[75] The CNKi was also aware of the second problem the administration had to deal with. It preferred the migration of a majority of Hutu (to provide labor) and a minority of Tutsi (to control the Hutu). However, things did not turn out as intended. In the first half of 1938, 72% of the migrants were Tutsi while only 28% were Hutu.[76] This was utterly the opposite of what the administration had hoped to achieve, causing a skeptical but fair remark by the CNKi's management:

> Up until now, the installation of these groups is not organized rationally. Families of notables have emigrated alone accompanied by a large herd of cattle, which has not contributed to improving the situation.[77]

The government reacted by restricting the migration of Tutsi elites and their cattle, resulting in a reversal of the proportions (85% Hutu or potential laborers) in the second half of 1938.[78] It should be stressed that in the beginning the number of migrants was low. In 1937, only 691 people settled in Gishari; but from 1943 to 1945 (25448 Rwandan settlers) people migrated massively,

---

73 Mathys, "People on the move. Frontiers, borders, mobility and history in the Lake Kivu region 19th–20th century": 180.

74 Mararo, "Land conflicts in Masisi, Eastern Zaire: the impact and aftermath of Belgian colonial policy (1920–1989)": 163.

75 René Bourgeois, *Témoignages*, vol. II (Tervuren: Musée Royal de l'Afrique Centrale, 1987): 2.

76 Mathys, "People on the move. Frontiers, borders, mobility and history in the Lake Kivu region 19th–20th century": 200–202.

77 AAB, Agri, Compagnies; sociétés; plantations, Documents CNKi (321), Rapport d'Assemblée générale, 6/10/1938.

78 Mathys, "People on the move. Frontiers, borders, mobility and history in the Lake Kivu region 19th–20th century": 202.

attempting to escape the Nyirahuku famine of 1943–1944.[79] This in turn caused oversaturation and degradation of the soil in the chieftaincy and resulted in the suspension of the program. However, this did not mean that people stopped moving around.[80] Moreover, attracting Rwandans did not solve the labor issue, as will be demonstrated in the next chapter. Mobilizing Rwandan labor proved to be very difficult. Consequently, plantations needed to attract more labor in local villages, which in turn caused problems and perturbations for local village life.

1.3.2 Limitation of Coffee Surfaces

I have already referred to this issue, in Chapter 1 when discussing the mobilization of coffee land in a quantitative way. As a consequence of overproduction and falling prices during the global crisis, Brazil, as the most important coffee producer, destroyed part of its stock in an unsuccessful attempt to stabilize prices on the international markets. The impact of such a decision was also felt in coffee production in Belgian Africa. The colonial and mandate governments tried to remedy this by limiting surfaces in the sense that no new concessions were granted. The aim was not to restrict production as such but rather to intensify cultivation and improve the quality of the coffee produced. The administrations' hope was that high-quality coffee would stabilize prices and, more particularly, would facilitate the export of coffee produced in Belgian Africa.

This possible solution to decreasing prices was mentioned for the first time in 1935. Agronomists and administrators alike debated the option of restricting *Robusta* plantations to the colony alone. It was argued that the *Arabica* sector in both the colony and the mandate was still too small and that, therefore, limitations would not have any impact.[81] This was a logical step because in the 1930s, and later, *Robusta* production indeed overshadowed *Arabica* cultivation. Furthermore, limiting the latter would have hampered both the emerging plantation sector in eastern Congo and the coffee campaigns in the mandate

79 Mararo, "Land conflicts in Masisi, Eastern Zaire: the impact and aftermath of Belgian colonial policy (1920–1989)": 150.

80 This resulted in a second phase of even more strictly controlled migrations (1948–1954). The Kivu administration tried to direct Rwandan migrants to areas with a low population density, such as Rutshuru, or the region surrounding Lake Mokoto in Masisi. Next to attracting Rwandans, this second phase is also characterized by controlled internal migrations, with, for example, Bashi emigrating from densely populated Kabare (Mathys, "People on the move. Frontiers, borders, mobility and history in the Lake Kivu region 19th–20th century": 246–247, and Mararo, "Land conflicts in Masisi, Eastern Zaire: the impact and aftermath of Belgian colonial policy (1920–1989)": 155).

81 AAB, Agri, Café, Limitations des plantations de café (342), Rapport "comité restreint au café," 20/3/1936.

(*infra*). However, the initial plan did not have the results hoped for as prices continued to be unstable, and in 1938, a formal limitation on both *Robusta* and *Arabica* plantations in both the colony and the mandate was promulgated.[82] Starting from June 1, 1938, it was prohibited to plant new coffee bushes outside the limits planted at that time. Replacing or regenerating unproductive bushes was still allowed within the existing limits. Furthermore, the intercropping of coffee with other crops was no longer allowed. Violating these stipulations was punishable by a prison term of a maximum of two months and/or a fine of 2000 Francs.

However, every rule has its exceptions. The INEAC (Institut National pour l'Etude Agronomique du Congo Belge), for example, could still plant coffee to a maximum of 20 hectares per year in order to continue scientific research. Individual colonists having obtained a concession where their workers were beginning to plant coffee before the decree became effective were allowed to complete the works on the condition that the planted surface did not exceed 50 hectares. In addition to the exceptions specified in the 1938 decree, *colons* could enjoy other benefits as well. Only one month after the enactment of the decree, the colonial administration decided to compensate European *Arabica* cultivators in both the colony and the mandate. Africans were excluded. Producers received a bonus of 1.5 Francs per kilo of exported *Arabica*. This measure was represented as support for colonists during the crisis, but administrators admitted that the bonus was equally intended to compensate colonists for the restrictions placed on their coffee surfaces which might have caused deficits.[83]

With the decree of December 19, 1944, new plantations were allowed again, although still in a limited way. Planters interested in *Robusta* cultivation had the right to plant a maximum of 150 hectares from then on, while *Arabica* producers had to be satisfied with a maximum of 50 hectares. In 1946, restrictions were cancelled completely and concessions could again be granted "freely."[84] It is hard to say whether these measures actually improved the quality of the coffee produced in Belgian Africa. What is certain is that, after World War II, prices on the international markets increased, which might have contributed to the decision to cancel the limitations altogether. Also, during and after the war several parastatal coffee quality control entities developed. Clearly, efforts

82 See Annex 1 for the entire decree.

83 AAB, Agri, Café, Correspondance (517), Conférence donné aux membres de l'Unaki à Costermansville par Sladden, 10/8/1938.

84 Ibid, Limitations des plantations de café (342), Note par Van den Abeele au ministre de la colonie, 2/10/1946.

were made to improve, classify and export the coffees produced in Belgian Africa.[85] As Chapter 1 shows, the size of land planted with coffee in the entire colony was smaller after this measure, most visibly in the European segment. But production (in tons) did not really grow until the mid-1950s. It is therefore doubtful that the decision indeed increased intensification in the coffee sector.

2 The Rwandan Kivu

2.1 *Customary Land Tenure and the German Period*

As argued in the previous chapter, a distinction is required between precolonial central Rwanda and the areas bordering Lake Kivu. Simultaneously with the expansionary drifts of the Central Court, the area around Lake Kivu developed into a transitional zone between the Congolese forest zone and central Rwanda. With the excursions of Rwabugiri in the second half of the nineteenth century, centralization and social stratification spread more and more to regions outside the central Nyiginya Kingdom.

It is important to stress this because land tenure systems from central Rwanda also spread, replacing or at least assimilating existing systems in the areas bordering Lake Kivu. The aim of this section is to sketch the situation on the threshold of colonialism. I am well aware that such a sketch is a bit superficial and may lack nuance, but it is outside the scope of this book to present an inventory of possible land tenure systems in precolonial Rwanda. At the end of the nineteenth century, the way control over land was "visible" on the ground often reflected the degree of penetration of the Central Court, leaving areas outside the Nyiginya Kingdom room for flexibility.[86] Furthermore, control over land is often intertwined with control over labor and cattle, which makes it sometimes difficult to make a claim about land as such.

Nevertheless, in central Rwanda, there was a hierarchical land tenure system with various categories. The first one, also existing in other parts of precolonial

85 The Office du Café Arabica, with headquarters in Costermansville, performed quality controls on *Arabica* produced in the Kivu district before exporting the cash crop from 1938 onwards. After World War II, the OCIRU (Office des Café Indigènes du Ruanda-Urundi), with headquarters in Bujumbura, equally performed quality controls for coffee produced in the mandate, although the OCIRU also had more impact and control over the production process itself (for more on these parastatal agricultural groups in Belgian Africa, see: ibid, Organismes paraétatiques, especially (50), (51), (52)).

86 Catharine Newbury, "*Ubureetwa* and *Thangata*: catalysts to peasant political consciousness in Rwanda and Malawi," *Canadian Journal of African Studies* 14, no. 1 (1980): 101.

Rwanda, is called *ubukonde*. This category of land was held independently from the Central Court.[87] It was land controlled by a lineage establishing its right to control by having cleared the land for the first time.[88] The land controlled within this constellation was distributed by lineage heads in exchange for tribute and sometimes *corvée* labor. The distributed land was hereditary. When there was no heritor (son), the plot returned to the lineage for redistribution.[89] Even "outsiders" seeking land could settle on an *ubukonde* and become land clients in exchange for tribute/labor. A second tenure system, referred to as *isambu*, was characterized by more "individual" control over land. In the nineteenth century, central Rwanda was already burdened with land shortage, causing the birth of a system where land was distributed to "nuclear families" in exchange for tribute and some *corvée* labor for a superior.[90] This individual tenure system increasingly but slowly encroached on and assimilated *ubukonde* land in the course of the nineteenth century.[91] Together with the introduction of other patron–client ties (for instance *uburetwa*; see Chapter 4), *isambu* eroded the power and former autonomy of the lineages.[92] In addition to these two types of land tenure, another category emerged as well. Cattle was a significant source of wealth and prestige, and until the first quarter of the nineteenth century, pasture land was public land. Every herder was allowed to place cattle on these lands. However, as a result of an increasing scarcity of pasture in central Rwanda, a new system of pasture land emerged: *ibikingi*, or "reserved pastures." Prominent chiefs, decorated warriors and loyal clients of the king were granted land domains by the Central Court. Some *ibikingi* included only pasture, but others also included people, who thus suddenly became land clients. Toward the end of the nineteenth century, they even had to pay tribute (food or labor) to the land lord, even though they were previously exempted.[93]

Regions removed from the Central Court enjoyed relative autonomy until the second half of the nineteenth century. Access to land was regulated through

87 Newbury, "Precolonial Burundi and Rwanda: local loyalties, regional royalties": 290.

88 Vansina, *Antecedents to modern Rwanda. The Nyiginya kingdom*: 40.

89 Villia Jefremovas, *Brickyards to graveyards. From production to genocide in Rwanda* (Albany: State University of New York Press, 2002): 65.

90 Mathys, "People on the move. Frontiers, borders, mobility and history in the Lake Kivu region 19th–20th century": 79.

91 Ibid: 82.

92 Newbury, *The cohesion of oppression. Clientship and ethnicity in Rwanda, 1860–1960*: 98.

93 Newbury, "*Ubureetwa* and *Thangata*: catalysts to peasant political consciousness in Rwanda and Malawi": 99–100, and Vansina, *Antecedents to modern Rwanda. The Nyiginya kingdom*: 131–132.

ubukonde. The areas bordering Lake Kivu usually had close commercial and social ties with areas west of the lake. I will come back to the commercial relations in Chapter 6, but in this context marriage ties, clientship and land ties are the most important.[94] In the course of the nineteenth century, especially during the second half, things started to change for those regions not yet incorporated into the Nyiginya Kingdom, albeit unequally. Before Rwabuguri (pre-1875), expeditions directed toward the west of what is now Rwanda resulted in the establishment or reinforcement of royal control over Kinyaga (south), Bwishaza (center) and Bugoyi (north).[95] In small parts of Kinyaga (around Shangi, for example), this also resulted in the establishment of control over land through *isambu*.[96] With Rwabugiri, centralization, hierarchy, *isambu* and more extractive control over land increasingly (albeit gradually and often contested) spread to or were extended in those regions, but homogenization was still lacking and complete centralization was not finalized until European colonization.[97]

In the last quarter of the nineteenth century, one of the novelties in regions previously unincorporated into the kingdom was the appointment of land chiefs by the Central Court.[98] That way, administrative control was extended to people loyal to the court who ruled over arable land and had the right to collect land exactions. Within a delimited area, land chiefs demanded periodic exactions from each kin group living in that area, but together with the court, which was gaining strength, chiefs could also demand additional services such as labor (*uburetwa*; see Chapter 4).[99]

This sketch reflects the complex land tenure systems in Rwanda at the time German colonization started. The German period was a time of great disruption, not because of the quantitative German presence but rather because of the reliance on "traditional" power structures and enhancement of the authority of the elites over the rural masses.[100] Germans needed the king to consolidate their power, whereas the king needed/used German colonialism to extend

94 Newbury, "Precolonial Burundi and Rwanda: local loyalties, regional royalties": 263.

95 Vansina, *L'évolution du royaume rwanda des origines à 1900*: 78.

96 Reisdorff, *Enquêtes foncières au Ruanda:* 57–58.

97 Vansina, *Antecedents to modern Rwanda. The Nyiginya kingdom*: 164–165 and 194–195.

98 And the creation of "chiefs of the long grass" who regulated access to pasture, probably following the introduction of *ibikingi* (Mathys, "People on the move. Frontiers, borders, mobility and history in the Lake Kivu region 19th–20th century": 83).

99 Newbury, "*Ubureetwa* and *Thangata*: catalysts to peasant political consciousness in Rwanda and Malawi" 100.

100 Ibid: 102.

the power and territorial basis of the kingdom.[101] However, since Germany did not interfere in internal affairs,[102] centralization and increasing control over land continued to force themselves upon rural communities. German colonial authorities also decided that, except for the bamboo forests in northwest Rwanda becoming German Crownland, all land would remain "property" of the king.[103] The fact that *ubukonde* land, for instance, was not granted by the court escaped German attention, thereby opening the way to this kind of land tenure being eroded and land tenure systems present in central Rwanda at that time being further extended. Similarly to in the Belgian Congo, complexities in customary land systems were not fully grasped by German administrators. However, the big difference was that in this part of German East Africa there was far less European demand for land – not only because this region was already relatively densely populated but also, and perhaps more importantly, because of the alleged lack of minerals (gold, diamonds).[104] This in turn lessened the urge to make customary land tenure more legible/controllable and to expropriate "vacant" land. Consequently, Germany opted to use the local labor supply, following the *modus operandi* of the British in Uganda. After experimenting with all kinds of cash crops (cotton especially, but also tobacco) coffee appeared to be most convenient for this region. Moreover, coffee could be cultivated on land previously considered useless by local farmers.[105] In contrast to cotton, for example, coffee thrives well in humid soil intercropped with banana trees (their leaves provide shade and protection from the wind). In the vicinity of their administrative-military post, Germans distributed coffee seeds to Africans; chiefs also produced on sometimes relatively large estates using *corvée* labor.[106] Missions were even more important, not only in distributing seeds to associated Christians but also in serving as an example to those first

101 Lemarchand, *Rwanda and Burundi*: 57; William Roger Louis, *Ruanda-Urundi, 1884–1919* (Oxford: Clarendon Press, 1963): 122.

102 Vansina, *Antecedents to modern Rwanda. The Nyiginya kingdom*: 179.

103 Louis, *Ruanda-Urundi, 1884–1919*: 151. Missions represent a notable exception. By appropriating land and using *corvée* labor, fathers actually followed patterns set by notables sent by the Central Court (see Des Forges, *Defeat is the only bad news: Rwanda under Musinga, 18961931*: 50 and 63).

104 Louis, *Ruanda-Urundi, 1884–1919*: 172–173. From the mid-1920s, however, mines (cassiterite) started to open in Rwanda. For an overview see Baudouin Paternostre de la Mairieu, *Le Rwanda: son effort de développement. Antécédents historiques et conquêtes de la révolution Rwandaise* (Bruxelles: Editions A. De Boeck, 1972): 136.

105 Louis, *Ruanda-Urundi, 1884–1919*: 174–175.

106 Chrétien, *The Great Lakes of Africa. Two thousand years of history*: 258.

planters.[107] German ambitions were quite great: from 1914 until 1920 they wanted to plant 1 million coffee bushes each year in Rwanda and Burundi.[108] But on the eve of World War I, these plans turned out to be overly ambitious, and in practice coffee cultivation was still in its infancy.[109]

2.2 *Belgium Enters the Scene*

After the Great War, diplomatic discussions and a series of compromises eventually ensured that Belgium became the mandatary of Ruanda-Urundi. The newly installed administration did not have the intention of hastily transforming customary land systems. It was supposed to be a slow but steady evolution toward individual property in a European legal sense.[110] Feeling the pressure of the League of Nations, the administration allowed access to land to continue to be regulated as in precolonial times, even though more exploitative control over land, centralization and homogenization were spreading to all areas of present-day Rwanda. For areas bordering Lake Kivu, this meant adaptations to existing land systems (more centralization and individualization) rather than continuity. Moreover, similarly to the colony and contrary to the former German policy, the mandate government also initiated a dual land tenure system. Alongside customary tenure, written law had to systematize access to land for non-Africans. Allegedly vacant land – lacking in most parts of Rwanda – became *terre domaniale*, despite the recognition of native rights over those lands and the opposition of a Dutch member of the Mandate Commission who unsuccessfully insisted that former German Crownland should return to the natives instead of becoming vacant land.[111]

107 Hatungimana, *Le café au Burundi au XXe siècle: Paysans, argent, pouvoir*: 103–105. From 1903–1904 onwards, White Fathers of Mibirizi (colonial Shangugu territory), for instance, were among the first and most important distributors of *Arabica* seeds, both to smallholders in Rwanda and to colonists in the Congolese Kivu.

108 Dorsey, "Rwandan colonial economy, 1916–1941": 34.

109 The failed German dream was also partly the result of sabotage by Rwandan notables and even King Musinga. There are examples of Musinga ordering his notables to drive their cattle through fields where Hutu were attempting to cultivate coffee, which resulted in the destruction of these fields (Des Forges, *Defeat is the only bad news: Rwanda under Musinga, 1896–1931*: 94).

110 S.N., *Le Ruanda-Urundi* (Bruxelles: L'Office de l'information et des relations publiques pour le Congo belge et le Ruanda-Urundi, 1959): 144.

111 De Clerck, "Le régime foncier, le régime minier et le droit des biens": 272, and AAB, RARU, Rapport à la Commission permanente des Mandats, Lettre de Orts (Belgian mandate member) au ministre de la colonie, 15/8/1921, no. 17(1).

2.2.1 European Access

In contrast to in the colony, in the mandate there was no parastatal entity such as the CNKi through which non-Africans could acquire land. Officially, colonists aiming to develop agricultural activity always had to turn to the government, although it is not unreasonable to assume that some negotiated directly with chiefs to buy land and thus bypassed the administration. Nevertheless, from 1925 onwards, no concessions were granted in densely populated regions if this would disrupt residential structures. Moreover, in these zones concessions were limited to 500 hectares.[112] To areas with a lower population density, as in parts of Shangugu, for example, this limitation did not apply. This enabled firms such as Protanag to demand a 7000-hectare concession. The question here, however, is: how did local administrators define "densely populated"?

Access to land that did not belong to the *terres dominales* was always preceded by a vacancy inquiry, and when land was not declared "vacant" it had to be purchased from native authorities. Thus, the same method was used as in the colony. It is unclear whether local Rwandan communities also considered the very start-up of an inquiry as an order to relinquish land. What is certain, however, is that giving up land equaled giving up power, and that even as late as the 1950s, the Belgian administration used moral pressure to influence native decisions, as the following quote referring to Gisenyi illustrates:

> an amount of 200 Francs per hectare is transferred of which 80% goes to the Chieftaincy's treasury and 20% to the State's treasury. If you [native authorities] think that the Chieftaincy is not appropriate for Europeans to settle on small plots (on payment of an amount and with the agreement of the owners), you oppose the valorization of the country. Those Europeans certainly do not pay taxes to the Chieftaincy but they pay heavy taxes to the Government, and moreover they make sure that industry and trade are running by investing capital in the country [*sic*].[113]

112 Dorsey, "Rwandan colonial economy, 1916–1941": 144. In the second half of the 1920s, the administration in Ruanda-Urundi also initiated "protective zones." In areas of usually 70000 hectares, a company received a monopoly for ten years to "cooperate" with Africans. The latter produced while the former, having unlimited access to African labor, processed and exported (ibid: 146). The Compagnie de la Rusizi, for instance, active in Shangugu and engaged in the cotton sector, is a perfect example of a firm "collaborating" with African cultivators.

113 AAB, RWA, Conseils de Territoire et de Chefferie, Bugoyi – Gisenyi, RWA(71), Compte rendu du conseil de chefferie, 29/10/1957.

2.2.2 African Coffee Land

More important for the mandate, however, is the way Africans mobilized coffee land, or were instructed to do so. Up until the 1930s, attempts to disperse coffee production among African farmers were unsuccessful. Both Tutsi and Hutu lacked enthusiasm. The former feared social upheaval, while the latter did not see the added value of a new crop with no immediate results (coffee bushes are productive only after four to six years).[114] On the other hand, notables forcing clients to cultivate on their personal plots were more successful. By using unpaid *corvée* labor, they ensured that profits from cultivation went directly into their pockets. Moreover, from 1925 onwards, chiefs were obliged to cultivate at least 0.5 hectare each in order to serve as a role model for "ordinary" farmers.[115] In 1930, chiefs, sub-chiefs and hill chiefs were ordered to tend to 1000, 500 and 250 bushes respectively, but in 1934, the mandate administration limited the surface notables could use to cultivate coffee to 1 hectare per 1000 taxpayers, likely to free people from *corvée* labor and enable them to produce themselves.[116]

Despite the initial reluctance of Rwandans to produce coffee, a serious effort was made by the government to try to fit land for cash crops into customary land systems. The annual report of 1923 announces the implementation of a program in which access to and control over coffee land resembled access to customary *isambu* land:

> Supervised by an agronomist or the *chef du poste*, the indigenous chief chooses a vast plot appropriate for coffee cultivation. This plot is parceled out to all the neighboring natives. Then, separately, everyone plow. When this is done, the natives go to the [administrative] post or to the chieftaincy's nursery and collect the required amount of plants (distributed for free). [...] The chief is charged with supervising the natives maintaining the young plants properly; he has the obligation to reprimand all those neglecting to take care of their lot.[117]

Land in this constellation clearly was not *ubukonde* land, because it was not controlled by a lineage; it was controlled by a chief and divided into individual plots. This was the first step of the mandate government to further expand

114 Uwizeyimana, "Rôle politique de la caféiculture au Rwanda": 176–177.
115 Ibid: 176.
116 Hatungimana, *Le café au Burundi au XXe siècle: Paysans, argent, pouvoir*: 136 and 162.
117 S.N., *Rapport sur l'administration Belge du Ruanda-Urundi pendant l'année 1923* (Bruxelles: s.n., 1923): 21.

isambu and to homogenize individual rights over land. However, the fact that coffee fields were placed together simplified control. In this respect this program resembles the coffee "gardens" introduced in colonial Java at the end of the eighteenth century.[118]

However, this program too did not excite Rwandan farmers, and in combination with a lack of sufficient administrative personnel, this persuaded the government to change tack. In 1933, the agronomist of the Residence Dohogne informed the administration that grouping coffee bushes on a plot or even isolated individual plots was not a good idea. According to Dohogne: "We must force the natives to surround them with food crops. That way weed will be removed, the native will visit his plantation more often and property rights will be established more easily."[119] By "encouraging" Africans to cultivate coffee in the vicinity of their habitations and among food crops, especially shade plants providing protection for the precarious coffee plants, another step to further individualize land rights was taken.[120] Moreover, by inducing people to produce a perennial crop, more permanent land occupation appeared either way. Furthermore, according to Uwizeyimana, coffee land escaped customary authority, including patron–client ties.[121] However, when land was abandoned, for instance when a farmer also worked as a wage laborer, some chiefs abused their power by expropriating and redistributing the plot. This happened in Kibuye as late as the mid-1950s.[122]

From a colonial point of view, this system was successful. The Shangugu territory coffee report of October 1937 stated that the bushes on the ancient fields had little or no value and also that "every future replacement of plants has to be done exclusively nearby the *ingos* [homesteads] of the natives. Very often it concerns a whole field that needs to be replaced. Bushes planted within the banana plantations develop very well in general."[123] With the start of the coffee campaigns each HAV received fifty-four plants, later raised to eighty on average (1949), then to 120–200 in regions where soil and land

118 Breman, *Mobilizing labour for the global coffee market. Profits from an unfree work regime in colonial Java*: 169–172.

119 AAB, RWA, Café, Rapports, RWA(442), Rapport d'inspection agricole édité par Dohogne, 25/4/1933.

120 However, initially, Africans were reluctant to include coffee in their production scheme, because it was considered a supplementary crop to cultivate with no direct results in addition (Hatungimana, *Le café au Burundi au XXe siècle: Paysans, argent, pouvoir*: 334).

121 Uwizeyimana, "Rôle politique de la caféiculture au Rwanda": 177.

122 AAB, RARU, Kibuye Territoire, Rapport Général, 1953, no. 82(3).

123 Ibid, RWA, Café, Rapports, RWA(437), Rapport mensuel Shangugu, Octobre 1937.

availability allowed it (mid-1950s).[124] On the one hand, it should be stressed that, even though the average quantity of crops per HAV increased during the Belgian era, the surface used for coffee was usually the smallest, as food crops prevailed.[125] On the other hand, in the 1950s in both Shangugu and Gisenyi, some large planters cultivated coffee as well. From 1955 onwards, producers in Gisenyi with 1000 or more plants were even exempted from other obligatory works, such as road maintenance. From 1959 onwards, the same measure was taken in Shangugu for planters with 500 or more bushes. In both territories chiefs agreed on the discharges, after consultation with the Belgian administration.[126]

Despite issues concerning land availability and debates about the pros and cons of intercropping (*infra*), coffee growing near people's habitations flourished, as is shown by the figures in Chapter 1. But in the mid-1950s, the idea of grouping coffee bushes returned and was effectively applied in areas bordering Lake Kivu as well as in central Rwanda. Although soil around peoples homesteads was more fertile and plants could be better maintained, reorganizing bushes between parallel contour lines (see Image 2) would facilitate their disinfection and pruning,[127] but above all their surveillance and control by African monitors and Belgian agronomists. Rather than cutting back individual land rights, this measure resulted in the opposite. As can be seen below, trying to rationalize coffee plots as well as land for habitations and food crops is probably the final step in the direction of mapping and registering land.[128] This intervention of the administration continued in the postcolonial period. In the 1970s, the majority of coffee fields were no longer placed around or within people's residential areas, and were sometimes as far as 1 kilometer away.[129]

---

124 Hatungimana, *Le café au Burundi au XXe siècle: Paysans, argent, pouvoir*: 205.

125 Dorsey, "Rwandan colonial economy, 1916–1941": 211.

126 AAB, RWA, Conseils de Territoire et de Chefferie, Kanage – Gisenyi, RWA(71), Procès-verbal de la réunion de conseil de chefferie, 4/3/1955, and ibid, Shangugu, RWA(72), Procès-verbal de la réunion plénière, 5/1/1959.

127 Ibid, RWA(443), Note aux superviseurs itinérants de café, éditée par H. Stainier, 17/4/1954.

128 A similar evolution toward more individual land rights for coffee smallholders can be found in other mandates as well – French Togo for example, even though in this mandate registering smallholder land was already underway in the early 1920s (Benoît Antheaume, "Le café au Togo. Chronique d'une émergence de la modernité rural (1920–1960)," *Etudes Rurales*, no. 180 (2007): 163–165).

129 Bart, "Le café dans l'agriculture rwandaise: l'exemple de Kidahiré (Runyinya)" 308–309.

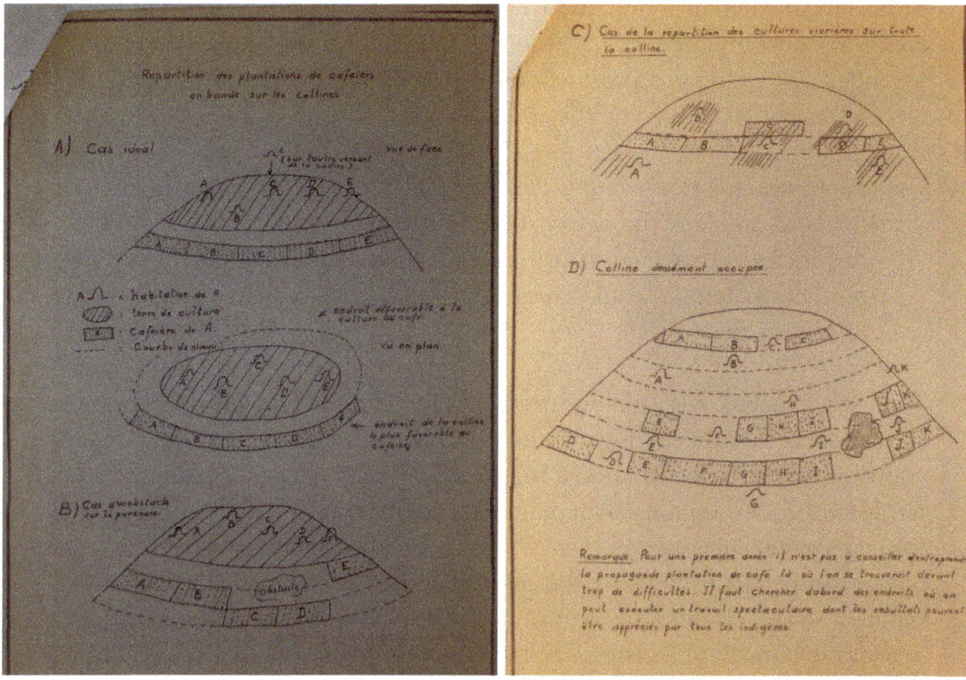

IMAGE 2 Sketches showing the rationalization of Rwandan coffee fields (mid-1950s)
SOURCE: AAB, RWA, CAFÉ, RAPPORTS, RWA(438), DOCUMENT D'INGÉNIEUR-AGRONOME J. JERNANDER, 15/3/1954

2.3 *Land-Related Tensions*

2.3.1 Availability

The installation of a smallholder mode of coffee production was a consequence not only of an already-existing customary "individualized" land system but also of a lack of land, which in turn stimulated individual land rights. Pressure on land increased even more during the 1940s and 1950s. In Gisenyi, at the end of the 1920s, for example, the average size of a family plot was about 2.5 hectares.[130] In parts of the territory, such as in central Bugoyi, fallow periods had to be shortened to one or two years, due to the high population density.[131]

130 AAB, RARU, Gisenyi Territoire, Rapport Général, 1929, no. 87(16). However, in areas close to Lake Kivu the size was smaller, while in the eastern part of the territory average sizes were larger. Furthermore, people moving especially from Gisenyi and Ruhengeri territories to Gishari were granted 5 hectares of land per family in the second migration phase (1948–1954) and even that was considered too small by contemporary observers (L. Bruyns and K. Pinxten, "De geleide immigratie van de Banya Ruanda in Kivu," *Zaïre: Revue Congolaise* (Mars 1952): 263).

131 AAB, RARU, Gisenyi Territoire, Rapport Agriculture, 1931, no. 90(8).

At the end of colonial period, the average size even halved to a mere 1.25 hectares.[132] A consistent decline in the amount of land caused problems not only for coffee cultivation but also, and perhaps especially, for food security, as the territorial agent of Gisenyi rightly observed in 1948:

> the overpopulation of almost all chieftaincies results in the acuteness of the land problem, the natives literally are living on top of one another; this situation explains and justifies the native's state of mind of being essentially materialistic and prosaic [*terre à terre*] because it concerns food to survive.[133]

The same tensions over land occurred in Kibuye. Similarly to in Gisenyi, pressure on land was already high in the late 1920s. Most fertile land was under cultivation, and the locals worked hard to clear additional land (pasture or less fertile land, for example), which indicates the precarity of the situation before the coffee campaigns even started.[134] It is no surprise, then, that land tensions only worsened in the course of the colonial period. According to the territorial report of 1953, soils in Kibuye were among the poorest in Rwanda – except for in the chieftaincies of Bwishaza and Rusenyi-Itabire, where coffee cultivation thrived.[135] In other parts of the territory, cultivatable fertile land for cash, as well as for food crops, was scarcer, troubling both European and African minds.[136]

The fact that pressure on land was a reality rather than a colonial invention had implications for coffee production. As mentioned, not all areas within a territory were equally appropriate for cultivating coffee. Moreover, already in the mid-1930s most chieftaincies bordering Lake Kivu were declared saturated, as Map 8 shows. This means that the idea of distributing new plants simmered for a while and that the mandate administration had to consent to replace bushes.

Initially, land pressure in Shangugu was relatively less urgent than in territories further north, resulting in the granting of supposedly vacant land by the bureaucracy to European *colons*. However, as Map 8 suggests, even here in areas bordering the southern tip of Lake Kivu, available fertile land was also diminishing as early as the mid-1930s. With an average size of only 1.31 hectares

---

132 Philippe Leurquin, *Le niveau de vie des populations rurales du Ruanda-Urundi* (Louvain: Editions Nauwelaerts, 1960). 121.

133 AAB, RARU, Gisenyi Territoire, Rapport Général, 1948, no. 88(8).

134 Derscheid Collection, University of Florida Digital Collection, Lubengera Territoire, Rapport avec réponses sur questions posé par M. le gouverneur du Ruanda-Urundi, 1929.

135 AAB, RARU, Kibuye Territoire, Rapport Général, 1953, no. 82(3).

136 Ibid, Rapport AIMO, 1957, no. 82(16).

MAP 8 Saturated coffee-planting regions in western Rwanda (mid-1930s)
Notes: Red: saturated end 1934; green: end 1935; orange: end 1936; gray-blue: expected end 1937
SOURCE: AAB, RWA, CAFÉ, RAPPORTS, RWA(438), LETTRE DU RÉSIDENT DU RUANDA AU VICE-GOUVERNEUR (ANNEXE), 3/7/1936

per family plot in the late 1950s, land availability had reached a critical point similar to that of the other Rwandan territories near Lake Kivu.[137] And even though after World War II the administration had restricted the granting of concessions in the entire mandate as a consequence of the high population density, the local Belgian government in Shangugu still conceded land to colonists (in Itshyesha, for example), albeit in small portions. This confounded United Nations representatives:[138] during the first visiting mission in 1948, the chief of the Agricultural Service in Ruanda-Urundi, Everaerts, was asked why in some parts of the mandate the number of colonists was rising while at the same time there was a lack of land. In a letter to the vice governor, Everaerts legitimized this using the same debatable "didactic" argument administrators used in the 1920s:

> I have highlighted the fact that the population is not spread uniformly, that the administration takes the necessary precautions, that [vacancy] inquiries are always carried out; [...] I have called attention to the value of the educational role of certain colonists.[139]

2.3.2 Converted Pasture

The importance of cattle in Rwanda is well known. Cattle was not only a source of wealth and status. Cattle clientship (*ubuhake* ties) "served as a key instrument for Tuutsi to gain and maintain control over the population. Through *ubuhake*, the elite gained support and services and, most important, control over cattle."[140] What is of interest here, however, is the land needed to pasture those herds. As a consequence of increasing pressure on agricultural land during the colonial period, pasture land was also curtailed. These lands were systemically converted into agricultural land – and certainly also used for coffee cultivation – demonstrating yet another factor of increasing pressure on land. These lands were supposedly available as public pasture, because *ibikingi* was specific to central Rwanda at least until the end of the nineteenth century and,

---

137 Leurquin, *Le niveau de vie des populations rurales du Ruanda-Urundi*: 121.

138 Similarly to Kabare, the mandate administration also relocated people from oversaturated regions in Rwanda to regions with a relatively lower population density, such as Imbo in southwestern Shangugu (A. Angladette, "Notes sur l'économie agricole du Ruanda-Urundi," *L'agronomie Tropicale* 9, no. 5 (1959): 585).

139 AAB, RARU, Rapport de la mission de visite de l'ONU au Ruanda-Urundi, Lettre de Everarts au vice-gouverneur, 24/7/1948, no. 25(oB).

140 Newbury, *The cohesion of oppression. Clientship and ethnicity in Rwanda, 1860–1960*: 125.

moreover, they were reserved for elite herders.[141] Nevertheless, transforming pasture was not a colonial innovation. In regions with a high population density and in exceptional circumstances, local notables allowed food crop cultivation by Hutu on cattle land; for instance, in Bwishaza (Gisenyi) this custom had existed since the reign of Rwabugiri and perhaps even earlier.[142]

The Gisenyi territory offers a perfect example of declining pasture and the way people reacted to it. According to the agricultural reports, in 1947 one animal still had an average of 1.16 hectares at its disposal, but in 1955 that average had dwindled to 0.97 hectares.[143] But even long before World War II, pressure on pasture was increasing. In combination with the proximity of the Congolese Kivu (where grazing land still was available – in Gishari, for instance), cattle owners and their retinue decided to cross the border in search of new land, which often led to conflicts with local Congolese notables.[144]

2.4 *Administrative Interventions*

2.4.1 Intercropping: Yes or No?

When the coffee campaigns started in the early 1930s, it was common to intercrop coffee with other crops (bananas, vegetables, fruit trees). Similarly to in colonial Tanzania, this method was successful because coffee could be integrated into existing food crop cycles.[145] Banana trees especially were considered benevolent for coffee bushes by colonial agronomists, because banana leaves provided shade, protection against heavy winds and fertile humus soils.[146] In addition, as in colonial Tanzania, intercropping coffee with bananas increased the value of land.[147] Colonial representatives discovered these ecological advantages not by intensive experiments or tests by agronomists, but by learning from the locals, at least in Shangugu:

> About four years ago, some natives, then at work with the Protanag, where they have stolen seeds, have planted coffee nearby their *rugo*

141 Vansina, *Antecedents to modern Rwanda. The Nyiginya kingdom*: 131–132.

142 Reisdorff, *Enquêtes foncières au Ruanda*: 71.

143 AAB, RARU, Gisenyi Territoire, Rapport Agriculture, 1947 and 1955, no. 90(21) and 90(29).

144 Ibid, Rapport Général, 1941, no. 88(1) and Mathys, "People on the move. Frontiers, borders, mobility and history in the Lake Kivu region 19th–20th century": 209–216.

145 Kenneth Curtis, "Smaller is better. A consensus of peasants and bureaucrats in colonial Tanganyika," in *The global coffee economy in Africa, Asia, and Latin America 1500–1989*, ed. William Gervase Clarence-Smith and Steven Topik (Cambridge; New York: Cambridge University Press, 2003): 320.

146 Hatungimana, *Le café au Burundi au XXe siècle: Paysans, argent, pouvoir*: 331–332.

147 Austen, *Northwest Tanzania under German and British rule. Colonial policy and tribal politics, 1889–1939*: 96.

> [homestead], I [territorial agent] have seen that these coffee bushes attain a height of 2 to 2.5 m, and the agent of Protanag who accompanied me assesses that they produced some 2 [kilograms] per tree. These coffee trees are manured with residues and composts coming from indigenous life. It is thus necessary to encourage the natives by any means possible to plant nearby their *rugo* on the most fertile plots of land.[148]

However, colonial thinking altered in the second half of the 1930s. Again as in colonial Tanzania, agricultural monitors considered it better not to intercrop banana and coffee trees any longer.[149] European specialists were convinced that banana trees, like sweet potatoes for example, housed insects which were especially detrimental to coffee bushes. Intercropping coffee with other crops, such as beans or peas, was still allowed – but not with bananas. Cultivators usually reacted to this measure by planting coffee bushes on the periphery of their individual plots while placing banana trees close to their habitations.

The decision made by the mandate administration confused not only coffee producers. After the introduction of coffee, cultivators had to reorganize their crops once again, but they often ignored orders from above by engaging in illegitimate intercropping. What Hatungimana stresses for Burundi in the colonial period also applies to Rwanda: "despite the vigilance of colonial representatives, coffee fields have never been homogeneous spaces: the cultivator has always intercropped, clandestinely, various vegetables and fruits."[150] The decision to abandon the intercropping of coffee with bananas in particular also confused colonial minds. After World War II, some African agricultural monitors in certain territories (including Shangugu and Gisenyi) had interpreted the "intercropping stop" to mean that banana trees should be removed from people's fields altogether, which provoked the intervention of the Resident. In a letter to the Rwandan head agronomist, the Resident clearly specified that total removal was not the intention. The idea was rather that banana trees should be thinned out if they were too dense and that removal only was required if they were planted too close to coffee bushes. After all, the Resident continued, coffee needs some shade in order to produce properly.[151]

In this context, "clarifying" banana trees should also be read figuratively. The fact that intercropping banana with coffee bushes was suddenly considered

148 AAB, RWA, Café, Rapports, RWA(440), Document: René Bourgeois, avis et considérations, 6/6/1933.

149 Weiss, *Sacred trees, bitter harvests. Globalizing coffee in Northwest Tanzania*: 153.

150 Hatungimana, *Le café au Burundi au XXe siècle: Paysans, argent, pouvoir*. 343–344.

151 AAB, RWA, Café, Rapports, RWA(444), Lettre du résident Sandrart à l'agronome Jernander, 26/1/1949.

negative for the latter indicates that agronomists and mandate administrators alike were meticulously trying to grasp control and increase legibility over the cultivation process.[152] The regrouping of coffee fields between parallel contour lines (*supra*) in, for instance, the territories bordering Lake Kivu from the mid-1950s only underlines this argument.

2.4.2 Restrictions on Smallholder Surfaces?

Even though the coffee campaigns were in full progress, overproduction and falling prices in the 1930s also had ramifications for the mandate. However, it was precisely the judicial constellation of Ruanda-Urundi that made the solution to this issue more complicated than in the Belgian colony, and merely limiting surfaces might have met with resistance. When debates concerning a possible solution for the mandate commenced in 1935, Belgian representatives were well aware of possible future criticism by the League of Nations – and likely also by other adversaries of unfair measures with regard to Rwandan planters, as the following quote seems to imply:

> I [General Governor Pierre Ryckmans] would not dare to take responsibility for giving you [Secretary of the Colony] the advice to spread the interdiction over Ruanda-Urundi. That would be unfair and it would be, I believe, deeply apolitical. Unfair because, at this moment, neither I nor anyone else can think of another remunerative activity for the natives. Apolitical because that would be deliberately scarifying the rights and interests of the natives in the mandate for the benefit of the European plantations in the Belgian Congo. How to justify such a measure to the Mandate Commission? I do not really see how.[153]

As mentioned above, in 1935, colonial officials in the Belgian Congo were still thinking of merely limiting *Robusta* surfaces. Pushing through such a restriction in the mandate would indeed have supported the *Arabica* plantation sector in neighboring Kivu. Moreover, some officials were concerned about the reaction of African cultivators. It would have been rather odd if native producers who risked punishment if they did not plant coffee suddenly, with one new measure, were to be punished for planting new coffee bushes.[154]

---

152 I follow James Scott's argument with reference to colonial Tanzania (Scott, *Seeing like a state. How certain schemes to improve the human condition have failed*: 242–243).

153 AAB, Agri, Café, Limitations des plantations de café (342), Lettre de Pierre Ryckmans au ministre de la colonie, 7/11/1935.

154 Hatungimana, *Le café au Burundi au XXe siècle: Paysans, argent, pouvoir*: 185.

After giving it some thought, the Colonial Council in Brussels came up with a solution that could (and did) satisfy the League of Nations. European surfaces were limited the same way as in the colony. On the other hand, rather than limiting smallholder surfaces in the mandate, the campaigns aimed at forcing Africans to establish coffee plots and produce for the world market were stopped abruptly in 1938.[155] No doubt some colonials must have imagined that stopping "encouragement" would have limited smallholder cultivation anyway. However, due to a lack of available data, especially African data, it is difficult to say whether halting the campaigns did indeed limit coffee surfaces in the mandate and subsequently intensify production. The figures for Shangugu (see Chapter 1) indicate that the total size of European surfaces was more or less constant from 1938–1940 onwards, while the total production capacity of the territory increased in the period between 1938 (the start of the official limitations) and 1946–1947 (the official end). A simple extrapolation shows that in the same period the production capacity of the entire mandate tripled, which was foremost a result of African production. Therefore, an increase of production coupled with an alleged maintenance of status quo in coffee land might lead to the conclusion that production indeed intensified. However, knowing that coffee bushes take four to six years to reliably produce, it is more likely that the rise in production in this period was the result of the earlier coffee campaigns.

3 Conclusion

This chapter has demonstrated, without ignoring nuances, that the Lake Kivu region belonged to one "land complex" in the precolonial period. Land tenure was organized and land was distributed via community-based principles (lineages and clans). From central Rwanda, a hierarchical land system with individual tenure spread westwards, but eastern regions bordering Lake Kivu remained relatively autonomous until the mid-nineteenth century. It was not until the colonial era that this land tenure system was fully implemented in the areas bordering Lake Kivu (and other regions not belonging to the Central Court in precolonial times).

In the colonial period, in both the colony and the mandate, dual land tenure emerged and the respective European administrations both attempted to homogenize land tenure systems as much as possible in order to facilitate control.

155 AAB, Agri, Café, Limitations des plantations de café (342), Lettre anonyme au ministre de la colonie, 2/6/1938.

Land mobilization for coffee production very much depended on state intervention. In eastern Congo, the colonial state created the CNKi, a parastatal entity in charge of conceding land to planters. The CNKi nevertheless lost power in the course of the colonial period, and the state regained a grip on "vacant" land. In the mandate, however, such a parastatal entity was absent and the European government conceded "vacant" land directly to Europeans. In both the colony and the mandate, colonists could also negotiate directly with local notables in order to acquire land. In the mandate, African coffee land was mobilized in consecutive stages: via chiefs using *corvée* labor and via expanding and finalizing individual land tenure in order to force smallholders to cultivate. Both processes were directed by the European regime. The way European agronomists conceived coffee land in the mandate altered a few times during the colonial period: from "gardens" to cultivation around the homestead to plots near the homestead, easier to control and to map.

Tensions over land were present in both eastern Congo and western Rwanda, albeit in different ways.[156] The quasi-monopoly position the CNKi enjoyed in the colonial Kivu often resulted in discussions and conflicts with settlers and the government. These conflicts very often involved money – mostly the price for land considered "vacant." In other words, mobilizing and commodifying land was a result of compromises. Conflicts also arose between European planters and Africans deprived of land. Such "feedback clashes" undoubtedly must have happened in the mandate as well, especially with an administration converting pasture land, but the sources I consulted are silent on this matter. What really troubled mandatary governments at all echelons was the limited amount of land appropriate for coffee (and food) production. Rwandan regions bordering Lake Kivu suffered from a lack of available land already in the early colonial stages, and the issue only worsened later on (colonial Kabare equally suffered from increasing pressure on land). Shangugu was an exception resulting in the establishment of European plantations (Chapter 2) but, especially after World War II, here too pressure on land increased.

The interference of the government in mobilizing land went even further in both the colony and the mandate. In colonial Masisi, for example, the administration created a chieftaincy in order to attract and settle immigrants (and

156 Conflicts over land continued in the postcolonial period, and some authors have linked the region's involvement in decades of violence to land tenure systems; see for instance: Paul Mathieu and Angelus Mafikiri Tsongo, "Enjeux fonciers, déplacements de population et escalades conflictuelles (1930–1995)," in *Conflicts et guerres au Kivu et dans la région des Grands Lacs*, ed. Paul Mathieu and Jean-Claude Willame (Paris: L'Harmattan, 1999), or Etienne Rusamira, "La dynamique des conflits ethniques au Nord-Kivu: une réflexion prospective," *Afrique Contemporaine*, no. 207 (2003).

potential coffee plantation labor) coming from densely populated areas in Rwanda. Governmental intervention in the mandate did not include the creation of an administrative unit, but rather involved the creation of uncertainty. From the mid-1930s onwards, agronomists believed that intercropping coffee with bananas was disadvantageous for the former. African coffee producers reacted not only by ignoring this measure but also by moving coffee to the edges of their plots, even though the intention of the mandate bureaucracy was merely to "enlighten" fields and make control easier. Besides "creating," administrative intervention also meant "limiting" on both sides of Lake Kivu, albeit in a different way. From 1938 to 1946, in both the colony and the mandate, European coffee concessions were not allowed to expand. European bureaucracies hoped to intensify production and improve quality in order to stabilize coffee prices. However, restricting Rwandan smallholders might have provoked criticism from the League of Nations. The solution to this was found in stopping the coffee "encouragement" campaigns. This perfectly shows that a common issue, such as coping with unstable prices on international markets, required different approaches and was solved in different ways as a result of the different legal statuses which enhanced existing dissimilarities.

CHAPTER 4

Mobilizing Coffee-Cultivating Labor

In a 1984 historiographical overview, Bill Freund stressed that "the most basic question of all concerning labor in Africa was how to get it."[1] This refers not only to people having the opportunity – within the constraints of a colonial context – to flee, but also to a common African factor endowment: land abundance and shortage of potential labor. As argued in Chapter 2, however, the region around Lake Kivu is a notable exception to this trend. However, this does not mean that it was easy for Belgians to mobilize labor for the coffee sector. Neither future plantation laborers nor future smallholders were passively waiting for coffee to be introduced so that they could finally enter the world market.

As with the mobilization of land discussed in the previous chapter, the colonizer/mandatory intervened directly or indirectly (through tax impositions, for instance). People with access to resources (land, animals, etcetera) usually do not have the urge to sell their labor. Moreover, recruitment of plantation laborers (primarily in eastern Congo) requires other means and interventions of the state than the mobilization of a smallholder sector (mainly in western Rwanda). The separation of producers and their means of production is much more manifest in a plantation sector. Yet, the mobilization of both coffee plantation workers and smallholders resulted in changing social, political and economic relationships.

Accordingly, the aim of this chapter is to analyze various ways in which labor was mobilized for the coffee sector around Lake Kivu. I will look at the role of the European and indigenous administrations in both the colony and the mandate. This means that I will examine not only "recruitment" as such but also governmental interventions aimed at facilitating *how to get* the coffee-producing labor force. I will focus on the differences between the colony and the mandate, but I will also highlight possible similarities.

1 Colonial Coffee Labor

Before Belgians arrived in the Kivu, several local communities suffered infractions on their way of life. Zanzibari raids caused not only material damage but also changes in systems of labor mobilization.

1 Bill Freund, "Labor and labor history in Africa: a review of the literature," *African Studies Review* 27, no. 2 (1984): 2.

 | DOI:10.1163/9789004428492_007

Permanent settlements of the Zanzibari were surrounded by plantations where slaves and people living in nearby villages cultivated crops such as rice and sesame. Labor conditions on these estates were harsh, and many plantation slaves died within a single year. The appearance of CFS agents did not alter this situation significantly in the sense that coercion and the commodification of the products of African labor continued and even were extended – rubber and ivory quotas had to be achieved by any means.[2] Moreover, the plantations erected by the Zanzibari continued to use slaves to produce food for the newly arrived Europeans until the mid-1890s. In the early twentieth century (and later), Islamicized Africans (*Arabisés*) or descendants of the Zanzibari continued to produce food for and engaged in trading with European officials. The CFS repurchased former slaves and employed them as wage laborers, or, to be more precise, forced them to work, for instance as soldiers in the Force Publique. On the other hand, many *Arabisés* freely entered state services, either as sentinels or as auxiliaries.

In sum, the Zanzibari started a process of forced labor that continued under the CFS, albeit in a different form and on a different scale. With the takeover by Belgium in 1908, labor mobilization was reframed once again, but at least until World War II *continuity* is a more appropriate term than *change*, as will be demonstrated in the following pages.[3]

1.1 *Entering the Plantations*

1.1.1 Spontaneously

The least that can be said is that free plantation entry was scarce before World War II and that even after the war a good deal of the mobilization continued to be unfree. The 1931 annual report of the Kivu district stated that some Africans were looking for a job in an agricultural enterprise but that some years before, not a single native presented himself spontaneously for wage labor of any kind.[4] The district administrator who wrote this report may have exaggerated with this last sentence. Africans with the opportunity to enter into wage labor were well aware of the advantages. It was not so much the wage level that was

2 Based on: Northrup, *Beyond the bend in the river: African labor in Eastern Zaire 1865–1940*: 42–43.

3 Northrup conceives those three distinct but overlapping periods as three "regional colonizations" with a certain continuation of practices and policy at least until 1910. As will be shown in this chapter, continuity of coercion lasted much longer and, rather, World War II proved to be a turning point; see: Northrup, "Slavery and forced labour in eastern Congo 1850–1910," in *Slavery in the Great Lakes region of East Africa*, ed. Henri Médard and Shane Doyle (Oxford: James Currey, 2007).

4 AAB, RACB, Kivu District, Rapport AIMO, 1931, no. 112.

important in this early period, but rather the possibility of escaping obligatory cultivation imposed by the colonial authorities, customary duties and/or the tyranny of customary chiefs.[5]

Spontaneous engagements did increase toward the end of the 1930s. The main reasons were not only the possible improvement of labor conditions in general (see following chapter) but also a more delicate and worsened situation in the villages themselves, as a consequence of rising compulsory cultivation demands, for instance.[6] Estimates made by the local government show that in Kabare in 1939, 50% of the labor force took up a job opportunity freely.[7] After the war, in 1946, free entries were still estimated at 50% but in 1949, the figure in the annual report rose to 80%.[8] Part of this labor force was formed by Rwandans crossing the border daily (*infra*). Figures from Masisi confirm this trend. According to the territorial reports, in 1939, 76% of the engagements were spontaneous while in 1949, 90% of the workers entered wage labor employment allegedly without extra-economic pressure.[9] Sources are unclear about whether Rwandans who were settled in Gishari entered freely or not. The only thing that is mentioned is that immigrants could not be recruited directly before they were settled definitely, which means that they entered either spontaneously or via local notables.[10]

Nonetheless, this is a substantial increase for both territories, and the aftermath of World War II proved to be crucial. However, caution is required when dealing with these figures. For example, data focusing only on coffee laborers are lacking. It can be argued, however, that the relative proximity of coffee plantations to local villages was an incentive for Africans to engage spontaneously, even though this sometimes resulted in reprisals by chiefs (*infra*). Furthermore, it is uncertain how these estimations are made: possibly by asking employers, in which case overestimations cannot be excluded. Nevertheless, even if 80 or 90% are correct estimates of spontaneous engagements, then at the end of the 1940s, 10 to 20% were still unfree (and thus coerced mobilization via chiefs or the administration). Already in 1936, the International Labor

---

5 Northrup, *Beyond the bend in the river: African labor in Eastern Zaire 1865–1940*: 204.

6 This was not unique to the Kivu district. A consequence of the global crisis was the extension of obligatory cultivation (kind of crops, people involved) throughout the entire colony and increased state control; see: Bogumil Jewsiewicki, "Rural society and the Belgian colonial economy," in *History of Central Africa. Volume two*, ed. David Birmingham and Phyllis M. Martin (London; New York: Longman, 1983): 101.

7 AAB, RACB, Kabare Territoire, Rapport AIMO, 1939, no. 99.

8 Ibid, 1946 and 1949.

9 Ibid, Masisi Territoire, Rapport AIMO, 1939 and 1949, no. 142 and 143.

10 Ibid, 1947, no. 143. The report of 1951 states that this term was fixed at two years (ibid, 1951).

Organization defined every operation to obtain workers who did not offer their labor spontaneously as unfree mobilization.[11] Knowing that in 1950, 16525 agricultural laborers were active in Kabare (Chapter 1), this means that, theoretically, some 3300 did not enter wage labor spontaneously in this territory, but were forced.

1.1.2 Via African Chiefs

The administrative reforms of 1910, which were aimed at concealing the most terrible atrocities of the CFS, were officially intended to restore and recognize the authority of customary chiefs, among other things. After the approval of district commissioners, chiefs received a medal; they received privileges, but they also could be (and often were) replaced by another more "benevolent" chief if they thwarted the Belgian local administration. However, what Gareth Austin argues for colonial Ghana also applies to Belgian Africa: colonial governments lacked the means to effectively control chiefs' behavior, and colonially installed chiefs could only gain support and legitimacy from their subjects if they defended the latter's interests.[12] Nonetheless, in contrast with the official aim of the reforms, chiefs thus became intermediaries between the people and the state charged with tasks such as collecting taxes and the mobilization of labor.[13] Chiefs had the right to recruit labor for public works, but the *Bulletin Officiel du Congo Belge* does not make any reference to chiefs being legalized to intervene in labor recruitment for private enterprises.[14] On the one hand, chiefs thus abused their legal power. But on the other hand, this reliance on customary power structures for mobilizing labor was the most cost-effective way to exercise control, and it is definitely not unique to Belgian Africa.[15] There is a vast literature highlighting this reliance in almost every other region in colonial Africa.[16]

---

11 Frederick Cooper, *Decolonization and African society. The labor question in French and British Africa* (Cambridge: Cambridge University Press, 1996): 55.

12 Austin, *Labour, land, and capital in Ghana: from slavery to free labour in Asante, 1807–1956*: 44.

13 Jean-Philippe Peemans, "Le rôle de l'état dans la mobilisation de la force de travail au Congo," *Contradictions*, no. 4 (1973): 117.

14 S.N., *Bulletin Officiel du Congo Belge* (Bruxelles: Hayez, Imprimeur des Académies Royales, 1910): 442–471.

15 This "cost-effective" argument is made by Sara Berry, "Hegemony on a shoestring: indirect rule and access to agricultural land," *Africa: Journal of the International African Institute* 62, no. 3 (1992): 329.

16 To give only a few examples: Ndobegang M. Mbapndah, "French colonial agricultural policy, African chiefs, and coffee growing in the Cameroun grassfields, 1920–1960," *International Journal of African Historical Studies* 27, no. 1 (1994): 43; Justin Willis, "'Men on the

In the colonial Kivu district, local chiefs enjoyed considerable authority, albeit with gradations.[17] The colonial government and the *colons agricoles* were well aware of this.[18] Because of continuing plantation labor demand and the role of chiefs as "suppliers," colonists were recommended to maintain good relationships with them, which they usually interpreted as a synonym for bribing them. The "normal" procedure for demanding plantation workers via chiefs was that a colonist – usually accompanied by a member of the local administration – asked for a certain number of people. The local chief then passed the command to the village heads, who subsequently ordered family heads to assemble the demanded quantity of labor.[19] However, in order to speed things up, colonists sometimes directed their demands immediately to lower-ranked notables.[20] By doing so, *colons* not only offended higher-ranked chiefs but also caused tension with the colonial administration, because the latter – convinced of its grip – lost control over the labor flow.

That chiefs were not always willing to "deliver" the requested labor is hardly a surprise. First of all, sending labor – particularly regular laborers (see next chapter) – to the plantations meant a loss of potential workers to complete *corvée* and/or other duties. Moreover, the social mobility of (regular) laborers could jeopardize the chief's authority.[21] This is why chiefs usually sent people living at the margins of the local communities (poor, orphans or people disliked by the chief). On the other hand, even at the end of World War II people

spot,' labor, and the colonial state in British East Africa: the Mombasa water supply, 1911–1917," *International Journal of African Historical Studies* 28, no. 1 (1995): 30; Andreas Eckert, "Comparing coffee production in Cameroon and Tanganyika, c.1900 to 1960s," in *The global coffee economy in Africa, Asia, and Latin America 1500–1989*, ed. William Gervase Clarence-Smith and Steven Topik (Cambridge; New York: Cambridge University Press, 2003): 290; and Emmanuel Tchumtchoua, "Caféiculture et pénurie de la main-d'œuvre au Sud-Cameroun sous régime du 'travail obligatoire' (1924–1945)," *Annales de la Faculté des Arts, Lettres et Sciences Humaines* 1, no. 11 (2010): 289.

17 Bishikwabo demonstrates that, in Kabare, some chiefs were certainly not keen on collaborating with the European administration but, on the contrary, overtly opposed colonial rule in trying to escape the degradation of their authority: see Chubaka Bishikwabo, "Deux chefs du Bushi sous le regime colonial: Kabare et Ngweshe (1912–1960)," *Etudes d'Histoire Africaine* VII (1975).

18 Bashizi, "Processus de domination socio-économique et marché du travail au Bushi (1920–45)": 17.

19 Sven Van Melkebeke, "Coerced coffee cultivation and rural agency: the plantation-economy of the Kivu (1918–1940)," in *On coerced labor: work and compulsion after chattel slavery*, ed. Marcel Van der Linden and Magaly Rodríguez García (Leiden, Boston: Brill, 2016): 195.

20 Bishikwabo, "Un aspect du colonat au Congo belge: le sort des travailleurs du Kivu (1900–1940)": 32.

21 Ibid: 38.

who were actually sent to the plantations experienced this kind of work as *corvée* labor.[22] However, in order to harmonize African and European interests some chiefs made agreements with colonists. In Rutshuru, for instance, it was not uncommon that:

> newly installed planters [...] are receiving help from the indigenous chief for six months. When they ask for it [labor], directly or via mediation of the territorial administrator. This help consists of delivering 25 or 50 day laborers and it stops automatically after six months, the time in which a colonist generally succeeds in establishing his provisional installation.[23]

At the other end of the spectrum, some chiefs rather preferred playing *cavalier seul*, which was disapproved of by the colonial administration. In Masisi in the 1930s, chief André Kalinda proved to be a constant thorn in the flesh of the local Belgian government. In 1934, the chief had sent laborers to some coffee plantations without even informing the administration. Even the district commissioner got involved, plainly stating that an intervention was required to teach Kalinda the proper way to deal with colonists: "We have to avoid that a chief gives the impression to particulars that the territorial administrator grants him 'every authority' in order to substitute for the administrator."[24] After World War II, the somewhat loose attitude of Kalinda vis-à-vis the *colons agricoles* began to work to his disadvantage. Rising demand for labor resulted in increasing pressure on this chief. Kalinda was not satisfied with this development and looked on colonists with increasing suspicion, because sending more labor to plantations meant fewer people at the disposal of the chief. Instead of frustrating the colonial administration, Kalinda now turned to the government in order to complain about colonists who were mistreating and insulting him. *Colons* lacking sufficient labor did not hesitate to spread the gossip – albeit unsuccessful – that he would be replaced by another chief if he did not obey their desiderata.[25] What this story demonstrates is that it was indeed hard, if not impossible, for the colonial state to control the actions of chiefs. Furthermore, the changing relations between local chiefs, colonists and

22 AAB, AIMO, MO agricole, Situation de la MO au Kivu, no. 1649/9236/10, Note sur le problème de la MO agricole dans le territoire de Kabare, éditée par M.C. Babilon, 19/3/1945.

23 Ibid, Inspections plantations européennes Rutshuru, no. 1653/13, Rapport d'ensemble sur la situation de la MO dans le territoire de Rutshuru, édité par Dubuisson (assistant du commissaire de district), 15/1/1938.

24 Ibid, RACB, Masisi Territoire, Rapport AIMO, 1934, no. 142; Commentaires du commissaire de district Kivu sur le rapport AIMO 1934, 24/1/1935.

25 Ibid, 1947, no. 143.

the colonial administration are also an indication that the state did not always back the wishes of colonists, even though the latter believed that this was exactly the *raison d'être* of the colonial state.[26]

The relationship between chiefs and subjects altered as well. People taking up employment without the consent of the chief or refusing to follow the chief's order to go to a plantation were often victims of reprisals, since both situations compromised the chief's authority. Consequently, deprivation of land or confiscation of cattle, for instance, were not uncommon. However, chiefs could compensate the loss of village labor in yet another way. In Katale (Rutshuru), laborers sometimes stayed for a few weeks on the plantation, after which they returned home to maintain their own crops. But as a colonist wrote in 1942, while the workers were back home, chiefs burdened them with *corvées*: not only those they had to do during their stay at home but also the *corvées* they were supposed to have done during the period they were working – even though escaping *corvée* labor was precisely a reason for people to engage in plantation labor in the first place.[27]

Local notables did not intervene in the mobilization only of male coffee labor. Women – young girls is more accurate – were also involved in the production process, especially during the harvest season, which lasted for about three months. These women were usually appointed by the chiefs. This kind of mobilization did not always go smoothly, as the following quote from a judicial report of 1943 – highlighting serious abuses of both local notables in Kabare and the coffee planter involved – suggests:

> He [the territorial administrator] has urged the notables to provide labor; every one of them had to procure a proportional contingent of the population they administer. The notables use their influence to convince the parents to send their girls to work. When this influence does not suffice, the notables make use of the services of their "Baganda" [...]. This is when the abuse begins; the "Baganda" are sent to the hamlets with the order to

26 Young, *The African colonial state in comparative perspective*: 119. There are other examples of local bureaucracies not backing Europeans (enough). In 1931, the SAAK complained about the lack of effort of the local administration in Kabare in trying to reverse the alleged idleness of the natives. According to the SAAK, this was the main reason that the firm had difficulties attracting local workers and that the firm was forced to recruit people in Ruanda-Urundi (AAB, AIMO, Recrutements Ruanda-Urundi, Recrutements pour le Kivu, no. 1603/9119, Lettre du président du CNKi au ministre de la colonie Rutten, 28/7/1931).

27 Ibid, MO agricole, Doléances colons de Rutshuru, no. 1653/6, Lettre du colon Mr de Menten de Horne au Noirot (gouverneur du province de Costermansville), 30/5/1942.

> "escort" a certain contingent of pickers to work. As volunteers are scarce and the "Muganda" [singular of Baganda] is or thinks he is supported, he beats, steals, arrests in order to force the parents to send their girls to work. [...] We [the judicial inspectors] observe that some girls are working with de la Kethulle for three years and sometimes for six years. When they are absent or are not present for the [morning] call, the "Baganda" are sent once again to the parents and this how these temporary female laborers are becoming moderate slaves. [...] We possess a whole series of accusations of girls and their parents, and these accusations are always the same: beating of girls or their parents, stealing of chickens or beer or illegal remunerations, or, eventually, arbitrary imprisonment of the parents until they agree to send their girls to work.[28]

1.1.3 Administrative Intervention

Chiefs, planters and the colonial administration very often had conflicting interests. As the then governor of the Oriental Province Moeller stressed in 1930: "for the chief, the indigenous is either his subject or the subject of the white."[29] This means that some chiefs were sometimes reluctant to send the number of laborers requested, or any laborers at all, especially regular workers (see next chapter for the diverse plantation labor categories), because this meant a loss of customary labor and control over these people. People could also refuse to enter wage labor – local economies usually were more vibrant – by deserting or migrating (see Chapter 6). In these situations local territorial administrators intervened directly, accompanied by the police or not, by "escorting" people (back) to the plantations. Even though direct state intervention in order to recruit people for private enterprises was officially prohibited by the Colonial Charter of 1908,[30] in some situations local administrations continued to "help" private firms to a greater or lesser extent. Recruitment of labor by the state for private purposes was also common in other colonies, but in the Belgian Congo administrators were sometimes actively encouraged by higher-ranked officials

28 Ibid, Dossiers individuels des plantations, no. 1655/9244, Extraits du rapport juridique "affaire de la Kethulle," 10/5/1943. In Bushi, Baganda were right-hand men of notables, although no notable themselves.

29 Jean-Luc Vellut, "Enquête sur la main-d'oeuvre au Kivu (1930)," *Enquêtes et documents d'histoire africaine* 3 (1978): 34. This is a published extract of a letter sent by Moeller de Laddersous on 3/21/1930.

30 Direct state recruitment of labor for public works (road building, for instance) has even been legalized since 1908 (Peemans, "Le rôle de l'état dans la mobilisation de la force de travail au Congo": 123).

to mobilize workers for mines and plantations.[31] In the Kivu district the "support" of the administration lasted up until the end of World War II. In 1931, direct governmental intervention was even legitimized by the Commission pour la Protection des Indigènes by referring to the backwardness of some regions – especially those only recently incorporated, such as the Kivu.[32]

Referring to colonial Africa in general, Frederick Cooper stresses that the common silence in the official records concerning recruitment by the state actually "speaks more loudly."[33] Silence, however, is something that was not present in the sources I consulted. There is ample evidence that, until the end of World War II, administrators intervened to provide plantations with workers. Nevertheless, agents' maneuvering space also had limitations. In a 1946 letter, the governor of the Costermansville Province speaks openly about the role of the state in recruiting workers in Kabare, but also recognizes that the administration has not done enough to create material needs:

> These primitive bashi do not feel the urge to go to work, we have not created needs for them. But as labor for the concessions is required, we have more or less constrained the indigenous to engage. Then, during the war, there was successively civil mobilization, then requisition. In the eyes of the indigenous, it is always the same system that continues: constraint labor.[34]

With this quote the governor refers not only to forced labor on plantations but also to forced food cultivation, both to support war efforts. During World War II, parts of the coffee plantations in the Kivu were placed under sequester, whereas agrarian labor requisition was important especially for quinine plantations.[35] Moreover, the war decree of July 28, 1942, obliged people to cultivate

31 Julia Seibert, "More continuity than change? New forms of unfree labor in the Belgian Congo, 1908–1930," in *Humanitarian intervention and changing labor relations. The long-term consequences of the abolition of the slave trade*, ed. Marcel Van der Linden (Leiden; Boston: Brill, 2011): 381.

32 Léon Guébels, *Relation complète des travaux de la Commission Permanente pour la Protection des Indigènes, 1911–1951* (Gembloux: Duclot, 1951): 425.

33 Frederick Cooper, "Conditions analogous to slavery: imperialism and free labor ideology in Africa," in *Beyond slavery: explorations of race, labor, and citizenship in postemancipation societies*, ed. Frederick Cooper, Thomas C. Holt and Rebecca J. Scott (Chapel Hill; London: The University of North Carolina Press, 2000): 135.

34 AAB, AIMO, MO agricole, Situation de la MO au Kivu, no. 1649/9236/10, Lettre du gouverneur de Costermansville Lardinois à Pierre Ryckmans, 19/12/1946.

35 For more information on Belgian Africa in World War II: H.A.A. Cornelis, "Belgisch Congo en Ruanda-Urundi tijdens de Tweede Wereldoorlog. De economische en financiële

food crops destined for Europeans.[36] For example, in Kabare people were forced to cultivate 20 ares of vegetables or 10 ares of wheat.[37]

Direct state intervention was not limited only to "simply" recruiting labor but also involved redistributing it, as happened in Rutshuru in the 1930s, for instance. The local administration recruited temporary workers and sent them to the most distinguished employers in the territory. Once every fifteen days these temporary workers were renewed, and this kind of recruitment "[took] the form of a payed *corvée*."[38] Because, as a result, people were migrating on a massive scale to Masisi in particular, the administration pushed the boundaries of this system and abandoned it in the early 1940s.[39]

That direct recruitment had its limits was also clear to labor inspectors in the 1930s. A report written in 1938 by inspector Cayen stressed that state intervention in the Kivu district had destroyed the mechanism in the sense that wages had not risen (wages indeed were quite stable during the 1930s; see next chapter), which would, according to the inspector, have eased the demand for administrative interference. On the contrary, more administrative pressure had been necessary to fulfill the rising demand for labor in general and, the inspector admitted, "nowadays, we are shattered, we have reached a limit we cannot cross without committing suicide."[40] The inspector refers to burdened villages with a good deal of the HAV at work, which in turn compromised village life.

Encouraging and legitimizing administrative intervention does not mean that local European agents had unlimited freedom. In 1938, for instance, the commissioner of the Kivu district suspended the assistant territorial administrator of Rutshuru for four days because he repeatedly exceeded the limits of this jurisdiction, which even agitated other agents.[41] The agent in question, Corbisier, coerced people not only morally but physically as well. Often by using brutal language, the agent made clear to potential workers that plantations

situatie," in *Le Congo belge durant la Seconde Guerre Mondiale* (Bruxelles: Académie Royale des Sciences d'Outre-Mer, 1983).

36 This is similar to other African colonies where an increase in forced labor (legitimized as war effort) has been demonstrated (Cooper, *Africa since 1940: the past of the present*: 35–36).

37 AAB, RACB, Kabare Territoire, Rapport AIMO, 1942, no. 99.

38 Ibid, Rutshuru Territoire, Rapport AIMO, 1933, no. 163.

39 Ibid, 1941, no. 163; Commentaires du commissaire de district Kivu sur le rapport AIMO 1941, 11/2/1942.

40 Ibid, AIMO, Recrutements MO Kivu, Instructions, no. 1647/9226/1, Le problème de la MO au Congo. La situation de 1934 à 1938 par H. Cayen, 10/12/1938.

41 Ibid, MO agricole, Dossier Corbisier, no. 1653/5, Lettre de J. Noirot au gouverneur général, 9/6/1938.

workers lived more happily than people who preferred the depressed village life. The report sent to the General Governor also mentions "the military way of escorting the workers" to plantations situated in Kagara. This shows that local administrators' behavior was not unrestricted. Moreover, the sources I consulted refer to direct state interventions in order to recruit people for the plantations, but this might only be the tip of the iceberg and excessive behavior by colonial agents might have been more prominent than sources hint at. On the other hand, as colonial states were rather skeletal and unable to control and/or direct everything, interventions in favor of plantations might have been reserved for only a few fortunate ones.

1.1.4 Taxation and Repurchasing Customary Duties

In order to make people engage in wage labor, colonial states could intervene directly by forcing Africans, which had limitations for the colonial system itself but also for nearly everyone involved, as shown above. Moreover, people could try to escape by fleeing, migrating or deserting (see Chapter 6). Furthermore, engaging in wage labor requires a need to earn a wage, and this was usually lacking in early colonial African societies. In order to solve this absence, bureaucracies in Africa created tax systems – at first in kind, followed by monetarized taxes. This indirect administrative intervention to push people into wage labor, linked to colonial state formation processes, has already been studied at length. Most recent studies find in common that tax-raising depended on local conditions and that, consequently, taxes not only varied between colonies but also within colonies.[42] In this chapter, I focus on head taxes in order to reveal the localized nature of tax-raising in eastern Congo and western Rwanda. Many scholars consider the imposition of a head tax system as vital to the working of the colonial state.[43] However, recently Van Waijenburg has claimed that the role of taxes in the form of *corvées* and/or tributes in early colonial states has been largely ignored.[44] Hence, in this section (and the comparable mandate section below), I emphasize more how colonizers tried to commodify and liberalize customary labor (*corvées* toward and tributes to chiefs) for the

---

42 See especially: Ewout Frankema and Marlous van Waijenburg, "Metropolitan blueprints of colonial taxation? Lessons from fiscal capacity building in British and French Africa, c.1880–1940," *Journal of African History* 55, no. 3 (2014): 388. See also: Leigh Gardner, *Taxing colonial Africa. The political economy of British imperialism* (Oxford: Oxford University Press, 2012), for a thorough focus on British Africa.

43 Richard Reid, *A history of modern Africa: 1800 to the present* (Malden: Wiley-Blackwell, 2012 [2009]); Young, *The African colonial state in comparative perspective*.

44 Marlous Van Waijenburg, "Financing the African colonial state: the revenue imperative and forced labor," *Journal of Economic History* 78, no. 1 (2018).

plantations (or the market economy in general), an aspect that also has been overlooked in most studies.

Throughout the colonial period, tax levels were the highest in Kabare, which indicates the concentration of plantations in this territory. The annual head tax was 28.5 Francs, against 27,5 Francs in Rutshuru in 1932.[45] At the end of World War II, taxes had increased to reach the level of 50 Francs in Kabare. In Ruthuru, Africans had to pay 36 Francs annually to the state, and in Masisi the level was set at 46 Francs.[46] The gap between the latter territories can be explained by the colonial state's need for revenue in order to finance the recently created Gishari chieftaincy. A major rise in tax levels happened after the war. Only one decade after it ended, tax levels had doubled or nearly doubled in all territories. In Kabare the head tax was 94 Francs, in Masisi 83 Francs and in Rutshuru 89 Francs.[47] Similarly to in other African colonies, this steep increase was a result not only of the greater governmental capacity to collect taxes but also of shifts in policy, with a greater focus on "development" and the financing of developmental programs (here, the ten-year plan initiated in 1949).[48]

Belgian colonial practices with reference to *corvées* mark an exception in colonial Africa. In 1910, the colonial administration established the rights of chiefs, declaring that they had to "rule in the measure and the way fixed by native customs, as long as it is not contrary to either universal public order, or legislative acts aimed at substituting other rules to customs."[49] While by the end of the 1920s such *corvées* were not officially advertised or no longer corresponded to a legal category in other colonies, in Belgian Africa the government decided to define *corvées* by fixing the amount of days chiefs could call upon customary labor to two, or 16 hours per month. Only in exceptional circumstances could this limit be exceeded.[50]

---

45 AAB, RACB, Kabare Territoire, Rapport AIMO, 1932, no. 99 and ibid, Rutshuru Territoire, no. 163.

46 Ibid, Kabare Territoire, 1943; Rutshuru Terriorie, 1943 and Masisi Territoire, 1943, no. 143.

47 Ibid, Kabare, 1953; Rutshuru, 1953; and Masisi 1953.

48 Frankema and van Waijenburg, "Metropolitan blueprints of colonial taxation? Lessons from fiscal capacity building in British and French Africa, c.1880–1940": 385 and 387 (footnote 52).

49 Quoted in: Benoît Henriet, "'Elusive natives': escaping colonial control in the Leverville oil palm concession, Belgian Congo, 1923–1941," *Canadian Journal of African Studies* 49, no. 2 (2015): 344 (original: S.N., *Bulletin Officiel du Congo Belge*: 463).

50 S.N., *Bulletin Officiel du Congo Belge*: 469. It has been demonstrated that in neighboring British colonies, *mulusa* labor *corvées* were still tolerated in 1928 but lacked legal foundation (see for instance: Henry S. Meebelo, *Reaction to colonialism: a prelude to the politics of independence in Northern Zambia, 1893–1939* (Manchester: Manchester University Press, 1971)).

The commodifying of tributes and *corvées* by the colonial administration was particularly intended to promote regular labor. The repurchasing of *corvées* was regulated on a local level and sometimes differed from one *chefferie* to another. This highlights not only local differences in labor mobilization, but also differences in chiefs' attitude toward the top-down imposed liberalization of a number of their subjects, and consequently the corrosion of their authority. In Rutshuru, redemption of *corvées* was first mentioned in the sources in the early 1930s, which is early compared with the other Congolese territories bordering Lake Kivu. In 1933, the territorial agent complained about the fact that, although in theory the *corvées coutumières* were set at twenty-nine days per year, in practice notables forced people to perform much more work than legally allowed. A good deal of the population of Rutshuru was already engaged in wage labor on plantations. Consequently, people who remained in the villages were burdened with double customary duties. Despite this, the number of days for performing customary duties was reduced to seven a year, while the local administration made sure that tributes and remaining *corvées* could be repurchased. Officially this seemingly bizarre measure was explained by the urge to stimulate people to produce more food.[51] However, there is a clear connection to the imposition of obligatory coffee cultivation, also starting in 1933 (*supra*). The aim of partly freeing coffee smallholders from *corvées* and providing them with an extra cash income incentive makes the allegedly illogical measure more logical. This connection was even more visible in the mandate (see *infra*).

In Kabare and Masisi, the redemption of *corvées* seemed to have been placed on the local administration's agenda only at the end of World War II, which unsurprisingly coincides with the rise of spontaneous engagements in those territories. In Kabare, tensions between *colons* and *chefs* initiated the discussion concerning tributes and *corvées*. The majority of the coffee labor force in this territory came from neighboring villages, offering workers the possibility to return home each day and continue at least part of their customary way of life. This did not really satisfy some chiefs; according to the territorial administration:

> agricultural workers [...] continue to live on customary land, they cultivate, or their wives cultivate, plots, they have cattle and consequently grass land, so they continue to live at the expense of customary traditions [*manger au ratelier coutumier*]; on the other hand we notice that those laborers are no longer available to customary *corvées* of any kind.[52]

---

51 AAB, RACB, Rutshuru Territoire, Rapport AIMO, 1933, no. 163.

52 Ibid, Kabare Territoire, Rapport AIMO, 1947, no. 99.

The solution the territorial administrator proposed was to introduce the possibility of repurchasing *corvées* and tributes, but this was easier said than done. Two years after the idea was launched, most chiefs still disagreed, not with redeeming duties as such but with the price to be paid in return. Only the chief of Ngweshe agreed with the amount. In the following years, redemption gradually spread to other *chefferies*, but it was not until 1953 that *corvées* and tributes could be fully repurchased in the entire territory.[53]

The situation in Masisi differed somewhat from that of other regions bordering Lake Kivu due to the presence of Gishari. The annual administrative report of 1949 mentions that every HAV could redeem 14 Francs' worth of *corvées* per year in the Wanianga *chefferie*, 26 Francs in Bahunde and 36.5 Francs in Gishari. In Bahunde, *corvée* labor consisted of public works and cultivating the chief's land by men and women. Villages delivered laborers who were replaced every fifteen days until the prescribed *corvées* were finished. In addition, people in Bahunde had to pay tribute in the form of beans, sorghum and banana beer.[54] That the repurchasing price for *corvées* was much higher in Gishari demonstrates the greater urge for labor and the government's hope of forcing people into plantation labor exactly by setting a high repurchase price. Moreover, in Gishari, emigrated Rwandan Tutsi notables also continued to impose "imported" *corvées* on their Hutu subjects.[55] Even though this issue is not mentioned any more after the report of the following year, chiefs in Masisi continued to impose *corvées* on their subjects as elsewhere at least until the mid-1950s, even if they were repurchased.

1.2 *It's All about the Numbers*

> [W]e cannot lay one finger on those 75%. Not we [colonists], nor the state. These 75% are kept in the village anyway where these blacks have to live almost exclusively off their [subsistence] plantations. They are forbidden to make money [...]. I myself was obliged to send away a number of blacks who were asking for employment. They do not understand. A lot of them then cross the border. [...] But, in the agrarian regions of the Kivu, keeping 75% of valid blacks or non-actives in the village is in my opinion illogical and inhuman. If recruitment was free, without limits, it would be a common good, to the advantage of everyone, whites and blacks. [...] In

53 Ibid, 1949 and 1953.

54 Viaene, "L'organisation politique des Bahunde": 25–26.

55 AAB, RACB, Masisi Territoire, Rapport AIMO, 1948, 1949 and 1950, no. 143. In Masisi, the possibility of redeeming *corvées* was initiated during World War II.

> Kivu, there are no industries yet, and there will not be a lot in this sector. [...] What will be the use of this population, these 75%? These blacks are simply kept in primitive conditions without resources.[56]

1.2.1 Crossing the Lines

One of the consequences of the CFS forced labor regime was the disturbing of demographic patterns in many Congolese villages. In order to avoid similar abuses, the colonial government installed in 1908, in close collaboration with comities created to deal with labor issues, puzzled out a recruitment maximum percentage system. From the mid-1920s onwards, a maximum of 5% of HAV of a native community could be mobilized for work at a distance (outside the territory of residence), another 5% for work no further than a two-day walk from the village, and 15% on the spot (within a 5-kilometer diameter around the village).[57] However, the very initiation of these percentages created a clash between economic and demographic interests. Despite the warning by the mid-1920s Labor Commission that exceeding these limits would disrupt local communities,[58] economic interests seem to have had the upper hand, because the introduced percentages were not seen as strict maxima but rather as guidelines adaptable to local conditions.[59] An obsession with numbers – or rather, how many people could be recruited while keeping up the appearance of a "civilized" colonial government – is not unique to the Belgian Congo. In British and French colonies alike, and at least until the mid-1930s, a focus on maximum percentages was present as well.[60] However, in the Belgian Congo the number issue continued until the end of the colonial period, although after World War II more attention was paid to labor conditions in general (see next chapter), as in other African colonies. Moreover, from the end of the 1930s only

56 Ibid, AI, MO et recrutement, Correspondance, no. 4379(111), "Quelques considérations sur la question de la MO agricole au Kivu," note éditée par un colon anonyme au Kivu, 14/10/1929.

57 Gudrun Van Pottelbergh, "Octave Louwers, 'Éminence grise' van het Belgisch koloniaal establishment. Achter de schermen van de koloniale politiek in de jaren 1920 en 1930," *Journal of Belgian History* 36, no. 3–4 (2006): 465.

58 S.N., "Rapport de la Commission pour l'étude du problème de la main-d'oeuvre au Congo belge (1924–1925)," in *Le problème de la main-d'oeuvre au Congo belge. Rapports (1) de la Commission pour l'étude du problème de la main-d'oeuvre au Congo belge (1924–1925); (2) du Comité consultatif de la main-d'oeuvre (1928)* (Bruxelles: Goemaere, 1928): 28.

59 AAB, Divers, Papiers Bertrand, no. 778/B/2/3, Rapport Général de Mr. le gouverneur Moeller, 21/3/1930.

60 Cooper, *Decolonization and African society. The labor question in French and British Africa*: 1.

one distinction remained: 15% mobilizable on the spot and 10% for work further than 5 kilometers from the residence village.

For the regions bordering Lake Kivu, the potential labor on the spot is of primordial importance to understanding the functioning of the plantation economy. Besides attempting to attract Rwandan migrants, coffee plantations recruited labor mainly in villages surrounding the estates or at least within the same territory, which resulted in serious transgressions of the recruitment restrictions and disturbances to village life. This was in part a consequence of the unsuccessful endeavor to mobilize Rwandan labor. In 1948 in Gishari, for instance, only 6% of HAV were at work. Hence, plantations had to seek labor elsewhere.[61] The fact that the limits were exceeded cannot be blamed on coffee plantations alone, as the percentages include *all* labor mobilizations (government, industry, commerce, etcetera). But given the importance of this sector in this area, the lion's share of labor mobilized in local villages was related to coffee. The most telling examples of excessive recruitment are to be found in Rutshuru. Already in 1933, about 30% of the HAV were employed on the spot in this territory.[62] With expanding colonization and given the distance between most plantations and local villages, things got even worse, especially in chiefdoms with a dense European segment. In a 1939 document, Colonel Bertrand – known in colonial circles for his outspoken criticism of labor policies – claimed that "in the Rutshuru territory, where the General Governor himself has declared that 52% of the men [HAV] are working on European plantations, certain chiefdoms are drained to 80%."[63] Bertrand is referring to Kisigari and, foremost, Bukumu, leaving the territorial agent to conclude that the situation was terrible and even that in these areas "customary life is destroyed or disappearing completely." Moreover, the Belgian agent was well aware of the ramifications on village level. Many workers left their villages in order to squat, which resulted in depopulation. This in turn left local notables in despair, because almost no people – except for the elite, the elderly, weak and sick, and women and children – remained to do *corvée* labor. Moreover, because of the lack of people in the villages, food production could not keep up with the demand, causing rising food prices.[64] It is striking that after World War II and after the attempts by the colonial bureaucracy to attract Rwandans to work on plantations, the labor situation remained precarious. Labor demand overran supply.

61 AAB, RACB, Masisi Territoire, Rapport AIMO, 1948, no. 143.

62 Ibid, Rutshuru Territoire, Rapport AIMO, 1933, no. 163.

63 Ibid, AIMO, MO: intervention administrative, Intervention au Kivu, no. 1708/9426, Extrait d'une session de la sous-commission de MO de la Province de Costermansville, 14/7/1939.

64 Ibid, RACB, Rutshuru Territoire, Rapport AIMO, 1937, no. 163.

For instance, in 1945 about 60% of HAV were at work, while in 1953 approximately 70% were working – or almost three times the recommended 25%.[65] Even more striking is that the local government in Rutshuru waited until after World War II to react, and to do even the minimum to try to solve this obvious over-recruitment (*infra*).

It would be tempting to assume that in more densely populated Kabare, labor demand and supply would be more harmonious. However, in this territory in particular, villages surrounding plantations were heavily solicited for labor.[66] The relative proximity of plantations also had an advantage in the sense that workers could return home each day and thus that village/family life was less disturbed. On the other hand, for employers the possibility of mobilizing workers locally reduced labor costs. In 1933, the 15% on-the-spot limit was already exceeded.[67] With expanding colonization, a similar evolution occurred in Kabare as in the other territories bordering the lake. At the end of World War II, in some villages 35% or more of HAV were working in the vicinity of their homestead.[68] Even more astonishing are the numbers for 1953. According to the annual report, Kabare housed 63374 HAV. Of these, 28357 (15066 agricultural workers) or 44.7% were at work. About 85% of these HAV were laboring on the spot and returned home each night or, for those who worked in Bukavu, each week.[69] Not only do these figures underscore the economic expansion of Kabare and in particular the area around Bukavu in the colonial period. The consistent and growing appeal to local labor also stresses the existence and importance of a relatively large labor reservoir.[70]

The above figures again require caution. It is not always clear whether percentages mentioned in the sources refer only to regular or to regular *and* temporary workers. Either way, if temporary laborers are included, percentages only represent a snapshot in time – likely the number of workers at the time the report was edited. However, as coffee plantations employed a lot of temporary workers, certain percentages might under- or overestimate the actual coffee labor force. Consequently, if temporary workers are not included, percentages clearly underestimate the coffee labor size. Moreover, in Kabare (and

65 Ibid, 1945 and 1953.

66 Bashizi, "Processus de domination socio-économique et marché du travail au Bushi (1920–45)": 19.

67 AAB, RACB, Kabare Territoire, Rapport AIMO, 1933, no. 99.

68 Ibid, 1944.

69 Ibid, 1953.

70 Northrup, *Beyond the bend in the river: African labor in Eastern Zaire 1865–1940*: 9. Northrup not only considers the regions bordering Lake Kivu as an important labor reservoir but for him the entire eastern Congo must be seen as "the colony's major labor pool."

Shangugu) a so-called *remplacement* system existed in which temporary and regular laborers were often replaced by other Africans (see next chapter). It was difficult, if not impossible, to count such replacers, and therefore they are not included in the figures. Finally, women and children are definitely not included in the percentages either, as they only refer to HAV. However, particularly during harvest season, many women and children also worked in the coffee sector. They should be included as well in order to get a better understanding of the actual impact on local life.

1.2.2 Restriction on Mobilizations

The above lines demonstrate that the development of a plantation sector affected regions bordering Lake Kivu with sometimes excessive over-recruitment. Local bureaucracies were well aware of this. As argued above, local representatives even helped to mobilize labor. However, when things went too far, the provincial government intervened. It restricted labor mobilization by not delivering recruitment permits to firms and/or colonists. According to a provincial directive, from 1939 onwards spontaneous engagements were no longer prohibited, even when the 25% limit was exceeded.[71] Territorial bureaucracies still had the right to adjust this provincial measure to local conditions and thus indeed prohibit free entries when deemed necessary. This resulted in contradictory situations, where a colonizer wanted people to engage in wage labor while on the other hand, they were limited in doing so. Furthermore, the involvement of the administration very often, if not always, came too late, as village life was already disrupted. Moreover, the question is whether such restrictions were effective on the ground. As governmental control was difficult, *colons* and chiefs might have "exchanged" workers mutually, despite the absence of permits.

In Kabare and Masisi, interdictions were proclaimed at the end of the 1930s, except for engagements on the spot and spontaneous engagements.[72] Partly as a consequence of war efforts and the end of mine recruitment restrictions (*infra*), the territorial agent of Kabare wanted to go one step further and, in 1946, reinstalled the prohibition of spontaneous recruitment in regions where 50% or more HAV were already at work.[73] His proposition was not completely rejected because from 1951 onwards, in regions where 50% of HAV were already engaged, recruitment was prohibited – except for free entries – even for labor

71 AAB, RACB, Kivu Province, Conseil de Province, 1939, no. 38(3).

72 Ibid, Kabare Territoire, Rapport AIMO, 1939, n°99 and ibid, Masisi Territoire, 1938, no. 142.

73 Ibid, Kabare Territoire, 1946, no. 99.

on the spot.[74] This implies that, for example, a coffee plantation wanting to recruit a certain number of laborers was blocked when a permit was refused on the basis of over-recruitment. Officially this plantation would have to wait until people engaged spontaneously or attract labors unofficially – for instance without a contract. In Masisi, on the other hand, spontaneous engagements were prohibited effectively after World War II. During the war, the 25% limit had to be respected, except in war industries (quinine plantations). The latter were permitted by the territorial bureaucracy to recruit even in villages where the 25% limit was already exceeded.[75] The delicate demographic situation in this territory not only urged the local administration to set up a *chefferie* destined for Rwandans in order to reconcile labor demand and supply. Since this attempt was rather unsuccessful, the government also even had to prohibit spontaneous recruitment in regions where 70% of HAV were working, and moreover in the whole Wanianga chiefdom from 1948 at least until 1954 (last available annual report).[76]

Further to the north of Lake Kivu, yet another pattern stands out. Similarly to in Masisi, recruitment and even spontaneous engagements were also prohibited in some parts of Rutshuru (Bukumu, for instance) from 1943 onwards.[77] Partly as a consequence of the rapid development of Goma and surroundings after World War II,[78] the disequilibrium between labor demand and supply only increased. Consequently, in 1949, the local government decided to forbid *all* recruitment in the entire territory. From then on, spontaneous engagements were only allowed where whole families were concerned.[79] This was clearly an attempt by the government to stabilize labor and unite productive and reproductive capacities. In a territory where squatting was an important way of mobilizing labor, this was not an illogical decision. Despite the success of this decision, labor demand remained massive. Consequently, colonists were advised to recruit in the neighboring Lubero territory, where no restrictions were in force, in order to attract more workers. However, relocating a problem is usually not a good decision, and from 1954 onwards recruitment in

74 Ibid, 1951.

75 Ibid, Masisi Territoire, 1942, no. 143.

76 Ibid, 1948. Wanianga chiefdom, with an important mining sector which also contributed to the high demand for labor, was located in western Masisi, although eastern Masisi was more significant as plantation region.

77 Ibid, Rutshuru Territoire, Rapport AIMO, 1943, no. 163; Commentaires du commissaire de district Kivu sur le rapport AIMO 1943, 7/2/1944.

78 Mathys, "People on the move. Frontiers, borders, mobility and history in the Lake Kivu region 19th–20th century": 230.

79 AAB, RACB, Rutshuru Territoire, Rapport AIMO, 1949, no. 163.

Lubero became increasingly difficult. Mining firms succeeded in attracting laborers more easily by paying higher wages, which, in turn, left a good deal of *colons* in Rutshuru with a labor shortfall.[80]

1.3 *Plantations versus Mines*

The plantation sector in eastern Congo was unable to survive without the interference of the administration. The restrictions on smallholder cultivation in many parts of the district is not the only factor that supports this argument. By creating *passeports de mutation*, the colonial government also tried to limit rural people's mobility, in particular to the expanding urbanized centers of Goma and Bukavu.[81] Higher wages, the possibility of becoming a skilled laborer, escaping deteriorating rural conditions, etcetera were possible incentives for people to exit rural areas. Besides these governmental attempts, a "battle for laborers" began in the mid-1930s between the agricultural sector and the mining industry (MGL: Compagnie Minière des Grands Lacs), especially in Kabare.[82] The battle lasted until the end of World War II, when it was settled in favor of the plantations, despite the much higher returns on investment in the mining sector.[83] That the administration intervened more actively in the agricultural than in, for instance, the mining sector is well known. However, in other parts of the Belgian Congo this interference usually involved granting credit/loans, fixing prices, enforcing obligatory cultivation, allocating land, etcetera.[84] In the Kivu, administrative involvement went even further.

The first signs of tension between plantations and mines appeared in 1935. Planters asked the administration for help, but the question was initially dismissed:

80 Ibid, 1954.

81 Attempts by colonial administrations to restrict people moving from the countryside toward cities were common throughout colonial Africa (see: Andrew Burton, *African underclass: urbanisation, crime and colonial order in Dar Es Salaam* (London: James Currey, 2005) for a comparative overview).

82 The MGL (created in 1923) was subdivided into northern, central and southern divisions. In this context, the latter is important and was active in Kabare. The other two mainly operated in Maniema (Bashizi, "Processus de domination socio-économique et marché du travail au Bushi (1920–45)": 7). Mining industry developed in Masisi as well, but in this territory there was a relative clear distinction between the eastern rural part and the western industrial part. Consequently, a "battle for labor" was less present. Sources do not mention any kind of competition in Masisi, as opposed to Kabare.

83 Guy Vanthemsche, *Congo. De impact van de kolonie op België* (Tielt: Lannoo, 2007): 174.

84 Jean-Luc Vellut, "Hégémonies en construction: articulations entre Etat et Entreprises dans le bloc colonial Belge (1908–1960)," *Canadian Journal of African Studies* 16, no. 2 (1982): 319.

> Planters believed they saw a danger in the recruitment of the MGL in the region of Ngweshe. This is untrue. Currently, planters are mobilizing three to four times more labor than necessary. On the contrary, recruitment by the MGL has nothing but a good influence on the labor destined for the plantations: work in the mines is an excellent training, and an improvement of the physical condition of the men they will engage.[85]

Moreover, Africans themselves preferred entering the mining sector, albeit not because of good working conditions. For instance, before World War II, workers were shaved when they left the mines in order to check whether they had stolen minerals.[86] The main reasons that people entered the mining sector were, according to Pierre Ryckmans, higher wages and, above all, the fact that mine workers received food, which was usually not the case in the plantation sector.[87] However, *colons agricoles* received help from an unexpected source. Labor inspector Cayen argued that the mining sector was more substantial, and that *petits colons* in particular were unable to support huge recruitment expenses. For the latter, labor potential "is synonymous with availabilities in the direct neighborhood."[88] What Cayen essentially proposed was that mines should be restricted from recruiting laborers in the vicinity of plantations. Apparently, the territorial, district and provincial governments accepted this argument.

In 1937, the first prudent steps were taken by the territorial government of Kabare: a restriction of mine recruitment in certain regions. That way, both the MGL and the CNKi were still able to find enough laborers, but "without provoking controversies and frictions with the numerous European concessions in the territory."[89] However, the mining sector reacted, and conflicts with colonists happened frequently. District commissioner Sand repeated once again that mines were only authorized to recruit in certain zones away from plantation areas.[90] However, as can be expected, these restrictions did not hold back the mines, and tensions with planters continued. Only one year after the call

85 AAB, RACB, Kivu Province, Conseil de Province, 1936, no. 37(7).

86 Bishikwabo, "Un aspect du colonat au Congo belge: le sort des travailleurs du Kivu (1900–1940)": 32.

87 AAB, AIMO, MO agricole, Dossier Unaki, no. 1653/10, Lettre de Pierre Ryckmans au ministre de la colonie, 27/12/1939.

88 Ibid, Recrutements MO Kivu, Instructions, no. 1647/9226/1, Le problème de la MO au Congo. La situation de 1934 à 1938 par H. Cayen, 10/12/1938.

89 Ibid, RACB, Kabare Territoire, Rapport AIMO, 1937, no. 99; Commentaires du commissaire de district Kivu sur le rapport AIMO 1937, 28/1/1938.

90 Ibid, 1938; Commentaires du commissaire sur le rapport 1938, 20/2/1939.

by the district commissioner, even the provincial council intervened. In a letter from governor Noirot to the General Governor, it is plainly detailed that the council aims to prohibit mine recruitment in colonization areas, or in other words "to give priority to the needs of agrarian enterprises."[91] Starting from the following year (1939), the provincial governor effectively proclaimed that in the Kabare territory, mine companies were forbidden to recruit in the proximity of plantations. The only exceptions were spontaneous engagements and the chieftaincies of Ngweshe and Nyangezi. That way, "colonists have every facility to recruit on the spot the labor required," according to territorial agent Willaert.[92]

The least that can be said is that the MGL in particular did not agree with such a settlement. In the same year that the decree was proclaimed, furious criticism was vented in the provincial council:

> Mr Callens [the manager of MGL] claims the right of the natives to take up employment wherever they please. He considers it unjustifiable to mobilize for the benefit of the colonists a whole population working only a few days per year [...], and so to speak keep them in serfdom, that is, wanting to prevent a whole population from working and creating resources, only to keep them available to a few planters. Moreover, the MGL employs barely 5% of the people in Kabare and believes it has the right to use more, especially because the MGL improves their skills and, after their contract has expired, sends them back to their village more vigorous, better fed and more healthy then when they left.[93]

Apart from these remarks, one should wonder whether the mining sector actually obeyed the law, foremost because the proclaimed provincial decree is rather fluid, as it is not specified what "proximity" means exactly. Secondly, even when for the antagonists everything was clear, control by the government still remained difficult. Thirdly, it is unclear whether it was the critics of the MGL or rather the confronting experiences of World War II, or both, that influenced the provincial administration. Nevertheless, already in 1946, prohibitions on mine recruitment were withdrawn, except for in a few localities where labor demand was very high.[94] However, sources do not make any reference to

91 Ibid, AIMO, Recrutements Ruanda-Urundi, Inspections MO, no. 2000, Lettre de gouverneur de Province de Costermansville au gouverneur général, 15/4/1938.

92 Ibid, RACB, Kabare Territoire, Rapport AIMO, 1940, no. 99.

93 Ibid, Kivu Province, Conseil de Province, 1939, no. 38(3).

94 Ibid, Kabare Territoire, Rapport AIMO, 1946, no. 99.

possible restrictions any more from 1947 onwards. Clearly the labor market had become more liberal, forcing planters to improve wages and working conditions, although they did not do so without discussion and frequent disagreement with the government.

2 Coffee Labor in the Mandate

As already demonstrated several times in the course of this book, in the mandate, smallholder cultivation was predominant. In some regions, however (Shangugu in particular), a minor plantation economy developed as well. The aim of this section is to analyze labor mobilization in both segments, although most attention will be given to the dominant production system. Previous chapters also showed that in the colonial Kivu, smallholder coffee cultivation was restricted in many ways, but was not absent. However, the issue here is that the sources I consulted are silent on everything relating to labor (mobilization, income, etcetera). As a result, this and the following chapter lack information concerning coffee smallholdings in the Congolese regions bordering Lake Kivu. Supposedly, small cultivators depended on family labor (women and children), as many other coffee smallholders did in other parts of the world.[95] The difference, however, was that from the 1930s, Congolese smallholders were not allowed to recruit fellow Africans, unlike smallholders in Ruanda-Urundi (*infra*).[96] Chiefs as smallholders likely made use of customary ways to mobilize labor, as did chiefs in the mandate (as I will argue in the following lines).

2.1 *Customary Labor Mobilization and "Chiefly" Cultivation*

In the previous chapter, I alluded to the birth of *uburetwa* in the second half of the nineteenth century, a patron–client tie relating directly to both land and labor. As with customary land systems, there were diverse ways of mobilizing labor, but this specific form is important to understanding the development of the coffee sector in the mandate. In central Rwanda, poor people had to deliver unpaid labor to chiefs two out of every four days of the Rwandan week from about 1870.[97] Similar to the expansion of land tenure systems, exactions of

95 Topik and Clarence-Smith, "Conclusion: new propositions and a research agenda": 394–395.

96 Jewsiewicki, "The great depression and the making of the colonial economic system in the Belgian Congo": 162.

97 Vansina, *Antecedents to modern Rwanda. The Nyiginya kingdom*: 134.

labor services by chiefs expanded under Rwabugiri, but on the eve of the European arrival uniformity was still lacking.[98] Moreover, *uburetwa* was imposed on Hutu lineages, but not all Hutu were forced to perform these services. Hutu able to enter a *ubuhake* (cattle) clientship escaped the often heavy burdening and humiliating *uburetwa*.[99] Alongside unpaid labor, there was also a precolonial system of day workers. According to Vidal, about half of the rural population performed day labor at the start of the twentieth century, because otherwise they would not be able to survive due to lack of land, the failure of harvests and/or plots that were too small to produce even at a subsistence level. Both men and women usually worked half a day, performing agrarian tasks for both Tutsi and Hutu. In return they received a wage consisting of, for example, beans and/or sorghum.[100] Vidal claims that the introduction of *uburetwa* made many poor people decide to enter day labor, because *uburetwa* was oppressive and did not leave space to cultivate food crops, for example.[101] Indeed, after the arrival of the Germans, *uburetwa* evolved to a more exploitative system:

> *Ubureetwa* was a residual category for the powerless. It is difficult to exaggerate the exploitative character of *ubureetwa*. The services performed were usually of the most menial kind – collecting and drying firewood for the use of the hill chief's household, serving as night watchman [in the chief's hut], fetching water, cultivating the hill chief's fields. Hutu were not only expected to perform such services without pay, but were often subjected to mistreatment as well.[102]

That chiefs were empowered during the German period is reflected not only in a greater reliance on Tutsi elites. The fact that chiefs initiated a new layer of mostly Hutu – called *ibirongozi* or *bamotsa* – underlines their increased capabilities. This new layer was responsible for duties previously accomplished by lineage heads, thereby further eroding the power of lineages. These *ibirongozi* were helpers of the chief without "official" status and had to perform tasks such as collecting taxes, assuring that people followed orders and seizing

98 Newbury, "*Ubureetwa* and *Thangata*: catalysts to peasant political consciousness in Rwanda and Malawi": 100–101.

99 Ibid.

100 Claudine Vidal, "Economie de la société féodale rwandaise," *Cahiers d'Etudes Africaines* 14, no. 53 (1974): 62–64.

101 Ibid: 67.

102 Newbury, *The cohesion of oppression. Clientship and ethnicity in Rwanda, 1860–1960*: 141.

labor.[103] The Belgian takeover did not improve the rural population's fate. Even though Belgium initially installed Hutu chiefs in some areas (northwestern Rwanda, for instance),[104] it was the expansion of *uburetwa* to all present-day Rwandan regions and the imposition of it on all Hutu HAV instead of lineages that formed the major changes.[105] However, the expansion encountered resentment, especially in regions not yet fully incorporated into the precolonial Nyiginya Kingdom, such as western Rwanda.[106] Similarly to land tenure, the early Belgian mandate bureaucracy clearly tried to individualize and standardize *uburetwa*. Nevertheless, there seems to have been some sort of regional differentiation. For instance, people in Kinyaga (Shangugu) referred to unpaid labor for chiefs as *uburetwa*, while in Bugoyi (Gisenyi) people called it *shiku* even though these were different labor forms, as the latter meant "obligatory planting on communal fields." This probably reflects the later introduction of *uburetwa* in Bugoyi.[107]

The focus on *uburetwa* is necessary because this system of unpaid labor continued until the late 1950s, despite its official abolition and replacement with a monetary tax in 1949.[108] Other kind of tributes and *corvées* were increasingly commodified from the 1930s onwards (*infra*). Moreover, *uburetwa* was also essential in initiating smallholder coffee cultivation. In 1927, the Belgian mandate bureaucracy changed the amount of time *uburetwa* was allowed to take to one day per seven-day week, or 52 days annually. In 1933 this changed once again to 13 days (three for the chief and ten for the sub-chief) per year per HAV. It can hardly be a surprise that abuses were common and that Hutu often had to perform more days than regulated, or that even family members were forced to perform *uburetwa*.[109] The mandate administration tried to control this, but

---

103 Mathys, "People on the move. Frontiers, borders, mobility and history in the Lake Kivu region 19th–20th century": 235–236, and Newbury, "*Ubureetwa* and *Thangata*: catalysts to peasant political consciousness in Rwanda and Malawi": 102.

104 Vervust, "The limits of colonial symbolic power. Ethnicization and racialization in Rwanda 1890–1960": 154–155. In some cases, existing Hutu chiefs were not expelled, as, for instance, in Shangugu as late as the 1930s. In other cases, some Hutu chiefs were replaced by Tutsi even though the former were seen as "good rulers" by their subjects.

105 Johan Pottier, *Re-imagining Rwanda. Conflict, survival and disinformation in the late twentieth century* (Cambridge: Cambridge University Press, 2002): 184–185.

106 Dorsey, "Rwandan colonial economy, 1916–1941": 67.

107 Mathys, "People on the move. Frontiers, borders, mobility and history in the Lake Kivu region 19th–20th century": 239.

108 Kamola, "The global coffee economy and the production of genocide in Rwanda": 578, and Newbury, *The cohesion of oppression. Clientship and ethnicity in Rwanda, 1860–1960*: 146. It should be stressed that regular laborers were able to redeem *uburetwa* much earlier.

109 Kamola, "*Ubureetwa* and *Thangata*: catalysts to peasant political consciousness in Rwanda and Malawi": 103, and AAB, RARU, Shangugu Territoire, Rapport Général, 1928, 100(7).

control was often limited to sample surveys and the way control mechanisms were introduced was often naïve, as this example for Shangugu shows:

> to Tutsi we have given the following order that will be implemented from 1-1-1935 onwards in order to establish efficient control over the [Hutu] labor batutsi use: when a muhutu works one day for them [...] he will take along his identity booklet; 75% of the batutsi are literate and the others can procure a clerk. On the first blank page there will be noted, through the agency of the beneficiary, the date on which the day of labor has taken place [...]. That way, a simple glance in the identity booklet will allow us [territorial bureaucracy] to control the work done by the bahutu for the benefit of the batutsi; abuses will be curbed severely.[110]

In an attempt to somewhat gloss over its own naivety, the territorial government of Shangugu started to advise – yet not compel – chiefs and sub-chiefs to progressively remunerate labor from 1938 onwards, in particular when the thirteen days were exceeded.[111] On the other hand, there are examples of territorial administrations equally using *uburetwa* for their own benefit in the early 1920s. In a letter to the Resident of Rwanda, the royal commissioner in Brussels clearly stated that Belgian bureaucracies had no right to use unpaid labor. Coffee plots surrounding administrative posts had no other purpose than to teach people how to cultivate previously unknown crops and diffuse the seeds of these crops to the indigenous people in order to start their own fields.[112]

Whether some functionaries (ab)used *uburetwa* intentionally or not, by expanding and legalizing a customary labor system – which is quite exceptional compared with other African zones of production – the mandate government nonetheless had given chiefs a powerful tool with which to exploit subjects, which they gratefully used to enrich themselves during the start of obligatory coffee cultivation in the early 1930s (see Image 3).[113] However, initially, many

110 Ibid, 1934, 100(13).

111 Ibid, RWA, Conseils de Territoire et de Chefferie, Shangugu, RWA(72), Réunion plénière, 31/5/1938.

112 Ibid, AIMO(346), MO agricole, Lettre du commissaire royal au résident de Rwanda, 22/11/1923. However, as I argued in the first chapter, coffee was not unknown but its cultivation was until the colonial period.

113 Newbury, *The cohesion of oppression. Clientship and ethnicity in Rwanda, 1860–1960*: 142. In Burundi as well, chiefs became the main beneficiaries of coffee cultivation, despite the absence of *uburetwa* (Hubert Cochet and Barnabé Ndarishikanye, "La production caféière au Burundi: agronomie, vulgarisation et rapports sociaux," *Canadian Journal of African Studies* 34, no. 2 (2000): 220).

IMAGE 3 Coffee estate of a chief in Kayanza (Burundi), 1949. Cultivation started in 1925, and when the picture was taken, the estate counted about 60000 bushes, which demonstrates the wealth some chiefs were able to gain in the Belgian mandate
SOURCE: SABI, INEAC, DOCUMENTS ET PHOTOS (546/5204)

notables were not enthusiastic about producing coffee. After all, why start to produce a crop that only yields after a few years? Hence, the first thing the mandate administration had to do was convince suspicious chiefs about the "delights" of coffee cultivation.

The regrouping of chieftaincies and the replacing of unwilling chiefs in the late 1920s certainly were incentives for the latter to collaborate more with the European enforced coffee cultivation scheme.[114] Subsequently, during the first coffee campaign (1931–1932) chiefs and sub-chiefs were ordered to plant 1000 and 250 plants respectively, but this campaign was not very successful, as about 25% of all fields in Ruanda-Urundi had to be destroyed due to bad cultivation/ maintenance methods.[115]

114 Nsavyimana, "La mobilisation de la force de travail au Burundi sous le mandate belge (1920–1940)": 217.

115 Molitor, "L'introduction et le développement de la culture du caféier Arabica chez les indigènes du Ruanda-Urundi": 166–172.

Nonetheless, the intention of the mandate government was rather to spread coffee cultivation among rural populations and make them produce for the world market. As Ryckmans already wrote in 1921, a mixture of measures was required to push Africans into the capitalist economy.[116] Ryckmans was referring not only to wages in proportion to effort or tax impositions. "A mixture of measures" also referred to specific proceedings in order to expand and make people cultivate coffee. By "encouraging" every HAV to plant coffee from 1932 onwards, the mandate administration vigorously started to unfold various procedures.

2.2 *Vulgarization and Mobilization of the Rural Masses*

2.2.1 How and By Whom?

Although some people knew how to cultivate coffee, the majority of HAV were unfamiliar with the production process.[117] By making chiefs and sub-chiefs principal producers during the first coffee campaign, the mandate administration especially wanted notables, accompanied by European agronomists, to function as role models. However, notables usually did not cultivate themselves; they used *uburetwa* labor. Hence, if the mandate government wanted rural people to produce coffee, other additional means were necessary. Missions were not important as coffee producers for the world market, but were more so as role models. In collaboration with local administrations, missions spread coffee cultivation not only by action but also by word.[118] Not only were the benefits of coffee production announced from the pulpit. Religious festivities also served as an excellent opportunity to convince people, and from 1933 onwards people were educated during special agricultural courses.

"Inspiration from above" alone was usually not enough to convince people to actually start producing coffee. Consequently, the mandate administration combined two more pressing inducements, imposing cultivation directly or indirectly.[119] The first method leaves little room for misinterpretation: the whip. Already used in the early 1920s as a disciplinary measure (four to twelve lashes),[120] the use of the *chicotte* intensified with the vulgarization of the coffee

116 Pierre Ryckmans, "Le programme économique dans le Ruanda-Urundi," *Bulletin de la Société Royale des Ingénieurs et des Industriels* 2, no. 1 (1921): 95.

117 This particularly refers to people who worked as seasonal workers in Uganda, where they learned how to produce coffee alongside other cash crops, such as cotton, for example (Leplae, *Les plantations de café au Congo belge: leur histoire (1881–1935), leur importance actuelle*: 218–219).

118 Hatungimana, *Le café au Burundi au XXe siècle: Paysans, argent, pouvoir*: 142–148.

119 Ibid: 175–177.

120 AAB, RARU, Rapport à la Commission permanente des Mandats, 1922, no. 17(2).

culture, as it was used not only to force people to start cultivating but also during the cultivation process itself (see following chapter). Moreover, in Gisenyi for example, it was only after World War II that the use of the whip was suppressed in the coffee sector.[121] In combination with corporal "stimuli," the administration also used indirect methods such as tax impositions in cash[122] and the possibility to increasingly repurchase customary tasks and tributes.

Incentives might indeed convince people to start cultivating, but since many in the mandate lacked the knowledge to produce coffee, orders from above on how to produce and maintain coffee plots had to reach the rural masses in one way or another. Territorial administrators receiving directives from either the Agricultural Service, created in 1929, or higher-ranked officials transmitted these directives to chiefs once every month (likely during territorial councils). Chiefs, sometimes accompanied by clerks and/or translators, returned home and then assembled their sub-chiefs in order to pass down the orders. The latter subsequently transmitted directives to their subjects on the hills. When important messages had to be delivered, chiefs summoned all adult men to come to a place close to their personal domain. During these meetings chiefs, sub-chiefs or even clerks told the orders from the mandate administration to all those present. Measures passed down were almost always accompanied by threats. Those recalcitrant in executing the orders or those dawdling too much risked punishment (whipping) by the notables.[123] That chiefs menaced their subjects is hardly a surprise. On the one hand, chiefs' power had been strengthened (*uburetwa*), and they received privileges and wages from the mandate regime. On the other hand, chiefs were also held responsible for the success or failure of coffee cultivation. Consequently, when harvests were bad or too many plants died due to poor maintenance, chiefs and sub-chiefs were the first to pay the price, which sometimes could result in intimidation by the European government, as happened in Kibuye in 1935:

> According to Mr Gvirtman [agronomist], these failures are caused by the manifest negligence of the sub-chiefs concerned in Bwishaza, and by

121 Ibid, Gisenyi Territoire, Rapport Général, 1949 and 1950, no. 88(9) and 88(10).

122 For the development and evolution of different taxes imposed on people in the mandate, see: Petra Vervust, "The relative importance of ethnicity, class and race in colonial Rwanda. The cases of prison policies, corvées, taxation, census and identity booklets," *Journal of Belgian History* 42, no. 4 (2012): 89–93. For a concrete case study of Shangugu, see: Newbury, *The cohesion of oppression. Clientship and ethnicity in Rwanda, 1860–1960*: 172–174.

123 This information is based on the situation in Burundi, but it is more than likely that a similar chain of command was used in Rwanda as well; see: Nsavyimana, "La mobilisation de la force de travail au Burundi sous le mandate belge (1920–1940)": 164–166.

> unwillingness of chief Ndakebuka [...]. On the other hand, it seems that chief Ndakebuka is seeking continuously, and by means of deceitful reasons, to deny European authority and his obligations. Thus, I [the Resident] want to ask you [the territorial administrator] to take boldly severe action against the recalcitrant sub-chiefs and against Ndakebuka, by making clear to the latter that at the moment Kibuye territory will be suppressed, he might not only lose Nyantango, but also Rusenyi, if he continues to behave badly.[124]

Chiefs may have been extremely important in passing down orders and directives, but they also had the responsibility for controlling coffee cultivation on the ground. However, notables or those loyal to them usually had other duties or lacked knowledge, and daily control was therefore difficult. The mandate administration anticipated such circumstances by engaging agricultural monitors as intermediaries between European agricultural agents and planters from the early 1930s onwards. Monitors were always Tutsi (sometimes sub-chiefs)[125] and often had received primary education in which they had learned how to write and measure, as well as the basics of cultivating coffee. When engaged by the government, monitors were trained by European agronomists in the dos and don'ts of coffee production.[126] However, it seems that over the course of time, the administration became more lax. Interviews conducted by Codere reveal that at the beginning of the 1940s, coffee monitors were sometimes appointed merely by a letter from the Resident, without any form of education and completely lacking cultivation know-how.[127] Nevertheless, with or without proper training, monitors were responsible for "encouraging" planters, for example by giving demonstrations,[128] and also for controlling the cultivation process very closely (see next chapter).

Due to a lack of staff, local governments in the entire mandate depended heavily on these monitors. Or to be more precise: bureaucracies had no other choice.[129] Monitors are therefore key in understanding the ways rural labor

124 AAB, RWA, Café, Rapports, RWA(439), Lettre du résident Sandrart au administrateur territorial de Kibuye, 27/5/1935.

125 Molitor, "L'introduction et le développement de la culture du caféier Arabica chez les indigènes du Ruanda-Urundi": 166–172.

126 AAB, RARU, Rapport à la Commission permanente des Mandats, 1931, no. 17bis(4).

127 Helen Codere, *The biography of an African society, Rwanda 1900–1960 based on forty-eight Rwandan autobiographies* (Tervuren: Royal Museum for Central Africa, 1973): 81.

128 AAB, RARU, Gisenyi Territoire, Rapport Général, 1937, no. 87(23).

129 Ibid, RWA, Café, Rapports, RWA(438), Lettre de l'agronome Dohogne au chef du service de l'Agriculture, 3/4/1935.

was mobilized and controlled. Gisenyi, for instance, counted twenty-nine monitors in 1933, but from 1944 onwards the territorial administration decided to engage monitors proportionally. From this point on, one monitor was appointed per 500 fields. When coffee cultivation grew, more monitors could be engaged, allowing the government to act more flexibly.[130]

The fact that coffee monitors were given substantial control over people often led to abuses by these governmental auxiliaries. In 1955, the manager of OCIRU sent a note to all European coffee agents complaining about monitors who cultivated coffee themselves on the fields of other owners – who perhaps were engaged in wage labor. As the manager wrote: this is not the task of monitors; they have to teach planters because otherwise cultivators will never know how to produce, and will never like it either.[131] It is unclear what the exact intentions of these monitors were: were they interested in the remunerations? Or, even worse, did they appropriate these fields? Either way, whatever the intentions of some monitors might have been, chiefs began to have serious doubts about the position and value of coffee monitors in the late 1950s. It cannot be denied that by holding on to the category of monitors the mandate bureaucracy not only enforced Tutsi authority but also attempted to double-check chiefs, and at the same time undermined chiefs' labor control mechanisms – and perhaps even control over land – by granting other notables (sub-chiefs) more authority. Accordingly, during one of the chieftaincy councils in Cyesha in 1957, some chiefs pleaded in favor of the abolition of monitors, even though it was framed as a cost-cutting measure: "those useless agents: given the fact that natives are more or less aware of how to maintain coffee bushes; and working the land in general."[132] The negative response of the territorial agent only underscores the argument that Belgians were forced to depend on these monitors.

2.2.2 Taxes and Monetization of Customary Tasks and Tributes

Besides the introduction of obligatory coffee cultivation, there were still more changes that were imposed on Rwandan rural populations in the early decades of the Belgian mandate. In 1923, for example, the mandate bureaucracy installed *akazi*-chiefs. After about three years this function was abolished and

130 Ibid, RARU, Gisenyi Territoire, Rapport Général, 1933, no. 87(19) and Rapport Agriculture, 1944, no. 90(19).

131 Ibid, RWA, Café, Rapports, RWA(443), Note aux agents de l'OCIRU (éditée par Stainier), 21/2/1955.

132 Ibid, Conseils de Territoire et de Chefferie, Cyesha – Shangugu, RWA(72), Procès-verbal du Conseil de Chefferie, 28/3/1957.

the tasks were absorbed by "regular" chiefs.[133] *Akazi* was meant to mobilize labor for European *corvées* such as infrastructure works, but this kind of labor was also used in the coffee sector (see next chapter). Moreover, *akazi* is not the same as *uburetwa*, but rather is yet another form of chiefly labor control. Clearly, chiefs' control had expanded while labor exactions on the rural population had increased. However, since the mandate government intended to incorporate these rural populations into the world economy by installing smallholder production, labor had to be emancipated. Consequently, the mandate bureaucracy imposed taxes and increasingly monetarized tributes and *corvées*, which occasionally caused tensions with the Colonial Council in Brussels. In a 1934 letter, the Secretary of the Colony urged the mandate bureaucracy not to act independently. The Secretary was correct that fixing the price should be done in dialogue with notables and their subjects (although their influence probably was very limited), but the administration in the mandate had legalized the repurchase of an unspecified *corvée* without the approval of Brussels.[134] This not only weakened its legal basis, but also undermined the authority of the colonial council, which explains the bold reaction of the Secretary of the Colony.

Tax imposition on the Rwandan side of Lake Kivu differed in some respects from that on eastern Congo. First, in the mandate several tax scales existed. Colonial administrators were convinced that Tutsi were more prosperous than Hutu. Consequently, Tutsi were supposed to pay higher taxes than Hutu. However, in practice, elites often forced people to pay taxes for them.[135] In this section, I focus on the scale most rural cultivators were classified in. Secondly, from the early 1920s onwards, people (mostly Tutsi) with ten or more cows had to pay an additional cattle tax. This cattle tax continued to increase during the colonial period. For instance in Gisenyi, in 1929, the cattle tax was set at 2 Francs; in 1944, the tax was 10 Francs whereas in 1958, large cattle owners were taxed 65 Francs.[136]

As for the head tax, the level Rwandans had to pay was the highest in Shangugu throughout the colonial period. The intention of the mandate administration – to force people into wage labor in this region with a European

133 Des Forges, *Defeat is the only bad news: Rwanda under Musinga, 1896–1931*: 193.

134 AAB, AIMO, Recrutements Ruanda-Urundi, Correspondance, no. 2003, Lettre du ministre de la colonie Tschoffen au gouverneur du Ruanda-Urundi, 16/2/1934.

135 Vervust, "The relative importance of ethnicity, class and race in colonial Rwanda. The cases of prison policies, corvées, taxation, census and identity booklets": 93.

136 AAB, RARU, Gisenyi Territoire, Rapport Général, 1929; 1944 and 1958, no. 87(16), 88(4) and 88(14).

segment larger than in Gisenyi – is reflected in these higher tax rates.[137] In 1937, Africans in Shangugu had to pay an annual head tax of 25 Francs, in Gisenyi 18 Francs.[138] Twenty years later, this gap still existed. In Shangugu the level of the tax was set at 166 Francs, in Gisenyi at 155 Francs per year.[139] Similarly to in eastern Congo, taxes rose steeply after World War II in order to subsidy developmental programs (the ten-year plan initiated in 1951). Moreover, after World War II, tax levels on the Rwandan side of Lake Kivu were higher than on the Congolese side. Stimulated by the bureaucracy, this might have been an incentive for Rwandans to migrate to the colony and hence reduce the increasing pressure on land, as discussed in the previous chapter.[140]

However, as opposed to in the Kivu, the intention of the government was not in the first place to promote wage labor in Rwanda. Rather, the mandate bureaucracy particularly aimed at allowing Africans to cultivate their own land more easily, which is similar to how France tried to stimulate smallholder production in its colonies after 1935.[141] Accordingly, in the regions bordering Lake Kivu, unsurprisingly, tributes in food were the first to be commodified. An example from Kibuye perfectly describes what people had to pay in kind to various hierarchical superiors.[142] Families grouped together on a hill had to deliver communally each year: in January, about 10 kilograms of peas or beans to both the chief and sub-chief; in May/June, about 10 kilograms sorghum to both the chief and sub-chief; one pot of *pombe* (honey or banana beer) to their chief and one to the sub-chief. Isolated families had to deliver half of these quantities to either the chief or the sub-chief. Extremely poor people were exempted from food tributes and only had to deliver an indigenous manufactured mat to the chief or sub-chief. Only a few years later, the redemption of tributes in food had already spread further, although it had by no means become the general rule. However, customary scales had apparently been abolished and harmonized by the mandate regime, thereby not only denying existing flexibilities in

---

137 Newbury, *The cohesion of oppression. Clientship and ethnicity in Rwanda, 1860–1960*: 172.

138 AAB, RARU, Shangugu Territoire, Rapport Général, 1937, no. 101(3). Ibid, Gisenyi Territoire, 1937, no. 87(23).

139 Ibid, Shangugu Territoire, 1958, no. 102(9). Ibid, Gisenyi Territoire, 1958, 88(14).

140 In colonial Mozambique, the Portuguese also stimulated migration by adapting tax scales to local labor needs; see: Kleoniki Alexopoulou and Dácil Juif, "Colonial state formation without integration: tax capacity and labour regimes in Portuguese Mozambique (1890s–1970s)," *International Review of Social History* 62, no. 2 (2017).

141 Cooper, *Decolonization and African society. The labor question in French and British Africa*: 74.

142 AAB, RARU, Lubengera Territoire, Rapport Général, 1930, no. 80(9).

socio-economic relations but also increasing the burden on the rural poor even more:

> Food tributes have been repurchased to a large extent (by 11759 bahutu) for the amount of 1 Franc for the provincial chief, and 2 Francs for the hill chief [...]. It would be prosperous if in the future – maybe near future – our watutsi would gain sufficient revenues from their coffee which, increased by the redemption of tributes previously paid in food, would permit them to pay labor *corvées* [*uburetwa*] their bahutu have to perform.[143]

The "large extent" the territorial administrator of Shangugu refers to is exaggerated. As shown in Chapter 1, in the mid-1930s this territory totaled about 25000 coffee cultivators, which means that less than half of that group (at the most) repurchased tributes in food. Moreover, remuneration of *uburetwa* labor is mentioned for the first time, and although advice to pay customary labor was still unsuccessful in the late 1930s (as argued above), making labor *corvées* marketable was on the table.

However, in Shangugu the territorial administration served a double goal. On the one hand, it supported European enterprises (for example plantations) and stimulated regular wage labor by exempting regular workers from taxes and customary obligations.[144] However, even when people were regularly engaged they (or their family) still were obliged to maintain their coffee bushes: if regular work ended for one reason or another, people could then resume coffee production.[145] On the other hand, the government in Shangugu also tried to free labor for compulsory smallholder coffee cultivation. According to the annual report of 1936, the payment of tribute for *ubutaka* land clientship had been commodified, and from then on the price was set at 1.5 Francs.[146] As mentioned above, *uburetwa* labor was replaced by a monetary tax only after World War II, except for regular workers, who had the possibility to repurchase *uburetwa* even before World War II. This was one way the territorial government tried to stimulate regular labor for Europeans. As early as 1929, people working for Europeans (or Asians) were exempted from paying tributes to their chiefs if they were employed for one month or longer.[147] Despite the fact

143 Ibid, Shangugu Territoire, Rapport Général, 1933, no. 100(12).

144 Newbury, *The cohesion of oppression. Clientship and ethnicity in Rwanda, 1860–1960*: 170 and 174.

145 AAB, RWA, AIMO(340), TEPSI, Procès-verbal de la réunion de la Commission, 18/11/1957.

146 Ibid, RARU, Shangugu Territoire, Rapport Général, 1936, no. 101(2).

147 Ibid, 1929, no. 100(8).

that in the 1930s regular workers could repurchase labor *corvées*, this measure seemingly did not convince Rwandans to enter wage labor for Europeans *en masse*, because many wanted to be exempted from labor *corvées* altogether: both labor as such and redemption.[148] Obviously, the administration did not endorse this purpose, but at the end of World War II an important step was nonetheless taken. From 1945 onwards, *all* Africans in Shangugu would have the possibility to repurchase *corvée* labor.[149] Even though redemption was possible after World War II, obligatory works (road maintenance, for example) still had to be performed and the same rule continued to be applied: only regular workers – now defined as those working at least 20 days a month for Europeans – were exempted from compulsory works, although laborers often circumvented this rule, as the following quote suggests:

> The sub-chief who ascertains that a native only once in a while takes up employment in a European firm, will have to make him work on the hill like the other natives, because decree no. 11 determines that those who do not have to cultivate [obligatorily] are those who are remunerated on a regular basis; he who works but 1-2-3-4 times a month for Europeans is not remunerated on a regular basis and is thus obliged to do the works as laid down in the decree no. 11.[150]

Further to the north, in Gisenyi, the European segment was very limited and this reflects the way redemption of *corvées* and tributes was organized. Unlike in Shangugu, there were no exemptions from taxes, not even for regular workers. Similarly to in Shangugu, however, the first thing the mandate administration started to commodify was tributes in food in order to emancipate land and labor. Framing it as a measure to end abuses, the territorial bureaucracy made tribute in kind (food plus a crafted product like honey) repurchasable in the vicinity of Gisenyi city from 1934 onwards.[151] By paying 1 Franc to the chief and 2 Francs to the sub-chief, people could redeem this tribute. The government followed the example of Shangugu in fixing the price level, and likely also eliminated customary scales. That in the mid-1930s only areas close to the border (here Bugoyi) could redeem this tribute might indicate the importance tobacco cultivation still had in this region, as well as the hope of the government

148 Ibid, 1938, no. 101(4).

149 Ibid, 1944, no. 101(10).

150 Ibid, RWA, Conseils de Territoire et de Chefferie, Impara – Shangugu, RWA(72), Procès-verbal du Conseil de Chefferie, 10/4/1952.

151 Ibid, RARU, Gisenyi Territoire, Rapport Général, 1933, no. 87(19).

to transform it into an export commodity. However, only two years later redemption was already harmonized for the entire territory, which in turn demonstrates the growing importance of coffee cultivation. Moreover, starting in 1936, research was conducted in order to examine the possibilities of expanding redemption of *corvée* labor.[152] The reason for this research is mentioned in the annual reports of the following years: only certain categories of workers were able to repurchase *uburetwa* and the majority of the potential labor force was still stuck with customary labor obligations. Only regular workers, catechists and people who had more than ten cows were able to pay 3 and 10 Francs respectively to their chief and sub-chief.[153] Both the scarcity in parts of Gisenyi that was a result of the 1943–1944 famine, and the fact that people often had to travel for a substantial amount of time to perform customary duties for their chiefs, convinced the territorial bureaucracy to change policy at the end of World War II:

> The majority of the chiefs are unable to obtain the three days of labor from natives living outside their "inyarulembo" […] it would be desirable for this to be valorized. In this way chiefs would really benefit from this duty which, in most cases, is only theoretical. It would be easier if chiefs themselves paid the labor they really require and that would avoid a considerable loss of days where no duties have been performed, and would reduce to a minimum the unbridled waste of labor days, nowadays performed as an utter obligation and without real advantages for the beneficiaries.[154]

This quote clearly expresses the territorial government's wish to make more labor available for remunerated work, and from 1944 onwards the measure of which it speaks was implemented. In 1948, about 70% of Hutu HAV had used the possibility to redeem *uburetwa*, but the following year redemption of every *corvée* was made compulsory.[155] This means that people had the possibility to repurchase labor duties vis-à-vis notables, or that notables would have to pay the workers they employed to perform customary tasks. Although it is doubtful that chiefs in Gisenyi actually paid sufficiently, making labor *corvées* expressible in money also happened in other territories in the mandate. According to the general report the Belgian government sent to the United Nations, from

152 Ibid, 1936, no. 87(22).
153 Ibid, 1937; 1938 and 1939, no. 87(23); 87(24) and 87(25).
154 Ibid, 1943, no. 88(3).
155 Ibid, 1948 and 1949, 88(8) and 88(9).

1948 onwards monetization – repurchase or remuneration – of all *prestations de travail* was made compulsory.[156]

2.3 *Other Kinds of Coffee Labor*

2.3.1 European Plantations

While in the Belgian Congo a vigorous focus on mobilization numbers and percentages was one of the major features of colonial labor policy, in the mandate such a focus seems to have been absent. An extract from the commission investigating labor conditions in the mandate at the end of the 1920s is clear in this respect: as opposed to the colony, Ruanda-Urundi is densely populated. Hence, the risks of over-recruitment are limited and therefore recruitment should be entirely free of any percentages.[157] Moreover, prohibiting people from entering salaried labor once a certain limit is exceeded – as happened in the colony – would never have been approved by the Mandate Commission. Despite the absence of maxima, Europeans still faced mobilization difficulties, particularly in Shangugu, not the least because wages in the Kivu were higher, resulting in many Rwandans crossing the border voluntarily (see Chapter 6).[158] Another reason was that enterprises from the Belgian Congo (such as the CNKi) recruited people in the Rwandan areas bordering Lake Kivu as well.[159] Protanag, for instance, asked the territorial administration to intervene and grant it a recruitment monopoly, thereby arguing that it was almost impossible for the firm to start up its activities: for a decent take-off at least twice the current labor force needed to be employed.[160] It goes without saying that recruitment from outside the territory only enhanced this problem. Nevertheless, Protanag's request was denied. However, apparently the territorial administration did apply some sort of labor mobilization limit in this territory. The annual report of 1941 still refers to difficulties European planters had finding sufficient labor on the spot, even though the 50% limit was not exceeded.[161] This indicates

156 Ibid, Rapport à la Commission permanente des Mandats, 1948, no. 20(4bis).

157 Ibid, AI, Zones économiques, no. 4370(13)2, Extrait du Procès-verbal de la Commission de la MO au Ruanda-Urundi, 5/12/1929.

158 See especially: Mathys, "People on the move. Frontiers, borders, mobility and history in the Lake Kivu region 19th–20th century."

159 That Shangugu supplied enterprises in the Kivu with manpower on a regular basis did not escape the attention of the territorial bureaucracy. In 1938, the territorial administrator even argued that Shangugu "*was in the Kivu's sphere*" (Dorsey, "Rwandan colonial economy, 1916–1941": 117).

160 AAB, AIMO, Recrutements Ruanda-Urundi, Recrutements pour le Kivu, no. 1603/9119, Lettre du manager de Protanag au député du résident du Rwanda, 2/6/1930.

161 Ibid, RARU, Shangugu Territoire, Rapport Général, 1941, no. 101(7).

that when only half of the HAV were at work in a certain chieftaincy, the territorial administration was instructed to restrict recruitment.

The way people entered the coffee plantation economy is similar to in the Kivu. People could enter spontaneously, to escape customary tasks (such as *uburetwa* for regular workers) or *akazi* labor for example. From the 1930s onwards, entering European wage labor freely meant a certain degree of independence for workers vis-à-vis their notables. Therefore, free entries were increasingly discouraged by (sub-)chiefs, for instance by the imposition of *uburetwa* on family members as mentioned above, the confiscation of land or the excommunication of those workers from the hill.[162] Plantations could also agree with chiefs in order to "deliver" laborers. The latter might have played an even more pronounced role in Ruanda-Urundi because of the increased authority given to them by the mandate government.[163] Although here too chiefs lacked formal regulation, they chose who they sent, as in the Kivu. Hence, it was often the outcasts or the people disliked by the chiefs who were forced to work for Europeans. On the other hand, and also similarly to in the Kivu, by sending people to plantations chiefs lost not only manpower but also, and especially, authority. This resulted in the increasing reluctance of notables in Shangugu,[164] but also in Gisenyi, where the European presence was even more limited. Although probably exaggerating, in 1952 the administrator of the latter territory criticized sub-chiefs in particular for their sabotage:

> In this particular labor domain we can say without fear of making a mistake that 90% of the sub-chiefs, instead of helping the Administration or the Colonists only a bit, are taking a sinful pleasure in "throwing a spanner in the works" and making workers and especially their wives suffer difficulties, in this way hoping to convince them that it is more interesting to cultivate their own fields than to enter European enterprises.[165]

This quote suggests that besides installing and controlling smallholder production, the government was also actively involved in the mobilization of laborers for private firms, despite the prohibition thereof. Similarly to in the colony,

162 Newbury, *The cohesion of oppression. Clientship and ethnicity in Rwanda, 1860–1960*: 168, and Dorsey, "Rwandan colonial economy, 1916–1941": 96–97.

163 Newbury, *The cohesion of oppression. Clientship and ethnicity in Rwanda, 1860–1960*: 167, and Dorsey, "Rwandan colonial economy, 1916–1941": 90.

164 Newbury, *The cohesion of oppression. Clientship and ethnicity in Rwanda, 1860–1960*: 168.

165 AAB, RARU, Gisenyi Territoire, Rapport Général, 1952, no. 88(12). Similar "sabotage" by sub-chiefs also occurred in Burundi; see: Nsavyimana, "La mobilisation de la force de travail au Burundi sous le mandate belge (1920–1940)": 301–302.

however, direct state intervention for public works was not prohibited, hence the creation of *akazi*. The difference is that, for the mandate, sources are much more tacit concerning this matter, in this way going along with Cooper's silence (*supra*). No doubt references to direct intervention in the annual reports or elsewhere would have encountered contrary winds from Geneva or New York. Still, I was able to find two references, the first one from Gisenyi, where the territorial agent not only refers to recalcitrant sub-chiefs but also admits that in 1947 forced mobilization of regular coffee workers was required … again:

> As has always been the case, European planters have not looked for permanent laborers. It was much easier, less expensive for them, to welcome each week or two times a month large groups coming from the sub-chieftaincies. […] In the eyes of the natives they are always seen as real representatives of the "Bula-Matari," of a severe and ungrateful "Bula-Matari" […] for which one should work without the ability to express the least desire. Planters' complaints have reached me quickly. I was left no choice, in order to avoid losses, but to intervene by coercing the natives once again to go to work.[166]

The second reference to direct state intervention comes from Shangugu, as late as 1957. The territorial administrator stressed that many people working for *colons agricoles* were dissatisfied, especially because of the low wages they received. This resulted in reluctance on the part of Africans to enter plantation labor and the need for plantations to appeal to the administration in order to mobilize labor. The territorial bureaucracy itself was not pleased with this situation, and argued that direct state intervention was a counterproductive provisional measure and that (non-agrarian) employers who paid higher salaries did not have such mobilization problems.[167]

2.3.2 To the Congo

A particular domain in which the territorial governments of the Rwandan areas bordering Lake Kivu have left their mark is the mobilization of workers for the plantation sector in the Kivu. In this part I will not focus on voluntary

166 AAB, RWA, AIMO(346), MO agricole, Lettre de l'administrateur territorial Gaupin (Gisenyi) au résident du Rwanda, 10/10/1947. During World War II, the mandate administration regularly obliged notables to requisition and send people to plantations (quinine and pyrethrum, mainly), but this quote suggests that direct state intervention was equally present in the coffee sector: before, perhaps during, and shortly after the war.

167 Ibid, RARU, Shangugu Territoire, Rapport AIMO, 1957, no. 103(10).

movements across the border, but rather on "directed" migration especially, but not only, to Gishari. In Gisenyi and even more in Shangugu, "labor contacts" between the colonial and mandate Kivu started very early. Even though *colons* vested in Rutshuru were trying to recruit people in Gisenyi as early as 1928, in 1937 labor movements were still weak.[168] Rwandans were not enthusiastic about being forcibly moved to the west, foremost because there were sufficient local resources, and a lack of incentives for people to enter the plantation sector in the Congo.[169] The same is true for migration to Gishari. Although in 1938 about 23% of the emigrants in Gishari were rooted in Gisenyi, people still preferred to cultivate their own plots rather than moving around and clearing new land.[170] Moreover, not only was the famine of 1943–1944 used by the territorial government of Gisenyi to increase propaganda in favor of Gishari. Some chiefs in Kibuye also encouraged people to leave for the Belgian Congo in order to escape poverty.[171] In the latter territory the relationship between emigration and food scarcity played out once again in the mid-1950s. Successive failures of pea harvests forced people – and sometimes entire clans – to leave for those regions in the Kivu destined for Rwandan migrants. According to the 1953 annual report, the number of people leaving Kibuye territory was so great that "the Administration has interrupted the emigration propaganda for those regions."[172]

The problem of finding people for Gishari, or for plantations in the Kivu in general, was even more notable in Shangugu. In the late 1920s, some 1000 people from Shangugu were working in Kabare – although only 154 possessed a permit to leave the mandate, which upset the administration in Shangugu. According to the latter, propaganda circulated by *colons* in the Kivu was successful, even though engaging people without permits was illegal.[173] People from Shangugu preferred working in and around Bukavu. As a result, recruiting people for Gishari was difficult. Moreover, many who were sent returned quickly because they believed that since Gishari was lacking banana fields, it

168 Ibid, Gisenyi Territoire, Rapport Général, 1928 and 1937, no. 87(15) and 87(23).

169 On the other hand, there were a lot of spontaneous movements to the Kivu. Rwandans who lived close to the border usually had certain ties (social, commercial) with people across the border, which resulted in regular border crossings. I will come back to this in Chapter 6. See also: Mathys, "People on the move. Frontiers, borders, mobility and history in the Lake Kivu region 19th–20th century": 254.

170 AAB, RARU, Gisenyi Territoire, Rapport Général, 1938, no. 87(24).

171 Ibid, 1944, no. 90(19), and Mararo, "Land conflicts in Masisi, Eastern Zaire: the impact and aftermath of Belgian colonial policy (1920–1989)": 140.

172 AAB, RARU, Kibuye Territoire, Rapport Général, 1953, no. 82(3).

173 Ibid, Shangugu Territoire, Rapport Général, 1927 and 1928, no. 100(6) and 100(7).

would exert too little attraction on emigrants.[174] In 1941, chiefs informed the territorial bureaucracy about the difficulties of finding people. They stressed that not only the appeal of Bukavu but also the presence of sufficient land in Shangugu stopped people from migrating, even though notables were not afraid to use force. In most cases, the people that were sent to Gishari were those disliked by chiefs, and "recruiting" such people often required coercion. Chiefs sometimes ordered their *ibirongozi* to pluck people from their fields and exile them to Gishari.[175] Nevertheless, as a result of the chiefly worries – indicating fear of losing manpower and thus authority, similar to the fears over providing laborers for firms in Rwanda – the Resident of Rwanda ordered the administration in Shangugu to stop propaganda for Gishari. His motivation was as follows:

> Because the emigration toward Gishari does not correspond with a real need for the people of Kinyaga. There is a natural movement of emigration toward the region of Costermansville. Understanding that creating an artificial movement toward Gishari will certainly cause damage to this natural flow, he decides: All "effective" propaganda with the intervention of the government will be stopped in Cyangugu territory. Only those who express the formal wish will depart.[176]

This quote not only manifestly shows that Belgian administrations in both mandate and colony had to take local conditions and existing power structures into account in order not to hamper their own economic goals. It also emphasizes a more general tendency in African colonial history with regard to how European bureaucracies often had to alter policies to fit realities on the ground.[177]

2.3.3 Africans Mobilizing Africans

As opposed to in the Belgian Congo, a constraint smallholders in the mandate did not have to face was the prohibition on engaging other Africans. In this section, I focus on people who did not belong to the elite, who could not

174 Ibid, 1940, no. 101(6).

175 Mathys, "People on the move. Frontiers, borders, mobility and history in the Lake Kivu region 19th–20th century": 208. Force used by chiefs was not absent in the other Rwandan territories bordering Lake Kivu either.

176 AAB, RWA, Conseils de Territoire et de Chefferie, Shangugu, RWA(72), Réunion plénière, 24/2/1941, quoted by ibid: 253.

177 Frederick Cooper, "Conflict and connection: rethinking colonial African history," *American Historical Review* 99, no. 5 (1994): 1531.

depend on *uburetwa* for example, but who still managed to employ people in order to produce – in this case coffee. This is not unique to Ruanda-Urundi, as there are several examples in colonial Africa of Africans engaging, paying and often establishing long-term ties with other Africans.[178] When, as in the regions close to Lake Kivu, (some) producers were able to successfully mobilize sufficient land and (paid and/or unpaid) labor, relative prosperity could be attained.[179] The territories bordering Lake Kivu and especially Shangugu usually had a higher living standard than those in central Rwanda.[180] This was not only due to the proximity of the Kivu (where wages were higher) but also because planters in those Rwandan areas were able to go beyond individual or household production. The relative prosperity of these Africans did not escape the attention of the government. In 1957, the territorial agent of Shangugu even talked about "a kind of aristocratic proletariat and peasantry."[181]

Coffee smallholders either engaged people coming from the east or people living on the same hill. Planters sometimes put others to work on their coffee plots while at the same time they were working in Bukavu.[182] Whether coffee smallholders were performing wage labor elsewhere or not, according to the annual report of 1946, the territorial bureaucracy had noticed once again that people from the Rwandan interior had offered their services to planters living in Kinyaga.[183] The words "once again" are particularly interesting because they indicate that such engagements were probably an older custom.[184] The second way that smallholders mobilized other Africans only starts to appear in the sources in the 1950s. During a chieftaincy meeting in 1954, the question was asked whether people desiring to produce coffee were able to engage wage

178 See, for instance, the cocoa planters in colonial Ghana: Anthony G. Hopkins, *An economic history of West Africa* (Harlow: Longman, 1993 [1973]): 216–219; the cotton planters in colonial Uganda: John Tosh, "Lango agriculture during the early colonial period: land and labour in a cash-crop economy," *Journal of African History* 19, no. 3 (1978); or for a general overview: John Iliffe, *Emergence of African capitalism* (London; Basingstoke: Macmillan Press, 1983): 23–43.

179 Eric Vanhaute, "Peasants, peasantries and (de)peasantization in the capitalist world-system," in *Routledge handbook of world-systems analysis: theory and research*, ed. Salvatore J. Babones and Christopher K. Chase-Dunn (London; New York: Routledge, 2012): 317–318.

180 Leurquin, *Le niveau de vie des populations rurales du Ruanda-Urundi*: 175.

181 AAB, RARU, Shangugu Territoire, Rapport AIMO, 1957, no. 103(10).

182 Ibid.

183 Ibid, Rapport Général, 1946, no. 101(12).

184 Mathys, "People on the move. Frontiers, borders, mobility and history in the Lake Kivu region 19th–20th century": 232. Hiring people from central Rwanda was not restricted to Shangugu; in Gisenyi as well, people engaged other Africans coming from the interior.

laborers living on the same hill. The answer of the territorial administrator was positive, as he stated:

> No objection provided that the total labor force contractually engaged by Europeans and by natives does not exceed the 50% of HAV on that hill. [...] Moreover, laborers have to be paid regularly with wages corresponding to prices in the region; there also has to remain sufficient land available so that part of the population is not prejudiced, because there is no need to grant large plots to some in order to expropriate others in the future.[185]

3 Conclusion

This chapter has demonstrated that mobilization of labor for the coffee plantation sector was largely similar in the colony and the mandate. People could enter in three ways: freely, via chiefs or via direct administrative intervention. The first way involves spontaneous entrance, the frequency of which increased after World War II. The second is via African intermediaries. Some chiefs' ability to coerce labor rested on the redeployment of existing authority structures.[186] However, customary chiefs were often replaced by more "cooperative" ones. Hence, other chiefs' ability rested on an elevated level of everyday violence (see next chapter), perpetrated with the silent approval of the colonial/mandate administration. Furthermore, people entering into wage labor often had to deal with reprisals, demonstrating the conflict of interests between African notables and European entrepreneurs. Thirdly, people could also be recruited with direct governmental "help." This kind of intervention declined after World War II, although in Shangugu, for example, evidence suggests that territorial administrators intervened directly until the end of the colonial period. This only underpins the difficulties European plantation owners faced in

185 AAB, RWA, Conseils de Territoire et de Chefferie, Impara – Shangugu, RWA(72), Compte rendu de la réunion, 11/5/1954. Smallholder cash-crop production relies on the unpaid help of community and/or family members – even more so in the start-up stage (John Tosh, "The cash-crop revolution in tropical Africa: an agricultural reappraisal," *African Affairs* 79, no. 314 (1980): 87). However, in this case, the emphasis on wage labor suggests that probably no, or not merely, family and/or community labor was involved and this indicates African entrepreneurs' agency.

186 Mamdani calls this the mobilization of "authoritarian possibilities in culture": see Mahmood Mamdani, *Citizen and subject: contemporary Africa and the legacy of late colonialism* (Princeton: Princeton University Press, 1996).

order to attract labor in the mandate. In combination with poor working conditions, Africans also had different ways of income-pooling (crossing the border, producing coffee, or cultivating and selling food crops, for example) and it was more difficult for local governments to restrict income alternatives, which was relatively easier in the colony (see next chapter).

In order to liberate labor and increase the need for cash, in both the colony and the mandate, administrations imposed taxes and gradually commodified customary tributes and duties. Differences in tax levels and in the monetization of *corvées* and tributes, between both sides of Lake Kivu and within each side, reflect the different local conditions to which colonial administrations had to adapt, as in other African colonies.[187] In both regions, bureaucracies also tried to homogenize existing labor systems. The difference between colonial and mandate Kivu is that in the latter, commodification started earlier. Because in the mandate a smallholder mode of production developed, both land and labor had to be stripped of customary obligations. However, chiefs often continued to impose *corvées* and tributes, which shows that pre-existing labor patterns and local power structures continued within the constraints of colonialism.

The continuation of precolonial labor patterns during the colonial period is clearly visible in the form of *uburetwa*. The Belgian administration not only expanded and legalized this form of labor mobilization: it also used it to introduce coffee cultivation in the mandate. By heavily relying on locals (chiefs, African monitors, but also missions), the mandate government hoped to persuade rural populations to cultivate coffee for the export market. Similarly to the attempted homogenization of land tenure, the mandate regime tried to harmonize labor systems, thereby augmenting chiefs' power.

As a consequence of different local conditions, territorial administrations in the colony and the mandate intervened in dissimilar ways as well. This chapter showed that in the colonial Kivu more emphasis was put on numbers and mobilization limits than in the mandate, although in practice such limits were often manipulated. On the other hand, it seems that on both sides of Lake Kivu limitations were respected by the respective territorial regimes, in particular when labor input endangered village life.[188] The lack of potential coffee

187 Frankema and van Waijenburg, "Metropolitan blueprints of colonial taxation? Lessons from fiscal capacity building in British and French Africa, c.1880–1940": 394.

188 Scholars disagree on the effects of the withdrawal of plantation labor from subsistence production. For instance, Wolpe emphasizes the destructive consequences, whereas Moore and Vaughan argue that rural households coped better than late-colonial anthropologists suggested; see: Harold Wolpe, "Capitalism and cheap labour-power in South Africa: from segregation to apartheid," *Economy and Society* 1, no. 4 (1972), and Henrietta

plantation labor in many areas in the colonial Kivu was addressed in two additional ways: by mobilizing people in neighboring Rwanda and by restricting competition. As has been argued, the mining sector, for instance, had to deal with limits on their labor mobilization efforts. However, such restrictions were relinquished after World War II, resulting in a relatively more liberal labor market. This shows that blocking alternative means of cash income was indeed easier in the colony. The presence of Africans engaging other Africans in the mandate to till the former's coffee land (unthinkable in the colony) only underscores this argument. Secondly, the mobilization of Rwandan labor involved territorial governments in both colonial and mandate Kivu, as well as local chiefs. Despite the efforts of many actors involved, however, shortage of labor did not disappear in many parts of the Kivu district – not even with the creation of Gishari.

Before focusing on the actual commodification of coffee labor and its consequences, I still have one final remark with which to conclude this chapter. Although free engagement in the coffee sector seems to have increased during the course of the colonial period and particularly after World War II, the mobilization of part of the labor force still was unfree until the end of the colonial period. However, the boundaries between free and unfree are unclear, and very often categories overlap.[189] A few examples: people might have entered plantation labor on a free basis but, when they returned home, could be forced to do *corvée* labor. Or, in Rwanda, smallholders ordered to cultivate coffee or to do *uburetwa* might have escaped both by crossing the border, in order to freely engage in colonial wage labor.[190]

L. Moore and Megan Vaughan, *Cutting down trees: gender, nutrition, and agricultural change in the Northern Province of Zambia, 1890–1990* (London: Pearson Education, 1994).

189 Marcel Van der Linden, "The 'globalization' of labor and working-class history and its consequences," *International Labor and Working-Class History*, no. 65 (2004): 142–143.

190 Newbury, *The cohesion of oppression. Clientship and ethnicity in Rwanda, 1860–1960*: 144.

CHAPTER 5

Coffee Labor on the Spot

In the previous chapter I demonstrated that the mobilization of labor can take different forms, even if people were mobilized to produce the same commodity. Drawing on Wallerstein, Van der Linden stresses that disparities in labor regimes are vital features of the capitalist world-system.[1] Different ways of organizing and controlling labor are as important as different systems of mobilization. After all, each administration in colonial Africa intended to incorporate part of the indigenous population "into the larger imperial economy either as independent producers or as wage-workers, and in all cases as consumers."[2]

Consequently, colonial states intervened not only to enable, harmonize and guarantee access to land, but also to enforce ways of structuring and supervising workplaces.[3] However, colonial states are often weak, and attempts to impose their will, rules and ideas unilaterally were usually unsuccessful, since people might resist in one way or another. This means that cooperation and compromises with other actors were necessary: with European firms, but also and above all with the African labor force itself.

Accordingly, this chapter will elaborate on the labor and labor relations of those who were actually producing coffee for the world market. The remark given in the introduction of the previous chapter is equally valid here: labor organization and control are different in plantation and smallholder economies, yet comparisons allow me to stress both differences and similarities. This chapter analyses labor organization on the ground and control of coffee workers, but also the ways in which laborers organized themselves – even though directed by the state – as well as ways of remunerating workers, purchasing power and the consequences of the introduction of salaried labor.

1 Marcel Van der Linden, *Workers of the world. Essays toward a global labor history* (Leiden; Boston: Brill, 2008): 291–292.

2 Immanuel Wallerstein, "The colonial era in Africa: changes in the social structure," in *Colonialism in Africa, 1870–1960. Volume 2: the history and politics of colonialism 1914–1960*, ed. Peter Duignan and Lewis Henry Gann (Cambridge; London; New York; Melbourne: Cambridge University Press, 1970): 408.

3 Wallerstein, *World-systems analysis. An introduction*: 56.

 | DOI:10.1163/9789004428492_008

1 Workforce West of Lake Kivu

1.1 *Dual Employment Categories?*

1.1.1 Regular Workers

A common feature in agricultural production processes is the need for both permanent and temporary labors. The first category is usually smaller, while the second consists of day, piece/task, seasonal workers, etcetera. The coffee sector around Lake Kivu required a large and flexible labor force, in particular during the initial (clearing the land and planting) and concluding (harvest and post-harvest) phases. During the intermediary phase (maintaining the estate), however, employment was more regular but considerably smaller.[4] As governor Moeller claimed in 1933: "in Kivu, temporary is the rule, regular the exception. For every 10000 workers, there are 8000 temporaries."[5] Before focusing on the different types and tasks of temporary workers, I will first take a deeper look at permanent labor.

The first thing that needs to be addressed is that regular labor was performed exclusively by men. Women – playing a primordial role outside the plantation economy (see following chapter) – "do not like to be incorporated [...]: they prefer to stay and leave freely."[6] European plantations owners usually confined themselves to supervising and managing their estate.[7] The actual control over the workforce on the ground was left to "team managers" or *capitas*, constituting the first category of permanent coffee workers.[8] Analogous to chiefs, *capitas* were intermediaries between the European owner(s) and the labor force. They were the ones making the morning calls, reporting absentees and work that was improperly done, to their superiors. In some cases *capitas* were promoted workers, but those people "do not have any prestige among the laborers and they are not afraid to either exploit workers or conspire with them in order to fool the

---

4 Van Melkebeke, "Coerced coffee cultivation and rural agency: the plantation-economy of the Kivu (1918–1940)": 192; see also the introduction in this book.

5 AAB, AIMO, MO agricole, Dossier Unaki, no. 1653/10, Lettre du gouverneur de la Province Orientale au ministre de la colonie, 31/1/1933.

6 Ibid, Planteurs de café au Kivu, no. 1653/14, Rapport d'inspection des entreprises agricole (Kabare), 15/5/1943. In the previous chapter I claimed that "free" is not always accurate, as women were sometimes forced to enter/remain in the planation sector.

7 P. Coppens, "La colonisation agricole au Congo Belge," *Bulletin Agricole du Congo Belge et du Ruanda-Urundi* 30, no. 1 (1939): 6.

8 Other African colonies also used middlemen in the agricultural sector in order to control the workforce: Luke Malaba, "Supply, control and organization of African labour in Rhodesia," *Review of African Political Economy*, no. 18 (1980): 19.

European."[9] Moreover, in order to raise competition among laborers, plantations often constituted ethnically heterogeneous work teams that, contrary to intentions, usually ended up in tensions and conflict.[10] In an attempt to counter these tensions and the lack of prestige of promoted people, some (usually larger) plantations recruited the children of local notables, educating them and granting them with a diploma before starting their career as *capitas*. In other cases mulattos or *évolués*, sometimes coming from outside the Belgian Congo, could be appointed as "team leaders" as well.[11]

Of greater interest here is the part of the workforce producing coffee for the export market. In most cases, people did not like to enter plantations on a regular basis and sign one- to three-year contracts.[12] As already argued, chiefs did not like this situation either. Apart from Africans deliberately trying to escape *corvées* or authoritarian chiefs, the only people who signed long-term contracts were those forced to do so (*infra*), or people disliked by their chief – referred to as "rebels" in the sources.[13] Either way, regular workers – or *fundi* – were engaged to maintain the plantations (and nurseries in some cases), which particularly means removing weed, but also the very important tasks of pruning bushes and searching for manure. Because pruning was a delicate affair, laborers started to specialize already in the early 1930s, and in the early 1940s about 20% of the regular workforce were pruning experts.[14] Successful harvests also depended on manuring coffee trees sufficiently. In Kabare, for instance, regular laborers could be ordered to search for cattle manure in the vicinity of the estate. Or, in other cases, plantation owners and local notables agreed to graze the latter's cattle on the

---

9 AAB, Agri, Compagnies, SAAK (4/13), Document "la MO indigène" de la SAAK, 1940.

10 Arthur Doucy and Pierre Feldheim, *Travailleurs indigènes et productivité du travail au Congo belge* (Bruxelles: Institut de Sociologie Solvay, 1958): 153.

11 See, for more on *capitas*: AAB, Agri, Compagnies, SAAK (4/13), Document "la MO indigène" de la SAAK, 1940.

12 As stipulated in the decree of March 3, 1922, on labor contracts, three years was the maximum legal limit of a contract term. A contract could, however, be renewed, again for a maximum of three years. See: Léon Strouwens and Pierre Piron, *Codes et lois du Congo belge: textes annotés d'après les rapports du Conseil colonial, les instructions officielles et la jurisprudence des tribunaux* (Léopoldville: Edition des codes et lois du Congo belge, 1943): 643. For more information on how this decree developed and on what motivations and interests of different players were involved, see: Vincent Vaessen, "Les législations sur le contrat de travail de 1910 et 1922 au Congo Belge: deux intentions et deux modes de décisions opposés," *Revue Belge de Philologie et d'Histoire* 79, no. 4 (2001).

13 AAB, Agri, Compagnies, SAAK (4/13), Document "la MO indigène" de la SAAK, 1940.

14 Ibid, AIMO, MO agricole, Planteurs de café au Kivu, no. 1653/14, Rapport d'inspection des entreprises agricole (Kabare), 15/5/1943.

estate while part of the *fundi* had to collect manure and spread it among the coffee trees.[15]

The not very attractive duties regular workers had to accomplish might have been a reason – alongside others (*infra*) – for people to prefer temporary plantation work, but in regions where labor was already hard to find this caused extra problems for *colons*. In such situations the administration intervened directly, not only to provide plantations with laborers but also to make sure that laborers stayed put.[16] The annual report of Masisi mentions the government "helping" colonists to keep laborers at work as late as the early 1940s.[17] But in Rutshuru where the labor potential was even smaller, contracting regular coffee laborers was an even bigger issue for plantations. There are references in the sources to people (squatters included) refusing even one-year contracts.[18] This in turn resulted in serious abuses at the end of the 1930s, when the aforementioned Corbisier not only exceeded limits in order to recruit people (see Chapter 4) but also forced people to sign three-year contracts by using (illegal) threats of imprisonment.[19] In this case, both the chiefs' preference for temporary workers and the laborers' preference for temporary labor were neglected. It is unclear whether such governmental "interventions" also happened in other regions bordering Lake Kivu. In any case, there are no references made in the sources I used. Furthermore, in Rutshuru, labor shortages and difficulties replacing workers whose contract had ended – whether combined with administrative force or not – resulted in "lifelong engagement" from the early 1940s onwards:

> the situation of the workers in the concessions is hardly enviable; in most regions, labor availability is far from sufficient in order to assure the replacement of workers. <u>The result is that theoretically a great deal of the</u>

15 Ibid, Dossier Kabare, no. 1653/7, Lettre de Castelein au gouverneur de Costermansville, 29/9/1937.

16 Ibid, Recrutement MO Kivu, Instructions, no. 1647/9226/1, Le problème de la MO au Congo. La situation de 1934 à 1938 par H. Cayen, 10/12/1938. In Kenya, the administration also intervened not only to recruit laborers but also to keep workers on the spot (see: B.J. Berman and J.M. Lonsdale, "Crises of accumulation, coercion and the colonial state: the development of the labor control system in Kenya, 1919–1929," *Canadian Journal of African Studies* 14, no. 1 (1980): 62).

17 AAB, RACB, Masisi Territoire, Rapport AIMO, 1940, no. 143.

18 Ibid, Rutshuru Territoire, Rapport AIMO, 1943 and 1947, no. 163.

19 Ibid, AIMO, MO agricole, Dossier Corbisier, no. 1653/5, Lettre de J. Noirot au gouverneur général, 9/6/1938 and ibid, Inspections plantations européennes Rutshuru, no. 1653/13, Rapport d'inspection Cafco par manager Beyer, 14/9/1937.

> laborers will never be able to extricate themselves from their obligations and have to be considered as engaged for life.[20]

The illegal prolongation of contracts was common in this territory. The 1952 annual report still refers to plantations lacking the ability to replace workers who had fulfilled their contract.[21] This practice of pushing workers into a kind of lifelong servitude resonates with the *serviçal* system used by the Portuguese from 1875 onwards. Cocoa and coffee laborers in Portuguese colonies were forced to sign five-year contracts that were continuously prolonged without their knowledge, which basically meant the persistence of slavery.[22]

1.1.2 Temporary Laborers

The majority of plantation laborers were temporary, and they included men as well as women and children. In some cases temporary workers (seasonal workers especially) signed contracts of one to three months, but in most cases they did not have written contracts at all. Usually, auxiliaries were engaged as day or task laborers via oral agreements between plantations and local notables, which annoyed territorial administrations until the end of the colonial period.[23] Although annual reports often refer to a waste of labor, in these cases it is clear that it was rather the lack of control of the labor force that frustrated the colonial government. Underscoring this argument is the fact that, in the early 1950s, the territorial administration of Kabare suggested contracting day laborers because that way anonymity would disappear.[24] I even found examples of plantations in Rutshuru where territorial agents intervened to force day workers to sign regular contracts.[25] To be sure, the colonial government was not opposed to temporary work as such but rather to the lack of control caused by the absence of contracts.

---

20 Ibid, RACB, Rutshuru Territoire, Rapport AIMO, 1941, no. 163. Underlined in the original document.

21 Ibid, 1952.

22 Catherine Higgs, *Chocolate islands: cocoa, slavery, and colonial Africa* (Athens (Ohio): Ohio University Press, 2013): 11–12.

23 AAB, RACB, Rutshuru Territoire, Rapport AIMO, no. 163, 1951, and ibid, Kabare Territoire, Rapport AIMO, 1952, no. 99. Colonists, represented by the Unaki, even protested against the efforts of the administration to regulate and contract coffee labor – likely because that would raise labor costs. The Unaki stressed that temporary labor should be not only maintained but also encouraged (ibid, Agri, Café, Revendications des Planteurs (515), Lettre de l'Unaki au premier ministre belge, 31/10/1930).

24 Ibid, RACB, Kabare Territoire, Rapport AIMO, 1950, no. 99.

25 Ibid, AIMO, MO agricole, Inspections plantations européennes Rutshuru, no. 1653/13, Rapport d'ensemble sur la situation de la MO dans le territoire de Rutshuru, édité par Dubuisson (assistant du commissaire de district), 15/1/1938.

Local notables, *colons* and workers alike all preferred auxiliary labor. For local notables, temporary labor meant not only a restriction on social mobility but also less of an infraction on their authority.[26] For colonists, temporary workers were beneficial because the nature of coffee production entails cyclical and temporary labor needs (particularly during planting and harvesting periods) and also because they reduced labor costs (*infra*). Finally, except for squatters, most temporary workers came from villages near the coffee estates. They preferred auxiliary work because this allowed them to combine salaried plantation work with communal and family duties and to preserve social relationships – which was more difficult for regular workers.[27]

Temporary workers were heavily in demand during the planting and harvest phases. During the latter phase, women and children were employed in particular to clear and prepare the land in order to prepare for planting seedlings or sowing, which in turn were tasks for auxiliary male laborers. In the early 1930s, some *colons* allegedly preferred day labor to fulfill these tasks, although piece work – also called the "Zeehandelaer system" – which was already in place in Shangugu (*infra*) had some unignorable advantages as well.[28] This system not only increased labor productivity, it also allowed people to leave the estate when the chores were accomplished rather than stay the entire day. In this way, workers were able to return more quickly to participating in village/family life. It is not unlikely that some colonists feared that a possible rise in labor productivity might invoke increasing wages, which in turn might have resulted in financial problems, especially during the 1930s. But at the beginning of World War II, still half of the temporary workforce were day laborers.[29] Day labor continued to be important in the 1950s, even though most planters seem to have realized that keeping laborers on their estate too long was counterproductive. Thus, in order to remedy the possible absence of auxiliary laborers:

> Generally, planters do not ask from their laborers an eight-hour presence at work (six hours of unremitting labor). They know that the Mushi [Kabare] prefer to be free in the afternoon in order to engage in personnel duties in their village.[30]

---

26 Bishikwabo, "Un aspect du colonat au Congo belge: le sort des travailleurs du Kivu (1900–1940)": 35 and 38.

27 Northrup, *Beyond the bend in the river: African labor in Eastern Zaire 1865–1940*: 171.

28 AAB, Agri, Compagnies, Dossiers individuels des plantations (654), Lettre de Mr Hanegraef à la direction de Crédit Agricole d'Afrique à Bruxelles, 31/12/1931.

29 Bashizi, "Processus de domination socio-économique et marché du travail au Bushi (1920–45)": 19.

30 AAB, RACB, Kabare Territoire, Rapport AIMO, 1953, no. 99.

In such cases and with the introduction of piece/task work, planters adapted to African needs rather than the other way around.[31] Another situation in which conflicting interests needed to be reconciled was during harvest (picking and sorting berries). As in other parts of the world, the most important segment of labor in this production phase was supplied by women and children, although the latter were also mobilized in earlier stages of the production process, for instance to search for and collect insects or chase away birds. Some planters may have believed that the "nimble fingers" of women and children were better suited to these kinds of jobs.[32] However, lower wages supposedly were a bigger incentive to engage women and children. Until the late 1920s, even children of less than twelve years old were mobilized to harvest berries. From that point on, however, it became legally prohibited to engage children below the age of twelve. Moreover, plantations had to make sure that children of between twelve and fifteen years old were only mobilized to do "light work" such as picking berries.[33] This suggests that, in the start-up stage of the plantation economy, children were also employed to perform heavy tasks such as clearing the land. That child labor was important to plantations is clear from an idea launched by Monseigneur Leys in the mid-1930s. In 1934, colonists asked to have school holidays coincide with the harvest period, but this was denied by the White Fathers. However, in order not to compromise either the education of children or the development of the coffee sector, Leys proposed that "the colonist who would like to engage children for one form of light work or another could, after agreement with the Mission, ask for volunteers who would work in the afternoon on the concession."[34]

Usually, but not exclusively, women and children were related to men already working – whether permanently or temporarily – on the coffee plantation.[35] Plantation laborers residing in bordering villages were accompanied by their wife and/or child(ren). In the case of squatters family ties were perhaps even more important, as this quote from a coffee plantation in Masisi proves:

31 In the 1950s, contemporary observers considered piece work outmoded, precisely because it allowed Africans to leave work as soon as their task was finished; see: M. Costier, "Note sur le rendement de la main-d'œuvre dans les plantations," *Bulletin de Documentation et de Technique Agricole* 8, no. 29 (1954): 15.

32 Not only in colonial Africa but also in Latin America, many planters believed in this advantage given by nature, although some scholars argue that "nimble fingers" are constructed historically rather than biologically; see for example: Diane Elson and Ruth Pearson, "'Nimble fingers make cheap workers': an analysis of women's employment in Third World export manufacturing," *Feminist Review* 7 (1981).

33 Vellut, "Enquête sur la main-d'oeuvre au Kivu (1930)": 38.

34 AAB, RACB, Kivu Province, Conseil de Province, 1935, no. 37(6).

35 Ost, "Agricultural laborers in Kivu, 1919–1939": 38.

> My brother and I employ a native labor force composed of families of which the family head is working voluntarily on our plantation. Due to the nature of the work and the attitude of the natives, certain jobs – harvest, manufacturing baskets and mats, separating coffee beans, [...] are performed by women [...]. Those families reside within the concession; they are not occupying a single village, but are organized in small village camps per family (*barza*). [...] It is incorrect that a relatively numerous population is living on our concessions; nonetheless no native is still living there who is not a son, daughter, wife, or supervised child or belonging to one of our workers and it is incorrect to say that our concessions are refuges for the single women and widows of the region. Labor is merely agricultural and essentially familial. That is the reason why every family member is employed according to their capacities and remunerated according to their work.[36]

This suggests that combined plantation wages were in many cases part of a household income strategy. However, food production (and the sale of surpluses) was also a part of the household economy (see Chapter 6). As women in most Sub-Saharan regions remained "the bedrock of food production,"[37] their attention was more directed to that activity. But in some cases, the harvesting of certain food crops (beans) coincided with the coffee harvest (June–August was especially demanding). In these circumstances women refused to harvest and planters lacked "nimble employees," especially in regions where labor was already scarce, such as Rutshuru. To force men to engage in the harvest, planters (or their *capitas*) threatened or deceived these potential workers, or called upon the territorial administration in order to recruit women.[38]

1.1.3 *Remplacement* System

In practice, the above categorization of labor categories was fluid, particularly in the southern regions of Lake Kivu (Kabare and Shangugu). In these territories an informal flexible replacement system existed until the early 1950s, and probably

---

36 AAB, AIMO, MO agricole, Situation de la MO au Kivu, no. 1649/9236/7bis, Rapport d'inspection concession Kishengo-Kimoo, 15/1/1941.

37 Cooper, *Africa since 1940: the past of the present*: 125.

38 AAB, AIMO, MO agricole, Doléances colons de Rutshuru, no. 1653/6, Extrait du rapport MO de Rutshuru, 24/6/1942, and ibid, Inspections plantations européennes de Rutshuru, no. 1653/13, Extrait de la réunion des planteurs, 7/5/1937. During this meeting, planters plainly asked the bureaucracy to coerce women and even children to harvest coffee. See also the previous chapter, where I demonstrated that notables too were involved in forcing women to enter plantations.

even longer.[39] Both regular and auxiliary coffee plantation workers were often substituted by family or community members.[40] In the first case, children, women, brothers, cousins or parents could replace the formal worker, but friends or older people from within the community could replace the actual hired plantation workers as well.

In practice, a worker entered into a contract (written or oral) or was forced to enter, and his name was registered. Consequently, he should be considered as *l'homme de base*. The latter was substituted for one or a few days by a *remplaçant*, who carried out the work of the contracted worker. As governor Moeller observed in the early 1930s, "the labor contract seems to be made with a community rather than with an individual."[41] Meanwhile, contracted employees performed other (community and/or family) tasks or other kinds of salaried work. Replacement laborers were thus completely unknown to plantation owners, *capitas* or the administration. They did not have a contract and did not receive a wage, as it was the *homme de base* or the chief who was supposed to distribute wages.

One of the reasons people engaged in wage labor was to escape *corvées* and/or their often strict notables (Chapter 4). But on the other hand, entering wage labor (especially on a regular basis) could mean reprisals by the latter, such as expropriation of land (Chapter 3). In regions with a relatively high population density, similar "revenge acts" by chiefs could get workers into serious trouble; it was noted by General Governor Ryckmans in 1945:

> that in particular the lack of fertile land [*bonnes terres*] make laborers fear that they will lose their plot in the village and pushes them to adopt the replacement system, which permits them to put in an appearance in the chieftaincy, but I can no longer tolerate the continuation of such a mistake.[42]

---

39 Ibid, RACB, Kabare Territoire, Rapport AIMO, 1950, no. 99. In parts replacement had disappeared, though.

40 Bashizi, "Processus de domination socio-économique et marché du travail au Bushi (1920–45)": 14–15.

41 Vellut, "Enquête sur la main-d'oeuvre au Kivu (1930)": 32.

42 AAB, AIMO, MO agricole, Situation de la MO au Kivu, no. 1649/9236/10, Lettre du gouverneur général Ryckmans au gouverneur de Costermansville, 14/8/1945. It is not surprising that a similar system did not exist in other regions bordering Lake Kivu. On the Congolese side the lack of land was less pronounced than in Kabare, while on the Rwandan side, in Kibuye and Gisenyi, the plantation sector was negligible.

The administration rejected the practice of laborers replacing each other on a regular basis. While Ryckmans framed governmental dislike as being about abuses by chiefs that needed to end, clearly the lack of control and hence of the legibility of the workforce was the main concern. Hired workers registered their name, but with that name several faces could correspond.[43] This blurriness must have given administrative agents a good few sleepless nights. Punishing someone who has a face but no name known to Europeans became extremely difficult, and tax impositions were impossible to collect properly. In order to deal with these problems the territorial government in Kabare tried to introduce a special kind of written interim contract (of fifteen days maximum) in the early 1930s, aimed at reconciling administrative and African interests:

> These short-term contracts create the possibility to punish delinquents, and would not harm native crop and customary requirements, nor their traditional obligations. They would allow the workers succeeding each other in every concession to be accurately counted.[44]

However, colonists were not fully convinced by the idea of giving *remplaçants* a contract, because that would inevitably raise labor costs. Moreover, when someone at least does the job without any extra cost, why should they complain? In the annual report of 1937, the territorial agent regretted that several *colons* and especially larger plantation firms still refused to use the contract template proposed by the government.[45] However, despite the reticence of many colonists the replacement system was subject to erosion over time. At the beginning of the 1930s, one laborer could have five to seven substitutes, or, "[a] worker, via replacement and adapting a communal identity, becomes a seven-headed hydra."[46] In the mid-1940s, the number of substitutes had been reduced to only one or two per worker.[47] According to one scholar, the system had evolved internally. He claims that colonization had encouraged individualism and that, consequently, collective-oriented replacement labor had shrunk.[48] However, external factors might also have contributed to this evolution. As life in the countryside

43 Bashizi, "Processus de domination socio-économique et marché du travail au Bushi (1920–45)": 16.

44 AAB, RACB, Kabare Territoire, Rapport AIMO, 1933, no. 99.

45 Ibid, 1937.

46 Ibid, 1933.

47 Ibid, AIMO, MO agricole, Planteurs de café au Kivu, no. 1653/14, Rapport d'inspection des entreprises agricole (Kabare), 15/5/1943.

48 Bashizi, "Pouvoirs publics, plantations européennes et réactions paysannes au Sud-Kivu (1920–1960)": 140.

deteriorated, spontaneous engagements increased from the end of the 1930s onwards (Chapter 4) and people might have chosen to abandon village life. Nevertheless, one might expect that urban employment/life probably had more appeal than working on coffee plantations. However, after World War II working conditions improved and employers might have finally preferred contracts, strengthened by the idea of stabilizing their labor force.

1.2 *Remunerating Laborers*

1.2.1 Men's Wages

In a general overview of the Belgian Congo, Peemans claims that in the period 1910–1960, nominal wages for unskilled workers multiplied on average by a factor of thirty-five.[49] However, when it comes to rewarding workers there is an important distinction between regular and temporary plantation workers. During the entire colonial period in the Kivu, the former category – paid per two weeks or per month – received higher remunerations than the latter. Auxiliaries were paid per week, per day or per task, and men always received higher wages than women, while women in turn were paid better than children. Wages were supplemented by a ration[50] – usually in the form of goods, but from the 1930s onwards increasingly in money. Moreover, a harmonization of wages was absent, and in some plantations wages even varied from month to month. Furthermore, minimum wages were not introduced until the end of World War II. From that point on, the provincial council fixed and adapted minimum wages based on the cost of living, similarly to in other African colonies (although in British colonies minimum wages were fixed without the interference of the government[51]). As a final note, attention is required since in most cases it was the employer who informed inspectors or the administration about wages. Hence, it is not unlikely that the figures in the sources are underestimations.

The consequence of all of this is that the sources sometimes present a confusing mishmash of figures. However, it is my intention not to burden this research with a profusion of numbers, but rather to work with samples and averages. I can correlate these wage samples to prices on local markets and in this way reveal

49 Jean-Philippe Peemans, *Diffusion du progrès économique et convergence des prix: le cas Congo-Belgique, 1900–1960: la formation du système des prix et salaires dans une économie dualiste* (Louvain: Editions Nauwelaerts, 1968); 270.

50 Until the end of the 1930s, the ration was not always paid or, on some plantations, the ration was paid but not the actual wage; see: AAB, RACB, Kivu Province, Conseil de Province, 1938, no. 38(2). After World War II, rations were in some cases only paid partially in an attempt by colonists to lower labor costs.

51 Cooper, *Decolonization and African society. The labor question in French and British Africa*: 324–326.

evolutions in real wages. This in turn allows me to shed light on workers' purchasing power, keeping in mind that, except for the 1950s, we are dealing with gross incomes here. Local market prices were regulated and controlled by the colonial state.[52] In doing so, the government implicitly legitimized poor wages at least until World War II. After the war, the wage question was reframed, resulting in tensions with *colons* (*infra*).

In 1928, wages for regular workers varied between 20 and 45 Francs (ration included) per month across the entire Kivu district; a skilled mason, for example, earned between 600 and 1000 Francs.[53] Based on average prices on local markets in the Kivu district, with his gross income and when the ration was paid in money, a regular male worker would be able to buy between 40 and 90 kilograms of potatoes (0.5 Francs per kilogram), or 10 to 20 kilograms of rice (2 Francs per kilogram).[54] However, in the wake of the global crisis, and combined with the devaluation of the Congolese Franc (1935), a drop in nominal wages and a rise in prices for imported goods occurred.[55] Since food prices were regulated by the colonial state, they did not increase but rather slightly decreased during the 1930s. In 1932, regular laborers in Kabare gained on average between 10 Francs per month plus 2 Francs ration per week (18 Francs in total) and 20 Francs monthly plus 3.5 Francs ration per week (totaling 34 Francs).[56] If the ration was paid in money, a laborer would be able to purchase between 72 and 136 kilograms of potatoes (0.25 Francs per kilogram), or between 17 and 30 kilograms of rice (1.1 Francs per kilogram).[57]

In the early 1940s, regular male workers earned between 30 and 48 Francs per month in Kabare (ration included), while at the end of the 1930s *capitas*' gross wages fluctuated between 100 and 120 Francs.[58] In Rutshuru, regular plantation laborers made an average of between 32 and 36 Francs.[59] At this point in time, a regular plantation worker in the Kivu district would be able to buy between 42 and 68 kilograms of rice (0.7 Francs per kilogram in 1939).[60] Based on the above figures, one might conclude that purchasing power rose in the 1930s. However,

52 Huybrechts, *Bilan économique du Congo*: 52–53.

53 AAB, GG, Kivu district, Rapport Annuel agriculture, 1928, no. 318.

54 Ost, "Agricultural laborers in Kivu, 1919–1939": 82.

55 Vanthemsche, *Congo. De impact van de kolonie op België*: 164.

56 AAB, AIMO, MO agricole, Dossier Unaki, no. 1653/10, Lettre du gouverneur de la Province Orientale au ministre de la colonie, 31/1/1933.

57 Ost, "Agricultural laborers in Kivu, 1919–1939": 82.

58 AAB, AIMO, Inspections plantations "La Linea" et "Dumont," no. 1653/12, Inspection des plantations européennes à Monvu, 28/4/1939, and ibid, Planteurs de café au Kivu, no. 1653/14, Rapport d'inspection des entreprises agricole (Kabare), 15/5/1943.

59 Ibid, RACB, Rutshuru Territoire, Rapport AIMO, 1942, no. 163.

60 Ost, "Agricultural laborers in Kivu, 1919–1939": 82.

taxes increased across the entire colony as well, so it is probably more cautious to say that, as with wages, purchasing power was rather stable.

A decade later nominal net wages had increased substantially, partly as a consequence of changes in governmental labor policy (setting minimum wages from 1945 onwards, for instance). In 1953 in Kabare, permanent workers earned on average of 180 Francs per month (ration included); a clerk in Bukavu made 600 Francs, while industrial laborers received 300 Francs. That same year, regular plantation workers in Masisi made 225 Francs and the net monthly salary in Rutshuru was 175 Francs (ration included as in Masisi).[61] A regular laborer would be able to buy 45 kilograms of potatoes in Kabare (4 Francs per kilogram), but 50 kilograms in Rutshuru (3.5 Francs per kilogram). In Kabare, the same workers could purchase 21 kilograms of rice (8.33 Francs per kilogram), but in Rutshuru only 19 kilograms (9.5 Francs per kilogram).[62] Even though wage averages can be deceptive and figures are based on only two food products, apparently the purchasing power of the regular coffee plantation workforce dropped during the course of the colonial period.

As argued above, the majority of Africans preferred temporary plantation work, so wages for these laborers indicate the purchasing power of the majority of the coffee labor force. Even though a distinction should be made between task and day workers, I focus only on day laborers, because their data is more coherent throughout the colonial period. Moreover, the following wages for day workers are all ration-inclusive. A male daily worker gained between 0.7 and 1 Franc in Kabare in the early 1930s.[63] During World War II, male day laborers in Kabare earned between 1 and 2 Francs, while in 1947, day laborers received a minimum of 3.5 Francs. In Bukavu, however, minimum wages fluctuated between 5 and 7 Francs a day, explaining the desire of many Africans to seek work in the city.[64] In the mid-1950s, the minimum day wage for agricultural workers was set at 8.5 Francs, while non-agricultural workers could earn at least 11.5 Francs per day.[65] Thus, a plantation worker in Kabare was able to buy 4 kilograms of potatoes (0.25 Francs per kilogram) or about 1 kilogram of rice (1.1 Francs per kilogram) in the

61 AAB, RACB, Kabare Territoire, Rapport AIMO, 1953, no. 99; Masisi Territoire, 1953, no. 143, and Rutshuru Territoire, 1953, no. 163.

62 Ibid, Kivu Province, Rapport Agri, 1953, no. 66. Prices in these sources are from markets in Bukavu and Goma respectively, both considered to be representative for the entire territory.

63 Ibid, GG, Kivu district, Rapport Annuel agriculture, 1933, no. 318.

64 Ibid, AIMO, MO agricole, Planteurs de café au Kivu, no. °1653/14, Rapport d'inspection des entreprises agricole (Kabare), 15/5/1943, and ibid, RACB, Kabare Territoire, Rapport AIMO, 1947, no. 99.

65 Ibid, 1953.

early 1930s. In the mid-1950s, an agricultural day wage was only sufficient to acquire about 2 kilograms of potatoes (4 Francs per kilogram) or 1 kilogram of rice (8.33 Francs per kilogram).

In the other territories bordering Lake Kivu the situation for temporary workers was different, because after World War II, a distinction was made between daily wages for Africans producing their own food and wages for Africans lacking their own means of food production. This indicates the lack of labor potential in areas with a lower population density than in the southern Kivu, and the desire to stabilize labor. It also shows that, as in many other parts of the world, wage labor income was buffered by a household subsistence economy.[66] For example, day laborers in Rutshuru earned between 0.5 and 1 Franc in 1937; five years later this had increased to 1.5 Francs, supplemented with 1 kilogram of beans a day for Rwandan laborers.[67] In 1953, the minimum daily wage of a worker with food crops of his own was set at 7.2 Francs; plantation laborers without their own food crops gained 8.61 Francs a day.[68] Thus, in 1937, a daily wage could result in 1 to 1.3 kilograms of rice (0.75 Francs per kilogram in 1937).[69] In the mid-1950s, workers with their own food crops could purchase 0.75 kilogram of rice (9.5 Francs per kilogram) or 2 kilograms of potatoes (3.5 Francs per kilogram); a worker without his own food crops could buy 0.9 kilograms of rice or 2.5 kilograms of potatoes at best. As for regular coffee plantation workers, there are clear indications that the purchasing power of day workers declined in the period under study.

During the colonial period nominal wages did not multiply by a factor of thirty-five, but rather by a factor of four to nine, indicating that plantation wages in the territories bordering Lake Kivu were extremely low compared with in the rest of the colony.[70] Comparisons made with other jobs in the same region only underline this argument. Nominal wages were not only low compared to other

66 This was also the case in Kabare: see Chapter 6 and Wilma A. Dunaway, "The centrality of the household to the modern world-system," in *Routledge handbook of world-systems analysis: theory and research*, ed. Salvatore J. Babones and Christopher K. Chase-Dunn (London; New York: Routledge, 2012).

67 AAB, AIMO, MO agricole, Inspections plantations européennes Rutshuru, no. 1653/13, Lettre du ministre de la colonie au gouverneur général, 17/3/1937, and ibid, RACB, Rutshuru Territoire, Rapport AIMO, 1942, no. 163.

68 Ibid, 1953.

69 Ost, "Agricultural laborers in Kivu, 1919–1939": 82.

70 See Louis Baeck, *Economische ontwikkeling en sociale structuur in Belgisch-Kongo* (Leuven: Centrum voor Economische Studiën, 1959): 223. Moreover, contemporary observers noticed that in general laborers' wages in the Belgian Congo were too low to even satisfy primary needs; see: Doucy and Feldheim, *Travailleurs indigènes et productivité du travail au Congo belge*: 47.

wages. At least until the mid-1950s, real wages seem to have decreased for regular workers and temporary workers alike, despite the introduction of minimum wages after World War II (*infra*). This runs counter to recent studies on African development stressing that rising urban wages are a sign of the rising purchasing power of large segments of the population.[71] The case of Congolese plantation workers suggests that urban developments should not be equated with developments in largely rural regions. Still, the consequences of wage labor – even if buffered by subsistence economic activities – were far-reaching. Firstly, while before World War II wages were primarily used to pay taxes and, if possible, to buy clothes, in the mid-1950s many agricultural workers even "possess[ed] bikes and sewing machines."[72] However, the question is whether these imported products were bought merely with plantation wages, since these were extremely low. As Peemans noticed, the growth of rural household income after World War II was largely a result of the expanding commercialization of food crops.[73] Secondly, the relationship with chiefs and other notables altered as well. One the one hand, chiefs were given more power by colonial authorities and often abused this, but on the other hand, wage labor allowed people to gain more freedom, as former customary tasks became increasingly commodified.

1.2.2 Women and Children

Unlike the data for male wages, there is a huge gap in information in the sources I consulted concerning wages for women and children. For the 1950s, for example, there is no data at all. Consequently, the following figures are circumstantial, but as incomes for women and children were probably part of a household revenue, they at least give some indications of the purchasing power of plantation workers' families.

At the end of the 1920s in Kabare, both women and children received nothing but a quantity of salt for their work, although sources do not specify the exact quantity.[74] In the early 1940s, women still received an amount of salt (between 200 and 380 grams), but they also got a salary. Women were paid 0.5 to 0.75 Francs per basket of picked coffee berries (this basket was 20 to 25 liters on average,

71 For instance: Sue Bowden, Blessing Chiripanhura and Paul Mosley, "Measuring and explaining poverty in six African countries: a long-period approach," *Journal of International Development* 20, no. 8 (2008).

72 Bashizi, "Processus de domination socio-économique et marché du travail au Bushi (1920–45)": 21, and AAB, RACB, Kivu Province, Conseil de Province, 1956, no. 41(2).

73 Peemans, *Diffusion du progrès économique et convergence des prix: le cas Congo-Belgique, 1900–1960: la formation du système des prix et salaires dans une économie dualiste:* 339.

74 AAB, GG, Kivu district, Rapport Annuel agriculture, 1928 and 1929, no. 318. As in precolonial times salt remained an important trade product on local markets.

which corresponds with the average yield of one day), or 1 to 2 Francs (or maximum 1.4 kilograms of rice) a day. In any case, they usually made less than their male co-workers. During World War II, children working on coffee plantations earned 2.5 to 5 Francs a week.[75] Evidence from Rutshuru suggests that wages for women and children there followed the same trend as in areas in the southern Kivu.[76]

1.2.3 Discussions on Remunerations

There is ample evidence in the sources that, throughout the colonial period, colonists were convinced that plantation labor productivity was insufficient, and for them this was the legitimization for maintaining extremely low wages. In order to enforce their arguments, colonists often compared coffee plantations in the Kivu with those in Kenya, arguing that coffee workers in Kenya deserved higher wages because their productivity was higher. While comparing labor output in Kivu and Kenya in 1945, for instance, the president of the Unaki even claimed that workers in the Kivu were paid too much in proportion to their productivity.[77] Up until World War II the colonial administration usually backed these arguments, but from that point on, more criticism emerged. Contemporary scholars were not the only ones who opposed the "low productivity" argument.[78] Some colonial agents too questioned *colons*' circular reasoning. As the administrator of Kabare declared in 1940:

> The colonists […] claim that they cannot pay more because they do not receive productivity, and we answer them that they cannot require productivity, if they do not increase the salary of their workers. It is a vicious circle.[79]

The government in the Kivu tried to break this vicious circle by showing willingness to pay higher wages. This started with the introduction of minimum wages,

75 Ibid, AIMO, MO agricole, Planteurs de café au Kivu, no. 1653/14, Rapport d'inspection des entreprises agricole (Kabare), 15/5/1943.

76 Ibid, Inspections plantations européennes Rutshuru, no. 1653/13, Rapport d'inspection Cafco par manager Beyer, 14/9/1937.

77 Ibid, RACB, Kivu Province, Conseil de Province, 1945, no. 195(1).

78 Doucy and Feldheim, *Travailleurs indigènes et productivité du travail au Congo belge*: 46. These scholars stress that Congolese laborers were well aware that they received a poor wage which did not allow them to improve their living standards. This, often in combination with harsh working conditions, provoked dislike and instability of the African labor force.

79 AAB, RACB, Kabare Territoire, Rapport AIMO, 1940, no. 99.

resulting in strains with colonists. However, none of these aspects are specific to the Belgian Congo. In other Africans colonies, both the governmental intention to pay higher revenues and opposition from European enterprises involved also influenced labor policy-making.[80]

Although discussions concerning minimum wages did not start until World War II, already in the 1930s colonists argued that labor costs should decrease, because the viability of many plantations was in danger as a consequence of the global crisis. One of the ideas they launched was to differentiate between industrial (*type fort*) and agricultural (*type faible*) workers – which happened after World War II. The latter, because they had to perform less physically demanding tasks, were in most cases able to return home each night or each week and continue to grow food crops, and they should therefore not get the same benefits industrial workers received, colonists argued.[81] Colonists were, among other things, referring to rations in kind, which in any case should be lower than rations for industrial workers. Despite the increasing monetization of rations from the late 1930s onwards, after World War II their levels continued to trouble European minds.

In 1940, the provincial council decided, in consultation with labor inspectors and the governor of Ruanda-Urundi, that when monthly wages were below 65 Francs a ration should be paid. However, mainly to satisfy *colons agricoles*, the following legal derogation was allowed: when the monthly wage was above 30 Francs, laborers coming from within a 5-kilometer range of the work spot would no longer receive a ration; when the monthly wage was above 30 Francs, laborers coming from outside a 5-kilometer range would no longer receive a ration if they were provided with 25 ares of land each and 25 days of paid leave in order to cultivate food crops.[82] As shown above, planters did not actually pay these wages; hence, discussions concerning revenues and ratios continued. In 1945, the Unaki, on behalf of the *colons agricoles*, and the administrators of the territories bordering Lake Kivu were polar opposites concerning the introduction of a minimum wage, as the following quote indicates:

80 Cooper, *Decolonization and African society. The labor question in French and British Africa*: 264.

81 Xavier Dierckx, "Note à M. le gouverneur général sur la culture du café au Kivu," *Agriculture et Elevage au Congo belge et dans les Colonies tropicales et subtropicales* 8 (1934): 25, and Leplae, *Les plantations de café au Congo belge: leur histoire (1881–1935), leur importance actuelle*: 228–229.

82 AAB, RACB, Kivu Province, Conseil de Province, 1940, no. 194(3). Moreover, in 1943, the limit to escape the payment of the ration was set at a wage of 90 Francs per month – or two to three times the average coffee plantation wage – which resulted in serious opposition from colonists (see: ibid, 1943, no. 194(4)).

> The administrators of the Colonization territories have already calculated this minimum which they assess at 46 frs per month [without ration] on average for singles [...]. The president [of the Unaki] thinks that in the Kivu the minimum should be set per day; at this moment it is 0.50 fr [without ration] [...]. The proposition of the Unaki is to fix a daily wage even lower than 0.50 fr, to which the Government is opposed. The president of the Unaki thinks that when a wage of 0.50 fr per day is too little, then 15 frs ration per week is manifestly too much; it is necessary to first readjust the level of the ration to the real costs of food products, and afterwards discuss wages.[83]

The solution was a compromise between colonists and the provincial government: the introduction of a minimum day wage of 3.5 Francs (ration included) in 1945. A decade later, the minimum wage had increased to 5.5 Francs a day (ration not included) but with agrarian colonists having the option to lower that minimum by 10% for laborers who performed "light work" (unspecified in the sources).[84] As demonstrated above, with rations included, minimum global wages in the 1950s differed from one territory to another – a consequence of either variations in food prices or the possibility of growing food crops of one's own.

However, the obligation to pay workers a minimum wage after World War II does not mean that employers always met their liabilities. One way of reducing labor costs was to pay the legal minimum wage and at the same time lower the ration.[85] Another way was to pay workers' wages below the legal minimum. Shortly after World War II, the Unaki argued that, apart from being insufficiently productive, workers did not need higher salaries because they (and their families) cultivated food crops of their own and, thus, there was no urge to buy food.[86] This was only partly true. Plantation workers also needed cash to pay taxes, for instance, but the argument *colons* used in order to legitimize low wages indicates that their primary concern was usually not the wellbeing of their laborers. Nevertheless, colonists avoiding their obligations were criticized in 1955 when the provincial governor of Kivu argued that "No justification whatsoever can be raised in order to maintain the present [wage] level, below subsistence level."[87] In the late 1950s, Congolese representatives also complained about

83 Ibid, 1945, no. 195(1).
84 Ibid, 1955, no. 41(1).
85 J. Nicaise, "Chronique sociale Congolaise," *Zaïre*, no. 1 (1954): 187.
86 AAB, RACB, Kivu Province, Conseil de Province, 1945, no. 195(1).
87 Ibid, 1955, no. 41(1).

poor revenues by stressing the expropriation of land by colonists. Consequently, according to the representatives, many villagers had no other option than to engage in plantation wage labor when salaries were up to four times lower than when those same villagers were still be able to cultivate and sell food crops.[88]

Because discussions on wage issues between the bureaucracy and colonists were usually settled to the disadvantage of the latter, *colons* had to find another way to reduce labor costs: introducing machines. Due to the high investment costs, initially most planters were not enthusiastic about mechanizing the crop-growing process. Furthermore, in some areas the mountainous environment did not permit the use of machinery. Moreover, as in Latin American coffee economies, it was not mechanization that was the key to success but rather the quality of the maintenance, harvesting, sorting and finally processing of the berries.[89] However, in regions with a lack of labor potential, such as Rutshuru, mechanization was more a must than a choice. According to the annual report of 1948, the majority of *colons* still refused, but some concessions attempted to mechanize aspects of the production process without reducing the workforce. The introduction of machines was accompanied by the expansion of their concession.[90] Only one lustrum later, mechanization was widespread and the initial repugnance of colonists allegedly had vanished:

> In the plantation sector, the carrying of products, coffee [...] has been reduced to an absolute minimum. Almost every colonist has a truck to transport coffee from the fields to the [processing] factory. Straw to cover the soil [an anti-weed measure] is no longer transported on the workers' back, but by vehicles. [...] A meeting is going to take place in order to decide the communal purchase of an airplane to spray insecticides over the concessions. This will result in a very serious reduction of labor and the worker will be relieved from a job he does not like. The colonists of Rutshuru do not quit improving labor methods and mechanizing in order to shrink the workforce.[91]

88 Ibid, 1958, no. 42(2).

89 Topik and Clarence-Smith, "Conclusion: new propositions and a research agenda": 390.

90 AAB, RACB, Rutshuru Territoire, Rapport AIMO, 1948, no. 163.

91 Ibid, 1954.

1.3 *Labor Conditions*

1.3.1 Violence and Insults

In his pioneering book on labor in eastern Congo, David Northrup argues that merely emphasizing wages would be imprudent.[92] For Africans, "pleasant work" and good treatment were at least as important as wages. The latter refers to food provisioning on the labor spot, lodgment for workers not able to return home, etcetera. There is ample evidence that at least until the end of World War II, plantation owners were reticent on these matters. The focus in this section will be on (physical and psychological) violence against plantation workers, which was omnipresent, again, at least until the end of World War II. Despite signing the International Labor Organization treaty on the abolition of coerced labor in the private sector in 1930, Belgium only ratified it in 1944. Before the end of World War II, this resulted in hidden forms of and a trivialization of forced labor, as Seibert calls it.[93]

Many colonial administrators and colonists were convinced that the use of the whip was the only effective measure for disciplining Africans.[94] In the second half of the 1920s, employers in the Oriental Province asked for the right to punish undisciplined workers corporally. This was agreed to by the provincial authorities at first, but after protest campaigns in the Belgian press the decree was nuanced and relaxed. The whip could still be used as a disciplinary measure, but the provincial council was "unanimous in repelling every arrangement that would allow the application of such punishments by the employer on the work floor, which would be the same as putting the natives outside the law." The provincial council decided that before employers could use the whip, a (European) police judge had to enforce its disciplinary use.[95] However, this does not mean

92 Northrup, *Beyond the bend in the river: African labor in Eastern Zaire 1865–1940*: 207.

93 Seibert, *In die globale Wirtschaft gezwungen. Arbeit und kolonialer Kapitalismus im Kongo (1885–1960)*: 185–186. For examples of forced labor regimes in other Congolese sectors, I refer to the extended work of Marchal, *L'histoire du Congo 1910–1945. Travail forcé pour le cuivre et pour l'or, pour le rail, pour l'huile de palme*. Things can always be worse. Portugal ratified this treaty only in 1956, resulting in abuses until the late 1950s; see for instance: Alexander Keese, "The constraints of late colonial reform policy: forced labour scandals in the Portuguese Congo (Angola) and the limits of reform under authoritarian colonial rule, 1955–1961," *Portuguese Studies* 28, no. 2 (2012).

94 Dibwe dia Mwembu, "La peine du fouet au Congo belge (1885–1960)," *Cahiers de Tunisie: revue de sciences humaines* 34, no. 135–136 (1968): 144–145.

95 See for the discussions: AAB, RACB, Province Orientale, Comité Régional, 1927; 1928 and 1929, no. 49(1bis), 49(1) and 49(2). It is not unlikely that colonists in the Kivu regarded courts as created to favor them. This is similar to Kenya, where settlers considered courts as an instrument not only to "teach" Africans new ways of working but also to impose

that employers obeyed this decree, and moreover, using the whip as a disciplinary measure was officially abolished only in 1951. This does not mean that, unofficially, the practice did not still continue.

In addition to the whip, unequal power relations between employers and Africans resulted in other forms of violence. A 1937 letter addressed to the General Governor mentions the common use of insults, threats and false promises by plantation owners vis-à-vis their workers in Kabare. One *colon* even "coerced the candidate laborers to enter and work for free for a month [...] meanwhile threatening to charge them with stealing."[96] Occasionally, physiological assaults went hand in hand with physical force against plantation workers. In Rutshuru for example, two charges were made against Europeans for beating and wounding Congolese coffee plantation laborers in 1932.[97] In several documents and as late as the 1940s, evidence can be found of workers in Kabare who were treated hard-handedly, with beatings which sometimes resulted in serious injuries.[98] Labor inspectors and (sometimes) officials were not the only ones to complain about the violent handling of coffee workers. Local chiefs expressed their displeasure as well. In 1932, a chief pressed a charge against a *colon* because the latter treated his workers brutally. The translation of the chief's plaint reveals, among other things, not only that plantation labors sometimes did not receive their wage but also that they "were beaten willy-nilly."[99]

However, things can always get worse. In Kabare, an Italian plantation owner was accused of manslaughter in the early 1930s. Even though the colonist was cleared of blame, it seems unlikely that a European would be accused of such a crime without serious indications.[100] The same repulsive atrocities were committed in Masisi. An inspection report of the early 1940s revealed two deaths at a certain specific concession; one was caused by heavy beatings resulting in fatal injuries. At the time the report was written legal proceedings were progressing, and it is uncertain whether the plantation owner was condemned or not.[101] After World War II, the sources I consulted no longer

extra-judicial sanctions on them; see: Brett Shadle, "White settlers and the law in early colonial Kenya," *Journal of Eastern African Studies* 4, no. 3 (2010): 510.

96 AAB, AIMO, MO agricole, Dossier Kabare, no. 1653/7, Lettre de Noirot au gouverneur général, 6/12/1937.

97 Ibid, RACB, Rutshuru Territoire, Rapport AIMO, 1932, no. 163.

98 Ibid, Kabare Territoire, 1940, no. 99, and ibid, AIMO, MO agricole, Dossier Unaki, no. 1653/10, Lettre anonyme au ministre de la colonie, 29/4/1940.

99 Ibid, Dossier Kabare, no. 1653/7, Dossier ex-chef de la chefferie de Kabare, 4/6/1938.

100 Ibid, Dossier Unaki, no. 1653/10, Lettre du gouverneur de la Province Orientale au ministre de la colonie, 31/1/1933.

101 Ibid, Situation de la MO au Kivu, no. 1649/9236/7bis, Rapport d'inspection concession Loashi, 14/1/1941.

make reference to violence against laborers. This might be the result of the ratification of the treatment on the abolition of forced labor (1944), causing a shift from an extra-economic to an economic coercive labor system.[102] Or the ratification might also have led to administrators/labor inspectors "forgetting" to write down possible assaults.

1.3.2 Fines and Bonuses

In addition to being subjected to violence, workers were often sanctioned for not following the rules in order to discipline them. If they were absent or failed to complete a task within a certain term, laborers could be punished either by withholding (part of) the wage or by means of fines.

In 1932, some chiefs in Kabare complained about harsh working conditions on the coffee plantations. They stated that, among other things, "when a laborer has to dig six holes a day [to plant bushes], and he only succeeds in doing five, he is not paid at all."[103] Whether workers were not able to dig more than six holes a day is not the issue here. The point is that coffee workers were fined heavily, sometimes exceeding a daily wage, as I will show below. Moreover, retention of salaries was still common in the early 1940s. Inspection reports of plantations in Kabare show that withholdings for absence oscillated between 1 and 1.5 Francs per day; the average male daily wage was between 1 and 2 Francs.[104] Even though retention of revenue no longer appears in the sources after the war, it is not unlikely that such practices continued as well, considering the discussions concerning the introduction of minimum wages and the retention of rations.

The practice of fining workers continued until the end of the colonial period and was feared by laborers. In 1951, workers in Masisi asked for the motive behind fine(s) not to be written down in their working booklet. This would probably put off possible future employers, and the workers' demand shows the continuation of a fining system.[105] People who were absent from work (for whatever reason, including illness) usually did not receive their wage. Laborers not completing their task (or not well enough to do so) were sometimes punished financially with fines of between 0.1 Francs and 1 Franc in the early 1940s in all regions

102 Van Melkebeke, "Coerced coffee cultivation and rural agency: the plantation-economy of the Kivu (1918–1940)": 207.

103 AAB, AIMO, MO agricole, Dossier Unaki, no. 1653/10, Rapport d'inspection édité par Dubuisson, 3/11/1932.

104 Ibid, Planteurs de café au Kivu, no. 1653/14, Rapport d'inspection des entreprises agricole (Kabare), 15/5/1943. For more examples see ibid, Dossier Unaki, no. 1653/10, Lettre anonyme au ministre de la colonie, 29/4/1940, and ibid, RACB, Kabare Territoire, Rapport AIMO, 1940, no. 99.

105 Ibid, Masisi Territoire, Rapport AIMO, 1951, no. 143.

bordering Lake Kivu, alongside withholding their revenue.[106] Furthermore, in addition to financial fines, *colons* sometimes used another, dubious way of sanctioning their workers: "When the laborers have not finished their task, a certain colonist locks them up during the night, in a chicken coop."[107] Clearly, penalties were heavy and plantation workers often retained little (if anything) from their already poor wages – a practice even contemporary observers did not fail to notice. In 1933, for example, governor Moeller made a lucid observation:

> the SAAK [...] applies a retention of 2 francs per day of absence to a worker who gains 1.33 fr per day [...] and a fine of 1 francs for a poorly conducted job [...] such a regime does not popularize working at a similar level of exploitation.[108]

It can hardly be a surprise that in such circumstances, the stabilization of the workforce was difficult to achieve for European employers. The African's supposed lack of discipline was, according to one African scholar, the reaction of laborers to poor working conditions and low wages.[109] These elements, in combination with the sometimes fierce handling of workers in the plantation sector as well as other sectors, mark the memory of many Africans, who started seeing wage labor as a form of "slavery."[110] However, in order to achieve more stability, employers also began to reward workers (with bonuses in kind or money and/or vacation days), starting from the end of the 1930s and increasingly after World War II.[111]

---

106 Ibid, AIMO, MO agricole, Situation de la MO au Kivu, no. 1649/9236/7bis, Rapport d'inspection concession Loashi, 14/1/1941; ibid, Inspections plantations "La Linea" et "Dumont," no. 1653/12, Inspection des plantations européennes à Monvu, 28/4/1939; and ibid, Planteurs de café au Kivu, no. 1653/14, Rapport d'inspection des entreprises agricole (Kabare), 15/5/1943.

107 Ibid, Dossier Unaki, no. 1653/10, Rapport d'inspection édité par Dubuisson, 3/11/1932.

108 Ibid, Lettre du gouverneur de la Province Orientale au ministre de la colonie, 31/1/1933. Fining heavily was also widespread in French and Portuguese colonies; see: Catherine Coquery-Vidrovitch, "The colonial economy of the former French, Belgian and Portuguese zones, 1914–1935," in *General history of Africa, Volume 7: Africa under colonial domination, 1880–1935*, ed. Albert Adu Boahen (Berkeley: Heinnemann Educational Books, 1985): 365.

109 Mwembu, "La peine du fouet au Congo belge (1885–1960)": 148.

110 Seibert, "More continuity than change? New forms of unfree labor in the Belgian Congo, 1908–1930": 385.

111 Bishikwabo, "Un aspect du colonat au Congo belge: le sort des travailleurs du Kivu (1900–1940)": 36. However, it seems that *capitas* received bonuses already in the early 1930s. When the workers they supervised succeeded in completing their task properly, *capitas* at the Lukayo concession (Kabare) received 2% of the wages paid to the workers as a bonus

Although bonuses were paid for achieving a task within a certain period, and even to allow the payment of taxes,[112] it seems that most of the efforts of plantations went to bonuses for re-engagements and regularity. At the end of the 1930s, workers from the Linea company who were present for an entire month without one day of absence received 1 Franc in addition to their wage. Moreover, workers extending their contract for one year received a bonus of 5 Francs, and those who extended it for two years got 15 Francs, with two days of paid leave every two months on top.[113] At the Loashi concession in Masisi in the early 1940s, bonuses were paid in kind. Laborers considered "productive" by the employer – which was an arbitrary criterion – received salt and soap, while workers whose women helped on a regular basis during harvest received a cup of salt.[114]

After World War II, these two systems (in kind and/or money) of rewarding plantation workers continued. Regularity bonuses continued to be paid in kind in both Masisi and, to a lesser extent, Kabare. In both territories, laborers with no absences during one month received an unspecified quantity of salt and oil at least until the mid-1950s.[115] Moreover, from the early 1950s onwards, some employers in Masisi granted their employees paid leave to cultivate food crops.[116] Similarly to in Rutshuru, this means of "rewarding" workers was also an attempt to reduce the instability of the workforce, which was a larger problem in regions with a small labor reservoir. In Rutshuru in the mid-1950s, every employer took paid leave two times per year to prepare the land – on the concession or in the villages – for cultivating food crops. Some employers even helped by allowing their workers to use tractors to plow the land.[117] Furthermore, as the lack of labor was especially pronounced in this territory, the level of various kinds of bonuses was inversely proportional, as the following quote indicates:

(see AAB, AIMO, MO agricole, Dossier Unaki, no. 1653/10, Rapport d'inspection édité par Dubuisson, 3/11/1932).

112 For instance: ibid, Inspections plantations européennes Rutshuru, no. 1653/13, Rapport d'inspection plantation Mbigo, 28/9/1937.

113 Ibid, Inspections plantations "La Linea" et "Dumont," no. 1653/12, Inspection des plantations européennes à Monvu, 28/4/1939.

114 Ibid, Situation de la MO au Kivu, no. 1649/9236/7bis, Rapport d'inspection concession Loashi, 14/1/1941.

115 Ibid, RACB, Kabare Territoire, Rapport AIMO, 1953, no. 99, and ibid, Masisi Territoire, 1954, no. 143. However, in Kabare, bonuses for regularity or productivity paid in money, were prevailing after the war.

116 Ibid, 1950.

117 Ibid, Rutshuru Territoire, 1953, no. 163.

> Engagement or re-engagement bonuses exist everywhere. They vary between 100 and 200 frs per contract year. When coffee is picked all employers pay a bonus proportional to the work delivered. During harvest periods certain workers receive daily salaries of between 15 and 20 frs. Working years and regularity bonuses are paid by some employers. Others pay [their workers'] taxes every year as a bonus.[118]

In addition to bonuses, international discussions arose about the payment of family allowances in an attempt to further enforce the idea of stabilization in the early 1950s. Belgium and France played a leading role in these debates. Both colonizing powers advocated monogamous families based on domestic examples with male wage earners and women who raised children.[119] Although this was particularly aimed at "detribalized" industrial workers, in rural regions bordering Lake Kivu the colonial state also induced employers to pay such allocations to regular laborers. Despite opposition among *colons agricoles*, who again used rising labor costs as an argument – in some cases 100 to 140% of the salary, according to them – family allowances were paid from 1952 onwards.[120] This was probably another reason why colonists continued to prefer temporary workers. Even though sources do not mention whether these familial bonuses were paid per child or how much actually was paid, at least in Masisi allowances were rendered in kind until 1954.[121] Whether family allocations halted the process of declining coffee wages is difficult to say, particularly because sources are scarce with information. But if allowances did improve workers' purchasing power, it was only in the final years of the colonial period.

1.3.3 Enterprise Councils

Another change disliked by colonists was one that reflected a growing interest in laborers and their concerns, as well as a wish of the state to increase participation: the creation of enterprise councils after World War II. After the example of the Belgian consultative model, consultations between state, employers and workers were organized in both the colony and the mandate. The decree of March 3, 1946, provided for the implementation of local comities and enterprise councils. The former consisted of state and employer representatives from vari-

118 Ibid, 1954.

119 Frederick Cooper, "From free labor to family allowances: labor and African society in colonial discourse," *American Ethnologist* 16, no. 4 (1989): 755–756.

120 AAB, RACB, Kivu Province, Conseil de Province, 1952, no. 39(5).

121 Ibid, Masisi Territoire, Rapport AIMO, 1954, no. 143.

ous sectors, while labor representatives could be called upon for consultation. These comities debated labor questions in general. The latter, on the other hand, were organized at an enterprise level and consisted of administrative agents, management and labor delegates. Every enterprise with at least 250 regular laborers was supposed to install such a council. It seems that agricultural firms, in particular, sometimes refused to hold meetings: "Agricultural associations are prompted to proceed to regular meetings of indigenous enterprise councils."[122] Even though more personal desiderata of workers were discussed during such councils, delegates were appointed by the management and their maneuvering space was limited and strictly defined.[123]

Information on enterprise councils is presented here schematically: first, because sources are not generous with details on how these councils functioned and what their impact ultimately was; second, because with the exception of larger firms, coffee plantations usually did not have 250 regular laborers. This might result in a biased picture, because workers active on small-scale plantations might have had other desires than laborers in a large-scale plantation company. Nevertheless, because enterprise councils were organized at a firm level, they allow us to determine what workers' wishes and complaints were. In general, in all areas bordering Lake Kivu, most demands were centered around wage increases, more vacation days, more bonuses, fewer tasks, etcetera. Evidently, not every demand of the workforce was met, but in some cases unusual things were asked for and even approved. For instance, in 1949, the management of the INEAC approved that workers with at least fifteen years of service would receive a cow.[124] In 1953, laborers from the SAAK in Rutshuru asked the management to install a food store on the concession. The SAAK approved this proposition, which suggests the will of the company to keep workers attached to the plantation while the firm equally attempted to increase profit margins.[125]

122 Ibid.

123 Baeck, *Economische ontwikkeling en sociale structuur in Belgisch-Kongo*: 231–232. From 1957 onwards, the worker limit at which enterprise councils had to be implemented was lowered to 100, which resulted in an increase in the number of councils. Furthermore, such organizations were not the same as syndicates. The latter were allowed from 1946, but strictly controlled and, consequently, with little success until 1957. In that year, the distinction between African and European unions was abandoned and the colonial state allowed African unions more room to maneuver.

124 AAB, RACB, Kabare Territoire, Rapport AIMO, 1949, no. 99.

125 Ibid, Rutshuru Territoire, 1953, no. 163.

2 Workforce East of Lake Kivu

2.1 *Coffee Production at Household Level*

2.1.1 Organization

The above categorization of laborers is not appropriate for smallholder cultivation. Producers are *de facto* responsible for every step in the production process, although unpaid assistance from family members is indispensable (*infra*), and some planters were also able to mobilize other Africans working for a wage (see Chapter 4). As explained previously, the organization of smallholder production on a family level only began in 1932–1933, with the second campaign. In order to distribute coffee, notables were supposed to deliver seeds or seedlings to their subjects, initially free of charge, but they often refused to do that.[126] In order to anticipate this, the government itself handed over coffee seedlings, also initially free of charge. Africans were obliged to pick up their plants (initially fifty-four) in the *chef-lieu* of the territory, transport them in self-constructed baskets and then finally plant them around their homestead.[127]

However, for many Africans the *chef-lieu* was far away from their home and therefore the mandate government relied on additional distribution channels. The state depended on missions to distribute seeds, and in some parts of Rwanda even allowed private firms to deliver the required seedlings to cultivators.[128] Experimental stations were of minor importance in this context. From 1935 onwards, African smallholders as well allegedly sold seeds (at 4 Francs per kilogram) to fellow producers.[129]

When cultivators have to travel around to pick up seeds/seedlings, they lose quite some time. Moreover, transportation in baskets can severely damage young plants. The mandate administration was well aware of these issues and allowed, simultaneously with the "individualization" of coffee land (Chapter 3), the installation of individual nurseries from the mid-1930s onwards, although the government discursively framed it as an "educational objective":

> I would propose the system of individual nurseries of 150 seeds […]; this system, already started by my predecessor on certain hills of Busozo and

126 Gahama, *Le Burundi sous administration belge: la période du mandat 1919–1939*: 185.

127 Molitor, "L'introduction et le développement de la culture du caféier Arabica chez les indigènes du Ruanda-Urundi": 167–168.

128 Dorsey, "Rwandan colonial economy, 1916–1941": 176.

129 AAB, RWA, Café, Rapports, RWA(438), Lettre du résident aux administrateurs territoriaux, 21/6/1935. This price was maintained up until 1952, when a rise of 1 Franc per kilo was implemented.

> Bukunzi [Shangugu], deserves particular attention; even if surveillance of individual nurseries is more difficult, then still, the application of this system is not contestable when it comes to educating the individual. [...] I would like to implement the following system: every nursery is divided into as many parcels as there are hills to be provided; and these parcels in turn will be subdivided per family; family chiefs will be responsible vis-à-vis sub-chiefs for maintaining the parcels, which will be considered as family property from the moment they are created. [...] The system I propose will have in particular the purpose of attaching to the natives the idea of property and consequently, of contributing to the success of the coffee campaign.[130]

As this quote already predicts, control of individual nurseries indeed proved to be very challenging. In order to overcome this, administrations in all territories bordering Lake Kivu decided to abandon this system and started to promote state nurseries from the mid-1950s onwards. People had to pick up plants themselves once again, but the change in policy was that seedlings were no longer distributed for free. They were now sold for maximum of 1 to 2 Francs per plant. Although in theory it was a presumed lack of care for plants distributed freely that motivated this decision, it is clear that control and an attempt to raise state revenue were more plausible reasons for bureaucracies to abandon individual nurseries.[131]

After planting, the next important step in the cultivation process was maintenance. In contrast to in the colony, where women were usually not involved in maintaining bushes, in the mandate women helped their men.[132] Moreover, when men were absent, for instance when they were engaged in wage labor, women maintained coffee bushes on their own, even though men returned home whenever possible to monitor the work.[133] Women were often assisted by their children, who caught bugs or removed weeds close to the trunk. Because

130 Ibid, RWA(440), Lettre agent territorial Feremans de Shangugu au résident, 10/5/1935.

131 Ibid, RWA(444), Lettre du vice-gouverneur général Harroy au résident du Rwanda, 19/4/1955.

132 Hatungimana, *Le café au Burundi au XXe siècle: Paysans, argent, pouvoir*: 386.

133 AAB, RARU, Gisenyi Territoire, Rapport Général, 1935, no. 87(21); ibid, Shangugu Territoire, Rapport Général, 1938, no. 101(4); and ibid, RWA, Café, Rapports, RWA(439), Lettre de l'administrateur territorial de Gisenyi au résident, 30/7/1949. In Cameroon, women often assisted men as well and, similarly to in Ruanda-Urundi, they sometimes cultivated when men were absent; see: J.H.B. den Ouden, "Incorporation and changes in the composite household: the effects of coffee introduction and food crop commercialization in two Bamiléké chiefdoms," in *The household, women and agricultural development*, ed. Clio Presvelou and Saskia Spijkers-Zwart (Wageningen: H. Veenmann & Zonen B.V., 1980): 61.

nearly every step in the maintenance process was(/is) proportional to the yield of the bushes, they were severely monitored by European agronomists and African intermediaries (*infra*). As mentioned in the Congolese part of this chapter, pruning in particular was a delicate affair. While in the Congolese Kivu some workers specialized in this, on the other side of the lake the administration used *akazi* labor to form pruning teams, at least in Kibuye, where the pruning of coffee bushes was done by specialized groups until the late 1950s.[134]

When the berries were harvested, growers had to wash and dry the beans. From the start of the coffee campaigns until the end of the colonial period, drying beans on the ground was prohibited. Africans were instructed either to fabricate mats or build fences a few centimeters above the ground, near their homestead.[135]

Finally, after drying, the coffee beans had to be sold. Similarly to in Burundi, until the end of World War II Rwandan producers had two options: an official and an informal way. The first was a market where cultivators or African intermediaries sold their coffee, usually to Greek or Arab traders.[136] Producers transported coffee not only by porterage but also by carts drawn by cattle.[137] On these formal markets, cultivators/intermediaries very often were deceived, for instance by using cooked fraud weights.[138] The informal method of selling coffee consisted of Africans purchasing coffee from the producers in exchange for money, but also for food or salt. Because the formal method of selling coffee was uncontrollable by the administration, the system of free markets was abandoned after the war. From this point on, producers had to bring their coffee to coffee markets. The territorial administration organized these markets within a time window that varied from year to year, while Africans were forced to sell their coffee at a fixed price. However, these controlled coffee markets were dis-

134 AAB, RARU, Kibuye Territoire, Rapport AIMO, 1959, no. 82(17). I have found no evidence of other regions with pruning teams.

135 Ibid, RWA, Café, Rapports, RWA(437) and (442), Rapport mensuel Shangugu, Juin 1935 and lettre du résident Dessaint aux administrateurs territoriaux, 20/4/1954.

136 Sources are unclear on who these intermediaries were. However, it is not unlikely that they were African Muslims, who were vital to the lower levels of coffee trade, similarly to Muslims in the Bukoba district in colonial Tanzania; see: Kenneth Curtis, "Cooperation and cooptation: the struggle for market control in the Bukoba district of colonial Tanganyika," *International Journal of African Historical Studies* 25, no. 3 (1992). Furthermore, it is not unlikely that the Arab traders were descendants of the previously mentioned nineteenth-century Zanzibari, active in eastern Congo.

137 AAB, RARU, Shangugu Territoire, Rapport Général, 1925, no. 100(4).

138 Hatungimana, *Le café au Burundi au XXe siècle: Paysans, argent, pouvoir*: 266–267, and Nsavyimana, "La mobilisation de la force de travail au Burundi sous le mandate belge (1920–1940)": 234.

liked by cultivators, not only because people often had to wait a very long time but also because their coffee was frequently rejected if a European inspector deemed the quality to be insufficient for the world market, and finally because the extras (cigarettes, for example) that were sometimes donated by informal African traders were no longer possible.[139] Because coffee often was excluded, a vibrant informal market developed and cultivators continued to sell coffee to informal intermediaries, sometimes during the night.[140] In 1949, the amount of coffee sold informally was estimated at 20% for the entire mandate.[141] Administrations in turn disliked this kind of deal and were keen on finding and judging touts (*racoleurs indigènes*).[142] From 1950 onwards, a sort of compromise was implemented: official "free" markets were established in negotiation or commercial centers, and these were the only places where producers would receive a "fair" fixed minimum price for their coffee. On the other hand, African (or Asian) intermediaries were allowed to purchase coffee directly from the cultivators if they had a license.

2.1.2 Paying the Producers

The elaborated attention paid to markets and additional ways of selling coffee is essential because the prices paid to Africans that can be found in the sources are those established by the vice general governor on official (controlled) markets. However, people could always sell coffee clandestinely, as happened frequently (see Chapter 6), or to licensed traders who usually paid less than the official price per kilogram. Because it is impossible to figure out what producer sold how many kilograms, I will only make estimations as to what Africans would be able to buy with the price received for 1 kilogram of coffee. Consequently, "It is a real ambition to calculate exactly monetary revenues of a product of which commercialization [...] was so complex."[143] Moreover, as in the colony, people usually had various kinds of income (Chapter 6). When reading the following lines, one should keep in mind that purchasing power represents no more than an indication and that the counter value for 1 kilogram of coffee is more appropriate.

Before talking about prices, some important additional remarks are required. The price producers received was half or even only one third of the average

139 Hatungimana, *Le café au Burundi au XXe siècle: Paysans, argent, pouvoir*: 284–287.

140 S.N., "La commercialisation du café au Ruanda-Urundi," *Bulletin de la Banque Centrale du Congo belge et du Ruanda-Urundi* 7, no. 8 (1958): 265.

141 AAB, RWA, Café, Rapports, RWA(443), Procès-verbal de l'assemblée délibérante d'OCIRU, 30/11/1949.

142 Ibid, Conseils de Territoire et de Chefferie, Gisenyi, RWA(71), Procès-verbal de la réunion plénière des notables, 30/6/1948.

143 Hatungimana, *Le café au Burundi au XXe siècle: Paysans, argent, pouvoir*: 305.

IMAGE 4 Present-day coffee dry fences in Shangi
SOURCE: PERSONAL COLLECTION, 2016

market price in Antwerp.[144] This was partly due to the expensive transport of coffee produce. Internal transport was difficult as a consequence of Rwanda's mountainous geography; external transport was expensive because of the long distance coffee had to travel to either the Atlantic or the Indian Ocean and because of poorly developed road infrastructure.[145] Moreover, prices on international markets oscillated from month to month. In general, "the history of coffee is a saw-toothed history, punctuated with periods of growth, stagnation and crises."[146] Furthermore, cultivators' coffee income was much higher during harvest and sale seasons than in other periods. Conversely, wage laborers' income was more equilibrated.[147]

In 1935, a producer in Kibuye received 3 Francs for 1 kilogram of coffee. With this money, he would be able to buy 6 kilograms of beans (0.5 Francs per kilogram) or 15 kilograms of potatoes (0.2 Francs per kilogram). In 1953 when the territory was reorganized, a cultivator was paid 22 Francs for 1 kilogram of coffee and with that amount he could buy 4 to 5 kilograms of beans (4 to 6 Francs per

144 Ibid. 222 for a diagram with average annual coffee prices in Antwerp and New York (1931–58).

145 AAB, RARU, Rapport de la mission de visite de l'ONU au Ruanda-Urundi, 1948, no. 25(0A).

146 Bernard Charlery, François Bart and Jean-Christian Tulet, "Introduction: le café, facteur de dynamisation ou de dislocation des sytèmes de production paysans," in *Paysanneries du café des hautes terres tropicales. Afrique et Amérique latine*, ed. Jean-Christian Tulet, et al. (Paris: Karthala, 1994): 36.

147 Leurquin, *Le niveau de vie des populations rurales du Ruanda-Urundi*: 288–291.

kilogram) or 10 kilograms of potatoes (2.5 Francs per kilogram).[148] This example illustrates that the counter value for 1 kilogram of coffee declined during the colonial period. In the 1950s, a coffee producer in Kibuye could buy less with the money received for this cash crop than in the mid-1930s.

However, this argument requires nuance, as there are some variations in the other territories bordering Lake Kivu. In both Shangugu and Gisenyi, counter values decreased during the 1930s and then increased again, at least until the early 1950s. However, while in Gisenyi a producer could buy more or less the same for 1 kilogram of coffee in the 1950s as he could in the 1930s, in Shangugu he could buy more in the 1950s. In other words, the latter territory is the only one bordering Lake Kivu where the counter value for 1 kilogram of coffee improved during the colonial period.

Before the start of the coffee campaigns (1931), a producer in Gisenyi received an average price of 2.8 Francs per kilogram. With this money he would be able to purchase 7 kilograms of beans (0.4 Francs per kilogram) or 14 kilograms of potatoes (0.2 Francs per kilogram). A decade later, the "same" producer gained 2.3 Francs per kilogram of coffee, which equaled a maximum of about 5 kilograms of beans (0.45 Francs per kilogram) or 11.5 kilograms of potatoes (0.2 Francs per kilogram). Another decade later, 1 kilogram of coffee fetched 24 Francs; thus, a cultivator could purchase about 8 kilograms of beans (2.5 to 3 Francs per kilogram) or 12 kilograms of potatoes (2 Francs per kilogram).[149]

Growers in the southern tip of the Rwandan Kivu were paid on average 3.15 Francs per kilogram in 1931. With this, the producers would be able to afford 4.5 kilograms of beans (0.7 Francs per kilogram) or 3.15 kilograms of potatoes (1 Franc per kilogram). Immediately after World War II (1946), a producer gained 5.5 Francs for 1 kilogram of coffee and was able to acquire about 2.2 kilograms of beans (2.5 Francs per kilogram) or about 1.8 kilograms of potatoes (3 Francs per kilogram). In 1952, "this" grower was paid on average 23 Francs for 1 kilogram of coffee, which equaled about 8 kilograms of beans (3 Francs per kilogram) or 6 kilograms of potatoes (4 Francs per kilogram).[150]

The above estimations do not take taxes into account. This means that the real counter value of 1 kilogram of coffee was even lower than indicated. Furthermore, because the coffee market was (and still is) volatile, cultivators often take or have to take serious risks. In order to reduce risks, the mandate

148 AAB, RARU, Kibuye Territoire, Rapport Général, 1935 and 1953, no. 82(2) and 82(3).

149 Ibid, Gisenyi Territoire, 1931; 1941; 1952, no. 87(17); 88(1); 88(12).

150 Ibid Shangugu Territoire, 1931; 1946; 1952, no. 100(10); 101(12); 102(5), and ibid, RWA, Affaires économiques, RWA(398), Shangugu (loose files), 1931.

administration introduced a so-called equalization fund, which became operational on January 1, 1949:

> Coffee production is one of the principal resources for the natives in the mandate. This is the reason why the Government, in order to protect planters from the consequences of a fall in prices on the global coffee markets, has decided to create a compensation fund. This fund has to grant to the native producer, in case of a drop in coffee prices on the exterior markets, a supplementary amount of money alongside the trading price paid so that his maintenance work, harvest of berries and removal of chorions is remunerated sufficiently. This compensation fund is nurtured by skimming off [...] a tax which was fr 1.24 per kilogram of coffee exported on December 31, 1948.[151]

When prices dropped below a certain level, cultivators were compensated. However, it is unclear exactly how low prices had to fall. Moreover, at least until 1958, no compensation was paid at all, although cultivators did receive better equipment from the taxes they paid.[152] Either way, coffee producers had to pay such a tax from 1949 onwards, which reduced real income even more. The question is whether this tax was not rather an attempt on the part of the mandate administration to increase control over and stabilize smallholder production, as well as to make coffee cultivation more attractive by giving Africans at least a glimpse of a back-up plan. In this way, the bureaucracy might have tried to change the minds of people who sometimes abandoned their fields in order to work as wage laborers, or who neglected maintenance of their plants.

Nevertheless, the introduction of a monetary economy resulted in fundamental changes: patron–client ties became harsher, and the gender division of labor changed as women sometimes produced cash crops instead of their absent men. However, in general, transformations in African peasantries as a consequence of the colonial period were less pronounced than they were, for instance, in Latin America.[153] Smallholder families cultivating coffee changed their material way of life during the colonial period, but there is a consensus that this change was slow and that the little income they gained was not used as reinvestment but

151 Ibid, RARU, Rapport à la Commission permanente des Mandats, 1948, no. 20(4). In 1957, the tax amounted to 4.45 Francs per kilogram exported, while cultivators in Shangugu received on average about 26 Francs per kilogram (ibid, 1957, no. 24(3), and ibid, Shangugu Territoire, Rapport AIMO, 1957, no. 103(10)).

152 S.N., "La commercialisation du café au Ruanda-Urundi": 273.

153 Newbury and Newbury, "Bringing the peasants back in: agrarian themes in the construction and corrosion of statist historiography in Rwanda": 834.

rather to improve their social standing.[154] To a question asked by a French United Nations representative in 1950, the Belgian consultant answered:

> With reference to the peasants, the evolution is very different [compared to that of wage earners in general]. The peasant is still convinced of traditional ideas. When he has sold his coffee or his cotton, he saves to buy a cow that will improve his social level. His daily existence changes only very little, and improvement only shows in his replacing old clothes in bovine skin with clothes made of imported tissues. We can say that his ambition is not to ameliorate his daily existence, but to acquire a certain prestige and maybe a certain capital by increasing the number of cattle in his possession, or by acquiring one if he did not possess one yet.[155]

Trying to increase social capital is not unique to coffee smallholders in Ruanda-Urundi. West African cocoa farmers, for instance, reacted in a similar way.[156] The consequence of this was that cultivators in the mandate were less able than wage laborers (*infra*) to shake off the oppressive yoke of notables. Coffee producers often bought cattle, but these "coffee cows" were sometimes expropriated by chiefs and considered to be *ubuhake* cattle. Consequently, the actual owner (the coffee cultivator) was left with nothing more than usufruct while chiefs enforced control over cattle, land and people. Such abuses resulted in severe tensions between the rural masses and notables. These tensions, in combination with others, exploded violently in 1959.[157]

2.2 *Working Conditions in the Smallholder Sector*

2.2.1 Rigid Rules, Rigid Control

"Coffee cultivation implied a panoply of regulations administered by local chiefs and agricultural officers to force cultivators to tend their coffee plants according to particular, colonially mandated criteria."[158] With these words Catharine Newbury could not have been more correct in defining the coffee sector in Ruanda-Urundi, as nearly every step in the production process was strictly regulated and

154 See for instance: Hatungimana, *Le café au Burundi au XXe siècle: Paysans, argent, pouvoir*: 422–426, and Uwizeyimana, "Rôle politique de la caféiculture au Rwanda": 178.

155 AAB, RARU, Rapport à la Commission permanente des Mandats, 1950, no. 21(3).

156 Cooper, *Africa since 1940: the past of the present*: 21.

157 Uwizeyimana, "Rôle politique de la caféiculture au Rwanda": 179. For an excellent overview of the events in 1959, see: René Lemarchand, "The coup in Rwanda," in *Protest and power in Black Africa*, ed. Robert Rotberg and Ali Mazrui (New York: Oxford University Press, 1970).

158 Newbury, *The cohesion of oppression. Clientship and ethnicity in Rwanda, 1860–1960*: 205.

controlled. In Chapter 3, I illustrated the rigid rules concerning intercropping and land division; here I will elaborate on how the mandate administration tried to regulate and control the production process.

Before the government allowed individual nurseries, people had to pick up young plants in self-made baskets. Guidelines for their construction were distributed to planters by European agronomists via chiefs and sub-chiefs. Africans were forced to manufacture these baskets, preferably from banana bark. Baskets were required to have a diameter of 15 centimeters and a depth of 30 centimeters. Subsequently, after returning home, seedlings needed to be fixed in pits of 60 centimeters' diameter and 60 centimeters' depth, dug before the first of November, while the young plants needed to be planted from the fifteenth of December onwards. Especially during the first weeks after planting, seedlings also needed to be covered from the sun. Resident Coubeau dispatching these instructions to all administrative agents in the early 1930s, insisted on the imperative character of the rules and, as he stated, "no derogation will be tolerated."[159]

As stressed before, maintenance was a primordial step in the success of the cultivation process. One process that was considered to be very important by European agronomists, and strictly controlled by agrarian monitors, was mulching: providing plants with manure (from cattle or from leaves from food crops or straw) in order to protect them from drought.[160] As mentioned above, pruning was very important as well. And alongside specialized teams in Kibuye, this step was done by cultivators themselves, again monitored closely by agronomists and monitors. However, pruning directives imposed by bureaucracies were not always followed by agronomists, and some regional variation developed that in turn frustrated the mandate government in the 1950s:

> Mister the vice general governor insists that these directives have to be known and followed everywhere and by everyone, without the least hesitation or the least inadequacy. During the last years, everyone has acted as they think fit; the most divers "techniques" are used, at this moment the number of ways of pruning in use truly corresponds with the number of agronomists in Ruanda. [...] Divers methods are not only prohibited radically, but I also insist on a total cooperation between the territorial Service and the agricultural Service.[161]

159 AAB, RWA, Café, Rapports, RWA(438), Lettre du résident Coubeau aux chefs de poste, 6/1/1931.

160 Ibid, RARU, Rapport à la Commission permanente des Mandats, 1936 and 1938, no. 18(1) and 18(5).

161 Ibid, RWA, Café, Rapports, RWA(442), Lettre du résident Dessaint aux administrateurs territoriaux et agronomes, 4/6/1953. Underlined in the original document.

Harvesting berries and preparing coffee beans for sale were equally subjected to severe regulations. Especially in years when prices on international markets peaked (such as in the mid-1950s), the enforcement of harvest rules was even more severe and more controlled than in "bad" harvest years. During this period – mostly June–August, although in some areas harvest periods were more extended (for instance in Bugoyi in Gisenyi) – cultivators were supposed to pick berries at least once a week. Only ripe berries had to be harvested; berries with green or bright red tints were not allowed to be harvested until they had matured. Within twenty-four hours after the harvest, chorions had to be removed, immediately followed by washing the beans. After this, the beans had to be dried for no longer than four to five days, and never on the ground. Finally, the beans needed to be sold as soon as possible after drying, because coffee stocked inside habitations could become moldy, and root or dust could decrease the quality and hence the value of the beans as well.[162]

Such stringent regulations required severe controls and punishments for those who did not obey the imposed cultivation rules. European agronomists were not the only ones tasked with inspecting and fining African planters: African coffee monitors and (sub-)chiefs were as well, even primarily so. Although the latter were also expected to serve as an example, they – or their workers – often neglected regulations, resulting in fines. While (sub-)chiefs were given more tools to strengthen their grip on cultivators, there is ample evidence in the sources that suggests a lack of chiefly interest in controlling coffee planters:

> Mediocre maintenance: the natives, despite our advice, neglect their plantations. The sub-chiefs, in turn, do not excise any surveillance: they despise [...] occupying themselves with that matter, despite the fines they have received.[163]

Notables not only disregarded cultivation orders or the task of controlling planters; they sometimes ignored imposed timings concerning the delivery of seedlings to producers as well. Though the young plants were no longer free of charge in the 1950s, five sub-chiefs in Shangugu were still selling them to cultivators in October 1957, even though selling season had closed already. For their obstinate

162 Ibid, Lettre du résident Dessaint aux administrateurs territoriaux, 20/4/1954.

163 Ibid, RWA(437), Rapport mensuel Gisenyi, Septembre 1936. See also ibid, RWA(442), Lettre du résident Dessaint aux administrateurs territoriaux, 20/4/1954, and ibid, RARU, Gisenyi Territoire, Rapport Général; Rapport Agriculture, 1947; 1954, no. 88(7); 90(28).

IMAGE 5 Young coffee plant mulched with straw, Astrida, s.d
SOURCE: SABI, INEAC, DOCUMENTS ET PHOTOS (546/5204)

behavior the sub-chiefs received a fine of 250 Francs each, while their names were passed on to the *mwami* in Kigali.[164]

However, coffee planters feared control not only by notables but also, and even in particular, by local African coffee monitors. The latter knew the country very well; they traveled around at certain points in time and went from hill to hill. The monitors were the ones giving whip lashes when planters disobeyed directives. Planters often prepared banana beer for them, hoping to put them in a good mood.[165] Despite close inspection of monitors, producers often ignored or misunderstood orders, especially before World War II, resulting in "constant punishments in order to achieve results, and obliging them against their will to follow the prescriptions of the Agricultural Service."[166] Physical assaults imposed from above on planters not following the rules – this also might have been used by notables as a legitimization of the use of physical force on their subjects – often went hand in hand with other kinds of punishment. From the start of the coffee

164 Ibid, RWA, Conseils de Territoire et de Chefferie, Shangugu, RWA(72), Procès-verbal de la réunion plénière, 14/10/1957.

165 Nsavyimana, "La mobilisation de la force de travail au Burundi sous le mandate belge (1920–1940)": 219.

166 AAB, RARU, Gisenyi Territoire, Rapport Général, 1938, no. 87(24).

campaigns in the early 1930s until the end of the mandate period, producers violating legal prescriptions could be fined, or worse. According to the decree of October 30, 1939, planters were not allowed to sell coffee with a humidity level above 12.5%. When planters, whether intentionally or not, did sell crops that were not dry enough, intermediaries (ambulant or in centers) as well as producers were fined, and the latter also risked prison sentences. In all cases, the coffee sold was confiscated.[167]

According to Scott, "estates were, in a word, far more legible."[168] In other words, plantations are easier to control than smallholders. Especially in a hilly region where even today houses are sometimes hardly accessible, control by European bureaucracies, even in close collaboration with Africans, was difficult. Administrations in the mandate were aware of this problem, and in order to somewhat facilitate control over the production process, planters were asked to place a post with their names carved on it in their fields.[169] However, people can, deliberately or not, forget to place such posts. Furthermore, considering the lack of European staff, fines and other punishments, the questions are: to what degree did cultivators obey the severe regulations and, perhaps even more paramount, to what extent did rules filter through to the rural coffee-producing masses? The Gisenyi agricultural report of 1951 suggests that the transfer of knowledge from central to local governments to agronomists to African monitors and notables was not a finished and established procedure:

> currently, there are 12 monitors who have to control 60000 coffee bushes each on average; it is difficult for them to bring this task to a favorable conclusion. Actually, the planter does not know all principles in use yet, pruning and other operations. There still is a necessity to surround the mass of planters with auxiliaries themselves trained by agronomists.[170]

2.2.2 Coffee Cooperatives

In Chapter 2, I referred to the creation of *paysannats indigènes* in both the colony and the mandate in an effort of European bureaucracies to extend control over native production. Another way of extending control over the output and

---

167 Ibid, RWA, Café, Rapports, RWA(444), Lettre de l'administrateur territorial de Shangugu au vice-gouverneur général, 6/7/1939, and lettre de l'administrateur territorial de Shangugu au résident, 7/12/1953.

168 Scott, *Seeing like a state. How certain schemes to improve the human condition have failed*: 190.

169 AAB, RWA, Café, Rapports, RWA(437), Rapport mensuel Gisenyi, Octobre 1935.

170 Ibid, RARU, Gisenyi Territoire, Rapport Agriculture, 1951, no. 90(25).

price of their cash crops was the establishment of cooperatives by Africans themselves.[171] Unlike in the Congolese regions bordering Lake Kivu, in the Rwandan part two coffee cooperatives developed in the 1950s. In Uganda, some coffee cooperatives were established as a reaction of planters against exploitative measures and price controls by the British.[172] According to the United Nations, the two cooperatives in Gisenyi (Nkora) and Shangugu (Shangi) were also founded by planters uniting, albeit governmentally approved and controlled:

> we notice among planters a growing tendency to associate themselves either in cooperatives with a legal status or in free associations, in order to, by grouping their individual production, directly address export commerce, with the intention of getting better prices. The [visiting] Mission has visited the Nkora cooperative in the territory of Kisenyi that has become operational in 1957, grouping 4700 cooperators.[173]

This quote eloquently explains the main reason why cultivators cooperated. In both Gisenyi and Shangugu, coffee cooperatives also succeeded in achieving higher prices for their associates than independent planters did. For instance, in 1957 the cooperative in Shangi (founded in 1954 and counting more than 5000 members at that time) was able to get 32 Francs per kilogram, which is 6 Francs more than planters who did not belong to the cooperative.[174]

Despite the benefits of cooperatives, not every cultivator was able to participate. In both Gisenyi and Shangugu, every associate had to donate an initial 200 Francs in order to fund the activities of the cooperative. According to Leurquin, rural incomes in both the colony and the mandate were 1420 Francs on average (coffee plus additional revenues) in 1957; hence, 200 Francs was a serious investment for most planters.[175] With the contribution of the members, machines to

171 For a general overview of agricultural cooperatives in both the Belgian Congo and Ruanda-Urundi, see: A.G. Baptist, "Quelques considérations sur les coopératives agricoles au Congo belge et au Ruanda-Urundi," *Bulletin Agricole du Congo Belge et du Ruanda-Urundi* 50, no. 3 (1959).

172 See for the Ugandan case: Stephen G. Bunker, *Peasants against the state: the politics of market control in Bugisu, Uganda, 1900–1983* (Chicago: University of Chicago Press, 1991 [1987]). Furthermore, there is evidence that in northern Tanzania cooperatives were established along ethnic lines; see: Catherine Baroin, "L'impact social de la caféiculture en Tanzanie du Nord," *Etudes Rurales*, no. 180 (2007): 97.

173 AAB, RARU, Rapport de la mission de visite de l'ONU au Ruanda-Urundi, 1957, no. 25(4). In 1957, only three coffee cooperatives existed in Rwanda, two of them in the territories bordering Lake Kivu. In 1958, two more became operational.

174 Ibid, Shangugu Territoire, Rapport AIMO, 1957, no. 103(10).

175 Leurquin, *Le niveau de vie des populations rurales du Ruanda-Urundi*: 274.

remove chorions were installed in villages and the drying of berries was increasingly mechanized, while beans were gathered, centralized and sold in homogenous lots.[176] All these factors contributed not only to rising productivity but evidentially also, and most importantly, to an increase in selling prices.

However, joining a cooperative did not always assure fair treatment. In 1957, a bribing scandal came to light in the Shangi cooperative. A letter from the planters involved reveals irregularities among clerks working for the association:

> we are really sad because our coffee is of no use. How? We transport our coffee and we add money so that the coffee is bought. He who has nothing to pay has to wait until late at night. When he arrives early in the morning he has to wait too; only those who have money are served quickly. We have to pay those who help us transport this coffee 15 to 20 frs. Once it has arrived at the cooperative, the coffee is not bought, which forces us to return home with it. He who has helped with the transport then claims twice [the price]; or knocks down the load. When we cannot bring back home this load we sell it [...] for an insignificant price of 150 frs, while from the cooperative we can receive 320 frs [...]. This forces everyone who can to pay a certain amount as a bribe.[177]

In addition to planters, notables also opposed these irregularities. When the manager of the cooperative was asked for a detailed explanation, he could hardly deny involvement. He replied that he engaged and fired people as he wished and that only planters with coffee of inferior quality had to return home, and not because the latter were unable to pay bribes.[178]

2.3 *Rwandan Plantation Workers*

2.3.1 Labor Categories

The organization of plantation labor in the Rwandan territories bordering Lake Kivu unsurprisingly shows great resemblance to that of the Congolese Kivu. Temporary labor – especially day labor as a continuation of a precolonial and early colonial trend (Chapter 4) – was far more important than regular work, although after World War II permanent engagements increased. Both employers and workers preferred temporary labor: the former because auxiliaries were

176 AAB, RARU, Rapport de la mission de visite de l'ONU au Ruanda-Urundi, 1951, no. 25(1), and ibid, Shangugu Territoire, Rapport Général, 1957, no. 102(8bis).

177 Ibid, RWA, Conseils de Territoire et de Chefferie, Impara – Shangugu, RWA(72), Réunion du conseil de Chefferie, 13/7/1957.

178 Ibid, Réunion du conseil de Chefferie, 27/5/1957.

cheaper, the latter because it allowed them to continue other activities (such as food growing, for example).[179] After the war, the mandate administration aimed at stabilizing the workforce and promoting monogamous marriages, similarly to what happened in the colony. People entering on a regular basis not only escaped oppressive chiefs and *corvées*, but in the 1950s they also benefited from tax reductions, at least when they were unmarried or had no more than one wife.[180] In some cases even *colons* started to see the benefits of engaging coffee workers permanently. As colonists in Shangugu argued in 1950, regular laborers' productivity is higher because they are more accustomed to different tasks than temporary workers.[181]

Shangugu was somewhat different from the other territories bordering Lake Kivu, not only because the majority of plantations were situated here but also because of the existence of a *remplacement* system. While day labor was preferred by the majority of workers and employers, the Protanag management preferred task work. The so-called "Zeehandelaer system" was introduced in the early 1930s by the then manager and based on the success of the piece work system in Java.[182] More striking for this territory, however, was the phenomenon of various people working under one and the same name: the multiple-headed hydra found in neighboring Kabare. As the territorial agent of Shangugu clarified in the early 1930s: "the natives do not like to be under contractual obligations. They work according to their monetary needs and, during a few days, are replaced by another member of the same family."[183] Alongside permanent employees with a contract, temporary workers, usually only with an oral contract at best, also used replacements. Some of these familial substitutes were children too young (minors of fifteen to sixteen years old) to perform heavy tasks.[184] Although sources are silent, it is not unlikely that, similarly to in Kabare, the significance of the replacement system also decreased due to internal and external factors.

Besides replacing family members, children were also engaged to perform tasks similar to those they performed in the Congolese plantation sector

179 Ibid, RARU, Gisenyi Territoire, Rapport Général, 1931 and 1935, no. 87(17) and 87(21), and ibid, Shangugu Territoire, Rapport Général, 1932, no. 100(11).

180 Newbury, *The cohesion of oppression. Clientship and ethnicity in Rwanda, 1860–1960*: 174–176.

181 AAB, RARU, Shangugu Territoire, Rapport Général, 1950, no. 102(3).

182 Ibid, Agri, Compagnies, Dossiers individuels des plantations (654), Lettre de Mr Hanegraef à la direction de Crédit Agricole d'Afrique à Bruxelles, 31/12/1931.

183 Ibid, RARU, Shangugu Territoire, Rapport Général, 1931, no. 100(10).

184 Ibid, RWA, Conseils de Territoire et de Chefferie, Shangugu, RWA(72), Réunion plénière, 1/3/1939.

(removing insects, helping with harvests, etcetera). At the end of the 1950s, only children between twelve and sixteen years old (fifteen in the Congo) could be engaged to perform "light work." Moreover, "The engagement has to be authorized by the father or the tutor. When there is no father or tutor, the written authorization of the territorial agent is required."[185] Despite these obligations and prohibitions, several inspection reports refer to children under the age of twelve who worked in the coffee plantation sector, with or without approval of the father, even in this late colonial stage.[186]

As demonstrated in the Congolese part of this chapter, women as well were involved in plantation activities, especially during harvest and the processing of beans. Even though Rwandan women preferred working for other Africans, younger women in particular were engaged in the plantation sector as well.[187] In the 1950s, in some cases, women even brought their babies while treating bushes with insecticides containing hazardous materials. However, notables complained about such practices and insisted on no longer "making women, who carried their children on their back, participate."[188]

2.3.2 Remunerating the Workforce

Some remarks made for plantations wages in the Congolese Kivu are valid for Rwandan plantations as well: there was no harmonization of salaries; minimum wages were only introduced in 1949 (later than in the colony) and fixed by the Resident; with reference to rations, after World War II a distinction was made between industrial and agricultural laborers; and finally, figures below are gross wages. There are major differences, however. Firstly, that unlike for *capitas* and clerks, for "ordinary" workers (permanent and auxiliary) sources do not always distinguish between monthly and daily wages, which makes comparison with, for instance, monthly coffee wages/purchasing power in the Congolese Kivu difficult. Secondly, although only available from the mid-1950s onwards, sources do not refer to wages for women. This can indicate two things: either women received the same wages as men (quite emancipatory), or more likely, since many young girls were engaged, they received the same wage as children.

185 Ibid, AIMO(339), Shangugu rapports d'inspection agricole, Rapport plantation Nemry, 17/9/1958.

186 Ibid, Rapport plantation Nemry, 24/12/1957; Rapport plantation Morandini frères, 15/9/1958; Rapport plantation Van De Voorde, 22/9/1958.

187 Ibid, RARU, Shangugu Territoire, Rapport Général, 1952, no. 102(5). Annexe de la parts de l'ONU.

188 Ibid, RWA, Conseils de Territoire et de Chefferie, Gisenyi, RWA(71), Procès-verbal de la réunion plénière des chefs et sous-chefs, 2/1/1956.

Data from Gisenyi show that nominal wages were comparable to average plantation wages in the colony. In 1929, a regular laborer gained on average 45 Francs per month while daily wages varied between 1 and 3 Francs, ration included. Skilled workers earned between 90 and 1100 Francs a month. With these revenues, permanent workers could afford 30 kilograms of beans (1.5 Francs per kilogram) or 75 kilograms of potatoes (0.6 Francs per kilogram), a day laborer 1 to 2 kilograms beans or 2 to 5 kilograms potatoes.[189] In the early 1940s, average monthly regular plantation wages were 35 Francs, while day workers received 1.5 Francs (both ration included). When the ration was paid in money, regular workers would be able to buy 87.5 kilograms of beans (0.4 Francs per kilogram) or 175 kilograms of potatoes (0.2 Francs per kilogram) while day workers could purchase 4 kilograms of beans or 7.5 kilograms of potatoes.[190] At the end of the 1950s, agrarian laborers made on average 13.6 Francs a day, *capitas* 22.6 Francs, coffee monitors 38 Francs and mechanics 60.6 Francs (all ration included).[191] This means that a plantation workers would be able to buy about 4 kilograms of beans (3.5 Francs per kilogram) or 3 kilograms of potatoes (4.6 Francs per kilogram) with his gross revenue.[192]

For Shangugu, sources only mention daily plantation wages. In 1929, Protanag paid an average of 1.8 Francs (ration included) a day. With this gross revenue a worker could obtain less than 1 kilogram of beans (2 Francs per kilogram) or 1.8 kilograms of potatoes (1 Franc per kilogram).[193] In the early 1940s, daily wages oscillated between 1 and 1.5 Francs per day. Rwandans working in Bukavu could earn between 1.5 and 2 Francs a day, while skilled laborers earned between 4 and 15 Francs a day. Per day, workers could buy a maximum of 2 kilograms of beans (0.75 Francs per kilogram) or about 8 kilograms of potatoes (0.15 Francs per kilogram) with their salary.[194] At the end of the mandate period, daily wages for workers varied between 10.75 and 11.25 Francs a day, while *capitas* earned on average 23 Francs and mechanics 40 Francs per day (all ration included).[195] A gross daily plantation wage might have equaled about 2 kilograms of beans (5.67

189 Ibid, RARU, Gisenyi Territoire, Rapport Général, 1929, no. 87(16).

190 Ibid, 1941 and 1942, no. 88(1) and 88(2).

191 Ibid, 1958, no. 88(14).

192 Prices drawn form: S.N., *Rapport sur l'administration Belge du Ruanda-Urundi pendant l'année…, 1920–61*: 1958.

193 AAB, RARU, Shangugu Territoire, Rapport Général, 1929, no. 100(8).

194 Ibid, 1940; 1941, no. 101(6); 101(7); and ibid, RWA, AIMO(346), MO agricole, Lettre de l'administrateur territorial Synave (Shangugu) au vice-gouverneur général, 6/11/1941.

195 Ibid, AIMO(339), Shangugu rapports d'inspection agricole, 1957–58, and ibid, RARU, Shangugu Territoire, Rapport Général, 1958, no. 102(9).

Francs per kilogram) or 2.5 kilograms of potatoes (4.6 Francs per kilogram) in 1958.[196]

In sum, in Gisenyi and Shangugu purchasing power allegedly increased during the 1930s, similarly to in the colony. However, in the mandate too, taxes increased. Hence, the same cautious provisional statement should be made: real plantation wages remained stable, not only during the 1930s but during the entire colonial period. There might even have been a slight decline in purchasing power because taxes continued to rise.

For women and children, the situation is more difficult to analyze. As opposed to figures from the colony, data are only available from the mid-1950s onwards, and sources only mention wages for children. However, wages for women and children were likely part of household revenues as in the colony. It seems that wages for these temporary laborers remained rather stable in the second half of the 1950s, varying between 3 and 7 Francs per day.[197]

In the previous chapter, I referred to Rwandans coming from the east or even from the same hill to work for prosperous Rwandan coffee cultivators, particularly in Shangugu. Information on these coffee workers is scarce. However, what is certain is that the former received a wage either in kind (mostly food) or in money, or both. According to the 1952 annual report of this territory, these Africans could receive up to 9–10 Francs per day, while minimum wages were set at 5.7 Francs per day, plus 1 kilogram of beans in addition.[198]

While wages for Africans working for Africans were comparable to wages European plantation owners paid, the same tendency toward underpaid coffee labor also existed in the mandate, as in the colony. In 1951, this trend of low wages in general provoked stinging criticism from a Russian representative in the United Nations:

> with the salary paid in the [mandated] Territory a worker and his family could not survive, not even in a chronic state of undernourishment. According to the report of the Visiting Mission, the salary of an unskilled laborer is between 5 and 8 francs per day. A similar amount does not even suffice to buy a box of matches, costing 7 to 7 fr 50. Petitions received by the Council reveal the existence of even lower salaries. […] Because of impossible living conditions more than 35000 natives have been forced to emi-

196 S.N., *Rapport sur l'administration Belge du Ruanda-Urundi pendant l'année…, 1920–61*: 1958.

197 AAB, RWA, AIMO(339), Shangugu rapports d'inspection agricole, 1953–1958.

198 Ibid, RARU, Shangugu Territoire, Rapport Général, 1952, no. 102(5).

> grate to Tanganyika, to the Belgian Congo and elsewhere in 1950. Workers are manifestly exploited.[199]

Even though the Russian representative could hardly hide his communist background, his analysis was not wrong. What's more, employers used the same kind of legitimation as in the colony to maintain low salaries. As the report of the United Nations' visiting missions of 1951 stated: "invoke the low productivity of the native workers to justify the current wage level."[200] Furthermore, also like in the colony, dissenting views on minimum wages and rations resulted in discussions between the administration, employers and workers involved. In 1949, with the introduction of minimum wages, debates regarding the level of this minimum lasted three days. The president of the TEPSI (Travail Et du Progrès Social Indigène) commission (founded to debate and advise administrations on issues such as wages and rations) backed by Catholic missions argued that in Rwanda, the minimum wage should be set at 3.5 Francs per day. Despite the absence of a lobby group such as the Unaki, agrarian colonists reacted by stressing the alleged low productivity of their workforce and considered 2 Francs a day a fair minimum. Finally, an agreement was reached with all parties involved, including African representatives: the minimum wage for workers with a contract was set at 3 Francs, and that for workers without a contract at 2 Francs a day.[201] Another point of resentment was the ration. Employers not only were convinced that the ration was too high. From the mid-1950s onwards, some employers no longer paid part of this ration in money. Instead regular workers received a ticket which they could exchange for meat (originally 400, but from 1957 onwards, 650 grams per week). Colonists argued that in this way workers would eat meat, increasing their strength and, hence, their productivity. However, most laborers were not satisfied with this measure. Their cash income not only decreased; workers had to pick up the meat at a self-chosen but administratively approved butchery; they did not always receive the amount they deserved; and the quality of the meat was often very low.[202]

Despite low wages (and likely decreasing purchasing power) and disagreements with employers, social relationships and the way of life of plantations

199 Ibid, Rapport à la Commission permanente des Mandats, 1951, no. 21(5bis).

200 Ibid, Rapport de la mission de visite de l'ONU au Ruanda-Urundi, 1951, no. 25(1).

201 See for the discussion: ibid, RWA, AIMO(340), TEPSI, Procès-verbal de la réunion de la Commission, 27–29/1/1949. A similar labor commission also existed in the Belgian Congo and in other African colonies (Cooper, *Decolonization and African society. The labor question in French and British Africa*: 274).

202 See for this discussion: AAB, RWA, AIMO(341), TEPSI, Documentation, Note du chef Seruvumbu (Kibuye), 22/2/1957.

workers altered during the colonial period. As Newbury convincingly shows, wage labor offered Rwandans an opportunity to more or less escape oppressive (sub-)chiefs and "to gain an economic base relatively autonomous from the chiefs' monopoly over the formerly crucial economic resources – cattle and land."[203] A similar evolution had occurred on the familial level as well, where the authority of family heads had eroded. Young people, in particular, engaged in wage labor, and thanks to a cash income they were no longer, or were much less, dependent on group solidarity. Moreover, family heads were sometimes beaten by younger men, which was unimaginable in precolonial times.[204] Wage labor also changed material demands/habits, as the territorial administrator of Shangugu noted at the end of the 1940s:

> Gaining salaries, [...] in an incontestable way, the native is looking to improve his standing: in general, he is far from being dressed like ten years ago [...]. The native is going to work [...] buys hats, raincoats, pullovers, jackets [...] and socks permitting him to resist bad weather in a Territory especially well-served with rain. [...] The native not only improves his clothing but he also alters his diet by adding a little dried fish.[205]

2.3.3 Working Conditions

The aim of the final part of this chapter is to analyze labor conditions in the same way as I have done for the colony. Consequently, the first issue addressed is the use of physical and psychological aggression against workers. Even though references to violence are much more limited in mandate sources, a remarkable contrast between the colony and the mandate is that in the colonial case sources are silent on violence against laborers after World War II, but for the mandate they are not. This might be the result of differences in development. As I have shown in Chapter 2, in Rwanda the peak of plantations was after World War II, whereas in the colony the plantation sector was already firmly established by then. It might also result from judicial changes (from mandate to trusteeship) and the greater focus on "democratization" after World War II,[206] urging European agents and labor inspectors to be more explicit about the abuses of chiefs and, possibly, European firms alike.

203 Newbury, *The cohesion of oppression. Clientship and ethnicity in Rwanda, 1860–1960*: 178.

204 AAB, RARU, Kibuye Territoire, Rapport AIMO, 1955, no. 82(14).

205 Ibid, Shangugu Territoire, Rapport Général, 1948, no. 102(1).

206 Mathys, "People on the move. Frontiers, borders, mobility and history in the Lake Kivu region 19th–20th century": 331.

Either way, as late as 1957, sources refer to agrarian colonists in Shangugu treating their laborers brutally and roughly.[207] In 1959, the manager of the INEAC station in Rubona (Gisenyi) was interpellated by the African labor representative regarding injuries inflicted on a worker by means of machete strokes.[208] However, other indications of violence refer to either other sectors or other regions. In 1958, for instance, workers of a construction company in Gisenyi complained about inconsiderate insults by members of the European staff.[209] In some situations, concession holders even applied "indirect violence." In 1946, plantation laborers traveled from Byumba territory to the office of the Resident in Kigali and filed a complaint against the owner Ortmans:

> Mister Ortmans coerces us to work. When he notices we do not succeed in our task, he gives us a note for our chief Rwigemera. The latter, after having seen this note, calls us and makes us lay down on the ground and gives us eight whip lashes each. We tell Rwigemera that we are not able to do a task surpassing our capacities and Rwigemera really insists that we return to Mr. Ortmans. Some return while others flee to Uganda [...]. We ask for your help and protection [...]. Moreover, we have to say that Mr. Ortmans, despite forced labor, does not pay us, we receive beatings and the work exceeds our capacities [...], nobody can live like this.[210]

Alongside assaults, employers also considered fines helpful tools to discipline their workforce. Although not specified, inspection reports from the second half of the 1950s reveal cutbacks in wages, particularly when daily tasks were not finished.[211] However, it seems that in the Rwandan regions bordering Lake Kivu, at least some employers paid more attention to rewarding plantations workers (in kind and/or in money) in order to stabilize the labor force. Rwandans seeking work outside the mandate because wages were higher there, or earning sufficiently by cultivating and selling crops, was all the more reason for employers to make agricultural work more appealing. At the concession of Jean Nemry, for example, workers who had not been absent for a single day during one month received a bonus of 40 Francs. A laborer renewing his contract for at least one

207 AAB, RARU, Shangugu Territoire, Rapport AIMO, 1957, no. 103(10).

208 Ibid, RWA, AIMO(342), TEPSI, Conseils d'entreprise, Procès-verbal de la réunion du Conseil d'entreprise INEAC, Gisenyi, 28/10/1959.

209 Ibid, Procès-verbal de la réunion du Conseil d'entreprise CCC (Congolese Construction Company), Gisenyi, 4/4/1958.

210 Ibid, AIMO(346), MO agricole, Plainte portée contre Ortmans, Byumba, 24/4/1946.

211 Ibid, AIMO(339), Shangugu rapports d'inspection agricole, 1953–1957.

year "receive[d] the amount of his taxes as gratification."[212] Several reports mention employees getting 1 kilogram of salt, but also an additional 1 kilogram of rice or 1 liter of palm oil when they worked at least 20 days a month.[213] Moreover, in the mid-1950s, two coffee plantations used a system of wage adjustments based on regularity. Colonists Van De Voorde and Vandersteene both paid salaries of 6 Francs while the minimum wage was set at 6.7 per day, but when workers were present for between 10 and 20 days per month they received 7 Francs, and those who worked 20 days or more were paid 8 Francs per work day.[214] Furthermore, similarly to in the colony, from the mid-1950s onwards regular workers were paid family allocations, although it is also unclear what the amount of these allowances was and whether they were paid in kind or in money.

Finally, in the mandate as well, after World War II the administration created enterprise councils in order to increase the participation of workers in decision-making processes at firm level. Companies with at least 250 regular laborers were supposed to organize meetings. However, up until 1957 the coffee sector in the areas bordering Lake Kivu did not have enterprise councils. Lowering the limit to 100 laborers (*supra*) created possibilities for agricultural workers. From 1957 onwards, some tea, pyrethrum and coffee plantations initiated councils. The same remarks that were made for the colony are also valid for the mandate, and the grievances and requests of plantations laborers are also similar. However, although not explicit in the following quote, one request in particular was made only in the mandate: vacation days to maintain personal coffee bushes:

> Bizimana [a coffee plantation worker] demands to only work five days per week – day off on Saturday – market day and tasks on their hill. Mister Morandini declares he does not agree, considering the size of his labor force. The A.T.A.P. [the administrative agent] answers that the workers are able to send their wives to the market and that there is no imposed work for [regular] employees on the hills any longer; those having coffee bushes to maintain can ask for vacation in this regard.[215]

212 Ibid, Rapport plantation Nemry, 16/6/1953.
213 Ibid, 1953–1959.
214 Ibid, Rapport plantation Vandersteene, 12/5/1954; Rapport plantation Van De Voorde, 12/5/1954.
215 Ibid, AIMO(342), TEPSI, Conseils d'entreprise, Procès-verbal de la réunion du Conseil d'entreprise Morandini frères, Shangugu, 23/1/1958.

3 Conclusion

This chapter has demonstrated that, regarding plantation workers, there were a lot of resemblances between the colonial and the mandate Kivu. On both sides of the lake, temporary workers outranked regular laborers, not only because the circular labor demand of coffee cultivation required this but also because planters, African notables and workers alike all preferred temporary jobs. European administrations did not dislike the latter category as such, but they mistrusted it due to a lack of control that was even more pronounced with regard to the informal system of substitutes (which was in place at least until after World War II in the southern Kivu).

The remuneration of plantation workers was similar as well, and not only in the sense that purchasing power decreased during the colonial period. Although my analysis has focused on only two food products and on the assumption that plantation wages were the only source of income (which was usually not the case), there are strong indications that the purchasing power of the plantation labor force (both temporary and regular) around Lake Kivu deteriorated. However, this conclusion requires caution. First, similarly to the conclusion of a recent paper on Uganda, a distinction should be made between rural and urban wages. Rising urban wages do not necessarily mean rising rural wages or rising purchasing power in general.[216] Second, declining purchasing power does not equal a decline in other social conditions after World War II. On the contrary, as in other African colonies, people around Lake Kivu also had access to better medical facilities, to unions (albeit strictly controlled), etcetera.[217] Nonetheless, on both sides of Lake Kivu, low wages were legitimized by colonists who stressed the low productivity of their laborers. This debatable argument was backed by European administrations, at least up until World War II. From that point on, however, there was a shift in approach, with the introduction of minimum wages, for example, which resulted in tensions with *colons*.

Finally, plantation workers on both sides of the lake were often treated harshly (with physical and psychological violence), although Rwandan sources are more silent on this matter. This shows that successful frontier development indeed went hand in hand with the use of coercion (see Introduction). In both areas, fines and bonuses were characteristic of the plantation economy, although after World War II there seems to have been more emphasis on rewarding workers than on punishing them, due to planters attempting to stabilize their labor

216 de Haas, "Measuring rural welfare in colonial Africa: did Uganda's smallholders thrive?": 627–628.

217 Cooper, *Africa since 1940: the past of the present*: 91.

force. Another attempt to stabilize labor and include workers was made by European governments: the installation of enterprise councils at least gave the impression of a more integrated labor system. Because data are scarce, only tentative conclusions concerning labor productivity can be made. The introduction of minimum wages, a greater focus on bonuses than on fines, family allowances, the introduction of enterprise councils, mechanization, etcetera all affected productivity, and suggest that plantation workers' productivity increased on both sides of Lake Kivu after World War II.

Labor organization, remuneration, etcetera, in the smallholder coffee cultivation sector differed significantly from that of the plantation sector, even though there are some similarities as well. First of all, it is impossible to distinguish between temporary and regular workers as smallholders were *de facto* responsible for every step in the cultivation process. However, as in to the plantation economy, women played an important role. The introduction of individual nurseries eased the burden on growers, but the lack of control urged the mandate administration to reintroduce central nurseries. A lack of control also resulted in the abolishment of a relatively free market for coffee sales, shortly after World War II. However, as those markets were disliked by Africans, informal trade thrived, resulting in a compromise with the reinstallation of both ambulant and fixed sales.

The way smallholders were paid also differed from that of plantation workers. The former had to sell their coffee and received an amount corresponding with the quantity sold. Because it is not possible to know what grower sold how many kilograms in a certain year, working with counter values offers a solution in order to make educated guesses regarding purchasing power. Although this analysis is also based on only two food products and does not take into account other sources of income, there seem to have been more profits for smallholders in comparison with the decreasing purchasing power for plantation workers. By this I mean that, except in Kibuye, purchasing power – that is, the counter value for 1 kilogram of coffee sold – was stable (Gisenyi) or increased (Shangugu) during the colonial period. The fact that in the latter territory the counter value rose only proves the conclusion drawn by the contemporary observer Leurquin, who referred to Shangugu as the territory with the highest living standard of all Rwandan territories in the 1950s – partly a result of the proximity of Bukavu.[218] However, because the coffee market was (is) volatile, the mandate bureaucracy initiated an equalization fund after World War II. Even though the underlying idea of giving producers a minimum revenue is questionable, this intervention is comparable to the introduction of a minimum wage in the plantation sector.

218 Leurquin, *Le niveau de vie des populations rurales du Ruanda-Urundi*: 175.

Coercion, severe control and rigid rules were the main features of the smallholder sector. Not only was every aspect of the production process accompanied by a set of strict rules, but also regulations were severely controlled by European agronomists, and especially by African coffee monitors and notables. Non-compliance with these stringent rules could result in punishments (fines, physical penalties and even confinement) for both African producers and controllers. Moreover, grassroots initiatives (cooperatives) were also controlled by the European governments in the 1950s, but these nevertheless resulted in pushing up prices for the Africans involved. Similarly to in the plantation sector, labor productivity seems to have increased, especially after World War II. The re-establishment of a free market, the introduction of an equalization fund, the emergence of cooperatives, etcetera are indications of increased smallholder productivity.

Finally, this chapter has demonstrated that in both the coffee plantation and the smallholder economy, social changes were major. Gender relations altered as women became an important part of the capitalist economy in both production systems. Relations vis-à-vis local notables also changed. On the one hand, (sub-)chiefs gained more control as supervisors of the production process and/or suppliers of labor. On the other hand, there was more independence for the rural poor as a result of the entrance of capitalism. However, it seems that the latter aspect was more pronounced for wage earners than for smallholder cultivators. Moreover, caution is required because categories such as wage laborers and smallholder growers are not always adequate. In many cases, such categories are better defined as "changing social fields."[219] This means that a smallholder could also be a wage worker and vice versa; and either way, both wage workers and smallholders around Lake Kivu were always active in the subsistence economy in the colonial period. This will be discussed in the following chapter.

219 Cooper, *From slaves to squatters. Plantation labor and agriculture in Zanzibar and coastal Kenya, 1890–1925*: 13–14.

CHAPTER 6

African Feedback

While the previous chapters of Part 2 focused on the way(s) Europeans tried to get access to (the output of) land and labor, this final chapter will emphasize the way(s) Africans around Lake Kivu experienced the entry and development of the coffee sector. In general Africans resisted, adapted to and reconfigured structures imposed on them.[1]

As opposed to the previous chapters, this chapter is not divided into a Congolese and a Rwandan part because most issues discussed below are either "cross-border" or similar on either side of the border. The colonially imposed border (1911) cannot be understood as a solely colonial implementation, as people living nearby the border were active agents in shaping it. In other words, people use(d) asymmetries created by demarcations. Around Lake Kivu, on the one hand, this means that precolonial relationships (economic, social, political) were maintained. On the other hand, it also means that new opportunities were explored that were often disliked by colonial bureaucracies.[2]

This chapter consists of two sections. Firstly, I will shed more light on the "weapons of the weak."[3] Borrowing ideas from James Scott, this section emphasizes the everyday forms of resistance of Africans involved in the coffee-cultivating sector around Lake Kivu. However, Isaacman warns us about the concept of "everyday resistance." He argues that it is somewhat misleading, because not all acts of resistance to colonial domination and exploitation happened every day or had the same intention (flight, for instance).[4] Moreover, sources usually do not refer to "everyday" acts of rebellion as such: colonial agents considered such acts as backward and sometimes anti-economic

1 Frederick Cooper, *Africa in the world: capitalism, empire, nation-state*: 55.

2 See: Mathys, "People on the move. Frontiers, borders, mobility and history in the Lake Kivu region 19th–20th century." 2. For a convincing example of Africans taking full advantage of the opportunities created by a (mandate-colony) border in West Africa, see: Paul Nugent, *Smugglers, secessionists & loyal citizens on the Ghana–Togo frontier: the lie of the borderlands since 1914* (Oxford: James Currey, 2002).

3 James Scott, *Weapons of the weak. Everyday forms of peasant resistance* (New Haven; London: Yale University Press, 1985). For an example of everyday resistance against colonialism in Tanzania, see: Göran Hyden, *Beyond Ujamaa in Tanzania: underdevelopment and an uncaptured peasantry* (London: Heinemann Educational Books, 1980).

4 Allen Isaacman, "Peasants and rural social protest in Africa," *African Studies Review* 33, no. 2 (1990): 31–32.

 DOI:10.1163/9789004428492_009

reactions. Finally, even though large-scale protest was very limited in the coffee-producing sector, it will not be ignored.

Secondly, this chapter will look at ways in which people involved in coffee production reconfigured colonial imposed structures. As Cooper argues, too much focus on resistance might "narrow our understanding of African history rather than expand it."[5] What Cooper means is that analysis of how people adapt to a changing context is essential. Both coffee plantations and small-scale production required land and labor, but how did people (whether plantation workers or smallholders) adapt to the entrance of capitalist production? That the entrance of capital altered social relationships with chiefs is demonstrated in Chapters 4 and 5, but how and to what extent did the existence of money affect pre-existing economies?

1 "Weapons of the Weak"

1.1 *The Cosyns Case*

According to Scott, most literature focuses on large-scale and well-organized revolts of rural populations, whereas small farmers usually lacked the possibility of organizing such upheavals and the means to do so. Moreover, even when ordinary people had the possibility, they rarely engaged in such acts: it was dangerous, would likely work to their disadvantage and almost always resulted in a more coercive and hegemonic state.[6] However, this does not mean that large-scale uprisings were completely absent. Zooming in on colonial Belgian Africa, the Pende revolt is probably the most famous case study of uprising in the agricultural sector (palm). In the summer of 1931, dislike among the Pende toward colonialism violently exploited. Early in June, two private recruiters of the HCB, accompanied by an administrative agent, committed abuses in the village of Kilamba. They took advantage of scarce local resources, confiscated cattle and raped women. These events were followed by a violent encounter on June 7 between village members and territorial agent Balot. When the latter visited the village in order to collect taxes, he was killed and dismembered, and his limbs were distributed among the chiefs of the area. In the following days, the colonial authorities reacted by means of a military occupation of the area, which lasted until the end of the summer. According to army reports, no

5 Cooper, "Conflict and connection: rethinking colonial African history": 1532.

6 Scott, *Weapons of the weak. Everyday forms of peasant resistance*: xv–xvi and 29.

soldiers or Belgian officers were killed, but between 300 and 500 Africans died, including more than thirty women and ten children.[7]

In the coffee sector around Lake Kivu, a large-scale revolt against European domination also occurred in the early 1930s. As argued in Chapter 4, chiefs usually were dissatisfied with plantations recruiting people as regular workers. When, in addition, customary rules, intentionally or not, were violated by *colons*, things got out of hand. This is what happened in December 1930, when a conflict – known as *Itumba lya Kabuga* – erupted between local African authorities and coffee plantation owner Cosyns in the village of Hongo (Kabare). The local notables accused regular plantation laborers of taking their cattle to the estate, which was inconsistent with customary law.[8] According to these laws, notables owned cattle and community members only had the right of use (through patron–client ties). One of the consequences was that laborers were forbidden to treat cattle as their private property and to displace them from communal lands. In order to return the cattle, furious notables, backed by more than 2000 community members, commanded the local police chief to head toward the plantation. Upon their arrival, pillaging started, the removed cattle was confiscated and the laborers were beaten ruthlessly, resulting in numerous injuries and thirteen or fourteen casualties.[9]

At first sight, this conflict looks like one within the local community. However, a report extensively referring to the outburst of violence states that the conflict was more complex than that. The report characterized the Belgian plantation owner Cosyns as "a European who mocks certain native customs in a shameless way." The report also warned *colons* that "there are certain customs which are dangerous to violate."[10] A few months later, in March 1931, the governor of the Oriental Province also commented on the incident:

> There is no moral foundation in telling the chiefs and the natives that the obligations between them do not exist any longer, following European colonization. And practically, it would be very maladroit vis-à-vis [...] chiefs regarding recruitment.[11]

7 For an extended overview and the consequences of this revolt, see: Louis-François Vanderstraeten, *La répression de la révolte des Pende du Kwango en 1931* (Bruxelles: Académie Royale des Sciences d'Outre-Mer, 2001).

8 Bashizi, "Pouvoirs publics, plantations européennes et réactions paysannes au Sud-Kivu (1920–1960)": 138.

9 AAB, RACB, Kivu District, Rapport Politique, 1930, no. 112.

10 Ibid.

11 Ibid, Rapport AIMO, 1931, no. 112, Lettre de Moeller à l'Unaki, 24/3/1931.

The key question here is whether workers deliberately violated customary rules, knowing that such violations would likely end up in retaliation by notables. Or, was the violation of customary laws a result of psychological abuse of workers by Cosyns and thus not solely a local conflict? On the one hand, regular work did not imply that customary cattle contracts expired, even if the governor of the Oriental Province seems to have believed it. On the other hand, in many cases European *colons* treated customary rules with disrespect – either intentionally or as a result of a lack of knowledge. However, as this case clearly shows, disregarding such customary arrangements could provoke local conflicts and turn them into acts of rebellion against European domination.[12]

1.2 *Migrations*

However, in the coffee sector around Lake Kivu most acts of resistance were small-scale and were not intended to subvert colonial rule but rather were banal actions and/or attempts to improve personal and familial living conditions. One of the most common "weapons of the weak" was running away – deserting the work spot, absence, etcetera; fleeing into the rain forest, for instance when plantations came to recruit people;[13] or migrating, whether permanently or not. This "weapon" was used by peasants all across Africa in order to maintain control over their labor.[14] This section focuses on people leaving their homestead in both the colony and the mandate. Since this chapter stresses Africans' feedback to colonialism, migrations supported and (partly) directed by African and/or European authorities, such as toward Gishari, will not be discussed here. The next section emphasizes people absenting themselves from their workplace.

The previous chapters already alluded to Congolese leaving the countryside to enter wage labor in the city (Bukavu in particular) and Rwandans traveling westwards to the shores of Lake Kivu in order to work in the coffee sector. There

12 As argued in Chapter 3, cases are known of notables protesting and sometimes even revolting against land grabbing by European colonists. There is also the Binji-Binji revolt in Kabare in 1931, instigated by a former plantation worker who advocated redistribution of European occupied land, among other things (see for instance: Koen Vlassenroot, "Violence et constitution des milices dans l'est du Congo: le cas des Mayi-Mayi," in *L'Afrique des Grands Lacs. Annuaire 2002–2003*, ed. Filip Reyntjens and Stefaan Marysse (Paris: L'Harmattan, 2003): 119–120). Moreover, in 1944, in Masisi, a religiously inspired Kitawalist uprising was repressed by the colonial bureaucracy and caused hundreds of casualties; see in particular: Maurice Lovens, *La révolte de Masisi-Lubutu: Congo belge janvier–mai 1944* (Bruxelles: Les Cahiers du CEDAF, 1974).

13 Bashizi, "Pouvoirs publics, plantations européennes et réactions paysannes au Sud-Kivu (1920–1960)": 138.

14 Isaacman, "Peasants and rural social protest in Africa" 34.

are even examples of people in Gisenyi migrating from one hill to another in an attempt to escape imposed coffee cultivation.[15] However, in most cases people crossed borders, seeking (better) income possibilities. In the 1930s, more than 12000 people left Rutshuru and settled in Gisenyi for several reasons: fear of oppressive chiefs, better taxation levels (which changed after World War II), dislike of work in the European plantation sector, and the psychological attraction of chiefs in Rwanda who had former ties with these returning people.[16] In Chapter 4, I argued that Rwandans were not keen on moving to Rutshuru on command, but many did so spontaneously because of existing socio-economic ties. As the example above shows, the opposite happened as well. The presence of sufficient resources in Gisenyi may have served as an additional incentive for people in Rutshuru to cross the border. In the early 1940s, the lack of labor potential in this Congolese territory and, in addition, the increased pressure on the population in order to supply plantations, caused the migration of more than 2300 Africans to Masisi and Rwanda.[17] Harsh labor exactions in Kabare, on the other hand, also caused migrations from Congolese toward Shangugu in order to escape forced recruitment or punishments when, for example, goals were not attained.[18]

The movement of Rwandans to the Kivu was nevertheless far more pronounced. People moved to developing cities, where wages were higher than in the mandate, as well as to the plantation sector. Already in the second half of the 1920s, many people in Gisenyi were attracted by the possibilities offered by the emerging plantation sector. They crossed the border and sometimes traveled as far as Sake (Masisi) in order to earn money to pay taxes, and then returned home. In the meantime their bond with the chiefs continued and their wives cultivated food crops and raised cattle.[19] This trend continued throughout the colonial period. In 1949, about 500 or half of all migrants from Gisenyi to the Congolese Kivu were working seasonally in the plantation sector, thereby continuing to maintain family ties.[20] Moreover, as a consequence of population growth in the 1950s, and the resulting lack of available land, people also moved: "Especially the fertile agricultural regions in the Masisi territory attract emigrants, discouraged by meager harvests [...] they settle on virgin lands."[21]

15 AAB, RARU, Gisenyi Territoire, Rapport Général, 1935, no. 87(21).
16 Ibid, 1937, no. 87(23).
17 Ibid, RACB, Rutshuru Territoire, Rapport AIMO, 1941, no. 163.
18 Mathys, "People on the move. Frontiers, borders, mobility and history in the Lake Kivu region 19th–20th century": 240.
19 AAB, RARU, Gisenyi Territoire, Rapport Général, 1929, no. 87(16).
20 Ibid, 1949, 88(9).
21 Ibid, Rapport AIMO, 1956, no. 89(9).

Similar trends – also lasting the entire colonial period – are visible at the southern side of Lake Kivu. The proximity of Bukavu, as well as the growing agricultural sector, attracted people from Shangugu, as mentioned in Chapter 4. As the annual report of 1936 stresses, the majority of people crossed the Rusizi river every day or every week in order to work for a European colonist.[22] That movements from Shangugu toward Kabare were important is suggested by the following quote:

> Little by little, an exodus of labor toward the Belgian Congo is created, and it is almost certain that part of the population of the Shangugu territory progressively sneaks off toward the Belgian Congo. [...] At the end of the year, departures are equally important (generally from October), a lot of natives engage temporarily in the agricultural enterprises of the Kivu in order to earn the required amount of money to pay the taxes.[23]

The *va-et-vient* of Africans from Shangugu toward the Congolese Kivu sometimes even jeopardized coffee cultivation in the mandate, especially in areas adjoining the colony. However, in such cases, women not only cultivated food crops but also maintained coffee bushes, as demonstrated previously (Chapter 5).[24] Furthermore, despite the possibilities of Shangugu, there were many reasons why people crossed the border. They not only tried to benefit from wage incentives and lower tax rates in the colony after World War II; in some cases they also tried to escape despotic chiefs, and, as in Gisenyi, pre-existing relationships mattered as well.[25]

Although trespassing the colonially demarcated border was an important way for people in the Lake Kivu area to try to maintain some level of freedom and exploit asymmetries within the constraints of the colonial system,[26] people from both the colony and the mandate also traveled much further to do so. The sources I consulted contain numerous references to people migrating to Uganda in order to earn cash. People traveled up to 200 kilometers, mainly because wages and working conditions in general were better in British-controlled areas. Contemporaries were aware of these migrations, and even of the causes,

22 Ibid, Shangugu Territoire, Rapport Général, 1936, no. 101(2).

23 Ibid, 1939, no. 101(5).

24 Ibid, 1952, no. 102(5). Annexe de la part de l'ONU.

25 Mathys, "People on the move. Frontiers, borders, mobility and history in the Lake Kivu region 19th–20th century": 237.

26 The idea of people, especially those living close to borders, exploiting asymmetries is central in Mathys' work (ibid).

as General Governor Ryckmans explained in a 1939 letter to the Secretary of the Colony:

> Every year one hundred thousand natives from Ruanda-Urundi migrate to Uganda for a few months: they ask for nothing better than to work in the Kivu, much closer to their home, if we succeed in offering them similar working conditions. It is a question of salary, lodgment and ration.[27]

Focusing on the territories bordering Lake Kivu, these movements mainly consisted of Africans coming from Rutshuru and Gisenyi. However, the annual report of 1934 also refers to people from Kibuye returning from Uganda after earning cash to pay for their taxes.[28] While people originating from these territories could earn about two to three times more in Uganda[29] (in the mining sector in particular), it seems that at the end of the 1930s, fear and economic regression caused a temporary diminution in movements. Many Rwandans residing in Gisenyi ignored Uganda and engaged in the Belgian Congo, not only because companies in the first colony went into liquidation but also because they feared conscription into the British army.[30]

In addition to being motivated by higher wages and better labor conditions in British areas, people also migrated to Uganda in order to escape the often brutal acts of notables. Similarly to Africans around Lake Kivu fleeing into other territories or crossing the border, some probably also used pre-existing networks and/or ties in order to migrate to Uganda. Sometimes these migrants even received wholehearted support from European colonists, even though labor was already scarce – for instance in Rutshuru in the early 1940s:

> Kassambi is the sub-chief of Busanza, an oppressor supported by Ndeze [chief]; I [colonist Menten de Horne] know that several administrators have tried to dismiss Kassambi, but they have not succeeded for whatever reason. Kassambi used and abused the whip for no reason and has certainly been one of the causes for displacing Busanza. A man unjustly or for no proper reason beaten or punished is disgusted and leaves for Uganda; in his position I would do the same. He leaves with his family, is satisfied with

27 AAB, AIMO, MO agricole, Dossier Unaki, no. 1653/10, Lettre du gouverneur général Ryckmans au ministre de la colonie, 27/12/1939.

28 Ibid, RARU, Kibuye Territoire, Rapport Général, 1934, no. 82(1).

29 Ibid RACB, Rutshuru Territoire, Rapport AIMO, 1937, no. 163. After decolonization, people still migrated to Uganda, where they still could earn up to three times more; see: Drevet, "Les plantations Européenes dans le Kivu d'altitude": 196.

30 AAB, RARU, Gisenyi Territoire, Rapport Général, 1939, no. 87(25).

his movement toward the other side of the frontier and makes his friends and acquaintances come over.[31]

1.3 *Desertions and Absenteeism*

As mentioned above, people migrated for various reasons: not only to benefit from wage differences across different regions but in some cases also to escape contracted labor. However, this does not imply that people who were engaged in wage labor – whether contracted or not – had no "weapons" with which to fight their often harsh labor conditions. Accordingly, this section merely deals with plantation workers. It could be argued that Rwandan smallholders abandoning their fields while working in the colony were also deserting. However, in many cases these "abandoned" fields were cultivated by family members, more particularly by their wives. Hence, it is likely that laboring in the colony was a means of income diversification rather than rebellion.

Nevertheless, plantation workers on the Rwandan side of Lake Kivu deserted their labor spots *en masse* at the end of the 1920s. As the territorial administrator of Shangugu clarified, about 450 to 500 workers deserted from Protanag in a period of only one year. According to the agent, desertions were not provoked by harsh labor conditions, but rather by the fact that people still lacked cash incentives.[32] In the 1950s, cash incentives – for instance, selling food crops was more lucrative than plantation labor (*infra*) – were available and, in combination with bad working conditions, prompted laborers to continue to desert plantations. For *colons* the problem of retrieving deserters proved to be an issue, because European authorities lacked the ability to help them while African notables no longer collaborated fully.[33]

On the Congolese side of Lake Kivu, desertions (unsurprisingly) also occurred. Even though they were present in all regions bordering the lake, Rutshuru territory offers a perfect case study to elucidate the evolution of this "weapon" used by African plantation workers. In the 1930s, people deserting in an area with a small labor reservoir were hunted and often retrieved *manu militari*. The colonial government therefore appealed to vagrancy legislation, similarly

31 Ibid, AIMO, MO agricole, Doléances colons de Rutshuru, no. 1653/6, Lettre du colon Menten de Horne au gouverneur de la Province Costermansville, 30/5/1942.

32 Ibid, RARU, Shangugu Territoire, Rapport Général, 1930, no. 100(9).

33 Ibid, RWA, AIMO(339), Shangugu rapports d'inspection agricole, Rapport plantation Willems-De Pauw, 18–19/7/1953; Rapport plantation Libera Oreste, 19/6/1959. It is not unlikely that, as in the Belgian Congo, employers made agreements with local chiefs not only to engage workers but also to help retrieve them when they deserted plantations (see: Doucy and Feldheim, *Travailleurs indigènes et productivité du travail au Congo belge*: 216–217).

to in French and Portuguese colonies. In May 1937, the territorial administrator received a list with names of workers who had deserted a coffee plantation. Subsequently, the agent sent the police accompanied by a *capita* of the plantation; they returned "with 13 men: the rope round their neck."[34] Not only were people in Rutshuru sometimes coerced to take three-year contracts; they were also treated badly, and forcibly retrieving a few deserters likely would not have helped to attract a sufficient amount of workers:

> repression of desertion is rarely a good solution for employers. After all, often we see that repressing desertions and retrieving deserters *manu militari* to their employers [...] definitely runs dry every source of recruitment. Sending a few deserters back to end their contract serves no purpose, if the use of such coercive measures scares off other natives from engaging.[35]

Not only did coercively retrieving a few deserters compromise future engagements but, in general, finding deserters in the first place was a difficult task for Europeans, especially when Africans did not or did not sufficiently cooperate. Deserters could flee into nearby forests, for example, and the administration was well aware of the fact that only few could be tracked and punished.[36] Even though after this episode desertions did not stop, it seems that colonists filed fewer complaints. In the 1950s, people deserting plantations mostly originated from Beni and Lubero, and according to the annual report of 1954, an estimated 0.74% of all contracted laborers still deserted their labor spot.[37]

A phenomenon closely linked to desertions is absenteeism. One could argue that the replacement system analyzed in the previous chapter was a way for people to absent themselves from work while in the meantime plantation tasks were carried out. However, as indicated, the system had more to do with land and the fear of losing it than with a class-conscious reaction to colonialism.[38] People might have stayed away from their workplace for several reasons. For example, not only did workers have to perform tasks they disliked or that were considered female tasks; there were also the heaviness of duties, harsh working

34 AAB, AIMO, MO agricole, Inspections plantations européennes Rutshuru, no. 1653/13, Rapport d'inspection Cafco par manager Beyer, 14/9/1937.

35 Ibid, Doléances colons de Rutshuru, no. 1653/6, Lettre du gouverneur général Ryckmans aux planteurs de café au Kivu, 2/10/1937.

36 Ibid, Lettre du commissaire de district Absil au gouverneur provincial, 9/5/1937.

37 Ibid, RACB, Rutshuru Territoire, Rapport AIMO, 1954, no. 163.

38 See in particular: Bogumil Jewsiewicki, "Political consciousness among African peasants in the Belgian Congo," *Review of African Political Economy*, no. 19 (1980).

conditions including low wages, and familial or communal obligations provoking absenteeism in both the colony and the mandate.[39]

Moreover, in 1954, the territorial administrator of Shangugu quoted yet another reason why people regularly absented themselves from plantation labor: "The sale of food crops and beer, and their coffee, procures for them revenues they deem sufficient."[40] As a consequence of diverse and more lucrative income possibilities, the level of absenteeism was sometimes high in the plantation sector. According to the TEPSI commission, there was a 10% level of absence in the mining sector, while agrarian colonists had to deal with 60 to 80% in 1955.[41]

Even though the bureaucracy in the Congolese Kivu limited income alternatives, it did not fully succeed. People still traveled to the city, engaged spontaneously in the mining sector and/or sold food crops as much as Rwandans did. This – in combination with other aspects – also resulted in laborers absenting themselves from coffee plantation work. In Masisi for instance, Rwandan settlers in particular preferred to leave the plantation early in order to cultivate their own food crops, inevitably resulting in absenteeism, irregularity and instability of the labor force.[42] In Rutshuru, the level of absenteeism was much lower in the mid-1950s when *colons* treated their workers properly (1 to 2%).[43] In this way labor scarcity and working conditions collaborated in pushing colonists not only to mechanize but also to improve labor relations in general.

It is difficult to say whether desertions and absenteeism decreased over time, in particular because source-based figures are usually lacking (except for circumstantial percentages). It might well have been the case that with improving working conditions (such as bonuses) the intensity of both African "weapons" dropped, especially after World War II. The only thing that can be said with certainty is that both occurred in all areas around Lake Kivu for the entire colonial period.

1.4 *Coffee Pilferage and "Illegal" Trade*

From the moment the coffee plantation economy in the Kivu district started to develop, plantation workers saw the benefits of this crop. At the end of the 1920s, smallholder cultivation in the mandate was still in its infancy. Coffee sales were not yet regulated and workers in the colony were well aware of the

39 Doucy and Feldheim, *Travailleurs indigènes et productivité du travail au Congo belge*: 204–219.

40 AAB, RARU, Shangugu Territoire, Rapport AIMO, 1954, no. 103(7).

41 Ibid, RWA, AIMO(340), TEPSI, Procès-verbal de la réunion de la Commission, 31/8/1955.

42 Ibid, RACB, Masisi Territoire, Rapport AIMO, 1953, no. 143.

43 Ibid, Rutshuru Territoire, 1954, no. 163.

potential of markets destined for smallholder coffee traffic established there, as the following quote shows:

> laborers on concessions situated close to the border, along the Ruzizi [Kabare], cross the border and sell stolen coffee on the markets in Ruanda-Urundi. Colonists declare that the pilferages are important. They ask that we authorize coffee sales only to planters or, as certain indigenous chiefs in the Kivu equally cultivate coffee, that we give the latter a certificate that indicates that they possess a plantation.[44]

However, despite colonists' demands, theft and "fraudulent" (from the colonial point of view) cross-border trade continued in the late 1930s. Some *colons* in Kabare estimated that about 6% of their harvest was stolen each year. This coffee was smuggled to, and sold in, Shangugu. Colonists insisted on more severe police control during harvest seasons, but the provincial council replied that such controls were impossible because of the size of some plantations. The council suggested that colonists themselves organize the control of their estate, for example by employing guards, building fences, using watchdogs or placing ambushes.[45] Despite this advice from the provincial council, it seems that at least some colonists either ignored the guidelines or had to abide by the fact that stopping pilferage was nothing more than wishful thinking as late as the end of the 1950s. Smuggling into the mandate continued as well, causing tensions between the bureaucracies of each side of Lake Kivu. A member of the provincial council declared that pilferage happened almost every day: plantation workers hid some coffee in their pockets and took it with them to their homestead, and when they had two or three sacks, they sold the coffee in Ruanda-Urundi. The latter's administration accused the provincial government in the Kivu of fencing, and the president of the provincial council urged for more and better road controls, not only in order to intercept coffee that lacked provenance but also to find the organizers of the fraud.[46] However, whether more severe road controls lessened, let alone stopped, smuggling is very doubtful. As efficient control of the border was lacking, it is more likely that people used roads where supervision was difficult or nonexistent, as also happened during the postcolonial period.[47]

44 Ibid, Province Orientale, Comité Régional, 1929, no. 49(2).
45 Ibid, Kivu Province, Conseil de Province, 1938, no. 38(2).
46 Ibid, 1958, 42(3).
47 Mukohya Vwakyanakazi, "Import and export in the second economy in North Kivu," in *The real economy of Zaire: the contribution of smuggling and other unofficial activities to national wealth*, ed. Janet MacGaffey (London: James Currey, 1991): 53.

Rwandan plantation workers also pilfered coffee,[48] and smuggling occurred the other way around as well. In addition, the territorial administrator of Shangugu extensively elaborated on coffee contraband from smallholders to the Congolese Kivu, and the ineffective measures against it at the end of the 1930s:

> An important export movement toward the Kivu has become visible, where certain buyers who have dry installations purchased green wet coffee, passages and fords [*gués*] usually used by the people of Ruanda-Urundi are now surveilled. [...] Usual passages and fords are turning impracticable, for clandestine departures by pirogue have taken place especially at night. I have established day and night guards along the Ruzizi. Despite this surveillance, clandestine departures continue. I have ordered that all the pirogues have to go ashore. Only known fishermen have the authorization to fish at night, but they are obliged to embark and debark at supervised points. [...] Despite all the measures taken, it would be adventurous to guarantee that all export of wet coffee is stopped. The extent of our shores makes surveillance extremely difficult.[49]

Although European governments in Rwanda were aware of coffee smuggling, they also realized that stopping it was impossible. As a consequence, "illegal" cross-border trade continued, and in the 1950s, estimations were even made of the amount of coffee likely to escape official statistics. For instance, agricultural services in Gisenyi calculated that 20 to 30 tons on average was smuggled to and sold in the Belgian Congo on a yearly basis in the mid-1950s.[50] Contraband in the southern part of the Lake Kivu region was even more extensive, and was often coupled to cross-border food trade. In 1940, the annual report of Shangugu clarifies that "the natives, accustomed to exporting their coffee directly to the Belgian Congo, begin to export food products at the same time."[51] However, it is more likely that food trade with the Belgian Congo preceded the trade in coffee (*infra*). Nonetheless, that the quantity of informally traded coffee was much larger than in Gisenyi is illustrated by figures from the mid-1950s. Agricultural reports estimate that approximately 200 tons on average were smuggled

48 AAB, AI, MO des plantations, no. 4378(91), Conférence donnée par Wilbaux à l'Unaki, 11/7/1954.

49 Ibid, RWA, Café, Rapports, RWA(444), Lettre de l'administrateur territorial de Shangugu au vice-gouverneur, 6/7/1939.

50 Ibid, RARU, Gisenyi Territoire, Rapport Agriculture, 1953–55, no. 90(27); 90(28); 90(29).

51 Ibid, Shangugu Territoire, Rapport Général, 1940, no. 101(6).

from Shangugu to the Belgian Congo each year, thereby illustrating the appeal of Bukavu in the first place.[52]

There are several reasons why people pilfered and smuggled coffee. It was not only a way to circumvent rigid regulations imposed on Africans (see also *infra*), but also, and perhaps foremost, a way of raising revenues. Plantation workers tried to increase their meager salary by selling the stolen coffee in the mandate, if necessary informally to intermediaries. That way the lack of a license to sell coffee was avoided. Smallholders from the mandate tried to increase their revenue by traveling to the colony, where they received two to three times more for 1 kilogram. When a sub-chief in Shangugu asked the territorial administration why it was forbidden for Rwandans to sell their coffee in the Belgian Congo, the answer was: to avoid Africans being fooled.[53] However, as stressed in the previous chapter, producers in the mandate often received only part of the market price, even on official markets, and therefore the question is who hoodwinked who by trading coffee "illegally" and out of administrative control.

1.5 *Various Kinds of Sabotage*

A final "weapon" Africans involved in coffee production could use to contest colonial rule was boycotting. Although overt uprisings or migration movements were easier to report for European agents, sabotage was likely to be more widespread, more difficult to discover and to control. And even when sabotage was revealed, colonial officers usually depicted it as laziness or as an uneconomic attitude of Africans.[54] I am well aware that sabotage is not a well-defined concept. In this context, it is rather a catch-all term for an assortment of random acts. Consequently, the aim of this section is to highlight some forms of boycott in the coffee sector rather than to present an exhaustive list of all possible acts of thwarting colonial domination.

First of all, people might refuse to pay taxes, although in such cases chiefs, responsible for tax collection, might use their authority to either collect the taxes or excommunicate defaulters. However, chiefs also opposed colonial rule and supported tax revolts, as happened in parts of Gisenyi in 1935. Military forces even had to occupy the region in order to force Africans to pay the required taxes.[55] Another way of financially sabotaging the European regime is

52 Ibid, Rapport Agriculture, 1954–55, no. 105(24); 105(258).

53 Ibid, RWA, Conseils de Territoire et de Chefferie, Biru – Shangugu, RWA(72), Compte rendu du conseil de Chefferie, 25/7/1952.

54 Isaacman, "Peasants and rural social protest in Africa": 17.

55 Dorsey, "Rwandan colonial economy, 1916–1941": 206207.

demonstrated by Rwandan smallholders crossing the border; they also circumvented periods and places in which sales of coffee were allowed. In the previous chapter, I referred to the existence of parallel sale circuits eventually legalized by the mandate administration in the 1950s. Moreover, territorial administrations were aware of both "fraudulent" practices. During a chieftaincy council in 1952, it was stressed that selling coffee was strictly forbidden for anyone (chiefs and commoners alike) before receipt of instructions from the government concerning the sales period.[56] However, as "illegal" sales continued, the year after, the Agricultural Service of Shangugu unsuccessfully demanded to advance the opening of the sales season in order to decrease such uncontrolled sales.[57] As the mandate bureaucracy stuck to their conviction that sales periods were rightly fixed, sabotage continued:

> I [Mister Van de Steene] have the honor to acquaint you [the vice general governor of Ruanda-Urundi] with the fact that numerous frauds are practiced in the territories of Ruanda bordering Lake Kivu. Those frauds are twofold: (1) purchases outside the season, closed for the trade of coffee between the first of March and the first of May every year; (2) purchases outside the centers established by the Resident; and to that has to be added the violation of the 1939 decree, fixing the maximum humidity level authorized for transactions of coffee.[58]

In addition to these forms of sabotage, smallholders used other means to contest imposed coffee cultivation. Chapter 3 argued that, despite prohibition and accompanying fines, coffee was always intercropped with other crops, including the allegedly detrimental banana trees. Apart from this, some growers managed to resist imposed coffee cultivation in a rather original way: by creating fake coffee plots. Africans gathered leaves from existing coffee bushes. Those leaves were set up as if they were real young plants. Subsequently, when an inspection passed by everything seemed normal. However, after a while these leaves rotted.[59] Africans resisted imposed cropping not only in the early stages of the production process, but also during the cultivation process. Bushes were sometimes

56 AAB, RWA, Conseils de Territoire et de Chefferie, Biru – Shangugu, RWA(72), Procès-verbal du conseil de la Chefferie, 24/4/1952.

57 Ibid, RARU, Shangugu Territoire, Rapport Agriculture, 1953, no. 105(23).

58 Ibid, RWA, Café, Rapports, RWA(444), Lettre de Van de Steene au vice-gouverneur général, 6/4/1956.

59 Hatungimana, *Le café au Burundi au XXe siècle: Paysans, argent, pouvoir*: 395.

destroyed, not to replace old and unproductive plants but rather to express dissatisfaction. This kind of resistance must have been common, especially in the 1930s, because in Shangugu anyone destroying a plant without authorization was fined 1 Franc per plant, or about the daily wage of a plantation worker in 1939.[60] Finally, before selling their coffee, producers sometimes drenched beans in water. This was likely an act of vengeance for the low prices they usually received, and it fooled African intermediary traders in particular, who purchased the semi-decayed coffee.[61]

Although I have not found direct references in the sources I used, we can expect that destruction of coffee plants also happened in the plantation sector. One way workers could destroy bushes was "by mistake," for instance by cutting roots underground.[62] Moreover, poor maintenance of bushes, often referred to in the sources, could be attributed to a lack of knowledge, but Africans could also deliberately ignore or poorly execute this important step in the coffee production process. Furthermore, foot-dragging was one of the "weapons" laborers around Lake Kivu used as well. Hence, the "low productivity idea" that was widespread among employers was partly a result of the agency of workers. For instance, in the previous chapter, I talked about laborers in Kabare who were fined because they were unable to dig six holes a day in order to plant seedlings. Comparison with other data suggests that these plantation workers intentionally slowed down. Inspections of plantations of similar sizes in Ngweshe in the same period reveal that workers managed to dig twelve to fifteen holes a day.[63] Plantation workers in the mandate equally dawdled over their work, as is proved by this illustrative quote from the Rwandan Resident: "We see them [plantation laborers] plodding a whole day long in order to dig 6 to 8 holes. […] Native planters easily manage to obtain an output of 15 to 20 holes a day."[64]

60 AAB, RWA, Conseils de Territoire et de Chefferie, Shangugu, RWA(72), Compte rendu de la réunion plénière des notbales, 30/5/1939.

61 Ibid, Café, Rapports, RWA(444), Lettre du gouverneur Jungers à l'administrateur territorial de Shangugu, 24/3/1937.

62 Bogumil Jewsiewicki, *Modernisation ou destruction du village africain: l'économie politique de la "modernisation agricole" au Congo Belge* (Bruxelles: Les Cahiers du CEDAF, 1983): 65.

63 AAB, AIMO, MO agricole, Dossier Unaki, no. 1653/10, "Note relative au travail à la pièce" par Ringoet, envoyée au gouverneur général, 29/5/1932.

64 Ibid, RWA, Café, Rapports, RWA(438), Lettre du résident Simon au vice-gouverneur général, 29/5/1933.

2 Lake Kivu Peasants

2.1 *How to Understand "Peasants"?*

Up until now, the focus of this book has been on the way coffee production for the export market developed around Lake Kivu and how it evolved during the colonial period. As in other parts of the world, a portion of the rural population became incorporated into capitalist production – as smallholders or plantation workers or both – but they never depended solely on wage labor revenues.[65] This means that subsistence economies remained important, and even more so in periods of economic contraction. These economies nevertheless were reconfigured and adapted to a "new" reality, a process referred to as "peasantization."

The aim of this section is not to engage in the theoretical debate concerning this process of "becoming peasants," but rather to present empirical evidence for the Lake Kivu region. However, similarly to other parts of the world, the African continent experienced several and distinct methods of peasantization.[66] In general, "becoming peasants" is a dynamic process and peasantries are the "historical outcome of an agrarian labor process which is constantly adjusting to surrounding conditions."[67] These conditions are diverse: from climate fluctuations to shifting political regimes to changing ecological, demographical and/or technological situations.

Scholars often struggle(d) to define African peasantries: some focus on commodity production, others on the essential role of women; but in all cases there were differences between the ways sharecroppers, plantation workers, forced commodity producers, etcetera coped with colonial exploitation and expanding commodification.[68] In order not to unnecessarily complicate the following lines, I borrow the conceptualization used by Vanhaute, who defines peasants as:

---

65 Joan Smith and Immanuel Wallerstein, eds., *Creating and transforming households: the constraints of the world-economy* (Cambridge: Cambridge University Press, 1992).

66 Eric Vanhaute, Hanne Cottyn and Yang Wang, "Peasantries," in *The world is out of joint: world-historical interpretations of continuing polarizations*, ed. Immanuel Wallerstein (London; New York: Routledge, 2015).

67 Deborah Bryceson, "Peasant theories and smallholder policies: past and present," in *Disappearing peasantries? Rural labour in Africa, Asia and Latin America*, ed. Deborah Bryceson, Christóbal Kay and Jos Mooij (London: Intermediate Technology Publications, 2000): 2–3.

68 Isaacman, "Peasants and rural social protest in Africa": 14–17.

> members of rural, agricultural households, who control the land they work, either as tenants or as smallholders, who are organized generally in households and in village communities that meet most of their subsistence needs (production, exchange, credit), who pool different forms of income, and who are ruled by other social groups, which extract a surplus either directly via rents, via (non-balanced) markets, or through control of state power (taxation).[69]

Key in this definition is: (1) the combination of subsistence activities and market activities. According to Bryceson, Africans had one foot in waged labor and one in subsistence farming out of necessity.[70] Partly as a result of low remunerations in the coffee sector, plantation workers and smallholders around Lake Kivu combined subsistence and (various) forms of income-pooling, which fueled a process of semi-proletarianization.[71] This means that Africans were able to hold on to a degree of autonomy within colonial constraints. (2) Household structures managed to meet their subsistence needs but also created surpluses that could be bartered or sold. For this case study, I add to this definition of peasants that in these household structures women played an important role. (3) People had control over the land they worked. In the previous chapters I already demonstrated that, in the colony and the mandate, people indeed controlled the land they tilled (usufruct). With the introduction of coffee (perennial crop), smallholders' control over land became even more permanent, although expropriation still happened. Control over land to work also existed in a specific way: concessionary subsistence plots for squatters or workers who were unable to return home on a regular basis. (4) Ruling social groups engaged in surplus extraction. In the precolonial region around Lake Kivu, tributes were paid to notables, usually in kind (food) but in the colonial period increasingly in a commodified way.[72] Moreover, monetary taxation was installed throughout the entire African continent. In addition, colonial regimes either installed, removed or shut down

69 Eric Vanhaute, "The end of peasantries? Rethinking the role of peasantries in a world-historical view," *Review* (*Fernand Braudel Center*) 31, no. 1 (2008): 42–43.

70 Bryceson, "African peasants' centrality and marginality: rural labour transformations": 40.

71 Bernstein, *Class dynamics of Agrarian change*: 55.

72 In most precolonial Sub-Saharan African regions, tributes had a social meaning. Tributes confirmed social stratification, and sovereigns directly consumed, accumulated or even destroyed them (Catherine Coquery-Vidrovitch, "The political economy of the African peasantry and modes of production," in *The political economy of contemporary Africa*, ed. Peter C.W. Gutkind and Immanuel Wallerstein (London; Beverly Hills: Sage Publications, 1976): 105).

(pre-existing) markets, hoping to control not only prices but also trade and trade routes.

When talking about peasants, it should be kept in mind that the relationship between capitalism and the people incorporated into it in one way or another is often very fluid, and that the definition of market or non-market activities is often open for debate:

> The peasant himself, when he regularly sells a part of his harvest and buys tools and clothing, is already a part of the market. But if he comes to the market town to sell a few items – eggs or a chicken – in order to obtain a few coins with which to pay his taxes or buy a plowshare, he is merely pressing his nose against the shop window of the marketplace.[73]

2.2 *Household (Plantation) Land*

Chapter 3 of this book analyzed methods of (changing) access to land and the *de facto* creation of a dual land system in both the colony and the mandate. This section discusses land on plantations put at the disposal of workers. The fact that plantation owners sometimes reserved a surface for their laborers' subsistence agriculture can be considered either a way of trying to tie the latter to the plantation (in this way hoping to reduce absenteeism, for instance), or as a way of keeping wages down and thus safeguarding cheap production and reproduction. However, instead of tackling this in Chapter 5, I consider concessionary subsistence land not as a way in which local economies were reconfigured and adapted to the emerging capitalist sector. Rather, I see it the other way around. Giving land to plantation workers is capitalism adapting to pre-existing local economic structures and trying to incorporate "new" people as cheaply as possible.

In the early periods of the establishment of the plantation sector around Lake Kivu, subsistence crops were usually cultivated between coffee bushes or on communal land on the concession. In the first case, it was not only more difficult for weed to grow; it was also a cheap way for estate owners to provide their workers with food (mostly bananas or maize) and hence to reduce labor costs.[74] In the second case, a surface is used merely to cultivate food crops. These surfaces were often extremely small (10 ares per regular worker in the Kivu district

73 Fernand Braudel, *Afterthoughts on material civilization and capitalism* (Baltimore: Johns Hopkins University Press, 1977): 19, quoted in: Vanhaute, "The end of peasantries? Rethinking the role of peasantries in a world-historical view": 43.

74 Leplae, *La culture et le rendement d'une plantation de café au Congo belge*: 67.

at the end of the 1920s), which may have resulted in employees stealing (communal) crops, sometimes even before they reached maturity.[75] Although in the early 1930s agricultural inspectors already urged plantation owners to create individual plots, it was not until the end of the 1930s that the latter actually changed the access to concessionary land reserved for their workers.[76]

In 1945, the territorial administrator of Masisi was convinced that in Sake no colonist had to purchase food for laborers who were unable to return home, because they all supposedly had an individual plot large enough to cultivate sufficient subsistence crops.[77] However, the following year, another agent nuanced this optimistic opinion by stating that, especially in CNKi blocs (see Chapter 3) workers' plots were too small:

> The native who takes service with a colonist generally does not receive enough land to assure his own subsistence. Colonists who have old concessions [before the creation of the CNKi], often very vast ones, can easily give 1/2 Hectare to every worker; this size is sufficient. A colonist asking for a plot (60 to 70 Hectares) in one of the CNKi blocs will not be able to do that because those plots are simply not large enough.[78]

For colonists to be able to grant their laborers, residing on the plantation, a subsistence plot of 0.5 hectares each, estates would have had to be on average at least three times larger than they actually were.[79] It thus goes without saying that no colonist would have granted a plot of this size, and the size of subsistence plots reserved for laborers must have been smaller. However, this development did not escape the attention of the provincial government. While debating this issue in 1952, the provincial council argued that subsistence land for workers and their families was indispensable. In 1951, the council even urged colonists to reserve at least 25 hectares, on either concessionary land or native land near their estate.[80] It is unclear whether *colons* followed the advice of 25 hectares, but in the mid-1950s, annual reports nevertheless stated that all

75 Leplae, *Les plantations de café au Congo belge: leur histoire (1881–1935), leur importance actuelle*: 232, and AAB, GG, Kivu district, Annuel agricultural report, 1929, no. 318.

76 Bishikwabo, "Un aspect du colonat au Congo belge: le sort des travailleurs du Kivu (1900–1940)": 36.

77 AAB, RACB, Masisi Territoire, Rapport AIMO, 1945, no. 143.

78 Ibid, 1946.

79 Ibid.

80 Ibid, Kivu Province, Conseil de Province, 1952, no. 39(5).

workers who were unable to return home had a plot, either on the estate or nearby on native land.[81]

The practice of colonists giving land outside concessionary terrain to workers was not new in the 1950s. According to a report from the CNKi, this practice already existed before 1949 and was tolerated by the colonial administration. The CNKi disputed not only turning *terres domaniales* (back) into native land in the 1950s ("economic conversion"; see Chapter 2) but also *colons* granting land illegally to African workers, and, moreover, the government tolerating such practices. Colonists sometimes agreed with chiefs that by paying a sum to the latter, their plantation workers had the right to reside on and cultivate native land near to but outside the concession. The CNKi's worst fear was that: "such practices have the indirect result of provoking the occupation, by the autochthones, of vacant land and thus *domaniales*, accordingly escaping its [the CNKi's] supervision."[82] In the mid-1950s the discussion was not over yet, and it seems that the fear of the CNKi was not unfounded. On the one hand, it was advocated that land belonging to the state but cultivated by workers and situated outside plantations required a vacancy inquiry before it could be granted to laborers. On the other hand, there were supporters (including the colonial bureaucracy) arguing that in such cases customary law should be applied. African workers tilling land outside plantations should address the local authorities directly and ask for access to these plots, while paying tributes in exchange. A crucial argument the promoters used was that by applying customary laws, customary ties and relationships were preserved much better.[83] This aspect in particular was something colonists rarely considered. I refer to the Cosyns case discussed previously, but also to plantation owners granting the ownership of concessionary subsistence plots to sons or widows of deceased workers.[84] Although in customary law user rights sometimes were hereditary, property never was, and women were excluded from land rights altogether.[85]

2.3 *Markets and Trade*

2.3.1 Markets in the Colonial Period

Before Europeans entered the region around Lake Kivu, there was already a widespread network of markets and trade. Markets were organized irregularly,

81 Ibid, Masisi Territoire, Rapport AIMO, 1953 and 1954, no. 143.

82 SAB2, Finoutremer, Documents CNKi (793), Procès-verbal Comité de Direction, 4/10/1949.

83 See for the discussion: AAB, RACB, Kivu Province, Conseil de Province, 1953, no. 40(1).

84 SAB1, INEAC, Rapports et notes (546/5210), Rapport sur l'improductivité des caféiers du Kivu Nord, 21/6/1939.

85 Koen Vlassenroot, *Households land use strategies in a protracted crisis context: land tenure, conflict and food security in eastern DRC* (FAO, 2006): 5.

and regional trade had already existed for several centuries and was not based on social/political ties, with the exception of local transactions.[86] Regional trade was organized in such a way that it did not interfere with agriculture. Intermediaries transported products and used their connections and ties to trade.[87] With reference to markets, especially (north) western Rwanda knew a lot of precolonial markets (see Map 9), while in Kinyaga (Shangugu) alone, for instance, at the end of nineteenth century there were six fixed and three seasonal markets.[88]

With the invasion of Tippu Tip, Lake Kivu regional trade became increasingly incorporated into long-distance trade connecting these networks to Eastern Africa during the last quarter of the nineteenth century. Lake Kivu traders exchanged ivory and slaves for Arab firearms, enabling local notables to increase control over markets and facilitating tribute collection from rural populations in the Lake Kivu region.[89] Even though local and regional trade characteristics continued to exist, the incorporation of this region into the world economy accelerated even more with the arrival of German and Belgian colonists, while the organization of markets altered as well.

During the colonial period, territorial governments reorganized, abolished and/or created markets, hoping to increase control in both the colony and the mandate. However, alongside authorized markets, difficult-to-control unofficial markets emerged or continued to exist. Usually, official markets coincided with small negotiation or larger commercial centers. In the former, traders had to own a license in order to trade; the situation was similar in the latter, but here licenses were much more expensive and trade was mostly limited to luxury goods and/or imported products.

On the Congolese side of Lake Kivu, numerous local markets existed in Kabare in the early 1930s, but the one in the Kabare chieftaincy outranked the others. Every Wednesday and Saturday, an average of 8000 Africans visited this market. Despite thriving markets, the colonial government decided to modify the existing network, by eliminating some markets (deemed useless) and relocating others in 1937.[90] The other Congolese territories bordering Lake Kivu went through the same evolution, even though in Masisi it seems that creating additional markets after World War II was an important activity of the colonial government. As a result of intensified colonization after the war, the labor force

86 Newbury, "Lake Kivu regional trade in the nineteenth century": 9, 17–18.

87 Ibid: 16.

88 Ibid: 35.

89 Chrétien, *The Great Lakes of Africa. Two thousand years of history*: 196–197.

90 AAB, RACB, Kabare Territoire, Rapport AIMO, 1932 and 1937, no. 99.

MAP 9 Precolonial markets in western Rwanda (end nineteenth century)
SOURCE: BASED ON BERNARD LUGAN AND ANTOINE NYAGAHENE, "LES ACTIVITÉS COMMERCIALES DU SUD KIVU AU XIXE SIÈCLE À TRAVERS L'EXEMPLE DE KINYAGA (RWANDA)," *CAHIERS D'OUTRE-MER* 36, NO. 141 (1983): 26

expanded. In 1946–1947, three new markets were opened in the eastern part of the territory in order to provide these workers with food they could not grow themselves – or not in sufficient amounts.[91]

That reorganizing existing markets was a risky undertaking for European regimes that was often subject to failure is very clear in the Rwandan Kivu. When, in 1925, the territorial administration decided to create a new market in Gisenyi

91 Ibid, Masisi Territoire, 1946, no. 143.

(the future city near the lake) and abolished the existing one nearby in Nyundo, chiefs were urged to send their subjects to this new market and make clear that trade no longer was allowed in the latter dismantled market: "Despite the chiefs, the natives, used to this market, are trying to continue to trade in Nyundo. A special surveillance has been installed in Nyundo, and little by little, but with dislike, the natives are going to Kisenyi."[92] While the administration continued to reorganize markets – in 1944, for instance, the territory counted eleven official markets – unofficial, uncontrollable trade continued as well.[93] In the early 1950s, rising food prices on official markets stimulated trade on unauthorized markets.[94]

In Shangugu the administration took even more drastic measures. In 1925, all (eight) existing markets were shut down. Only the market in Kamembe – three times per week and frequented by thousands of Africans coming from as far as central Rwanda, Burundi and the Belgian Congo – and Bugarama (merely for food) were still allowed.[95] The rather predictable result of this measure was that a lot of unofficial trade ensued in the territory. Furthermore, many people from the colony crossed the Rusizi plain with products bought in Rwanda, forcing the territorial administrator of Shangugu to plea for a border control post.[96] However, in the following decades the government in Shangugu reinstalled markets alongside roads. The result was that at the end of the 1950s, Gisenyi counted thirteen official markets, while in Shangugu seven existed (versus nine at the end of the nineteenth century) (see Maps 10 and 11). Although reduced in both territories and relocated toward roads, the precolonial tendency of more markets in Gisenyi continued throughout the colonial period.

2.3.2 Commerce in the Lake Kivu Region

On the eve of colonization,[97] trade around Lake Kivu consisted of various products, but the most important ones were food (beans, peas, butter, fish, sorghum and eleusine), livestock, salt and hoes. Before the second half of the nineteenth century, the northern axis was the more important trade route, but then a shift occurred toward the south, partly as a result of political events (for instance, the

92 Ibid, RARU, Gisenyi Territoire, Rapport Général, 1925, no. 87(13).
93 Ibid, 1944, no. 88(4).
94 Ibid, 1950, no. 88(10).
95 Ibid, Shangugu Territoire, Rapport Général, 1925, no. 100(4).
96 Ibid, 1930, no. 100(9).
97 This paragraph is primarily based on: Newbury, "Lake Kivu regional trade in the nineteenth century."; Lugan and Nyagahene, "Les activités commerciales du sud Kivu au XIXe siècle à travers l'exemple de Kinyaga (Rwanda)", and Leurquin, *Le niveau de vie des populations rurales du Ruanda-Urundi*: 13–56.

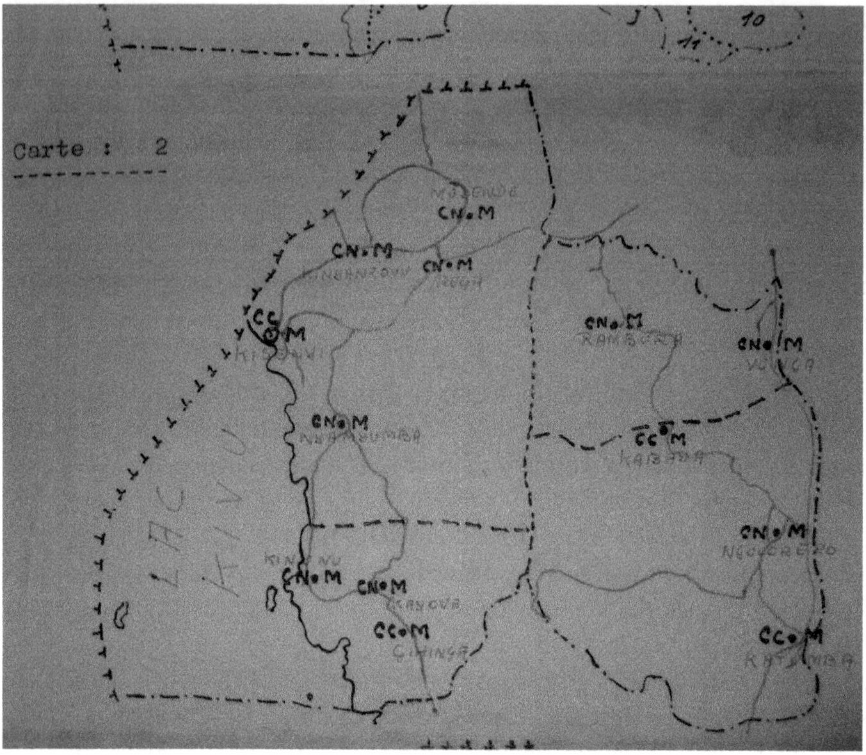

MAP 10 Official markets (M) and commercial (CC) and negotiation centers (CN) in Gisenyi, 1958
SOURCE: AAB, RACB, GISENYI TERRITOIRE, RAPPORT GÉNÉRAL, 1958, NO. 88(14)

expansion of political control from central Rwanda toward the southwest). Food was traded from the west of Lake Kivu toward the east and vice versa, depending on local or seasonal variations. Salt was coming from the Katwe network around Lake Edward to the northern tip of Lake Kivu,[98] but in the second half of the nineteenth century, trade in salt shifted. From that moment on, salt traded in the Kivu network originated in the Tanganyika network. As argued in the previous chapter, especially in the early stages of development, the coffee sector also used salt as a ration because of its importance in the local diet and trade. Trade in hoes (and iron in general) was mostly (but not solely) west–east directed. West of Lake Kivu, people were specialized in iron melting and

98 For more, see: Joseph Nzabandora Ndimubanzi, "Le commerce du sel mineral de Katwe au Nord-Kivu précolonial (1830–1911)," in *L'Afrique des Grands Lacs: cultures et civilisations* (Bukavu: CERUKI, 1982).

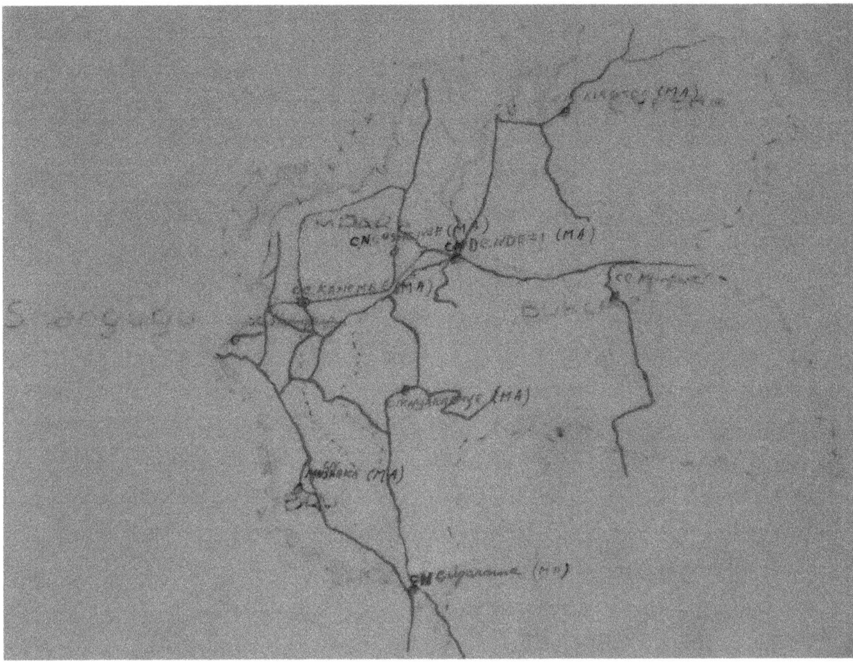

MAP 11 Official markets (MA) and commercial (CC) and negotiation centers (CN) in Shangugu, 1958
SOURCE: AAB, RACB, SHANGUGU TERRITOIRE, RAPPORT GÉNÉRAL, 1958, NO. 102(9)

forging.[99] Hoes and iron imported in Kinyaga were often redistributed to central and eastern Rwanda. Finally, a very important trade product was livestock, usually following an east–west orientation. People traded sheep and goats but also cattle, or at least unfertile cattle not involved in cattle contracts. A significant role in trade around Lake Kivu was played by *butega* (bracelets made of raffia fibers woven into a unique pattern). These bracelets were fabricated west of the lake, where they were used not only to barter but also as currency in local trade.[100] *Butega* had an economic rather than a socio-political role, and were distributed via the northern and southern route. In (central) Rwanda, the demand for *butega* was large. Social stratification encouraged the demand for

99 For more information, see: bin Mubibi Mugaruka, "La circulation des produits de la forge et de l'artisanat au Bushi ancien, leur rôle dans le développement du commerce dans la région interlacustre," *Actes du colloque L'Afrique des Grands Lacs* II (1982).

100 This currency was still used in the 1930s and 1940s, but then its importance started to decline as monetization of commercial transactions increased.

these bracelets as prestige goods as well. It was not uncommon for rich women to wear *butega* in order to display wealth.

Although during the colonial period a border was delineated between the Belgian Congo and Rwanda, trade around Lake Kivu continued. Administrations in both the mandate and the colony initially tolerated these movements of goods, but after World War I, they increasingly opposed "illegal" cross-border trade.[101] For Africans living in the vicinity of the lake, commercial transactions continued to exist. The only thing that was different was that the content of trade products expanded – in size and variety. Rice, for example, but also coffee, became part of the array of products traded between people around the lake. Trade during the colonial period went mainly, but not exclusively, from east to west. Rwandans sought to exploit asymmetries[102] (higher prices in the colony), but also the surplus of "freedom" as a consequence of the mandate structure.

Masisi offers a good example of how precolonial routes and colonial policy sometimes intertwined. At the end of nineteenth century, *butega*, manufactured in the Kivu, passed the lake either via the north or via the south in order to arrive in Bugoyi or Kinyaga, where they were exchanged for cattle or salt.[103] During the famine of 1943–1944, food was transported "clandestinely" from Masisi to both Gisenyi and Shangugu. As the territorial administrator reported in 1943, about 4000 tons of food left the territory, by boats crossing the lake, by trucks (from the CNKi, for instance), by Africans coming from Rutshuru and Kabare, or by Rwandans returning home after having worked temporarily in Masisi.[104] Rutshuru fulfilled the same food supply role in these years of crisis. As in Masisi, a prohibition on the export of food was promulgated in 1943, but food trade continued "illegally" and some traders from Rutshuru were able to make great profit. The annual report of 1943 cited an extraordinary case: a Rwandan consumer who was starving due to the famine exchanged a heifer for an imported basket of sorghum.[105] Circumventing colonial laws, using asymmetries and simultaneously gaining an income also happened in other ways. In 1936 for instance, the territorial bureaucracy in Rutshuru tried to increase labor productivity by combating an alleged excess of alcohol. In order to achieve this goal,

---

101 Mathys, "People on the move. Frontiers, borders, mobility and history in the Lake Kivu region 19th–20th century": 267.

102 As mentioned before, I borrow this concept from: ibid.

103 Lugan and Nyagahene, "Les activités commerciales du sud Kivu au XIXe siècle à travers l'exemple de Kinyaga (Rwanda)": 28.

104 AAB, RACB, Masisi Territoire, Rapport AIMO, 1943, no. 143. In the early 1950s, food (beans and peas) was still exported from Masisi to Gisenyi (ibid, RARU, Gisenyi Territoire, Rapport Général, 1951, no. 88(11)).

105 Ibid, RACB, Rutshuru Territoire, Rapport AIMO, 1943 and 1944, no. 163.

the government introduced a tax on banana beer (*pombe*), but, since then: "The natives are selling their produce in Ruanda, in places where no tax is levied."[106]

However, as mentioned above, the main direction of trade during the colonial period was from the mandate to the colony. In 1925, the territorial agent of Gisenyi noticed that trade toward the Kivu was immense. It consisted mainly of food crops, but also tobacco and cattle.[107] In 1933, about 560 tons of food (peas, sorghum, maize, potatoes, manioc and carrots) was exported to the Kivu, partly to supply European concessions. These crops were transported not only on foot but also by pirogue. Despite the continuing importance of food export, trade in livestock declined in this period, due to the rinderpest and the closure of the border.[108] However, the situation improved rapidly, because already in 1936 – as well as tobacco, pottery, woven baskets, chickens and eggs – some 1200 tons of food was traded to the colony, in addition to about 200 heads of cattle and nearly 3000 sheep and goats per month.[109] The famine of 1943–1944 resulted in a reversal of food trade, as during this period import prevailed over export. Due to bad weather conditions and persistent bad harvests, people in Gisenyi were left with no other choice than to consume food surpluses of especially beans and sweet potatoes, causing a temporary slump. As a consequence of declining revenues during this crisis period, barter (food in exchange for small livestock) had the upper hand, despite the increasing monetization of commercial transactions.[110] In the 1950s, Gisenyi recovered and trade toward the colony re-amplified. Just as before the crisis, not only were food, tobacco and livestock (including pigs) sold but also animal skins and, increasingly, vegetables (onions, tomatoes, leek and cabbages).[111] The latter were particularly meant to cater to European consumer demands in Goma.

More to the south, Kibuye shows a similar tendency in products traded (mostly food and livestock), though mainly with Idjwi Island and by pirogue. However, I should stress that people from Kibuye often traveled on foot as far as Shangugu, Gisenyi and even Bukavu to trade food surpluses, livestock and manufactures.[112] Until the mid-1930s, commercial transactions between Kibuye and Idjwi consisted largely of barter. As the administrator of Kibuye stipulated in 1931, people from Idjwi brought beans, sorghum and coins in

106 Ibid, 1936.
107 Ibid, RARU, Gisenyi Territoire, Rapport Général, 1925, no. 87(13).
108 Ibid, 1933 and 1934, no. 87(19) and 87(20).
109 Ibid, 1936, 87(22).
110 Ibid, 1943 and 1944, no. 88(3) and 88(4).
111 Ibid, 1950, no. 88(10), and ibid, Rapport Agriculture, 1951, no. 90(25).
112 Ibid, Lubengera Territoire, Rapport Général, 1928, no. 80(7), and ibid, Kibuye Territoire, Rapport Général, 1935, 82(2).

order to exchange these for peas, tobacco and goats.[113] In the 1950s, after the reinstallation of the territory, trade with Idjwi still was important: people coming from the island by boat purchased small livestock and fowl, and sold mainly beer and beans.[114]

As a continuation of precolonial trends, commercial transactions between Shangugu and the colonial pendant were intense in the early 1920s.[115] In 1927, the annual report elaborated on food scarcity in parts of neighboring Kabare that caused a rise in food export toward the colony, but also an increase in food prices in Shangugu.[116] After a regression in trade with the Kivu in the early 1930s, followed by export restrictions due to the rinderpest, commerce revived from the mid-1930s. Even though the territorial government advised against food export to the colony, food was increasingly traded once again, together with beer and cattle.[117] The trade of the latter especially was very important in Shangugu – although cattle trade also existed in Gisenyi, albeit to a lesser extent. On the Kamembe market, local traders often acted as intermediaries for transiting cattle coming from central Rwanda, mostly toward the colony.[118] Similarly to Gisenyi and Goma, the increased urbanization of Bukavu created an additional incentive for Africans in Shangugu to transport and sell products after World War II. Among the products traded were small livestock, food, beer, chickens and eggs.[119] Although commercial transactions were increasingly monetized, barter continued until at least the early 1950s: people from Kabare traveled to Shangugu and not only sold their animal skins but also exchanged them for food crops and banana beer.[120] That the growth of Bukavu as an urban center (and the Kivu in general), combined with higher prices, exerted a great attraction on people living in the mandate is illustrated by figures from the mid-1950s. In 1954, for example, Shangugu exported in total, among other things, 145 tons of beans, 300 tons of sweet potatoes, 500 tons of bananas and 150000 eggs to the colony.[121]

---

113 Ibid, Lubengera Territoire, Rapport Général, 1931, 80(10).
114 Ibid, Kibuye Territoire, Rapport Général, 1953, no. 82(3).
115 Ibid, Shangugu Territoire, Rapport Général, 1924, no. 100(3).
116 Ibid, 1927, no. 100(6).
117 Ibid, 1935 and 1936, no. 101(1) and 101(2).
118 See, for more information on cattle trade and markets: Mathys, "People on the move. Frontiers, borders, mobility and history in the Lake Kivu region 19th–20th century": 271–288. While in Gisenyi about two hundred heads of cattle passed the border monthly in 1936, it is estimated that in the same year some 35000 heads of cattle were transited via Shangugu.
119 AAB, RARU, Shangugu Territoire, Rapport Général, 1945, no. 101(11).
120 Ibid, 1951, no. 102(4).
121 Ibid, Rapport Agriculture, 1954, no. 105(24).

2.4 *Income Diversification and the Role of Women*

While in the previous section the focus was on regional trade, this final section emphasizes local trade and the people selling products on local markets. While both kinds of trade were part of household income strategies, the former often covered considerable distances, sometimes involving intermediaries. In local trade, on the other hand, Africans went to nearby markets and mostly sold subsistence food surpluses, but also banana beer and, in later periods, vegetables, thereby catering to European demands. Even though the commodification of food surpluses gained importance after World War II, its impact remained rather modest in both the colony and the mandate. According to estimations made by Leurquin, in Rwanda only 4.7% of the total bean production and 15.7% of manioc flower production, for example, was sold on the market in the 1950s.[122] Nevertheless, selling food surpluses contributed substantially to household revenues and supplemented meager coffee remunerations.[123] Moreover, there is ample evidence that in all areas bordering Lake Kivu, the commercialization of food was more lucrative than revenues in the coffee sector. Furthermore, in this local trade women were pivotal because they usually went to markets to sell food surpluses.

In Kabare, plantation households supplemented wages by selling food crops (beans and manioc, for instance), but also eggs, chickens, butter, milk, honey and wood – the latter was lucrative, according to the annual report of 1933.[124] In addition to food surpluses, selling manufactured goods (skins, hoes, mats and pots, for example) on local markets also contributed to household incomes.[125] In the early 1940s, the administrator of this territory was aware that low wages

122 Leurquin, *Le niveau de vie des populations rurales du Ruanda-Urundi*: 225–226.

123 See for Kabare: Elinor Sosne, "Colonial peasantization and contemporary underdevelopment: a view from a Kivu village," in *Zaïre. The political economy of underdevelopment*, ed. Guy Gran (New York: Praeger, 1979): 192. Income diversification is not unique to the coffee sector around Lake Kivu. There is a vast literature on how people in colonial Africa supplemented low remunerations with other income sources. To cite only a few examples: Nkasa Yelengi, "Labor policies and household economic strategies among the railway workers in Katanga, Belgian Congo, 1928–1960," *Africa: Rivista Trimestrale di Studi e Documentazione Dell'Istituto italiano per l'Africa e l'Oriente* 55, no. 4 (2000), and Erik Green, "Diversification or de-agrarianization? Income diversification, labor, and processes of agrarian change in Southern and Northern Malawi, mid-1930s to mid-1950s," *Agricultural History* 82, no. 2 (2008). For other coffee-producing regions: Charles W. McClellan, "Land, labor, and coffee: the South's role in Ethiopian self-reliance, 1889–1935," *African Economic History*, no. 9 (1980); Roger Van Zwanenberg, "The development of peasant commodity production in Kenya, 1920–40," *Economic History Review* 27, no. 3 (1974); and Curtis, "Smaller is better. A consensus of peasants and bureaucrats in colonial Tanganyika."

124 AAB, RACB, Kabare Territoire, Rapport AIMO, 1933, no. 99.

125 Ibid, 1938.

deterred Africans and that, consequently, they rather engaged in "every occupation they deemed sufficiently remunerated and that conflicts with labor demands."[126] The agent referred not only to the commercialization of food and vegetables but also to that of milk and cattle, while equally acknowledging the agency of Africans who saw the benefits of small-scale trade. That Africans saw the advantages of selling food surpluses was also noticed by the territorial bureaucracy of Masisi. According to the annual report of 1942: "every cultivator sells every year more than half a ton of food to the mines, more or less the same quantity on the markets, and consumes the rest."[127] Although the northern tip of the colonial Kivu had to deal with wild pigs and elephants destroying food crops from the end of the 1930s onwards, local markets were vibrant and even frequented by people from Rwanda and Uganda. Like in Kabare, food crops formed the bulk of trade goods, but baskets, pots, hoes and small livestock were traded as well.[128] Also similar to developments in Kabare is the insight European agents gained that low wages did not encourage Africans to enter or stay in the plantation economy, because:

> the revenues the native living in his customary environment can procure by selling food crops on the markets are exceeding those he can procure by selling his labor in exchange for a little elevated salary.[129]

Consequently, exchanges on local markets were intense in the 1950s, despite the loss some people suffered from wild animals destroying part of their crops (and hence additional revenues).[130]

In Rutshuru's counterpart Gisenyi, local markets were frequently visited by Rwandans coming from the north and northeast, but also by numerous Congolese from as far as Masisi. People mostly bought food crops and livestock, but also tobacco, for example. The importance of the latter cannot be underestimated. In the early 1920s, Africans were producing and selling cigars to the few Europeans residing in the territory.[131] Alongside tobacco, people also sold small livestock and surpluses of beans, maize and potatoes.[132] That local markets in Gisenyi were commercial hubs can be illustrated by this quote from 1931:

126 Ibid, 1941.
127 Ibid, Masisi Territoire, Rapport AIMO, 1942, no. 143.
128 Ibid, Rutshuru Territoire, Rapport AIMO, 1932, no. 163.
129 Ibid, 1941.
130 Ibid, 1950 and 1951.
131 Ibid, RARU, Gisenyi Territoire, Rapport Général, 1923, no. 87(12).
132 Ibid, 1928, no. 87(15).

> The market of the administrative post continues to be frequented by about a thousand natives composed of 75% Banyarwanda, 25% natives from the Congo, Bahunde from the territories of Masisi and Rutshuru [...]. The Bagoyi [people from Bugoyi] sell to them numerous heads of small livestock, cattle, coming from their tobacco trade with people from the Rwandan interior [...]. The market, by itself, daily counts some hundred goats and sheep for sale; the great majority are bought by indigenous people from the Kivu. Some twenty galliforms follow the same route every day. Another product from Gisenyi sought after by the Bahunde is the pottery dish – the nature of their soil does not allow its fabrication – of which they every day equally take some twenty with them for the price of 1.50 to 2 Francs.[133]

The same trends continued after World War II, with numerous and intense transactions on local markets in order to supplement coffee incomes. However, the urbanization of Goma resulted in a higher European demand for vegetables from the late 1930s onwards, which in turn resulted in additional income possibilities for Africans living near the border.[134] Kibuye was an exception compared with Gisenyi and Shangugu, primarily because this territory lacked a network of markets at least until the early 1950s. Trade (mainly in beans, peas and banana beer) occurred mainly in ambulant exchange centers or in people's homesteads.[135] Despite the absence of organized markets, Kibuye still managed to be an excellent food trader during the famine of 1928–1929 – Shangugu played a similar role in 1943–1944 (*infra*). The annual report of 1929 speaks of an intensive commerce of food, with Africans coming from other territories in order to buy expensive beans, maize and eleusine.[136] As in the other territories bordering the lake, here too commerce was more lucrative than working for Europeans (publicly or privately). According to a calculation made in 1958, the commercialization of African-produced crops (food but also coffee) yielded about 500 Francs per year more than the average wage paid by Europeans.[137] Similarly to other markets in the Kivu region, local markets in Shangugu mainly

133 Ibid, 1931, no. 87(17).

134 See for instance ibid, 1951, no. 88(11).

135 Ibid, Lubengera Territoire, Rapport Général, 1925, no. 80(4); ibid, Kibuye Territoire, Rapport Général, 1935 and 1953, n°82(2) and 82(3). This was a result of trading routes bypassing Kibuye. For instance, cattle coming from central Rwanda went directly to Gisenyi and to Shangugu in particular.

136 Ibid, Lubengera Territoire, Rapport Général, 1929, no. 80(8).

137 Ibid, Kibuye Territoire, Affaires économiques, 1957–58, no. 82(22).

sold food surpluses, banana beer and livestock. These markets were animated and well populated, as the annual report of 1925 claims:

> It is impossible to give a figure, even approximatively, for the number of transactions between natives realized on the market of Kamembe. Three days a week the market is frequented by thousands of natives coming from the territory, from the Belgian Congo, from Urundi and even from Nduga [central Rwanda]. All indigenous products are sold there, except for butter and milk.[138]

The global crisis and the dismissal of many wage laborers in both Shangugu and the Kivu had serious repercussions for the hitherto flourishing food trade. Prices on local markets dropped, but food transactions continued, albeit in an altered way. People in Shangugu sold products at their homesteads instead of spending energy and time to travel to the nearest market.[139] The importance of Shangugu as a food producer and supplier was accentuated during the famine of 1943–1944. Although some regions also suffered from scarcity, food and seeds were sold to victims of deprivation coming from other territories.[140] After World War II, Shangugu in particular benefited greatly from the development of Bukavu. Not only did people go to Bukavu to sell products and sometimes make three times more than at local markets, but these local markets in Shangugu thrived as well. Moreover, selling products there was more lucrative than wages in the European sector because "beans, manioc, [...] bananas, beer, are sold very expensively on the markets and in Bukavu."[141]

It is impossible to understand the functioning of the coffee sector around Lake Kivu without paying attention to the central role of women. Even though the sources I consulted are usually rather silent on their role, and fieldwork is absolutely required to expand our knowledge, some tentative remarks are possible. Foremost, even when women were not directly involved in coffee production, their subsistence activities "underpinned the profitability of coffee cultivation."[142] However, as demonstrated in the previous chapter, women were involved in the coffee sector around Lake Kivu. In the plantation economy they were important during harvests, while smallholders sometimes left cash-crop

138 Ibid, Shangugu Territoire, Rapport Général, 1925, no. 100(4).

139 Ibid, 1931, no. 100(10).

140 Ibid, 1944, no. 101(10); also: Singiza, "Les réactions des autorités belges et locales face à la famine Ruzagayura (Rwanda, 1943–1944). Heuristique, méthodologie et premiers résultats": 196.

141 AAB, RARU, Shangugu Territoire, Rapport AIMO, 1955, no. 103(8).

142 Topik and Clarence-Smith, "Conclusion: new propositions and a research agenda": 395.

cultivation to their wives, for instance when they worked as wage laborers. This nuances the static view of women in the subsistence and men in the market sector.[143] Rather, alongside subsistence activities (most steps in food provisioning, but also fabricating clothes, for instance), women also contributed to household incomes. Moreover, women were also active in local trade and the commercialization of subsistence surpluses (but also in some forms of petty trade) in order to supplement coffee revenues and thus improve total incomes.

According to Catharine Newbury, few technological changes entered local subsistence agriculture, even though local agriculture changed drastically during the colonial period. The introduction of new crops (coffee and tea, but also potatoes, for example) altered agriculture. Moreover, as a consequence of increasing commodification (especially after World War II), the social relations of production altered as well and there was a shift in women's work toward food production for the market.[144] It should be stressed, however, that food commodification also resulted in changing gender relations on the household level. Women could earn an income, although this was usually part of a household revenue, but it could result in a certain degree of freedom. On the other hand, men earning wage or cash-crop incomes could (or sometimes had to) buy food, and thus women lost a certain degree of authority.[145]

The fact that women were employed in the coffee sector sometimes even caused problems for food production. In Kabare, a huge demand for female plantation workers during harvest periods compromised food crop cultivation in some areas at the end of the 1930s.[146] Furthermore, some European agents seem to have been surprised by the vital role of women in food production,

143 Recent literature on coffee production in colonial Africa supports this argument: Patrick Mbataru, "Women in the coffee society: the case of Nyeri, Kenya," *Etudes Rurales*, no. 180 (2007), and Hélène Guetat-Bernard, "Cultures du café et dynamiques des rapports de genre en pays Bamiléké au Cameroun: effet de similitude avec la situation Kikuyu au Kenya," *Cahiers d'Outre-Mer* 61, no. 243 (2008).

144 Catharine Newbury, "Ebutumwa Bw'Emiogo: The tyranny of cassava a women's tax revolt in Eastern Zaïre," *Canadian Journal of African Studies* 18, no. 1 (1984): 37.

145 Some authors focus on the negative results of coffee cash production – for example: J.H. Konter, "The deteriorating position of African women in the development from a subsistence economy towards a market economy," in *The household, women and agricultural development*, ed. Clio Presvelou and Saskia Spijkers-Zwart (Wageningen: H. Veenmann & Zonen B.V., 1980): 24 – and others on the positive impact: Guetat-Bernard, "Cultures du café et dynamiques des rapports de genre en pays Bamiléké au Cameroun: effet de similitude avec la situation Kikuyu au Kenya": 348–349. Some are more nuanced, stressing both positive and negative results: Mbataru, "Women in the coffee society: the case of Nyeri, Kenya": 104.

146 AAB, RACB, Kabare Territoire, Rapport AIMO, 1938, no. 99.

although in both the colony and the mandate women fed plantation workers (temporary and regular) as well, whether by cultivating customary land or plantation land. As the territorial agent of Shangugu wrote in 1930, referring to employees of Protanag:

> These workers are going home in the evening and find there food crops coming from their fields. When men are engaged in wage labor, women are tilling the land. The crops [the extent of the land] of the workers are not less extensive than those of the natives never leaving the hill.[147]

3 Conclusion

This chapter was divided into two sections, both intended to demonstrate ways in which Africans provided feedback to the incorporation into the capitalist world-system. The previous chapters (land and wage issues) already showed occasions on which Africans' interests were met and how those concerns contributed to the development of the coffee sector around Lake Kivu. In the final chapter of this book, the focus was on two specific forms of interaction: resistance and adaptation.

Even though open and large-scale resistance against colonialism was limited, the Cosyns case shows that aversion to ignorance of existing customary rules was not absent. However, by using Scott's ideas on the "weapons of the weak," I showed that other forms of resistance were more widespread. People involved in coffee production for the world market questioned this economic system in various ways. First and foremost, they migrated, mostly by following precolonial patterns. Although people from the colonial Kivu also migrated to the mandate, it seems that movement in the other direction was more pronounced during the colonial period. This indicates that Rwandans living near the border indeed exploited asymmetries and especially higher wages in the colony. Secondly, plantation laborers on both sides of the lake often deserted or absented themselves from their work. While workers were sometimes returned hard-handedly by territorial administrators or African intermediaries, harsh working conditions in the plantation sector and more lucrative income sources are but two reasons why these "weapons" were often used by Africans. A third "weapon" used by both smallholder and plantation workers was pilferage and "illegal" coffee trade in an attempt to increase revenues. Seeking higher incomes across borders, desertion and absenteeism, theft and "illegal" sales all point to

147 Ibid, RARU, Shangugu Territoire, Rapport Général, 1930, no. 100(9).

low wages resulting in low productivity. Attempts to improve labor productivity, discussed in the previous chapter, must have affected these issues as well. For instance, even though data are scarce, desertions probably declined as a result of improved working conditions, which in turn improved labor productivity after World War II. Finally, both smallholders and plantation employees consciously sabotaged coffee production in order to show their disproval. As explained previously, smallholders not only continued to intercrop coffee with other crops despite the prohibition, they also sold coffee outside selling seasons or via informal circuits. In addition, smallholders sometimes destroyed plants or moistened them before sale. Intentionally bad maintenance, hinted at in previous chapters, could also be a form of resitance. Plantation workers probably destroyed plants as well, and foot-dragging was a "weapon" commonly used.

Resisting coffee production was one way in which Africans faced the emergence of an export sector. However, the entrance of capital also modified, and created possibilities for, existing local economies. During the colonial period, a process of peasantization progressed on both sides of Lake Kivu. Africans involved in the coffee sector combined subsistence with capitalist activities – as either smallholders or wage laborers. Part of their income was skimmed off by the introduction of monetary taxes, but also by the commodification of tributes and customary tasks. They had control over land (through usufruct or individual rights), either in local communities or on concessions. Furthermore, markets and trade around Lake Kivu were already vibrant in precolonial times and continued to be in the colonial period, despite the efforts of European governments to reorganize markets and their dislike of "illegal" cross-border trade on both sides of the lake. As with migration patterns, trade mostly went from the mandate to the colony. A major exception here is during the famine of 1943–1944, when large amounts of food were transported from eastern Congo to afflicted areas in Rwanda. This demonstrates the flexibility of peasants in adapting to new circumstances. In general, however, trade flows went from east to west, which was partly a result of the attraction of Goma and, particularly, Bukavu. This, in turn, illustrates again that (Rwandan) peasants exploited opportunities created during the colonial period. For Africans, trading was an important way to supplement coffee incomes. On many occasions the surplus of subsistence food crops was sold, and this was also done with manufactured goods, cattle or banana beer, for instance. In light of meager coffee incomes for both smallholders and plantation workers, small-scale trade was often more lucrative than working in the coffee sector, which partly also explains why many Africans deserted or absented themselves from work.

Women were vital in the coffee economy around Lake Kivu. Next to many subsistence activities, they worked in the coffee sector and, especially by selling food surpluses on local markets, they contributed to the household income in yet another way.

To conclude this chapter, I have shown that both migration patterns and trade around Lake Kivu largely continued during the colonial period, albeit modified. It seems that precolonial structures were maintained, albeit reconfigured. The transformed continuity indicates African feedback in response to the arrival of capitalism, but also the manifestation of rural populations thwarting a skeletal colonial state incapable of controlling and directing such issues as markets and trade.[148]

148 In a recent published article, Henriet comes to a similar conclusion with reference to palm oil cutters in the Congo basin: Henriet, "'Elusive natives': escaping colonial control in the Leverville oil palm concession, Belgian Congo, 1923–1941": 356.

CONCLUSION

A Merger Based on Diversity and Compromise

The contribution of this book is twofold. Firstly, my research fills a thematic and geographical lacuna in the historiography of Belgian Africa: the lack of attention to the Kivu in the literature.[1] Moreover, on the one hand, by focusing on this region as a historical region, and on the other, by using the colonially imposed border as a mirror in order to compare the two sides of Lake Kivu, I have tried to transcend this border. Furthermore, coffee production too has been overlooked by the greater part of the historiography on Belgian Africa. While cotton and palm oil, for instance, have already received sufficient attention, literature on Belgian Africa has remained mostly silent about coffee. However, (*Arabica*) coffee was of major importance for the Kivu region. Hence, a study of this commodity is justified.

Secondly, by supplying empirical evidence, this book has also contributed to two interrelated historical-theoretical concepts: commodity frontiers and empire. The expansion of capitalism was accompanied by the incorporation of "new" peripheral rural zones into the modern world-system. While "new" zones are being incorporated, a process of interaction takes place. Hence, frontier processes are fueled by feedback from local actors (incorporated populations, but also settlers, for example), albeit in a context of unequal power relations. Even though frontier has to be understood as a process between formerly unattached socio-economic/political/cultural systems, this process also has a spatial component, referred to as the frontier zone. While focusing on one commodity (in this case coffee), and how this commodity was produced, this book offers empirical evidence on what happened with land and labor in the Lake Kivu region throughout the process of incorporation and commodification. The development of a commodity frontier zone is backed by a territorial power (in this case Belgium), which results in unequal power relations between the incorporator and the incorporated. By applying the concept of empire to this territorial power, diversity (vital in empire-building) and the role of actors on the ground (similar to their role in frontier development, but in this case indigenous populations) within the coffee commodity frontier can be fully grasped. Empire is created out of diversity, but the concept does not necessarily make

1 Besides path-breaking work by both David and Catharine Newbury, primarily focusing on socio-political and economic aspects, and the recent dissertation by Mathys, who also emphasizes socio-political issues, there is little literature available.

 | DOI:10.1163/9789004428492_010

diversity visible. Therefore, in this book, I have used a reciprocal comparative method in order to apply a similar set of questions to both sides of Lake Kivu, aimed to discover the different sets of rules used on the two sides.

The combination of these two theoretical concepts enabled me to formulate the main research question: how did the coffee production sector develop in the region around Lake Kivu throughout the colonial period? Using a comparative framework, I have answered the following sub-questions: how were labor and land mobilized and commodified on both sides of the lake? What factors influenced this labor and land mobilization/commodification (policy, coercion, agency)? What role did different colonial powers (the state, but also feedback from African chiefs, ordinary Africans and European planters) play in these processes? This book argues that the emergence and evolution of dissimilar coffee commodity frontier zones around Lake Kivu after World War I was the result of pre-existing local differences, enhanced during the colonial period, and of compromises between and feedback from several local actors. Despite the harmonizing tendencies of capitalism, both difference and compromise resulted in diverging modes of production, methods of labor/land mobilization and empire-building (sets of rules), even though the very nature of empire equally resulted in "internal diversity."

1 On Differentiation

The development and growth of the Kivu coffee commodity frontier zone, as analyzed in Chapter 1, not only revealed that the coffee sector became more significant on a global scale (from 1 to 2% in the late 1950s; global production multiplied by 1.5) throughout the colonial period. This chapter also quantitatively underpinned the diversity of production systems (and hence labor and land input) in the Lake Kivu region – mainly plantations in eastern Congo and mostly smallholders in western Rwanda.

It has been argued that the differentiation of dominant production systems was a result of three prevailing factors. The first is a difference in land tenure systems. Individual land tenure (*isambu*) existed in central Rwanda before colonization and was spreading to western Rwanda in the last quarter of the nineteenth century, but the process was only completed during the colonial period. In eastern Congo Kivu, such a process of "individualization" was lacking. The second factor explaining the difference between the western and eastern sides of Lake Kivu is land availability. As opposed to in most regions in eastern Congo, in many parts of precolonial Rwanda land was already scarce

(Shangugu was a notable exception), which made it difficult for European powers to establish a plantation economy (supposing that this was indeed the ambition). As shown, up until the "rush of colonists," smallholder cultivators in eastern Congo were more "encouraged" than plantations. However, these two differences between the two sides of Lake Kivu are still insufficient to explain the sustained differentiation during the colonial period. For example, a lack of land in a colonial context does not necessarily mean that plantations cannot emerge. The Kabare territory in the colonial Kivu is a perfect example of this. Existing local differentiation was enhanced throughout the colonial period as a result of deviating judicial objectives. The mandated territory of Ruanda-Urundi could not be ruled with the same sets of rules as the colony. This resulted in different methods of labor and land mobilization for the coffee sector, even though similarities (indicating the uniforming tendencies of capitalism) were not absent either.

With regard to land mobilization, in both eastern Congo and western Rwanda, dual land tenure emerged during the colonial period. On both sides of the lake, indigenous land was distinguished from vacant land (not cultivated or occupied land). European access to vacant coffee land differed in the sense that in eastern Congo, the colonial administration granted a lot of authority to a parastatal entity (CNKi), which was lacking in western Rwanda. In the latter, more emphasis was put on African coffee land. The spread of the individualized *isambu* system was completed during the colonial period, and this land tenure system firmly embedded smallholder production. Although European administrations in the mandate and the colony tried to increase control over coffee land, there is a clear distinction between individualized land tenure in western Rwanda and coffee estates in eastern Congo. Furthermore, the way respective administrations in the colony and the mandate intervened differed as well. In the colonial Kivu, a chieftaincy (Gishari) was created in order to attract Rwandan labor, while in the 1930s serious limitations on coffee land mobilization were initiated. Similar limitations would not have been approved by the League of Nations, which resulted in a different method of restricting coffee expansion in Rwanda: by stopping the coffee campaigns, but not explicitly by limiting smallholder cultivation.

There are great similarities between the colonial and the mandate Kivu in the ways people entered the plantation economy. Despite local differences, tax obligations and the commodification of tributes and customary duties for both plantation workers and smallholders were an attempt by European bureaucracies to free labor for the coffee sector and to create financial incentives on both sides of Lake Kivu. Voluntary entries increased from the 1940s onwards, but plantations also relied on intermediaries (chiefs) in order to mobilize labor, while respective administrations intervened directly as well, not only to recruit labor but also to make sure that workers stayed on the spot and to return them if they deserted. However, plantations were not the only ones to rely on intermediaries to mobilize coffee laborers. Administrations in western Rwanda did so as well, albeit in a different manner. The initial stage of coffee cultivation was characterized by chiefs and sub-chiefs using customary labor systems (*uburetwa*) while in the later stages, notables and African coffee monitors in particular were responsible for the prosperity of the production process. Differentiation between the two sides of Lake Kivu manifested itself not only in the possibility for Rwandans to mobilize other Africans, as opposed to people in the colony who were unable to do this. It also became clear in the attempts of European governments to "transplant" Rwandan labor toward eastern Congo. As mentioned, population density was higher in Rwanda, and hence the efforts to counterbalance this disequilibrium and provide plantations in the colonial Kivu with sufficient labor in order to decrease over-recruitment – which were sometimes excessive despite restrictions on mobilizations in particular periods and areas.

The least that can be said with reference to the actual commodification of labor is that underpayment for both coffee plantation workers and smallholders was characteristic of the whole colonial period around Lake Kivu. Purchasing power hardly increased. However, extremely low remunerations were backed by household subsistence economies and other sources of income. A greater emphasis on bonuses (including family allowances) in order to stabilize labor after World War II, combined with the introduction of minimum wages and the installation of an equalization fund, suggest improved coffee labor productivity and are clear indications of a shift in colonial thinking – or in empire-building with a greater focus on development.[2] Furthermore, throughout the area, labor conditions were harsh and violence was common, especially before World War II. Eastern Congo and western Rwanda differed in the way these features manifested themselves. Severe working conditions in the plantation sector were related to Europeans treating their labor force violently[3] on both sides of Lake Kivu, while in the smallholder sector violent handling was

2 Even though Cooper mainly refers to French and British colonialism, this shift also happened in the Belgian colonial sphere: see Cooper, *Africa in the world: capitalism, empire, nation-state*: 60–61.

3 This was already hinted at by Mathys, who stated that in the Belgian Congo, people identified violence in general more with European than with African authorities: Mathys, "People on the move. Frontiers, borders, mobility and history in the Lake Kivu region 19th–20th century": 236.

usually committed by African intermediaries (notables and/or monitors). The two sides of Lake Kivu also differed in the way coffee labor was organized and paid. Even though, as a result of the cyclical labor demand of the coffee production process, most labor was temporary, smallholder households were responsible for every step in the cultivation process, while the plantation labor force was more diverse in the sense that one laborer likely did not perform every single step in the production process. Moreover, in eastern Congo workers received a wage (with an added ration), while in western Rwanda smallholders had to sell their coffee themselves. Contrary to in colonial Kivu, coffee growers in the mandate Kivu managed to establish coffee cooperatives in the 1950s in order to increase prices, thereby using their judicial advantage of greater "freedom."

Difference between the eastern and western side of Lake Kivu is one thing, but difference within these two regions is another – "plantations and smallholders" instead of only "plantations versus smallholders." This indicates that empire also builds on diversity within particular localities ("internal diversity"). Despite a lack of data, this book suggests that in eastern Congo, smallholders were not absent, even though their number was very low from the end of the 1920s onwards. In the 1950s, limitations were lessened, which resulted in increased smallholder coffee production. This indicates not only a moving commodity frontier but also a shift in empire-building, more inclined toward development, and a corresponding shift in sets of rules. Diversity in western Rwanda has been highlighted in more concrete terms (Rwandan sources are more explicit on European economic activities than Congolese sources on African market engagement). Although this was limited in scale, in Shangugu in particular, a plantation sector developed next to a successful smallholder coffee sector. The presence of supposedly vacant land (local conditions) in this territory enabled the granting of concessions.

2 On Compromise

The historical outcome of frontier-based development differs from one region to another. It is a result not only of existing differences between localities but also of the reaction of people absorbed into the world-system, as well as feedback provided by other local agents and/or intermediaries. The result of this is an array of hybrid systems based on compromises. Some of the points illustrated above equally apply here. For instance: the creation of cooperatives on the eastern shores of Lake Kivu – lacking in eastern Congo – was a result of the agency of Africans involved in coffee production. In other words, in this final part, I focus on the paradox of capitalist incorporation – attempting to harmonize but encountering interplay and feedback, which results in compromises and the development of hybrid systems.

The final chapter of this book abundantly demonstrated that populations around Lake Kivu both resisted and adapted to the development of the coffee commodity frontier and, hence, integration into the world-system. Most resistance was undertaken with the "weapons of the weak." Large-scale organized resistance against European domination was uncommon and not widespread. For example, people resisted coffee production by migrating, deserting or absenting themselves from work, by sabotaging colonialism in various ways (for instance disobeying rules), or by exploiting the entrance of capital by means of stealing and selling coffee where profits were highest. People around Lake Kivu also reconfigured capitalist structures. In the colonial period, rural populations involved in coffee production experienced the process of peasantization. Having control over land – usufruct or property – in the villages, on the hills or on plantation estates, Africans succeeded in seizing the paradox of capitalism. Throughout the entire colonial period, coffee labor – whether plantation or smallholder – was combined with subsistence activities. Moreover, meager coffee remunerations were supplemented with additional income sources (in which women played a vital role). By continuing precolonial markets and precolonial trade routes – even though European administrations disliked and/or attempted to reorganize them – people around Lake Kivu provided feedback to their entrance in the world-system. Furthermore, peasants around the lake adapted rapidly to changing circumstances, for instance during the famine of 1943–1944. The availability of additional income sources – although more limited in the colonial Kivu than in the mandate – in turn resulted in adaptations of the coffee sector: improving working conditions, bonuses, etcetera.

The final chapter was not the only one that revealed a "negotiated periphery"; other chapters too unmasked various ways in which Africans (chiefs and commoners alike), as well as European planters, shaped and reshaped the coffee sector. Firstly, I showed that up until the 1950s, the development of a coffee plantation sector and the limitation of smallholders in eastern Congo very much depended on the presence of settlers and their lobby association (Unaki). In turn, "economic conversion," starting in the mid-1950s, resulted in more focus on the development of African cash-crop production west of Lake Kivu, which caused tensions with colonists.

Compromises regarding coffee land manifested themselves in the presence of squatters in eastern Congo (most pronounced in Rutshuru), indicating attempts to facilitate labor mobilization. Tensions between the CNKi and colonists with reference to land commodification, and conflicts between *colons* and Africans with the latter resisting land appropriation, are also clear indications of compromise and feedback in the periphery. It can be argued that coffee land in western Rwanda was even more a result of compromise. Firstly, although modified, coffee land was much more based on customary land tenure than it was on the colonial side of Lake Kivu. Secondly, due to a lack of fertile land in many parts of Rwanda, pasture land was converted by mandate administrations, thereby continuing precolonial practices. Finally, the vagueness concerning intercropping, but especially Africans continuing to plant food crops and coffee together, despite the prohibition, once more points to feedback.

Mobilizing labor partly depended on intermediaries on both sides of Lake Kivu. I have argued that (sub-)chiefs were given extended power in order to recruit people, whereas in western Rwanda, initial coffee cultivation drew heavily on existing labor systems (*uburetwa*). Mostly, control of labor was left to intermediaries – *capitas* in the plantation economy and notables in the smallholder sector. On the other hand, escaping *corvées* by entering plantation labor on a regular basis, for instance, was a way in which Africans exploited the mere presence of wage labor and the opportunities provided by it. But compromise also turns up in the way bureaucracies – at least in theory – restricted labor mobilization on both sides of Lake Kivu. Moreover, by backing plantations and restricting mining mobilizations up until World War II, a compromise was made with the plantation sector west of Lake Kivu.

As for the commodification of labor, nearly the entire colonial period is characterized by constant compromises (concerning wages and rations) between plantation owners and administrations. With the introduction of an equalization fund in Rwanda and of minimum wages on both sides of Lake Kivu after World War II, European governments no longer supported colonists' arguments, and at least gave a glimpse of an intention of improving Africans' purchasing power. Moreover, the commodification of labor was hampered by the existence of a *remplacement* system in both Kabare and Shangugu. While this labor system clearly reflects the continuation of precolonial patterns, European governments tried to counter it by introducing short-term contracts in an attempt to increase labor control. Finally, the initiation of enterprise councils after World War II not only indicated a shift in empire (more toward development) but also increased African participation (feedback) in the further evolution of the coffee commodity frontier around Lake Kivu.

To conclude, this book has provided empirical evidence for two interrelated theoretical concepts: commodity frontiers and empire. It has shown that frontier development depends on context. This means both (differing) existing socio-economic/political structures, and feedback provided by many local actors involved (incorporated people, but also settlers for example). However, this book has also shown that contexts shaped within the colonial period (judicial distinctions, or in this case a mandate) contribute to differences in development as well. As such, my research provides more insight into the complexities of frontier development, and the expansion of capitalism in general. Future (comparative) research should take into account *all* of these features. Only then will a better understanding of economic diversity (in labor and land regimes, for instance) within the standardizing tendencies inherent in capitalism emerge.

ANNEX 1

Decree on Coffee Limitations (1938)

Leopold III,[1]

Roi des Belges,

A tous présents et à venir, salut,

Sur la proposition de Notre Ministre des Colonies:

Nous avons arrêté et arrêtons:

Notre Ministre des Colonies est chargé de soumettre en Notre Nom, à l'avis du Conseil Colonial, le projet de décret dont la teneur suit:

Article premier.- A dater du Ier juin 1938 il est interdit dans toute l'étendue du territoire du Congo belge et du Ruanda-Urundi:

1°) de créer ou de faire créer à quelque titre que ce soit des nouvelles plantations de caféiers en dehors des superficies actuellement plantées.

Tous travaux quelconque de remplacement, de régénération ou autres restent donc permis dans les limites de ces superficies.

2°) d'interplanter ou de faire interplanter de caféiers en tout ou en partie toutes autres plantations ou cultures existantes ou à créer.

Article 2.- Sont exceptés des interdictions prescrites à l'article précédent:

1) Les plantations de l'Institut National pour l'Etude Agronomique à établir en exécution de son programme de sélection et d'expérimentation culturale à concurrence de 20 Ha au maximum par an.
2) Les extensions imposées par les Commissions de Crédit agricole prévus aux arrêtés royaux du 9 juillet 1931, du 26 juillet 1937 et du 24 août 1937, avant la date de mise en vigueur du présent décret, et pour la réalisation desquelles des prêts ont été concédés.
3) Pour les colons individuels, l'achèvement à concurrence d'une superficie totale de 50 Ha par colon, d'une plantation commencée sur une concession agricole à la date de la mise en vigueur du présent décret.

    L'autorisation d'extension ou d'achèvement dont font mention les deux derniers alinéas, sera constatée par un permis spécial dont la forme et la modalité de délivrance seront déterminées par une ordonnance du Gouverneur Général.

1 AAB, Agri, Café, Correspondance (517), Projet de décret sur la limitation temporaire des plantations de café au Congo et au Ruanda-Urundi, 1938.

 | DOI:10.1163/9789004428492_011

Article 3.- Les infractions aux dispositions du présent décret sont punies de 2 mois de servitude pénale au maximum et d'une amende qui ne dépassera pas 2000 francs ou d'une de ces peines seulement.

Article 4.- Notre Ministre des Colonies est chargé de l'exécution du présent décret.

Donné à le

Par le Roi:
Le Ministre des Colonies

Archives

1 African Archives Brussels (AAB)

1.1 *Belgian Congo*

1.1.1 Rapports

- Rapports Annuels des Provinces
  - Agri 66: 1953
- Rapports Annuels des Districts
  - AIMO 112: 1924–1934
- Rapports Annuels des Territoires
  - AIMO 99 Kabare: 1932–1953
  - AIMO 103 Kalehe: 1945–1953
  - AIMO 142 and 143 Masisi: 1932–1939 and 1940–1954
  - AIMO 163 Rutshuru: 1932–1954
- Conseil de Province Kivu: 1934–1959: 37(5), 37(6), 37(7), 38(1), 38(2), 38(3), 38(4), 39(2), 39(3), 39(4), 39(5), 40(1), 40(2), 41(1), 41(2), 42(2), 42(3), 43(2), 194(3), 194(4), 194(5), 195(1)
- Comité Régional Province Orientale: 1927–1933: 49(1bis), 49(1), 49(2)

1.1.2 Agri

- Café
  - Café au Ruanda-Urundi: 119/80
  - Correspondance: (340), (517)
  - Limitations des plantations de café: (342)
  - Revendications des Planteurs: (515)
  - Statistiques: (516)
- Compagnies
  - CNKi: (650)
  - Dossiers individuels des plantations: (654)
  - SAAK: (4), (649)
- Compagnies, sociétés, plantations
  - Colonisation au Kivu: (657)
  - Documents CNKi: (321)
- Organismes paraétatiques
  - (50), (51), (52)
- Paysannats Indigènes
  - Kivu: (82)

 | DOI:10.1163/9789004428492_012

1.1.3 Affaires Indigènes et Main-d'œuvre (AIMO)
- MO agricole
  - Situation de la MO au Kivu: 1649/9236
  - Dossier Corbisier: 1653/5
  - Doléances colons de Rutshuru: 1653/6
  - Dossier Kabare: 1653/7
  - Dossier Unaki: 1653/10
  - Inspections plantations "La Linea" et "Dumont": 1653/12
  - Inspections plantations européennes Rutshuru: 1653/13
  - Planteurs de café au Kivu: 1653/14
  - Dossiers individuels des plantation: 1655/9244
- MO: intervention administrative
  - Intervention au Kivu: 1708/9426
  - Recrutements MO Kivu
  - Instructions: 1647/9226
  - Recrutements Ruanda-Urundi
  - Correspondance: 2003
  - Inspections MO: 2000
  - Recrutements pour le Kivu: 1603/9119

1.1.4 Other
- Papiers Bertrand: 778

1.1.5 Gouvernement Général (GG)
- Rapports Annuels agriculture District Kivu: 1927–1933: 318

1.2 ***Ruanda-Urundi***

1.2.1 Rapports
- Résidence du Vice Gouvernement général d'Usumbura – Rapports sur l'administration belge au Ruanda-Urundi à la Commission permanente des Mandats
  - 1921–1939: 17(1), 17(2), 17(4), 17bis(4), 18(1), 18(5)
  - 1947–1961: 19(2), 20(4), 20(4bis), 21(3), 21(5bis), 24(3)
- Résidence du Vice Gouvernement général d'Usumbura – Rapports des missions de visite de l'ONU au Ruanda-Urundi
  - 1948–1961: 25(0A), 25(0B), 25(1), 25(4)
- Résidence du Ruanda – Rapports Annuels des Territoires
  - Gisenyi: 1921–1959: 87(12), 87(13), 87(14), 87(15), 87(16), 87(17), 87(18), 87(19), 87(20), 87(21), 87(22), 87(23), 87(24), 87(25), 88(1), 88(2), 88(3), 88(4), 88(6), 88(7), 88(8), 88(9), 88(10), 88(11), 88(12), 88(14), 89(9), 90(8), 90(9), 90(11), 90(15), 90(16), 90(17), 90(18), 90(19), 90(20), 90(21), 90(22), 90(23), 90(24), 90(25), 90(26), 90(27), 90(28), 90(29)

  - Kibuye: 1930–1959: 82(1), 82(2), 82(3), 82(5), 82(14), 82(16), 82(17), 82(22) 82(23), 82(24), 82(25)
  - Lubengera: 1922–1932: 80(4), 80(7), 80(8), 80(9), 80(10), 80(15A+B), 80(16), 80(17), 80(18) 80(19)
  - Shangugu: 1921–1959: 100(2), 100(3), 100(4), 100(6), 100(7), 100(8), 100(9), 100(10), 100(11), 100(12), 100(13), 101(1), 101(2), 101(3), 101(4), 101(5), 101(6), 101(7), 101(8), 101(9), 101(10), 101(11), 101(12), 102(1), 102(2), 102(3), 102(4), 102(5), 102(8bis), 102(9), 103(7), 103(8), 103(10), 103(12), 104(3), 105(1), 105(2), 105(3), 105(4), 105(5), 105(7), 105(8), 105(10), 105(11), 105(12), 105(13), 105(14), 105(15), 105(16), 105(17), 105(18), 105(19), 105(20), 105(21), 105(22), 105(23), 105(24), 105(25)

1.2.2 RWA

- AIMO:
  - RWA(346): MO agricole
  - RWA(339): Shangugu rapports d'inspection agricole
  - RWA(340), (341), (342): TEPSI
- Conseils de Territoire et de Chefferie
  - Gisenyi: RWA(71)
  - Shangugu: RWA(72)
- Café:
  - Rapports: 1927–1961: RWA(437), (438), (439), (440), (442), (443), (444)
- Colonisation
  - RWA(510)
- Affaires économiques
  - RWA(398)

1.2.3 Affaires Indigènes (AI)

- Zones économiques: 4370(13)
- MO et recrutement: correspondance: 4379(111)
- MO des plantations: 4378(91)

2 Other Collections

Derscheid Collection: University of Florida Digital Collection (accessed via http://ufdc.ufl.edu/derscheid)

Royal Museum for Central Africa (RMCA): Collection Privé : Papiers Pierre Staner (79.6)

State Archives of Belgium (SAB1): INEAC (546)

State Archives of Belgium (SAB2): Finoutremer – Documents CNKi (792), (793)

United Nations Organization Geneva (UNOG): Fonds du Secrétaire – Section des Mandats (1), n° 9/1025

White Fathers Archives Rome (WFAR): Diaires de Rugari, Kabare, Mibirizi et Nyamasheke

References

Acemoglu, Daron, Simon Johnson and James A. Robinson. "The colonial origins of comparative development: an empirical investigation." *American Economic Review* 91, no. 5 (2001): 1369–1401.

Acemoglu, Daron, Simon Johnson and James A. Robinson. "Reversal of fortune: geography and institutions in the making of the modern world income distribution." *Quarterly Journal of Economics* 117, no. 4 (2002): 1231–1294.

Alexopoulou, Kleoniki, and Dácil Juif. "Colonial state formation without integration: tax capacity and labour regimes in Portuguese Mozambique (1890s–1970s)." *International Review of Social History* 62, no. 2 (2017): 215–252.

Angladette, A. "Notes sur l'économie agricole du Ruanda-Urundi." *L'agronomie Tropicale* 9, no. 5 (1959): 573–599.

Antheaume, Benoît. "Le café au Togo. Chronique d'une émergence de la modernité rural (1920–1960)." *Etudes Rurales*, no. 180 (2007): 155–170.

Antippas, Georges. *Pionniers méconnus du Congo belge*. Bruxelles: Interprint, 2007.

Arrighi, Giovanni. "Labor supplies in historical perspective: a study of the proletarianization of the African peasantry in Rhodesia." *Journal of Development Studies* 6, no. 3 (1970): 197–234.

Austen, Ralph A. *African economic history: internal development and external dependency*. Oxford: James Currey, 2003 [1987].

Austen, Ralph A. *Northwest Tanzania under German and British rule. Colonial policy and tribal politics, 1889–1939*. New Haven; London: Yale University Press, 1968.

Austin, Gareth. *Labour, land, and capital in Ghana: from slavery to free labour in Asante, 1807–1956*. Rochester: University of Rochester Press, 2005.

Austin, Gareth. "Reciprocal comparison and African history: tackling conceptual Eurocentrism in the study of Africa's economic past." *African Studies Review* 50, no. 3 (2007): 1–28.

Austin, Gareth. "Resources, techniques, and strategies south of the Sahara: revising the factor endowments perspective on African economic development, 1500–2000." *Economic History Review* 61, no. 3 (2008): 587–624.

Austin, Gareth. "The 'Reversal of Fortune' thesis and the compression of history: perspectives from African and comparative economic history." *Journal of International Development* 20, no. 8 (2008): 996–1027.

Baeck, Louis. *Economische ontwikkeling en sociale structuur in Belgisch-Kongo*. Leuven: Centrum voor Economische Studiën, 1959.

Baptist, A.G. "Quelques considérations sur les coopératives agricoles au Congo belge et au Ruanda-Urundi." *Bulletin Agricole du Congo Belge et du Ruanda-Urundi* 50, no. 3 (1959): 727–751.

Barbier, Edward B. *Scarcity and frontiers. How economies have developed through natural resource exploitation*. Cambridge; New York: Cambridge University Press, 2011.

Barnes, Carolyn. "An experiment with coffee production by Kenyans, 1933–48." *African Economic History*, no. 8 (1979): 198–209.

Baroin, Catherine. "L'impact social de la caféiculture en Tanzanie du Nord." *Etudes Rurales*, no. 180 (2007): 85–100.

Bart, François. "Le café dans l'agriculture rwandaise: l'exemple de Kidahiré (Runyinya)." *Cahiers d'Outre-Mer* 33, no. 132 (1980): 301–317.

Bashizi, Cirhagarhula. "Pouvoirs publics, plantations européennes et réactions paysannes au Sud-Kivu (1920–1960)." In *Ambiguités de l'innovation: sociétés rurales et technologies en Afrique Centrale et Occidentale au XXe siècle*, edited by Bogumil Jewsiewicki and Jean-Pierre Chrétien, 125–145. Québec: SAFI Press, 1984.

Bashizi, Cirhagarhula. "Processus de domination socio-économique et marché du travail au Bushi (1920–45)." *Enquêtes et Documents d'Histoire africaine* 3 (1978): 1–29.

Beghin, Paul. *Geleide verandering in een Afrikaanse samenleving. De Bushi in de koloniale periode*. Brussel: Koninklijke Academie voor Overzeese Wetenschappen, 1974.

Berman, B.J., and J.M. Lonsdale. "Crises of accumulation, coercion and the colonial state: the development of the labor control system in Kenya, 1919–1929." *Canadian Journal of African Studies* 14, no. 1 (1980): 55–81.

Bernstein, Henry. *Class dynamics of Agrarian change*. Sterling: Kumarian Press, 2010.

Berry, Sara. "Hegemony on a shoestring: indirect rule and access to agricultural land." *Africa: Journal of the International African Institute* 62, no. 3 (1992): 327–355.

Bhattacharya, Bhaswati. "Smallholdings versus European plantations: the beginnings of coffee in nineteenth-century Mysore (India)." In *Embedding agricultural commodities using historical evidence, 1840s–1940s*, edited by Willem van Schendel, 55–77. Oxon; New York: Routledge, 2017.

Bishikwabo, Chubaka. "Deux chefs du Bushi sous le regime colonial: Kabare et Ngweshe (1912–1960)." *Etudes d'Histoire Africaine* VII (1975): 89–111.

Bishikwabo, Chubaka. "Un aspect du colonat au Congo belge: le sort des travailleurs du Kivu (1900–1940)." *Genève-Afrique* 16, no. 2 (1977–78): 25–44.

Bishikwabo, Chubaka. "Le Bushi au XIXe siècle: un peuple, sept royaumes." *Revue Française d'Histoire d'Outre-Mer* 67, no. 246–247 (1980): 89–98.

Bishikwabo, Chubaka. "Mythes d'origine et croyances religieuses, bases d'une communauté de royauté interlacustre dans l'est du Zaïre." In *La civilisation ancienne des peuples des Grands Lacs. Colloque de Bujumbura (4–10 septembre 1979)*, edited by Unesco and Centre de la Civilisation Burundaise, 64–80. Paris: Karthala, 1981.

Bishikwabo, Chubaka. "La politique indigène au Congo-belge et son application au Kivu: de la légitimé à l'illégitimé (1900–1945)." *Zamani* 1 (1984): 38–88.

Bishikwabo, Chubaka, and David Newbury. "Recent historical research in the area of Lake Kivu: Rwanda and Zaïre." *History in Africa* 7 (1980): 23–45.

Bourgeois, René. *Témoignages*. Vol. II, Tervuren: Musée Royal de l'Afrique Centrale, 1987.

Bowden, Sue, Blessing Chiripanhura and Paul Mosley. "Measuring and explaining poverty in six African countries: a long-period approach." *Journal of International Development* 20, no. 8 (2008): 1049–1079.

Breman, Jan. *Mobilizing labour for the global coffee market. Profits from an unfree work regime in colonial Java*. Amsterdam: Amsterdam University Press, 2015.

Bruyns, L., and K. Pinxten. "De geleide immigratie van de Banya Ruanda in Kivu." *Zaïre: Revue Congolaise* (Mars 1952): 251–271.

Bryceson, Deborah. "African peasants' centrality and marginality: rural labour transformations." In *Disappearing peasantries? Rural labour in Africa, Asia and Latin America*, edited by Deborah Bryceson, Christóbal Kay and Jos Mooij, 37–63. London: Intermediate Technology Publications, 2000.

Bryceson, Deborah. "Peasant theories and smallholder policies: past and present." In *Disappearing peasantries? Rural labour in Africa, Asia and Latin America*, edited by Deborah Bryceson, Christóbal Kay and Jos Mooij, 1–36. London: Intermediate Technology Publications, 2000.

Buelens, Frans. *Congo 1885–1960. Een financieel-economische geschiedenis*. Berchem: EPO, 2007.

Bunker, Stephen G. *Peasants against the state: the politics of market control in Bugisu, Uganda, 1900–1983*. Chicago: University of Chicago Press, 1991 [1987].

Burbank, Jane, and Frederick Cooper. *Empires in world history. Power and the politics of difference*. Princeton; Oxford: Princeton University Press, 2010.

Burton, Andrew. *African underclass: urbanisation, crime and colonial order in Dar Es Salaam*. London: James Currey, 2005.

Campbell, Gwyn. "The origins and development of coffee production in Réunion and Madagascar, 1711–1972." In *The global coffee economy in Africa, Asia, and Latin America 1500–1989*, edited by William Gervase Clarence-Smith and Steven Topik, 67–99. Cambridge; New York: Cambridge University Press, 2003.

Chabouis, Lucette. *Le livre du café*. Paris: Bordas, 1988.

Charlery, Bernard, François Bart and Jean-Christian Tulet. "Introduction: le café, facteur de dynamisation ou de dislocation des sytèmes de production paysans." In *Paysanneries du café des hautes terres tropicales. Afrique et Amérique latine*, edited by Jean-Christian Tulet, Bernard Charlery, François Bart and Jean Pilleboue, 13–48. Paris: Karthala, 1994.

Charlip, Julie. "Small farmers and coffee in Nicaragua." In *The global coffee economy in Africa, Asia, and Latin America 1500–1989*, edited by William Gervase Clarence-Smith and Steven Topik, 236–253. Cambridge; New York: Cambridge University Press, 2003.

Chrétien, Jean-Pierre. "Le 'désenclavement' de la région des Grands Lacs dans les projets économiques allemands au début du XXe siècle." In *Histoire sociale de l'Afrique de l'Est (XIXe–XXe siècle)*, edited by Département d'histoire de l'Université du Burundi, 335–362. Paris: Karthala, 1991.

Chrétien, Jean-Pierre. *The Great Lakes of Africa. Two thousand years of history*. New York: Zone Books, 2006 [2003].

Clarence-Smith, William Gervase. "Plantation versus smallholder production of cocoa: the legacy of the German period in Cameroon." In *Itinéraires d'accumulation au Cameroun*, edited by Peter Geschiere and Piet Konings, 187–216. Paris: Karthala, 1993.

Clarence-Smith, William Gervase. "Rubber cultivation in Indonesia and the Congo from the 1910s to the 1950s: divergent paths." In *Colonial exploitation and economic development. The Belgian Congo and the Netherlands Indies compared*, edited by Ewout Frankema and Frans Buelens, 193–210. London; New York: Routledge, 2013.

Clement, Piet. "The land tenure system in the Congo, 1885–1960: actors, motivations and consequences." In *Colonial exploitation and economic development. The Belgian Congo and the Netherlands Indies compared*, edited by Ewout Frankema and Frans Buelens, 88–108. London; New York: Routledge, 2013.

Cochet, Hubert, and Barnabé Ndarishikanye. "La production caféière au Burundi: agronomie, vulgarisation et rapports sociaux." *Canadian Journal of African Studies* 34, no. 2 (2000): 218–248.

Codere, Helen. *The biography of an African society, Rwanda 1900–1960 based on forty-eight Rwandan autobiographies*. Tervuren: Royal Museum for Central Africa, 1973.

Colle, Pierre. *Essai de monographie des Bashi*. Bukavu: Centre d'Etude de Langues Africaines, 1971.

Colson, Elizabeth. "The impact of the colonial period on the definition of land rights." In *Colonialism in Africa, 1870–1960. Volume 3: profiles of change: African society and colonial rule*, edited by Victor Turner, 193–215. Cambridge; London; New York; Melbourne: Cambridge University Press, 1971.

Comaroff, John L. "Reflections on the colonial state, in South Africa and elsewhere: factions, fragments, facts and fictions." *Social Identities: Journal for the Study of Race, Nation and Culture* 4, no. 3 (1998): 321–361.

Cooper, Frederick. "Africa and the world economy." In *Confronting historical paradigms. Peasants, labor, and the capitalist World System in Africa and Latin America*, edited by Frederick Cooper, Allen Isaacman, Florence E. Mallon, William Roseberry and Steve J. Stern, 84–201. Madison: University of Wisconsin Press, 1993.

Cooper, Frederick. *Africa in the world: capitalism, empire, nation-state*. Cambridge (Massachusetts): Harvard University Press, 2014.

Cooper, Frederick. *Africa since 1940: the past of the present*. Cambridge: Cambridge University Press, 2002.

Cooper, Frederick. *Colonialism in question. Theory, knowledge, history*. Berkeley; Los Angeles; London: University of California Press, 2005.

Cooper, Frederick. "Conditions analogous to slavery: imperialism and free labor ideology in Africa." In *Beyond slavery: explorations of race, labor, and citizenship in postemancipation societies*, edited by Frederick Cooper, Thomas C. Holt and Rebecca J. Scott, 107–150. Chapel Hill; London: The University of North Carolina Press, 2000.

Cooper, Frederick. "Conflict and connection: rethinking colonial African history." *American Historical Review* 99, no. 5 (1994): 1516–1545.

Cooper, Frederick. *Decolonization and African society. The labor question in French and British Africa*. Cambridge: Cambridge University Press, 1996.

Cooper, Frederick. "From free labor to family allowances: labor and African society in colonial discourse." *American Ethnologist* 16, no. 4 (1989): 745–765.

Cooper, Frederick. *From slaves to squatters. Plantation labor and agriculture in Zanzibar and coastal Kenya, 1890–1925*. Portsmouth: Heinemann, 1997.

Cooper, Frederick. "What is the concept of globalization good for? An African historian's perspective." *African Affairs* 100, no. 399 (2001): 189–213.

Coppens, P. "La colonisation agricole au Congo Belge." *Bulletin Agricole du Congo Belge et du Ruanda-Urundi* 30, no. 1 (1939): 3–11.

Coppens, Paul. "De la propriété collective vers la propriété individuelle." In *Vers la promotion de l'économie indigène. Compte rendu du colloque colonial sur l'économie indigène (9–13 janvier 1956)*, edited by Henri Janne, 413–421. Bruxelles: Institut de Sociologie Solvay, 1956.

Coquery-Vidrovitch, Catherine. "The colonial economy of the former French, Belgian and Portuguese zones, 1914–1935." In *General history of Africa, Volume 7: Africa under colonial domination, 1880–1935*, edited by Albert Adu Boahen, 351–381. Berkeley: Heinnemann Educational Books, 1985.

Coquery-Vidrovitch, Catherine. "The political economy of the African peasantry and modes of production." In *The political economy of contemporary Africa*, edited by Peter C.W. Gutkind and Immanuel Wallerstein, 90–111. London; Beverly Hills: Sage Publications, 1976.

Cornelis, H.A.A. "Belgisch Congo en Ruanda-Urundi tijdens de Tweede Wereldoorlog. De economische en financiële situatie." In *Le Congo belge durant la Seconde Guerre Mondiale*, 51–87. Bruxelles: Académie Royale des Sciences d'Outre-Mer, 1983.

Cornevin, Robert. *Historie du Zaïre. Des origines à nos jours*. Bruxelles; Paris: Hayez, 1989.

Costier, M. "Note sur le rendement de la main-d'œuvre dans les plantations." *Bulletin de Documentation et de Technique Agricole* 8, no. 29 (1954): 14–19.

Cottyn, Hanne. "Renegotiating communal autonomy. Communal land rights and liberal land reform on the Bolivian altiplano. Carangas, 1860–1930." Unpublished PhD dissertation, Ghent University, 2014.

Cottyn, Hanne. "A world-systems frontier perspective to land: exploring the uneven trajectory of land rights standardization in the Andes." *Journal of World-Systems Research* 23, no. 2 (2017): 515–539.

Courcelles, J. "Etablissement d'une plantation de café arabica au Kivu." *Bulletin Agricole du Congo Belge* 28, no. 2 (1937): 302–318.

Curry-Machado, Jonathan. "Global histories, imperial commodities, local interactions: an introduction." In *Global histories, imperial commodties, local interactions*, edited by Jonathan Curry-Machado, 1–14. Houndsmills; New York: Palgrave Macmillian, 2013.

Curtis, Kenneth. "Cooperation and cooptation: the struggle for market control in the Bukoba district of colonial Tanganyika." *International Journal of African Historical Studies* 25, no. 3 (1992): 505–538.

Curtis, Kenneth. "Smaller is better. A consensus of peasants and bureaucrats in colonial Tanganyika." In *The global coffee economy in Africa, Asia, and Latin America 1500–1989*, edited by William Gervase Clarence-Smith and Steven Topik, 312–334. Cambridge; New York: Cambridge University Press, 2003.

D'Hoore, J.L. *Soil map of Africa scale 1 to 5 000 000. Explanatory monograph*. Lagos: Commission for Technical Co-operation in Africa, 1964.

De Clerck, Louis. "Le régime foncier, le régime minier et le droit des biens." In *L'ordre juridique coloniale Belge en Afrique Centrale. Eléments d'histoire*, edited by Emile Lamy and Louis De Clerck, 253–309. Bruxelles: Académie Royale des Sciences d'Outre-Mer, 2004.

de Dampierre, Eric. "Coton noir, café blanc. Deux cultures du Haute-Oubangui à la veille de la loi-cadre." *Cahiers d'Etudes Africaines* 1, no. 2 (1960): 128–147.

De Haan, Leo. *La région des savanes au Togo. L'état, les paysans et l'intégration régionale (1885–1985)*. Paris: Karthala, 1993.

de Haas, Michiel. "Measuring rural welfare in colonial Africa: did Uganda's smallholders thrive?" *Economic History Review* 70, no. 2 (2017): 605–631.

de Haas, Michiel. "Measuring rural welfare in colonial Uganda: Why farmers would not work for wages." In *African Economic History Working Papers Series no. 18/2014*, 2014.

De Roo, Bas. "Colonial taxation in Africa. A fiscal history of the Congo through the lens of customs (1886–1914)." Unpublished PhD dissertation, Ghent University, 2016.

den Ouden, J.H.B. "Incorporation and changes in the composite household: the effects of coffee introduction and food crop commercialization in two Bamiléké chiefdoms." In *The household, women and agricultural development*, edited by Clio Presvelou and Saskia Spijkers-Zwart, 41–67. Wageningen: H. Veenmann & Zonen B.V., 1980.

Depelchin, Jacques. *From the Congo Free State to Zaire (1885–1974). Towards a demystification of economic and political history*. London: CODESRIA, 1992.

Des Forges, Alison Liebhafsky. *Defeat is the only bad news: Rwanda under Musinga, 1896–1931*. Madison: University of Wisconsin Press, 2011.

Dierckx, Xavier. "Note à M. le gouverneur général sur la culture du café au Kivu." *Agriculture et Elevage au Congo belge et dans les Colonies tropicales et subtropicales* 8 (1934): 25–26.

Dorsey, Learthen. "Rwandan colonial economy, 1916–1941." Unpublished PhD dissertation, Michigan State University, 1983.

Doucy, Arthur, and Pierre Feldheim. *Travailleurs indigènes et productivité du travail au Congo belge*. Bruxelles: Institut de Sociologie Solvay, 1958.

Douzant-Rosenfeld, Denise, and Pernette Grandjean. "Planteurs et plantations. Le système de l'exploitation caféière en Amérique latine." *Etudes Rurales*, no. 180 (2007): 71–84.

Drachoussof, Vladimir, ed. *Le developpement rural en Afrique Centrale 1908–1960/1962. Synthèse et réflexions*. 2 vols. Bruxelles: Fondation Roi Baudoin, 1991.

Drevet, Jean-François. "Les plantations Européenes dans le Kivu d'altitude." Unpublished PhD dissertation, Université de Paris, 1977.

Dunaway, Wilma A. "The centrality of the household to the modern world-system." In *Routledge handbook of world-systems analysis: theory and research*, edited by Salvatore J. Babones and Christopher K. Chase-Dunn, 453–461. London; New York: Routledge, 2012.

Eckert, Andreas. "Comparing coffee production in Cameroon and Tanganyika, c.1900 to 1960s." In *The global coffee economy in Africa, Asia, and Latin America 1500–1989*, edited by William Gervase Clarence-Smith and Steven Topik, 286–311. Cambridge; New York: Cambridge University Press, 2003.

Eggers, Nicole. "Kitawala in the Congo: religion, politics and healing in 20th–21st century Central Africa." Unpublished PhD dissertation, University of Wisconsin, 2013.

Elson, Diane, and Ruth Pearson. "'Nimble fingers make cheap workers': an analysis of women's employment in Third World export manufacturing." *Feminist Review* 7 (1981): 87–107.

Fairhead, James Robert. "Fields of struggle: towards a social history of farming knowledge and practice in a Bwisha community, Kivu, Zaire." Unpublished PhD dissertation, School of Oriental and African Studies, 1990.

Fieldhouse, David Kenneth. *Unilever Overseas: the anatomy of a multinational 1895–1965*. London: Croom Helm, 1978.

Forbes Munro, J. *Africa and the international economy, 1800–1960: an introduction to the modern economic history of Africa south of the Sahara*. London; Totowa: Dent, 1976.

Frankema, Ewout, Erik Green, and Ellen Hillbom. "Success and failure of European settler farming in colonial Africa." In *African Economic History Working Papers Series no. 16/2014*, 2014.

Frankema, Ewout, and Marlous van Waijenburg. "Metropolitan blueprints of colonial taxation? Lessons from fiscal capacity building in British and French Africa, c.1880–1940." *Journal of African History* 55, no. 3 (2014): 371–400.

Freund, Bill. "Labor and labor history in Africa: a review of the literature." *African Studies Review* 27, no. 2 (1984): 1–58.

Gahama, Joseph. *Le Burundi sous administration belge: la période du mandat 1919–1939*. Paris: Karthala, 1983.

Galaty, Michael L. "World-systems analysis and anthropology: a new détente?." *Reviews in Anthropology* 40, no. 1 (2011): 3–26.

Gardner, Leigh. *Taxing colonial Africa. The political economy of British imperialism*. Oxford: Oxford University Press, 2012.

Goffin, Joseph. "Les facteurs de développement et d'intégration des économies indigène et européenne au Congo belge et au Ruanda-Urundi." In *Vers la promotion de l'économie indigène. Compte rendu du colloque colonial sur l'économie indigène (9–13 janvier 1956)*, edited by Henri Janne, 315–328. Bruxelles: Institut de Sociologie Solvay, 1956.

Green, Erik. "Diversification or de-agrarianization? Income diversification, labor, and processes of agrarian change in Southern and Northern Malawi, mid-1930s to mid-1950s." *Agricultural History* 82, no. 2 (2008): 164–192.

Guébels, Léon. *Relation complète des travaux de la Commission Permanente pour la Protection des Indigènes, 1911–1951*. Gembloux: Duclot, 1951.

Guetat-Bernard, Hélène. "Cultures du café et dynamiques des rapports de genre en pays Bamiléké au Cameroun: effet de similitude avec la situation Kikuyu au Kenya." *Cahiers d'Outre-Mer* 61, no. 243 (2008): 339–354.

Gunst, Brecht. "Het Institut National pour l'Étude Agronomique du Congo belge. De integratie van de Congolese peasant in het kapitalistische wereld-systeem." Unpublished Master thesis, Ghent University, 2012.

Hall, Thomas D. "Frontiers, ethnogenesis and world-systems: rethinking the theories." In *A world-systems reader. New perspectives on gender, urbanism, cultures, indigenous peoples, and ecology*, edited by Thomas D. Hall, 237–270. Lanham (Maryland): Rowman & Littlefield Publishers, 2000.

Hall, Thomas D. "Incorporation into and merger of world-systems." In *Routledge handbook of world-systems analysis: theory and research*, edited by Salvatore J. Babones and Christopher K. Chase-Dunn, 47–55. London; New York: Routledge, 2012.

Hall, Thomas D. "Lessons from comparing the two Southwests: Southwest China and Northwest New Spain/Southwest United States." *Journal of World-Systems Research* 19, no. 1 (2013): 24–56.

Hall, Thomas D. "Puzzles in the comparative study of frontiers: problems, some solutions, and methodological implications." *Journal of World-Systems Research* 15, no. 1 (2009): 25–47.

Hall, Thomas D. "(Re)periphalization, (re)incorporation, frontiers, and non-state societies: continuities and discontinuities in globalization processes." In *Globalization and global history*, edited by Barry Gills and William Thompson, 96–113. London; New York: Routledge, 2006.

Hatungimana, Alexandre. *Le café au Burundi au xxe siècle: Paysans, argent, pouvoir*. Paris: Karthala, 2005.

Hecq, J., A. Lefebvre, E. Vercruysse, and A. Van Wambeke. *Agriculture et structures économiques d'une société traditionnelle au Kivu (Congo)*. Bruxelles: Publications de l'Institut National pour l'Etude Agronomique du Congo, 1963.

Hempstead, William H. *The history of coffee in Guateamla*. Bogota: Villegas Asociados, 2001.

Henriet, Benoît. "'Elusive natives': escaping colonial control in the Leverville oil palm concession, Belgian Congo, 1923–1941." *Canadian Journal of African Studies* 49, no. 2 (2015): 339–361.

Henriet, Benoît. "The concession experience. Power, ecology and labour in the Leverville circle (Belgian Congo, 1911–1940)." Unpublished PhD dissertation, Université Saint-Louis Bruxelles, 2016.

Herbst, Jeffrey. *State and power in Africa: comparative lessons in authority and control*. Princeton: Princeton University Press, 2000.

Higgs, Catherine. *Chocolate islands: cocoa, slavery, and colonial Africa*. Athens (Ohio): Ohio University Press, 2013.

Honke, Gudrun, ed. *Au plus profond de l'Afrique: le Rwanda et la colonisation allemande 1885–1919*. Wuppertal: Peter Hammer Verlag, 1990.

Hopkins, Anthony G. *An economic history of West Africa*. Harlow: Longman, 1993 [1973].

Hopkins, Anthony G. "The new economic history of Africa." *Journal of African History* 50, no. 2 (2009): 155–177.

Huybrechts, André. *Bilan économique du Congo*. Paris: L'Harmattan, 2010.

Hyde, David. "'Paying for the emergency by displacing the settlers': global coffee and rural restructuring in late colonial Kenya." *Journal of Global History* 4, no. 1 (2009): 81–103.

Hyden, Göran. *Beyond Ujamaa in Tanzania: underdevelopment and an uncaptured peasantry*. London: Heinemann Educational Books, 1980.

Iliffe, John. *Emergence of African capitalism*. London; Basingstoke: Macmillan Press, 1983.

Isaacman, Allen. "Peasants and rural social protest in Africa." *African Studies Review* 33, no. 2 (1990): 1–120.

Jefremovas, Villia. *Brickyards to graveyards. From production to genocide in Rwanda*. Albany: State University of New York Press, 2002.

Jewsiewicki, Bogumil. "African peasants in the totalitarian society of the Belgian Congo, 1917–1960." In *Peasants in Africa, historical and contemporary perspectives*, edited by Martin A. Klein, 45–75. Beverly Hills; London: Sage Publications, 1980.

Jewsiewicki, Bogumil. "Le colonat agricole européen au Congo-belge, 1910–1960: questions politiques économiques." *Journal of African History* 20, no. 4 (1979): 559–571.

Jewsiewicki, Bogumil. "The great depression and the making of the colonial economic system in the Belgian Congo." *African Economic History*, no. 4 (1977): 153–176.

Jewsiewicki, Bogumil. *Modernisation ou destruction du village africain: l'économie politique de la "modernisation agricole" au Congo Belge*. Bruxelles: Les Cahiers du CEDAF, 1983.

Jewsiewicki, Bogumil. "Political consciousness among African peasants in the Belgian Congo." *Review of African Political Economy*, no. 19 (1980): 23–32.

Jewsiewicki, Bogumil. "Raison d'etat ou raison du capital: l'accumulation primitive au Congo belge." *African Economic History*, no. 12 (1983): 157–182.

Jewsiewicki, Bogumil. "Rural society and the Belgian colonial economy." In *History of Central Africa. Volume two*, edited by David Birmingham and Phyllis M. Martin, 95–125. London; New York: Longman, 1983.

Kalemaza, Kavuha. "Le développement de l'agriculture au Kivu colonial (1903–1940)." Unpublished Master thesis, Université nationale du Zaïre (campus Lubumbashi), 1973.

Kamola, Isaac A. "The global coffee economy and the production of genocide in Rwanda." *Third World Quarterly* 28, no. 3 (2007): 571–592.

Kanogo, Tabitha. *Squatters and the roots of Mau Mau 1905–63*. Nairobi: East African Educational Publishers, 1993 [1987].

Kardulias, Nick. "Negotiation and incorporation on the margins of world-systems: examples from Cyprus and North America." *Journal of World-Systems Research* 13, no. 1 (2007): 55–82.

Katzenellenbogen, S.E. *Railways and the copper mines of Katanga*. Oxford: Clarendon Press, 1973.

Keese, Alexander. "The constraints of late colonial reform policy: forced labour scandals in the Portuguese Congo (Angola) and the limits of reform under authoritarian colonial rule, 1955–1961." *Portuguese Studies* 28, no. 2 (2012): 186–200.

Kermans, H. "Les cafés du Congo belge." *Bulletin Agricole du Congo Belge* 21, no. 3 (1930): 954–956.

Kestergat, Jean. *Quand le Zaïre s'appelait Congo. L'aventure coloniale belge.* Bruxelles: Paul Legrain, 1985.

Kieran, J.A. "The origins of commercial Arabica coffee production in East Africa." *African Historical Studies* 2, no. 1 (1969): 51–67.

Konter, J.H. "The deteriorating position of African women in the development from a subsistence economy towards a market economy." In *The household, women and agricultural development*, edited by Clio Presvelou and Saskia Spijkers-Zwart, 17–25. Wageningen: H. Veenmann & Zonen B.V., 1980.

Kuété, Martin. "Café, caféiculteurs et vie politique dans les hautes terres de l'Ouest-Cameroun." *Cahiers d'Outre-Mer* 61, no. 243 (2008): 285–302.

Lawrence, Benjamin N. *Locality, mobility and "nation." Periurban colonialism in Togo's Eweland (1900–1960).* Rochester; New York: University of Rochester Press, 2007.

Lemarchand, René. "The coup in Rwanda." In *Protest and power in Black Africa*, edited by Robert Rotberg and Ali Mazrui, 877–923. New York: Oxford University Press, 1970.

Lemarchand, René. *Rwanda and Burundi.* London: Pall Mall Press, 1970.

Léonard, Guillaume. "Un divorce belge. Expériences contrastées du planteur belge de café au Kivu (1945–1960)." In *L'Afrique belge aux XIXe et XXe siècles. Nouvelles recherches et perspectives en histoire coloniale*, edited by Patricia Van Schuylenbergh, Catherine Lanneau and Pierre-Luc Plasman, 207–228. Bruxelles; Berne; Berlin: P.I.E. Peter Lang, 2014.

Leplae, Edmond. "La collaboration agricole entre Indigènes et Européens." *Bulletin Agricole du Congo Belge* 22, no. 4 (1931): 566–570.

Leplae, Edmond. "La colonisation agricole belge au Congo." *Bulletin Agricole du Congo Belge* 9, no. 1–4 (1918): 3–28.

Leplae, Edmond. *La culture et le rendement d'une plantation de café au Congo belge.* Bruxelles: Imprimerie industrielle et financière, 1928.

Leplae, Edmond. "Faut-il, en Afrique centrale, repousser le salariat et les plantations européennes?" *Bulletin Agricole du Congo Belge* 22, no. 4 (1931): 570–574.

Leplae, Edmond. *Histoire et développement des cultures obligatoires de coton et de riz au Congo belge de 1917 à 1933.* Bruxelles: Goemaere, 1933.

Leplae, Edmond. "Native agricultural policy and European agriculture in the Belgian Congo." *Journal of Royal African Society* 38, no. 152 (1939): 357–369.

Leplae, Edmond. *Les plantations de café au Congo belge: leur histoire (1881–1935), leur importance actuelle.* Bruxelles: Van Campenhout, 1936.

Leplae, Edmond . "Prix de revient et rendements probables de plantations au Congo belge." *Bulletin Agricole du Congo Belge* 14, no. 4 (1923): 675–710.

Leurquin, Philippe. *Le niveau de vie des populations rurales du Ruanda-Urundi.* Louvain: Editions Nauwelaerts, 1960.

Likaka, Osumaka. *Rural society and cotton in colonial Zaire.* Madison: University of Wisconsin Press, 1997.

Louis, William Roger. *Ruanda-Urundi, 1884–1919*. Oxford: Clarendon Press, 1963.

Lovens, Maurice. *La révolte de Masisi-Lubutu: Congo belge janvier–mai 1944*. Bruxelles: Les Cahiers du CEDAF, 1974.

Lugan, Bernard. "Causes et effets de la famine 'Rumanura' au Rwanda, 1916–1918." *Canadian Journal of African Studies* 10, no. 2 (1976): 347–356.

Lugan, Bernard. *Cette Afrique qui était allemande*. Paris: Jean Picollec, 1990.

Lugan, Bernard. "Les pôles commerciaux du lac Kivu à la fin du XIXe siècle." *Revue Française d'Histoire d'Outre-Mer* 64, no. 235 (1977): 176–202.

Lugan, Bernard, and Raphaël Mutombo. "Le tabac du Bugoyi dans le Rwanda ancien: une culture commerciale dans une société d'autosubsistance." *Africa-Tervuren* 29, no. 1–2 (1983): 51–60.

Lugan, Bernard, and Antoine Nyagahene. "Les activités commerciales du sud Kivu au XIXe siècle à travers l'exemple de Kinyaga (Rwanda)." *Cahiers d'Outre-Mer* 36, no. 141 (1983): 19–48.

Makana, Nicholas E. "Metropolitan concern, colonial state policy and the embargo on cultivation of coffee by Africans in colonial Kenya: the example of Bungoma district, 1930–1960." *History in Africa* 36 (2009): 315–329.

Malaba, Luke. "Supply, control and organization of African labour in Rhodesia." *Review of African Political Economy*, no. 18 (1980): 7–28.

Mamdani, Mahmood. *Citizen and subject: contemporary Africa and the legacy of late colonialism*. Princeton: Princeton University Press, 1996.

Mararo, Bycyalimwe. "Land conflicts in Masisi, Eastern Zaire: the impact and aftermath of Belgian colonial policy (1920–1989)." Unpublished PhD dissertation, Indiana University, 1990.

Mararo, Bycyalimwe. "Occupation économique du Kivu (1945–1959)." Unpublished Master thesis, Université nationale du Zaïre (campus Lubumbashi), 1974.

Marchal, Jules. *L'histoire du Congo 1910–1945. Travail forcé pour le cuivre et pour l'or, pour le rail, pour l'huile de palme*. 3 vols. Borgloon: P. Bellings, 1999–2001.

Mathieu, Paul, and Angelus Mafikiri Tsongo. "Enjeux fonciers, déplacements de population et escalades conflictuelles (1930–1995)." In *Conflicts et guerres au Kivu et dans la région des Grands Lacs*, edited by Paul Mathieu and Jean-Claude Willame, 19–62. Paris: L'Harmattan, 1999.

Mathys, Gillian. "Bringing history back in: past, present, and conflict in Rwanda and the Eastern Democratic Republic of Congo." *Journal of African History* 58, no. 3 (2017): 465–487.

Mathys, Gillian. "People on the move. Frontiers, borders, mobility and history in the Lake Kivu region 19th–20th century." Unpublished PhD dissertation, Ghent University, 2014.

Mauro, Frédéric. *Histoire du café*. Paris: Editions Desjonquères, 1991.

Mbapndah, Ndobegang M. "French colonial agricultural policy, African chiefs, and coffee growing in the Cameroun grassfields, 1920–1960." *International Journal of African Historical Studies* 27, no. 1 (1994): 41–58.

Mbataru, Patrick. "Women in the coffee society: the case of Nyeri, Kenya." *Etudes Rurales*, no. 180 (2007): 101–116.

Mbuluyo, Mokili K. "La culture du café et le développement de l'Uele." *Cahiers d'Outre-Mer* 39, no. 154 (1986): 143–156.

McClellan, Charles W. "Land, labor, and coffee: the South's role in Ethiopian self-reliance, 1889–1935." *African Economic History*, no. 9 (1980): 69–83.

McMichael, Philip. "Incorporating comparison within a world-historical perspective: an alternative comparative method." *American Sociological Review* 55, no. 3 (1990): 385–397.

Médard, Henri. *Le royaume du Buganda au XIXe siècle. Mutations politiques et religieuses d'un ancien Etat d'Afrique de l'Est*. Paris; Nairobi: Karthala; IFRA, 2007.

Meebelo, Henry S. *Reaction to colonialism: a prelude to the politics of independence in Northern Zambia, 1893–1939*. Manchester: Manchester University Press, 1971.

Mendiaux, E. "Le Comité National du Kivu." *Zaïre*, no. 10 (1956): 803–813.

Mertens, Myriam. "Chemical compounds in the Congo: pharmaceuticals and the 'crossed history' of public health in Belgian Africa (ca. 1905–1939)." Unpublished PhD dissertation, Ghent University, 2014.

Mignolo, Walter D. *Local histories/global designs: coloniality, subaltern knowledges, and border thinking*. Princeton: Princeton University Press, 2000.

Miracle, Marvin P. *Traditional agricultural methods in the Congo Basin*. Stanford: Food Research Institute, 1964.

Mokili Danga Kassa, Jeannôt. *Politiques agricoles et promotion rurale au Congo-Zaïre (1885–1997)*. Paris: L'Harmattan, 1998.

Molitor, Georges. "L'introduction et le développement de la culture du caféier Arabica chez les indigènes du Ruanda-Urundi." *Le Matériel Colonial* 27, no. 6 (1937): 156–175.

Moore, Henrietta L., and Megan Vaughan. *Cutting down trees: gender, nutrition, and agricultural change in the Northern Province of Zambia, 1890–1990*. London: Pearson Education, 1994.

Moore, Jason W. *Capitalism in the web of life. Ecology and the accumulation of capital*. London; New York: Verso, 2015.

Moore, Jason W. "Madeira, sugar, and the conquest of nature in the "first" sixteenth century, Part II. From regional crisis to commodity frontier, 1506–1530." *Review (Fernand Braudel Center)* 33, no. 1 (2010): 1–24.

Moore, Jason W. "Sugar and the expansion of the Early Modern world-economy: commodity frontiers,ecological transformation, and industrialization." *Review (Fernand Braudel Center)* 23, no. 3 (2000): 409–433.

Mosley, Paul. *The settler economies. Studies in the economic history of Kenya and Southern Rhodesia 1900–1963*. Cambridge; New York: Cambridge University Press, 1983.

Mugaruka, bin Mubibi. "La circulation des produits de la forge et de l'artisanat au Bushi ancien, leur rôle dans le développement du commerce dans la région interlacustre." *Actes du colloque L'Afrique des Grands Lacs* II (1982): 114–132.

Mutibwa, Phares M. "White settlers in Uganda: the era of hopes and disillusionment, 1905–1923." *Transafrican Journal of History* 5, no. 2 (1976): 112–122.

Mwembu, Dibwe dia. "La peine du fouet au Congo belge (1885–1960)." *Cahiers de Tunisie: revue de sciences humaines* 34, no. 135–136 (1968): 127–153.

Nayenga, Peter F.B. "Commercial cotton growing in Busoga district, Uganda, 1905–1923." *African Economic History*, no. 10 (1981): 175–195.

Ndaywel è Nziem, Isidore. *Histoire générale du Congo. De l'héritage ancien à la République Démocratique*. Paris: Duclot, 1998.

Nelson, Samuel H. *Colonialism in the Congo basin, 1880–1940*. Athens (Ohio): Center for International Studies, 1994.

Newbury, Catharine. *The cohesion of oppression. Clientship and ethnicity in Rwanda, 1860–1960*. New York: Columbia University Press, 1988.

Newbury, Catharine. "Ebutumwa Bw'Emiogo: The tyranny of cassava a women's tax revolt in Eastern Zaïre." *Canadian Journal of African Studies* 18, no. 1 (1984): 35–54.

Newbury, Catharine. "Ethnicity in Rwanda: the case of Kinyaga." *Africa: Journal of the International African Institute* 48, no. 1 (1978): 17–29.

Newbury, Catharine. "*Ubureetwa* and *Thangata*: catalysts to peasant political consciousness in Rwanda and Malawi." *Canadian Journal of African Studies* 14, no. 1 (1980): 97–111.

Newbury, David. "'Bunyabungo': the Western Rwandan frontier, c.1750–1850." In *The African frontier: the reproduction of traditional African societies*, edited by Igor Kopytoff, 164–192. Bloomington: Indiana University Press, 1987.

Newbury, David. *Kings and clans: Ijwi Island and the Lake Kivu Rift, 1780–1840*. Madison: University of Wisconsin Press, 1991.

Newbury, David. "Lake Kivu regional trade in the nineteenth century." *Journal des Africanistes* 50, no. 2 (1980): 7–30.

Newbury, David. "Precolonial Burundi and Rwanda: local loyalties, regional royalties." *International Journal of African Historical Studies* 34, no. 2 (2001): 255–314.

Newbury, David. "The 'Rwakayihura' famine of 1928–1929. A nexus of colonial rule in Rwanda." In *Histoire sociale de l'Afrique de l'Est (XIXe–XXe siècle)*, edited by Département d'histoire de l'Université du Burundi, 269–285. Paris: Karthala, 1991.

Newbury, David, and Catharine Newbury. "Bringing the peasants back in: agrarian themes in the construction and corrosion of statist historiography in Rwanda." *The American Historical Review* 105, no. 3 (2000): 832–877.

Nicaise, J. "Chronique sociale Congolaise." *Zaïre*, no. 1 (1954): 181–192.

Nkundabagenzi, F. *Rwanda politque, 1958–1960*. Bruxelles: CRISP, 1961.

Northrup, David. *Beyond the bend in the river: African labor in Eastern Zaire 1865–1940*. Athens (Ohio): Center for International Studies, 1988.

Northrup, David. "Slavery and forced labour in the Eastern Congo 1850–1910." In *Slavery in the Great Lakes region of East Africa*, edited by Henri Médard and Shane Doyle, 111–123. Oxford: James Currey, 2007.

Nsavyimana, Deogratias. "La mobilisation de la force de travail au Burundi sous le mandate belge (1920–1940)." Unpublished PhD dissertation, Université Catholique de Louvain, 1989.

Nsengimana, Innocent. *Le Rwanda et le pouvoir européen (1894–1952). Quelles mutations?* Bern: Peter Lang, 2003.

Nugent, Paul. *Smugglers, secessionists & loyal citizens on the Ghana–Togo frontier: the lie of the borderlands since 1914*. Oxford: James Currey, 2002.

Nunn, Nathan. "Historical legacies: a model linking Africa's past to its current underdevelopment." *Journal of Development Economics* 83, no. 1 (2007): 157–175.

Nunn, Nathan. "The long-term effects of African's slave trades." *Quarterly Journal of Economics* 123, no. 1 (2008): 139–176.

Nzabandora Ndimubanzi, Joseph. "Le commerce du sel mineral de Katwe au Nord-Kivu précolonial (1830–1911)." In *L'Afrique des Grands Lacs: cultures et civilisations*, 279–292. Bukavu: CERUKI, 1982.

Nzigire, Bulakali. "Problème des terres dans l'occupation économique du Kivu (1918–1930)." Unpublished Master thesis, Université nationale du Zaïre (campus Lubumbashi), 1972.

Nzongola-Ntalaja, Georges. *The Congo: from Leopold to Kabila: a people's history* London; New York: Zed Books, 2002.

O'Brien, Patrick Karl. "Colonies in a globalizing economy, 1815–1948." In *Globalization and global history*, edited by Barry Gills and William Thompson, 248–291. London; New York: Routledge, 2006.

Ogutu, M.A. "Dualism and the development of coffee in Meru, Kenya, in 1930s." *Transafrican Journal of History* 8, no. 2 (1979): 140–159.

Ost, Michael B. "Agricultural laborers in Kivu, 1919–1939." Unpublished Master thesis, University of Wisconsin, 1979.

Page, Melvin E. "The Manyema hordes of Tippu Tip: a case study in social stratification and the slave trade in Eastern Africa." *International Journal of African Historical Studies* 7, no. 1 (1974): 69–84.

Pagès, Albert. *Au Ruanda sur les bords du Lac Kivu (Congo Belge): un royaume hamite au centre de l'Afrique*. Bruxelles: Hayez, 1933.

Palacios, Marcos. *Coffee in Colombia, 1850–1970. An economic, social, and political history*. Cambridge: Cambridge University Press, 1980.

Paternostre de la Mairieu, Baudouin. *Le Rwanda: son effort de développement. Antécédents historiques et conquêtes de la révolution Rwandaise*. Bruxelles: Editions A. De Boeck, 1972.

Peemans, Jean-Philippe. *Diffusion du progrès économique et convergence des prix: le cas Congo-Belgique, 1900–1960: la formation du système des prix et salaires dans une économie dualiste*. Louvain: Editions Nauwelaerts, 1968.

Peemans, Jean-Philippe. "Le rôle de l'état dans la mobilisation de la force de travail au Congo." *Contradictions*, no. 4 (1973): 101–125.

Pereira de Melo, Hildete. "Coffee and development of the Rio de Janeiro economy, 1888–1920." In *The global coffee economy in Africa, Asia, and Latin America 1500–1989*, edited by William Gervase Clarence-Smith and Steven Topik, 360–384. Cambridge; New York: Cambridge University Press, 2003.

Perrings, Charles. *Black mineworkers in Central Africa: industrial strategies and the evolution of an African proletariat in the copperbelt, 1911–1941*. London: Heinemann, 1979.

Piret, Bérengère. "Reviving the remains of colonization – the Belgian colonial archives in Brussels." *History in Africa* 42 (2015): 419–431.

Pottier, Johan. "'Customary land tenure' in Sub-Saharan Africa today: meaning and contexts." In *From the ground up: land rights, conflict and peace in Sub-Saharan Africa*, edited by Chris Huggins and Jenny Clover, 55–75. Pretoria: ISS, 2005.

Pottier, Johan. *Re-imagining Rwanda. Conflict, survival and disinformation in the late twentieth century*. Cambridge: Cambridge University Press, 2002.

Pryor, Frederic L. "The plantation economy as an economic system." *Journal of Comparative Economics* 6 (1982): 288–317.

Reid, Richard. *A history of modern Africa: 1800 to the present*. Malden: Wiley-Blackwell, 2012 [2009].

Reisdorff, I. *Enquêtes foncières au Ruanda*. s.l.: s.n., 1952.

Renton, David, David Seddon, and Leo Zeilig. *The Congo: plunder and resistance*. London; New York: Zed Books, 2007.

Reyntjens, Filip. *Pouvoir et droit au Rwanda: droit public et évolution politique, 1916–1973*. Tervuren: Musée Royal de l'Afrique Centrale, 1985.

Reyntjens, Filip. "Statut international et droit constitutionnel du Ruanda-Urundi." In *L'ordre juridique coloniale Belge en Afrique Centrale. Eléments d'histoire*, edited by Emile Lamy and Louis De Clerck, 67–120. Bruxelles: Académie Royale des Sciences d'Outre-Mer, 2004.

Rumiya, Jean. *Le Rwanda sous le régime du mandat Belge: 1916–1931*. Paris: L'Harmattan, 1992.

Rusamira, Etienne. "La dynamique des conflits ethniques au Nord-Kivu: une réflexion prospective." *Afrique Contemporaine*, no. 207 (2003): 147–163.

Ryckmans, Pierre. "Le programme économique dans le Ruanda-Urundi." *Bulletin de la Société Royale des Ingénieurs et des Industriels* 2, no. 1 (1921): 89–98.

S.N. *Bulletin Officiel du Congo Belge*. Bruxelles: Hayez, Imprimeur des Académies Royales, 1910.

S.N. *Comité National du Kivu 1928–1953. Vingt-cinquième anniversaire*. Bruxelles: Editons L. Cuypers, 1953.

S.N. "La commercialisation du café au Ruanda-Urundi." *Bulletin de la Banque Centrale du Congo belge et du Ruanda-Urundi* 7, no. 8 (1958): 263–273.

S.N. "Le développement de la culture du café dans les milieux indigènes du Ruanda-Urundi." *Servir* 10, no. 3 (1949): 106–107.

S.N. *FAO statistical pocketbook coffee 2015*. Rome: FAO, 2015.

S.N. "http://data.un.org/CountryProfile.aspx?crName=Burundi."

S.N. "http://data.un.org/CountryProfile.aspx?crName=Rwanda."

S.N. "https://monusco.unmissions.org/sites/default/files/north_kivu.factsheet.eng_.pdf."

S.N. "https://monusco.unmissions.org/sites/default/files/south_kivu_factsheet._eng.pdf."

S.N. *Rapport annuel sur l'activité de la Colonie du Congo Belge pendant l'année…, 1920–58*. Bruxelles.

S.N. "Rapport de la Commission pour l'étude du problème de la main-d'oeuvre au Congo belge (1924–1925)." In *Le problème de la main-d'oeuvre au Congo belge. Rapports (1) de la Commission pour l'étude du problème de la main-d'oeuvre au Congo belge (1924–1925); (2) du Comité consultatif de la main-d'oeuvre (1928)*: 9–34. Bruxelles: Goemaere, 1928.

S.N. *Rapport sur l'administration Belge du Ruanda-Urundi pendant l'année…, 1920–61*. Bruxelles.

S.N. *Rapport sur l'administration Belge du Ruanda-Urundi pendant l'année 1923*. Bruxelles: s.n., 1923.

S.N. *Le Ruanda-Urundi*. Bruxelles: L'Office de l'information et des relations publiques pour le Congo belge et le Ruanda-Urundi, 1959.

Samper, Mario, and Radin Fernando. "Historical statistics of coffee production and trade from 1700 to 1960." In *The global coffee economy in Africa, Asia, and Latin America 1500–1989*, edited by William Gervase Clarence-Smith and Steven Topik, 411–462. Cambridge; New York: Cambridge University Press, 2003.

Sassen, Saskia. "When the center no longer holds: Cities as frontier zones." *Cities* 34 (2012): 67–70.

Schuerkens, Ulricke. *Du Togo allemand aux Togo et Ghana indépendants. Changements social sous régime colonial*. Paris: L'Harmattan, 2001.

Scott, James. *Seeing like a state. How certain schemes to improve the human condition have failed.* New Haven; London: Yale University Press, 1998.

Scott, James. *Weapons of the weak. Everyday forms of peasant resistance.* New Haven; London: Yale University Press, 1985.

Seibert, Julia. *In die globale Wirtschaft gezwungen. Arbeit und kolonialer Kapitalismus im Kongo (1885–1960).* Frankfurt; New York: Verlag, 2016.

Seibert, Julia. "More continuity than change? New forms of unfree labor in the Belgian Congo, 1908–1930." In *Humanitarian intervention and changing labor relations. The long-term consequences of the abolition of the slave trade*, edited by Marcel Van der Linden, 369–386. Leiden; Boston: Brill, 2011.

Seti Gableame, Gbédémah. "L'échec de la politique française d'integration au Togo sous tutelle (1946–1960)." In *Les Togolais face à la colonisation*, edited by Nicoué Lodjou Gayibor, 111–147. Lomé: Presses de l'Université de Bénin, 1994.

Shadle, Brett. "White settlers and the law in early colonial Kenya." *Journal of Eastern African Studies* 4, no. 3 (2010): 510–524.

Shlomowitz, Ralph. "Plantations and smallholdings: comparative perspectives from the world cotton and sugar cane economies, 1865–1939." *Agricultural History* 58, no. 1 (1984): 1–16.

Sigwalt, Richard. "The early history of Bushi. An essay in the historical use of genesis traditions." Unpublished PhD dissertation, University of Wisconsin, 1975.

Singiza, Dantès. "Les réactions des autorités belges et locales face à la famine Ruzagayura (Rwanda, 1943–1944). Heuristique, méthodologie et premiers résultats." In *L'Afrique belge aux XIXe et XXe siècles. Nouvelles recherches et perspectives en histoire coloniale*, edited by Patricia Van Schuylenbergh, Catherine Lanneau and Pierre-Luc Plasman, 193–205. Bruxelles; Berne; Berlin: P.I.E. Peter Lang, 2014.

Smith, Joan, and Immanuel Wallerstein, eds. *Creating and transforming households: the constraints of the world-economy.* Cambridge: Cambridge University Press, 1992.

Sokoloff, Kenneth L., and Stanley L. Engerman. "History lessons: institutions, factor endowments, and paths of development in the New World." *Journal of Economic Perspectives* 14, no. 3 (2000): 217–232.

Sosne, Elinor. "Colonial peasantization and contemporary underdevelopment: a view from a Kivu village." In *Zaïre. The political economy of underdevelopment*, edited by Guy Gran, 189–210. New York: Praeger, 1979.

Sosne, Elinor. "Of biases and queens: the Shi past through an androgynous looking glass." *History in Africa* 6 (1979): 225–252.

Staner, Pierre. "Les paysannats indigènes du Congo belge et du Ruanda-Urundi." *Bulletin Agricole du Congo Belge et du Ruanda-Urundi* 46, no. 3 (1955): 467–551.

Stengers, Jean. *Le Congo, mythes et réalités. 100 ans d'histoire.* Gembloux: Duculot, 1989.

Strizek, Helmut. *Geschenkte Kolonien: Ruanda und Burundi unter deutscher Herrschaft.* Berlin: Christoph Links Verlag, 2006.

Strouwens, Léon, and Pierre Piron. *Codes et lois du Congo belge: textes annotés d'après les rapports du Conseil colonial, les instructions officielles et la jurisprudence des tribunaux.* Léopoldville: Edition des codes et lois du Congo belge, 1943.

Taringana, Takesure. *Agrarian capitalism and the development of the coffee industry in colonial Zimbabwe 1900–1980.* Newcastle upon Tyne: Cambridge Scholars Publishing, 2018.

Tchumtchoua, Emmanuel. "Caféiculture et pénurie de la main-d'œuvre au Sud-Cameroun sous régime du 'travail obligatoire' (1924–1945)." *Annales de la Faculté des Arts, Lettres et Sciences Humaines* 1, no. 11 (2010): 277–311.

Topik, Steven. "The integration of the world coffee market." In *The global coffee economy in Africa, Asia, and Latin America 1500–1989*, edited by William Gervase Clarence-Smith and Steven Topik, 21–49. Cambridge; New York: Cambridge University Press, 2003.

Topik, Steven, and William Gervase Clarence-Smith. "Conclusion: new propositions and a research agenda." In *The global coffee economy in Africa, Asia, and Latin America 1500–1989*, edited by William Gervase Clarence-Smith and Steven Topik, 385–410. Cambridge; New York: Cambridge University Press, 2003.

Topik, Steven, and William Gervase Clarence-Smith. "Introduction: Coffee and global development." In *The global coffee economy in Africa, Asia, and Latin America 1500–1989*, edited by William Gervase Clarence-Smith and Steven Topik, 1–17. Cambridge; New York: Cambridge University Press, 2003.

Topik, Steven, and Allen Wells. *Global markets transformed, 1870–1945.* Cambridge (Massachusetts); London: Harvard University Press, 2012.

Tosh, John. "Lango agriculture during the early colonial period: land and labour in a cash-crop economy." *Journal of African History* 19, no. 3 (1978): 415–439.

Tosh, John. "The cash-crop revolution in tropical Africa: an agricultural reappraisal." *African Affairs* 79, no. 314 (1980): 79–94.

Tucker, Catherine M. *Coffee culture: local experience, global connections.* New York; London: Routledge, 2011.

Uwizeyimana, Laurien. "Rôle politique de la caféiculture au Rwanda." *Etudes Rurales*, no. 180 (2007): 171–186.

Vaessen, Vincent. "Les législations sur le contrat de travail de 1910 et 1922 au Congo Belge: deux intentions et deux modes de décisions opposés." *Revue Belge de Philologie et d'Histoire* 79, no. 4 (2001): 1213–1254.

Van Acker, Frank. "Where did all the land go? Enclosure & social struggle in Kivu (D.R. Congo)." *Review of African Political Economy* 32, no. 103 (2005): 79–98.

Van den Abeele, M. "Edmond Leplae." In *Biographie coloniale belge*, 515–518. Bruxelles: Académie Royale des Sciences Coloniales, 1955.

Van der Linden, Marcel. "The 'globalization' of labor and working-class history and its consequences." *International Labor and Working-Class History*, no. 65 (2004): 136–156.

Van der Linden, Marcel. *Workers of the world. Essays toward a global labor history*. Leiden; Boston: Brill, 2008.

Van der Straeten, Edgar. *L'agriculture et les industries agricoles au Congo belge*. Bruxelles: Editons L. Cuypers, 1945.

Van Melkebeke, Sven. "'Changing grounds.' The development of coffee production in the Lake Kivu region (1918–1960/62). The colonial state, labor, land and production for the world market." Unpublished PhD dissertation, Ghent University, 2017.

Van Melkebeke, Sven. "Coerced coffee cultivation and rural agency: the plantation-economy of the Kivu (1918–1940)." In *On coerced labor: work and compulsion after chattel slavery*, edited by Marcel Van der Linden and Magaly Rodríguez García, 187–207. Leiden, Boston: Brill, 2016.

Van Melkebeke, Sven. "Divergence in rural development: the curious case of coffee production in the Lake Kivu region (first half twentieth century)." *African Economic History* 46, no. 2 (2018): 117–146.

Van Melkebeke, Sven. "Dualisme ou dynamisme? Une analyse de l'économie rurale congolaise durant l'Entre-deux-guerres." *Journal of Belgian History* 43, no. 2–3 (2013): 152–177.

Van Melkebeke, Sven. "*More continuity than change*. Arbeid en arbeidsrelaties in de koffieplantagesector van Kivu tijdens het interbellum." Unpublished Master thesis, Ghent University, 2012.

Van Pottelbergh, Gudrun. "Octave Louwers, 'Éminence grise' van het Belgisch koloniaal establishment. Achter de schermen van de koloniale politiek in de jaren 1920 en 1930." *Journal of Belgian History* 36, no. 3–4 (2006): 453–494.

Van Reybrouck, David. *Congo. Een geschiedenis*. Amsterdam: De bezige bij, 2010.

van Schendel, Willem. "Embedding agricultural commodities: an introduction." In *Embedding agricultural commodities using historical evidence, 1840s–1940s*, edited by Willem van Schendel, 1–10. Oxon; New York: Routledge, 2017.

Van Waijenburg, Marlous. "Financing the African colonial state: the revenue imperative and forced labor." *Journal of Economic History* 78, no. 1 (2018): 40–80.

van Zwanenberg, Paul. "Kenya's primitive colonial capitalism: the economic weakness of Kenya's settlers up to 1940." *Canadian Journal of African Studies* 9, no. 2 (1975): 277–292.

Van Zwanenberg, Roger. "The development of peasant commodity production in Kenya, 1920–40." *Economic History Review* 27, no. 3 (1974): 442–454.

Vanderstraeten, Louis-François. *La répression de la révolte des Pende du Kwango en 1931*. Bruxelles: Académie Royale des Sciences d'Outre-Mer, 2001.

Vandewalle, Gaston. *De conjuncturele evolutie in Kongo en Ruanda-Urundi van 1920 tot 1939 en van 1949 tot 1958*. Ghent: RUG. Hogere school voor handels-en economische wetenschappen, 1966.

Vandewoude, Emile. *Documents relatifs à l'ancien district du Kivu, 1900–1922*. Léopoldville: Section Documentation Bureau Archives, 1959.

Vanhaute, Eric. "The end of peasantries? Rethinking the role of peasantries in a world-historical view." *Review (Fernand Braudel Center)* 31, no. 1 (2008): 39–59.

Vanhaute, Eric. "Peasants, peasantries and (de)peasantization in the capitalist world-system." In *Routledge handbook of world-systems analysis: theory and research*, edited by Salvatore J. Babones and Christopher K. Chase-Dunn, 313–321. London; New York: Routledge, 2012.

Vanhaute, Eric, Hanne Cottyn and Yang Wang. "Peasantries." In *The world is out of joint: world-historical interpretations of continuing polarizations*, edited by Immanuel Wallerstein, 55–68. London; New York: Routledge, 2015.

Vanhee, Hein, and Geert Castryck. "Belgische historiogafie en verbeelding over het koloniale verleden." *Journal of Belgian History* 32, no. 3–4 (2002): 305–320.

Vansina, Jan. *Antecedents to modern Rwanda. The Nyiginya kingdom*. Madison: University of Wisconsin Press, 2004.

Vansina, Jan. *Being colonized: the Kuba experience in rural Congo, 1880–1960*. Madison: University of Wisconsin Press, 2010.

Vansina, Jan. *L'évolution du royaume rwanda des origines à 1900*. Bruxelles: Académie Royale des Sciences d'Outre-Mer, 2000.

Vansina, Jan. "Les régimes fonciers Ruanda et Kuba – une comparaison." In *African agrarian systems*, edited by Daniel Biebuyck, 348–363. London: Oxford University Press, 1963.

Vanthemsche, Guy. *Congo. De impact van de kolonie op België*. Tielt: Lannoo, 2007.

Vanthemsche, Guy. *Genèse et portée du "Plan décennal" du Congo belge (1949–1959)*. Bruxelles: Académie Royale des Sciences d'Outre-Mer, 1994.

Vanthemsche, Guy. "The historiography of Belgian colonialism in the Congo." In *Europe and the World in European historiography*, edited by Csaba Lévai, 89–119. Pisa: CLIOHRES, 2006.

Vellut, Jean-Luc. "Enquête sur la main-d'oeuvre au Kivu (1930)." *Enquêtes et documents d'histoire africaine* 3 (1978): 30–38.

Vellut, Jean-Luc. "Hégémonies en construction: articulations entre Etat et Entreprises dans le bloc colonial Belge (1908–1960)." *Canadian Journal of African Studies* 16, no. 2 (1982): 313–330.

Vellut, Jean-Luc. "La misère rurale dans l'expérience coloniale du Zaïre, du Rwanda, et du Burundi. Crises de subsistance et insuffisances alimentaires dans les possessions coloniales de la Belgique (ca.1920–1960)." In *The annual meeting of the African Studies Association*. Boston, December, 7–10, 1983.

Vervust, Petra. "The limits of colonial symbolic power. Ethnicization and racialization in Rwanda 1890–1960." Unpublished PhD dissertation, Ghent University, 2010.

Vervust, Petra. "The relative importance of ethnicity, class and race in colonial Rwanda. The cases of prison policies, corvées, taxation, census and identity booklets." *Journal of Belgian History* 42, no. 4 (2012): 74–109.

Viaene, Leo. "L'organisation politique des Bahunde." *Kongo-Overzee* 18, no. 1 (1952): 8–34.

Viaene, Leo. "L'organisation politique des Bahunde (II)." *Kongo-Overzee* 18, no. 2–3 (1952): 111–121.

Vidal, Claudine. "Economie de la société féodale rwandaise." *Cahiers d'Etudes Africaines* 14, no. 53 (1974): 52–74.

Vijgen, Ingeborg. *Tussen mandaat en kolonie. Rwanda, Burundi en het Belgische bestuur in opdracht van de Volkenbond (1916–1932)*. Leuven: Acco, 2005.

Vlassenroot, Koen. *Households land use strategies in a protracted crisis context: land tenure, conflict and food security in eastern DRC*. FAO, 2006.

Vlassenroot, Koen. "Land and conflict: the case of Masisi." In *Conflict and social transformation in Eastern DR Congo*, edited by Koen Vlassenroot, Timothy Raeymaekers, Anna Verhoeve, Luca Jourdan and Jeroen Cuvelier, 81–102. Ghent: Academia Press, 2004.

Vlassenroot, Koen. "Violence et constitution des milices dans l'est du Congo: le cas des Mayi-Mayi." In *L'Afrique des Grands Lacs. Annuaire 2002–2003*, edited by Filip Reyntjens and Stefaan Marysse, 115–152. Paris: L'Harmattan, 2003.

Vos, Jelmer. "The first African coffee boom: Angolan Robusta, c.1820–c.1900" In *II CHAM International Conference*. Universidade Nova de Lisboa, 2015.

Vries, Peer. *Escaping poverty. The origins of modern economic growth*. Goettingen: V & R Unipress, 2013.

Vwakyanakazi, Mukohya. "Import and export in the second economy in North Kivu." In *The real economy of Zaire: the contribution of smuggling and other unofficial activities to national wealth*, edited by Janet MacGaffey, 43–71. London: James Currey, 1991.

Wallerstein, Immanuel. "The colonial era in Africa: changes in the social structure." In *Colonialism in Africa, 1870–1960. Volume 2: the history and politics of colonialism 1914–1960*, edited by Peter Duignan and Lewis Henry Gann, 399–421. Cambridge; London; New York; Melbourne: Cambridge University Press, 1970.

Wallerstein, Immanuel. *World-systems analysis. An introduction*. Durham; London: Duke University Press, 2007 [2004].

Watt, Carey. "'A world of history in your cup': teaching coffee as global commodity c.1400–2000." *World History Bulletin* 28, no. 2 (2012): 16–19.

Watteyne, R.P. "Le café du Kivu." *Bulletin Agricole du Congo Belge* 21, no. 3 (1930): 939–941.

Weiss, Brad. *Sacred trees, bitter harvests. Globalizing coffee in Northwest Tanzania.* Portsmouth: Heinemann, 2003.

West, Paige. *From modern production to imagined primitive: the social world of coffee from Papua New Guinea.* Durham (North Carolina): Duke University Press, 2012.

Wild, Antony. *Coffee: a dark history.* New York; London: W.W. Norton & Company, 2004.

Williamson, Jeffrey G. "Land, labor and globalization in the Third World, 1870–1940." *Journal of Economic History* 62, no. 1 (2002): 55–85.

Willis, Justin. "'Men on the spot,' labor, and the colonial state in British East Africa: the Mombasa water supply, 1911–1917." *International Journal of African Historical Studies* 28, no. 1 (1995): 25–48.

Wolpe, Harold. "Capitalism and cheap labour-power in South Africa: from segregation to apartheid." *Economy and Society* 1, no. 4 (1972): 425–456.

Wringley, Gordon. *Coffee.* Harlow: Longman, 1988.

Yelengi, Nkasa. "Labor policies and household economic strategies among the railway workers in Katanga, Belgian Congo, 1928–1960." *Africa: Rivista Trimestrale di Studi e Documentazione Dell'Istituto italiano per l'Africa e l'Oriente* 55, no. 4 (2000): 463–487.

Young, Crawford. *The African colonial state in comparative perspective.* New Haven; London: Yale University Press, 1994.

Index